# Ballet
## in
## Western Culture

## A HISTORY OF ITS ORIGINS AND EVOLUTION

### CAROL LEE

University of South Florida

WITHDRAWN FROM STOCK

i

Routledge
New York and London

4518774

Published in 2002 by
Routledge
29 West 35th Street
New York, NY 10001

Published in Great Britain by
Routledge
11 New Fetter Lane
London EC4P 4EE

Routledge is an imprint of the Taylor & Francis Group.
Copyright © 2002 by Routledge

Pearson Education, Inc. previously published this book.

Printed in the United States of America on acid-free paper.

All rights reserved. No part of this book may be reprinted or reproduced or utilized in any form or by any electronic, mechanical, or other means, now known or hereafter invented, including photocopying and recording, or in any information storage or retrieval system without permission in writing from the publisher.

10 9 8 7 6 5 4 3 2 1

Cataloging-in-Publication Data available from the Library of Congress.

ISBN 0-415-94256X—ISBN 0415-94257-8 (pbk)

# CONTENTS

iv

v

## 12  The Ballets Russes from the Pursuit of the Avant-Garde to Neoclassicism    254

## 13  Ballet in the Twentieth Century    277

## 14  The Development of Ballet in the United States    312

viii

# ℱOREWORD

Dance literature is enriched with the publication of this comprehensive presentation of the evolution and development of classical dance. With *Ballet in Western Culture,* Carol Lee has distilled and integrated an enormous and diverse amount of historical, biographical, and artistic information with precision and clarity. The fascinating story of ballet is told anew with the insight of one who has spent a lifetime dancing herself. The author illuminates the many periods of dance, each in its historical setting, eloquently linking the ages from antiquity to present. Her colorful treatment of medieval and Renaissance dancing as expressions of society and politics is both informative and factual.

The origins of classical ballet have been carefully described in a manner that almost suggests the author's firsthand experience at the court of the Sun King. Jean Georges Noverre's passion for the art of dance and his vehement efforts to revitalize it take on additional relevance in Carol Lee's account of Romantic ballet two generations later. In writing about the excitement, novelty, and scope of the Diaghilev years, she sheds light on the art of dance in our own time. From the masterful Jules Perrot to the innovations of Marius Petipa and the streamlined works of Mikhail Fokine, from Western Europe to Russia and the New World, her smooth handling of the transference of creative and technical ideas across the centuries relates directly to the repertory still before us.

*Ballet in Western Culture* does much to narrow the schism of misunderstanding between classical dance and modern dance, which started out as ballet's rebellious alternative. Chapters 11 through 14 emphasize the similarities of ballet and modern dance, rather than the differences, in how they combine techniques from the early twentieth century onward. The future lies in a blending of ballet and modern dance, indeed, in an amalgamation of the many forms of dance, including historical, jazz, ethnic, and street idioms. We see this trend occurring in companies everywhere as choreographers take their inspirations from the entire range of human experience. Classical companies add works of modern choreographers to their repertories; modern ensembles are often formed with classically trained artists, a natural step forward in the evolution of dance.

Ballet is both re-examining its past and adapting to modern aesthetics as it prepares to enter into the next millennium. The inclusion of works by Jiri Kylian into the repertoire of the Stuttgart Ballet is as important as the performance of Nureyev's revived baroque ballets at the Paris Opera. The creation of contemporary ballets, the descendants of the great repertory of the past, are witness to this. Of these works, only time will prove which will prevail and become the classics of our era.

In addition to serving dance students in courses on ballet history, *Ballet in Western Culture* will be of special interest to the growing audience of balletomanes, and to all readers dedicated to the performing arts. The author's inclusion of a chronology of significant events is especially helpful, as exemplified by her account of ballet during the reign of Louis XIV and the years of the French Revolution. A sizeable amount of dance information is integrated within the broader historical setting when massive changes have been so relevant to the international growth of ballet. The attractive illustrations, some of which have never before been published, will be especially appreciated by lovers of dance. A glossary of critical and uncommon terms will also greatly assist in the study of ballet history.

Arlette van Boven
*Executive Artistic Director, NDT III*
*Nederlands Dans Theater*
*The Hague*

# PREFACE

In recent years, ballet has generated a growing curiosity and prevailing interest among the American public. There is an eagerness to learn more about theatrical dance: its origins, the players, places, and the artistic product that comprises its heritage. *Ballet in Western Culture* is dedicated to all serious students of ballet and the liberal arts. While intended primarily as a book for college and university dance history courses, it is also designed to appeal to all who love and cherish classical ballet in all its splendor as an art form.

In sharing my understanding of ballet's marvelous story over the past two decades with students in university and college dance programs, with ballet teachers and professional dancers in ballet seminars, and with adolescent and adult ballet students in private studios, I have been amazed and delighted with the public's taste for the subject of ballet history. I have also been impressed with the interest in ballet history expressed by artists, writers, and musicians, as well as with the excitement voiced by high school students and parents at dance festivals and workshops. Consequently, a substantial rendering of the history of ballet seems to be in order.

An overview of ballet's history was provided by an earlier book, *An Introduction to Classical Ballet* (Lee, 1983), which also included a technical discussion of ballet's classroom work, but a thorough chronicle of ballet history seemed fascinating enough to merit a fuller accounting. This volume begins with the earliest seeds of dance in Western civilization, traces its development during the Middle Ages and the Renaissance through the appearance of classical ballet in the seventeenth-century court of Louis XIV, and continues with a discussion of the monumental contributions of Lully and Beauchamp. The eighteenth century witnessed the presence of theatrical dance, which grew in technical knowledge consistent with the scientific spirit of the era. Ballet emerged in the nineteenth century as a perfect expression of Romanticism. Its extraordinary expansion on Russian soil during the nineteenth century achieved a supreme level of excellence. And with the exodus of Russian dancers in Diaghilev's company, ballet returned to the West and the stage was set for the present state of the art.

In the United States, it was not until after World War II and the subsequent development of the communications media that ballet experienced its phenomenal growth. By the 1970s, it seemed that "all America was dancing," to paraphrase Agnes de Mille. Not only has national prosperity increased enrollment in neighborhood dancing schools around the country, but federal and private endowments to national, state, and local ballet companies have supported their presence in American society.

An understanding of ballet, like anything else, cannot be had outside the context of appreciating the particular world it inhabits. Classical dance's unbroken line of development over 350 years is highlighted by the professional work of the dancers, choreographers, and teachers who created ballet for the present. Hopefully, *Ballet in Western Culture* will inform and instruct the reader by presenting ballet history in light of the most significant artistic, political, and social currents of its times. Although ballet arrived late in Western culture, the story of its formation in regard to the color, glamour, and sheer drama surrounding its establishment is unparalleled in the annals of art. As cultural historian Walter Sorell often reminds us in his luminous writing, dance is inextricably related to the ebbs and flows of its own times.

A number of people and institutions have been most helpful in providing inspiration and assistance for this volume; but for their generosity and thoughtfulness, this book would not have been possible. I am especially indebted to my teachers for making my early dance career a reality. The refined deportment and beauty of Felia Doubrovska, one of Diaghilev's last ballerinas, greatly influenced me in classes at the American School of Ballet. Muriel Stuart also inspired with her elegant teaching and her memories of Pavlova and Maestro Cecchetti. During the annual programs at Jacob's Pillow, Antony Tudor instilled in me, early on, the relationship between classroom work and the efforts of the choreographer. I am forever in his debt for sharing his unique insights into the creative process.

I would also like to thank Benjamin Harkarvy for his extraordinary patience as a teacher, and for his careful and personalized classes that benefited my work so much. By the time I began my dancing career in Europe, Ben was in Holland, founding Nederlands Dans Theater. I never imagined then what a haven and source of artistic inspiration that great company would be during the happy times I spent in The Hague.

My lifelong interest in French history and its subsequent relationship to the Romantic ballet was initially fueled by French ballerinas Ludmilla Tcherina and Violette Verdy. Violette, who wrote the preface for my first book, has done so much in a variety of ways to advance the cause of ballet in America, and the profession will always be grateful to her. In the 1970s when Violette was a guest with Tampa Ballet, she and her dynamic partner, Edward Villella, generated so much enthusiasm for ballet that the company crossed the threshold from a regional group to a full-fledged professional organization.

For their meticulous comments, I am most grateful to Judith Chazim-Bennahum and Catherine Turocy who generously lent their scholarship to the final reading of the manuscript. I am indebted to Elizabeth Gibbons, Graham Hempel, Rhythm McCarthy, Isabel Schleeter, and Marc Ozanich, my former partner and colleague at Florida State University, who made many suggestions during the various stages of completing the book. Thanks are also in order to publishers Lawrence Erlbaum of Erlbaum & Associates and Charles Woodford of Princeton Books who provided me with valuable direction and reassurance.

For calling my attention to little-known etchings of sixteenth-century folk dancing, I am grateful to Mme Nicole Walch, curator of the Bibliothèque Royale in Brussels. During the early preparation for this book, Mme Gilberte Cournand expertly guided me through the maze of literature on French court ballet and eighteenth- and nineteenth-century theater architecture in the Bibliothèque National in Paris. A very warm thanks to Ann Barzel for her extensive comments on Chapter 14 after which she delighted me with the dance treasures in the Barzel collection of Chicago's Newberry Library. To the extent that this project was a pleasurable undertaking, I thank Jos Hooghuis of the Netherlands Institute for Advance Studies for his long-distance support and Joke van Pelt of Amsterdam's Toneelmuseum who made invaluable materials available to me. My task was immeasurably facilitated because of the thoughtfulness of the research staff at the Victoria and Albert Museum. I am indebted to Jack and Linda Vartoogian, and the Chicago Institute of Art, the Isabella Stewart Gardner Museum, and the Dance Collection at the New York Public Library for the Performing Arts for permission to use drawings and photographs of dance luminaries and events. The backing and enthusiasm of my gracious chairman, Dr. Timothy Wilson, have facilitated the later stages of this book.

For our many stimulating discussions during the past eight years, I am beholdened to Erkki Tann, distinguished graduate of the Moscow State Institute of Theatrical Art (GITIS), choreographer, and teacher. His profound insights into Russian ballet history and its current pedagogy, music, and art, have informed and inspired. Numerous conversations with the great Bolshoi dancer Mikhail Lavrovsky, and with Konstantin Russu and his dynamic wife, Uté Mitreuter, both faculy members at the John Cranko Ballet School in Stuttgart, have broadened my understanding of Russia's past and present contributions to ballet. Special thanks are in order to the late Jurgen Schneider who introduced me to the wonders and science of the Vaganova syllabus, a technical system that has posed many questions for me to ponder and has revealed so many doors to open.

I would like to express my gratitude to Virginia Berch, who has been a significant help in producing numerous manuscript drafts over many months. For her generous aid in sleuthing out minute-but-wonderful fragments of information, verifying dates, and suggesting solutions to technical problems, I am indebted to the the University of South Florida Library research staffer Jana Futch. For their comments and careful technical assistance, I thank my colleagues Susan Taylor, Megan McDonald, Fiona Ferrie, Sveinbjörg Alexanders, and Victoria Schneider. Not least, I wish to thank my editors Richard Carlin and George Zimmar at Routledge for their guidance and goodwill.

To my husband, Charles Spielberger, I am profoundly grateful for his enormous support and encouragement. Without the luxury of accompanying him on his extensive travels over the past twenty-five years, I would not have had t he opportunity to experience the actual court theaters, opera houses, and schools where ballet grew. Nor would I have seen or held the objects that are the precious ballet memorabilia that abound in European collections and the historical archives of cultural life long gone. And finally, I would like to thank my dear son, Nicholas, for his patience and good grace in having to grow up with all the madness that goes with a dancing mother.

Carol Lee

*Great nations write their autobiographies in three manuscripts, the book of their deeds, the book of their words and the book of their art.*

JOHN RUSKIN

# 1

# $\mathcal{O}$rigins of $\mathcal{D}$ance

Throughout the ages, a wealth of documentation in the form of cave paintings, Egyptian hieroglyphics, descriptions of ancient Olympic games, and Old Testament references have attested to the importance of dancing in society. From time immemorial people have danced in response to an instinctual need for emotional expression. Dance figured prominently as an essential component in the rituals of primal religions, which formally celebrated all aspects of human life and its relationship to nature. Dancers performed to assure the continuation of traditional ways of living, to honor their gods and each other, and to affirm their tribal identities. Early humans were confronted by a world filled with natural calamities that they could not understand; their very existence was threatened daily. An indispensable part of early religious rituals, dancing represented an effort on the part of prehistoric people to deal with their limitations in making sense out of the terrifying environment in which they lived.[1]

The primal thinking process led to a belief that spirits controlled life in mysterious ways to bring about birth, sickness, death, wars, and violent acts of nature. The spirits could be influenced in magic activities, especially that of dance. The rhythmic basis for dance was percussive, stamping into the earth to attract the attention of a deity in order to ask for intervention in human concerns. Therefore, making contact with the spirits in trance-inducing dances was a means for early people to calm fears and gain control over the course of events that affected life.[2] Echoed in all dance down through the ages are the two fundamental rhythms of the human body. The heartbeat is reflected in stamping feet and breathing is expressed in the sung melodic phrase. Millenniums later, when men and women wanted to dance they held out their arms to companions, whereby they linked hands and sang.

# THEATRICAL DANCE IN ANCIENT GREECE

Ancient civilizations expanded the religious use of dance, and in time, dance was employed as a part of general education, festival games, military training, and theatrical entertainment.[3] The potent devotion accorded to ancient Greece's sunlit ideals of perfection in philosophy, science, and art have allowed no sphere of spiritual or intellectual activity in Western culture to be untouched by its living flame. This remarkable and continuing impact is a tribute to the inspiration of the Greek example that has affected men and women for 2,500 years and enabled them to discover new truths about themselves, their condition, and their capacities. Greek ideals, temporarily swept aside by the triumph of Christianity in the Middle Ages, survived the new faith, humanized it during the Renaissance, and reasserted themselves again in the New World.

At a time when humankind was still in the initial stages of civilization and thought processes had not yet consciously come to serve objective truth, the resort to myth was the only way to provide answers to questions, to interpret natural phenomena, and to preserve experiences and imagined events for posterity. Greek mythology owes its timelessness to the fact that it was cultivated for 1,400 years in the places where it was given life by a host of epic, lyric, and dramatic poets who intended it to be a vehicle for Greek ideals. Many characteristics of the Greek spirit are imprinted on the myth—the affirmation of life, the worship of beauty, and the centrality of the person that led to the idealization of humans and served to promote general rules of life.

An analysis of beauty that Friedrich Nietzsche derived from Greek culture and formulated in *The Birth of Tragedy* (1872) is helpful in understanding Western art. According to the German philosopher, all art works are comprised of Apollonian and Dionysian phenomena. Their Apollonian elements reflect ideals of solemn and ordered perfection, analogously attributed to the sun god, Apollo. Dionysian elements in an art work or in the context of performance, on the other hand, derive from the irrational, passionate, and wildly sensual nature of Dionysius, the god of wine. Dionysian tendencies represent a negative but necessary dialectic action without which the creation of aesthetic values would be impossible. Viewing art according to its Apollonian and Dionysian tendencies provides a rich framework for understanding and weighing notions of artistic form and content. In all art objects or events, Apollonian and Dionysian elements are present, but rarely equal, to one another. One of the poetic constructs generally dominates the other in any given work or event. When, however, these divergent tendencies are perceived to be in balance, the result is commonly understood to be a masterpiece. Some of the most perfect examples of a harmonious integration of Apollonian and Dionysian characteristics in ballet are found in *Giselle*, *Sleeping Beauty*, *Les Sylphides*, and *Apollo*.

Throughout the classical period of Greek history (540–300 B.C.), dance gained an especially important place in its vibrant theater. Scattered references of many ancient writers describe the characteristic dance in the great tragic plays of Aeschylus, Sophocles, and Euripides as the *emmeleia*, stately and noble in bearing and suitable to the drama at hand. The Greeks regarded songs accompanied by gestures as a form of dance. An entire body of symbolic gestures, called *cheironomia*, was one aspect of the dance. In Greek dramas, a highly trained chorus of masked performers supported an unfolding plot of riveting human experience by visibly responding in song, dance, and gesture to the speech of the actors.[4] The brilliant comedies of Aristophanes also included dance, mime, and gesture. One specific kind of dance, the popular *kordax*, was lascivious, ignoble, and obscene.[5] Other colorful dances also enriched the presentation of comic plays; they included animal and victory dances, dances of pure joy, spirited processions, and even burlesques of religious rituals.

In fourth-century B.C., Greek civilization was spread far and wide by Alexander the Great with the establishment of Greek colonies throughout the Mediterranean area, especially in southern Italy. Around the same time, Rome was beginning to emerge as the dominant military power in the known world. The Romans looked upon Greece and its colonies in Italy as bearers of civilization, greatly admiring its art and science. The Greek glorification of humanity as reflected in its civic philosophy, architecture, and sculpture was particularly appreciated by the Romans. Absorbing many elements of Greek life and style, the Romans adjusted Greek ideals and customs to fit their own needs and tastes.

When the Romans conquered the Greek settlement of Tarentum in southern Italy in 272 B.C., they opened the way for Greek drama to enter into their capital city. Livius Andronicus, a noted actor and playwright from Tarentum, was familiar with Athenian theatrical methods. He was invited to the festival of *Ludi Romani* in 240 B.C. where annual games and general entertainment were held in the city. He presented a tragedy and a comedy in Latin that followed the Greek dramatic format that incorporated a swaying and gesturing chorus. Thereafter, theatrical presentations were included in all holiday festivals, and Roman drama was committed to Greek forms.[6] Of the Roman playwrights, Plautus and Terence became the most famous writers of comedy, the preferred Roman form of plays. Later, Roman playwrights succumbed to the massive audiences' increasing demands for violent spectacle, coarse humor, and farce in theatrical performances.

Shortly after the introduction of Greek style plays at the *Ludi Romani*, legend has it that Livius Andronicus, becoming hoarse after too many performances, had a boy perform the songs required in his role. Finding himself freed from the task of singing, Livius Andronicus was able to present a more expressive and powerful performance through silent acting alone.[7] Quintilian, a teacher and rhetorician of first century A.D., left this description of the style of miming that Livius Andronicus had introduced:

> Their hands demand and promise, they summon and dismiss, they translate horror, fear, joy, sorrow, hesitation, confession, repentance, restraint, abandonment, time and number. They excite and they calm. They implore and they approve. They possess a power of imitation which replaces words. To suggest

3

Grecian dancer with cymbals.
(Courtesy of Jerome Robbins Dance
Division, The New York Public
Library for the Performing Arts, Astor,
Lenox and Tilden Foundations.)

illness, they imitate the doctor feeling the patient's pulse; to indicate music they
spread their fingers in the fashion of a lyre[8]

Thus, the seed of Roman pantomime may have been planted.

# ROMAN PANTOMIME

Two freed Greek slaves who came to Rome in 22 B.C. are credited with inventing
a perfected form of pantomime that reached such a level of refinement that
miming was elevated to an art form. Pylades of Cilicia and Bathyllus of
Alexandria, the first professional mimes known by name, became enormously
famous for their presentations of skits in which they conveyed meaning through
gestures and symbolic movements. Pylades, lionized for his beauty and skill in
tragic roles, exemplified a noble genre. Bathyllus, in marked contrast, was much

loved for his voluptuous and effeminate burlesque style, denoting him a performer of the grotesque sort.[9]

At their highest level of development, Roman pantomimes were constructed with four or five scenes portrayed by one performer in episodes that were separated by musical interludes. The performance was introduced by a herald who told the audience the story to be presented. This was followed by a chorus singing an introduction to the story. The pantomime artist then appeared sumptuously costumed in jewels and silk. He wore a mask with a closed mouth to signify a story without words. By way of gestures, symbolic movements, and occasionally, cape tricks to add theatrical interest, he conveyed nuances of the story to the end of the episode. At this point, a musical interlude gave the artist time to change costume and mask for the next segment of the story.[10]

The last episode of the pantomime ended with a final burst of music that created a frightful pandemonium consisting of drums, metal rattles, castanets, pipes, lyres, trumpets, cymbals, and *scabella* which were boards fastened to the players' feet. After the applause, an encore was given and there were often virtuoso displays of leaping, acrobatic balances, and statuesque poses of great beauty.[11] At some of the *Ludi Romani* it was not uncommon for a pantomine to be accompanied by as many as 6,000 dancers and singers.[12] As accomplished by Pylades, Bathyllus, and their imitators, the pantomime skits were said to display grace, flexibility, and strength, the results of long and exact training and good diet. Pantomime became the most important form of Roman theatrical art and maintained its popularity for the next four centuries.

5

# ⟨𝒟⟩ANCE AND CHRISTIANITY

When the over-extended and exhausted Empire finally collapsed in 476, Western civilization as it had been wrought by the Greco-Roman world came within a hair's breadth of disappearing. Although the eastern domain of the Empire in Byzantium thrived as an intellectual and cultural repository of learning, for several hundred years the European part of the Empire came under the ravaging swords of marauding barbaric tribes. Parallel in time, the growing Christian culture, shaped by the deeply spiritual writings of St. Augustine, offered itself as an alternative organization for a world in chaos. Despite the violence of living and rigorous persecutions, Christianity's attractive religious message gained a following. It provided the masses who lived on the edge of existence with a creed based on hope and a code of behavior based on love.

By the sixth century, the Church found itself in the dominant position of overseeing the restructuring of Europe's damaged social and economic life, and did so by integrating new religious values into the fabric of its polyglot society. Having replaced Roman epicureanism with pious spiritual discipline, life in general was considered to be a preparation for the next world. All human pleasures were regarded as distractions to contemplating holy thoughts such as the martyrdom of Christ and the mysteries of Christian doctrine. The human body and certainly dancing were considered evil temptations that turned people's attention away from death and eternal life in heaven.

Ever on guard to prevent relapses into the degenerate lifestyle of pagan ways, the Church established bans on social activities that might contaminate Christian mores. Outlawed were the popular low-life comedies, pantomime skits, and circuses, which had been spectacular entertainments attended by the general populace throughout the Roman Empire. Circuses included everything from chariot races to blood-letting gladiator fights, while the Roman theaters featured comedies and pantomimes performed by dancers, mimes, acrobats, and jugglers. Over the years, these displays had escalated into vulgar demonstrations of nudity and devastating cruelty, testifying to the decadence of the Empire.[13] To ensure that the new order of Christianity would never again be tainted by the old ways, clergymen discouraged all large public gatherings including theatrical performances and the dancing that was included in them. The great arenas and coliseums were abandoned, turned into grazing grounds, or, in many cases, their stones were used to construct churches and monasteries.

When the Christian Emperor Justinian I closed all the entertainment sites in Byzantium around 530, the art of theater took to the street. Actors, singers, dancers, and mimes became wandering vagabonds so that their breed and their art never totally disappeared. The Christian aversion to public revelry spread and in 544 Childebert, a converted Frankish king, outlawed dancing in his territories as a pagan activity.[14] When the papacy forbade all forms of dance in 744, theater people were cast out of society, out of the Church, and denied Christian burial by ecclesiastical edict. The mimes were particularly vulnerable to Church sanctions since their often erotic skits frequently parodied Christian ritual and the holy sacraments. The Church condemned performers and their art alike.

The theatrical dance that was once an intrinsic part of the Greek theater, along with the art of Roman pantomime, lost its showcase for a thousand years, a critical blow to its development. While public entertainment locales fell into ruins, the largest buildings yet built by Western civilization sprang up. As concrete manifestations of the Christian faith, cathedrals were erected across the face of Europe. These massive stone structures were designed to house the business of religion and in this sense they became "theaters" for the one great medieval spectacle, the Mass.

# DANCE IN THE MIDDLE AGES

A considerable amount of medieval documentation records the periodic condemnation of dance by watchful prelates, a confirmation of its frequent reappearance and universal popularity in people's lives. Despite the official disapproval, churchmen realized that dancing could not be entirely suppressed. The natural proclivity for self-expression through the activity of movement was too obvious and the simple pleasure that people took in village dances on days of religious celebration seemed harmless. Consequently, the Church held a divided attitude toward dance. The clergy was confronted with a number of biblical references that spoke of dance as a natural occurrence in human expression. For example, the Old Testament recorded that during the sacred processional of King David, "all the house of Israel danced with all their might before Jehovah." Strong precedent for dance in Christian ritual was indicated as far back as A.D. 160; a hymn, appearing in the Acts of John, recalls Christ as a *choregus*[15] at the Last Supper, leading his disciples in song and circle dance.

St. Ambrose, a powerful fourth-century Bishop of Milan, had written "And just as he who dances with his body, rushing through the rotating movements of the limbs, acquires a right to share in the round dance, in the same way, he who dances the spiritual dance, always moving in the ecstasy of faith, acquires a right to dance in the ring of all creation." In the same century, the Bishop of Caesarea, St. Basil, linked his flock to the angels when he sermonized that nothing was more blessed than imitating on earth the circle dances of angels while raising voices in prayer and song to glorify the Creator. With characteristic moderation, St. Thomas Aquinas sanctioned dancing for special occasions and even wrote that it was a healthy form of exercise, provided it was kept decent. On a wall in Siena's Palazzo Pubblico, a fresco shows nine noble women singing and performing a circle dance to the accompaniment of a tambourine. What the artist Lorenzetti was expressing in the fresco was the presence and popularity of dancing as one aspect of the good life that resulted from the Christian city's well-organized government.

The medieval mind envisioned God on his heavenly throne surrounded by dancing "rounds of angels," a favorite theme represented over and over again in medieval painting. The notion that dancing was the principal pastime for the saints in heavenly regions was a medieval idea lingering from the ancient Greek mystery cults. Fra Angelico confirmed his own belief in a number of paintings by depicting with the sentiments of a master painter the dancing and music-making of saints and angels. As a result, the Church wisely incorporated small amounts of highly disciplined and formalized dance in its most profound religious services, thereby preserving as well as sanctifying its presence in medieval culture. The most famous dance to survive, Spain's *baile de los seises* (dance of the six), was introduced some time after Christendom's third largest cathedral was completed in Seville around 1450. The clergy attempted to forbid this dance and ruled that when its special costumes wore out, it could no longer be performed. The congregation, however, so loved the traditional *baile* that the costumes were secretly patched and kept in tack by the women of the town. A beautiful embellishment of the *Corpus Christi* services, the dance continues to be performed by young boys in front of the high altar to this day.[16]

Liturgical dances took other forms as well. Labyrinths designed in colored stone on the floors of the basilica of St. Mark's in Venice and in the cathedrals of Chartres and Auxerre were the sites for symbolic Easter Day chain dances lead by the senior members of the clergy. Proceeding in a three-step rhythm called a

7

*tripudium*, the priests wound their way through the labyrinth representing the path or dance of the sun during the year. Analogous to the path or dance of the incarnate Christ from his birth to his death, burial, and resurrection as the Christ-Sun, the ritualistic significance of the movement was clearly grasped by the faithful.[17]

During the rule of Justinian I (527–565), the restricted use of dance in medieval religious ceremonies acquired an additional dimension when the Church absorbed the technique of pantomime to strengthen the communication of Christian beliefs to its faithful. Itinerant performers, some descending from the Roman mimes, were colorful players at village fairs and festivities, keeping the tradition of entertainment alive throughout the Middle Ages. These players enacted nonverbal storytelling in the form of skits and plays, a technique lingering from the past when pantomime had been a highly refined art and an essential part of the Roman theater. In a period when few people understood Latin, the Church recognized that the expressive gestures of these mimes could be meaningfully employed to dramatize the liturgy and religious parables for the congregation. Appropriate gestural movements were duly selected by churchmen who then regulated and codified their liturgical usage.

While dance as a public entertainment did not exist in the Middle Ages due to prohibitions imposed by the Church, everyday life was not devoid of dancing. Medieval guilds,[18] under the patronage of specific Christian saints, had been created to guarantee the quality of the various goods and services produced by the town's craftsmen. Guilds purposely restricted open-market competition, and with painstaking detail protected the public and the workers in one profession or another by demanding high standards of craftsmanship. Becoming rich, powerful, and important to the community, guilds were authorized to hold celebrations during the pre-Lenten carnival. Members participated in festivities held in the town's center by performing dances that were specifically related to the guilds they represented. Competing with each other, they paraded through the streets, skipping and prancing, costumed in merry attire and masks. Processions often ended in the impressively decorated guildhalls where social dancing took place among the wealthier citizens. The dances themselves ranged from vigorous but simple line and circle dances to more complex forms that were accompanied by flutes and stringed instruments.

Toward the end of the Middle Ages, musicians began to organize themselves into guilds from which their services were purchased by wealthy clients. In their capacity to provide the music for social dances of the upperclass, musicians largely controlled the content and teaching of dance for centuries. Guilds, founded by royal decree, had the right to grant licenses for the teaching of dance to aspirants after they had exhibited a thorough knowledge of the subject including music, execution of dances, creation of new dances, and the ability to notate them. On becoming a master, the guild member as licensed teacher was then permitted one or two apprentices whom he took under his roof for several years. During this time, the apprentice had to prove to the guild that he was prudent and loyal; he must demonstrate, like his master before him, a full

The picture invokes the high-spirited and pantomimic *Hoppaldei* in which rustic couples give themselves up to the motor and sensory pleasures of dancing. (Courtesy of the author.)

knowledge of dance and music for dance; he must produce and present a "masterpiece"; and he must swear to uphold the guild's laws and customs. Finally, he was required to pay a fee that went not to the guild, but to the sovereign.[19]

Although their activities were frowned upon by the priests, generations of wandering musicians, acrobats, and jugglers performed street dances. Wayfarers and gypsies from India, making their way westward through southern France and northern Italy and Spain, also contributed to the gaiety of the marketplace with tightrope dances, magic tricks, and fortune-telling. On the move from town to town, these free-spirits were much in demand because their songs and amusing antics spread good humor and merriment in village squares. They have been variously remembered as *minnesingers*, *spiëlmann*, *joglars*, and minstrels, and were often the possessors of extensive and varied knowledge acquired in their travels.

Whenever possible, the common people of the Middle Ages lived their daily lives outdoors. Only the harshest weather contained them in the dank and smoky cottages that served as their dwellings. In cases of war or natural catastrophe, they took shelter in the feudal overlord's walled and moated castle. When the Church's bans on dancing were overlooked, farmers and townsfolk alike reveled in highlighting their humble celebrations of religious feasts with simple dances. Not having an official organizer, these dances were little more than spontaneous and passionate outpourings of energy performed to singing, handclapping, and perhaps to the tune of a shepherd's flute. All ages participated in these activities because they were essentially pleasurable, expressing the joy people felt at a gathering to proclaim a good harvest or a country wedding. The stomping and circling of the dancers provided a heightened sense of community among the participants and a robust means of breaking the tedium of their daily labors. People, then as now, were social animals, and, considering the fearful medieval times, their dancing must have been a consolation.

Yet, more often than not, an overly zealous prelate would chastise his flock, railing at them that dancing was the devil's business, that it encouraged lasciviousness, and that the gaiety of dancing made people forgetful of the overriding importance of life hereafter. Still, the most popular songs and dances survived and were handed down from old to young. Eventually, folk dances became more organized, gaining names that indicated a gradual ordering of steps, patterns, and their accompanying rhythms. In the hands of dancing masters centuries later, elegant Renaissance court dances, and eighteenth- and nineteenth-century ballroom dancing, would acquire many of the forms from the dances of medieval folk.

The earliest dances in tribal societies had a central focus, a symbolic object such as a sacred tree, stone, animal, or person around which the worshipful dance was aimed. By the millennium the *carole*,[20] with its roots traceable to Minoan civilization, was the basic form of folk dance. The *caroles* were chain dances that included a leader who led hand-linked dancers in circles and lines. Having lost their religious connotation, these dances omitted the central focal point and were fairly freewheeling. At first they evolved of themselves, but eventually their popularity and frequent repetition lent them a definite structure. Peasants always sang their accompaniment to *caroles* with spritely rhythms that caused feet to beat together and advance forward and backward to the tune of a flute or a drum. Occasionally, the dancers performed hops and leaping movements, all the while yodeling or making rhythmic sounds with their lips and tongues to imitate bagpipes, flutes, and drums.

An example of a specific *carole* is the maypole dance,[21] still widely performed today in Europe, as well as in North American towns that have maintained their early settler traditions. The maypole dance is a carryover from Druid times around 300 B.C. when it had served as a magical fertility dance in the springtime of the year. A large tree trunk was decorated and worshiped during a ritual that included encircling dances by the Druid leader and his followers. The Middle Ages, having forgotten the full pagan significance of this phalli-

10

cally symbolic ceremonial dance, retained and adapted its colorful external elements. Creating their movements from the source of all dance, peasants gave into kinetic pleasure with exuberance, enjoying the ultimate "feeling of life." Descriptions of thirteenth-century dances denote their essential characteristics. The shoulder-rolling *ahselrotten* was vigorous and flirtatious, while the *gimpelgampel* and the *springeltanz* were boisterous with leaps and skips. In the *hoppaldei*, couples wildly rushed about with shoulders heaving and arms waving, while the *houbelschotten* called for sliding movements, head shaking, and the shoulder shrugging.[22]

More advanced than the *carole*, the couple dance was a pantomimic form that medieval people enjoyed as a part of courting activities. Just as some steps and rhythms of the spirited peasant dances crept into social gatherings of the nobility, most upper-class dances eventually trickled down to the commoners. Improvised couple dances were seen less often than round dances because they were only performed for mate seeking. The dances were often erotic in nature and offered the opportunity for wanton behavior and sacrilege as a legacy from pagan days.[23] Condemned by churchmen, dances were heartily disapproved of as licentious behavior, but that had little effect on their popularity. Musically, couple dances shared characteristics of the round dances. Like the people who performed them, the dances were ribald, lusty, and abundantly energetic. As to the spatial patterns of early folk dances, precision and beauty were probably secondary objectives due to the dancers' spontaneity as well as their lack of training. What mattered was that male and female had the occasions for flirtatious encounters.

11

## DANSEOMANIA

An ominous phenomenon referred to as *danseomania* occurred in the Middle Ages. It was characterized by large numbers of people, often entire town populations, dancing until they collapsed or died of exhaustion. For the most part, this dance was formless and nameless in the usual sense of organized dancing. It seems that it was one of improvisation urged on by the effects of mass psychology. People thought that this mania for dancing was the result of witchcraft, the bite of the tarantula spider, or intervention of the devil. More enlightened men, however, diagnosed *danseomania* as resulting from group hypnosis, sexual excitement, contaminated food, or hysterical symptoms of merriment.[24] In any event, people were again expressing themselves in the most instinctive manner known to them—movement. It is worth mentioning here that the Hans Christian Andersen fairy tale, which was the basis for the British film *The Red Shoes* (1947), enchantingly dramatized a tale reminiscent of a victim of *danseomania*. The children's story, *The Pied Piper of Hamelin*, inspired by a 1284 account surrounding the departure and fate of the town's children, was also said to have its plot based on the notion of *danseomania*. After ridding the town of an infestation of rats, the city fathers refused to pay the piper his fee. For this injustice, the piper spellbound the town's children, and skipping and prancing they followed him and his music to oblivion.

Toward the end of the medieval era, the Christian obsession with death led to an aberrant but popular game-like form of dance, which arose out of a horrifying social phobia. When bubonic plague swept Europe the first time in 1347, half the population was ravaged within a few years by the disease. The Church-dominated mentality of the peasant population in the Middle Ages had always been preoccupied with death, and now this so-called Black Death became the great leveler of humanity.[25] No one could escape from its jaws, no wealth or power, no prayer or pious living was assurance of deliverance from the dreaded disease. These notions were infused with beliefs that the dead returned to haunt the living, and many thought that the dead themselves danced nocturnal dances until the cock crowed.[26]

The result of all this was that people, elderly superstitious folks and youthful pranksters alike, gathered in the graveyards to perform game-like round dances at wakes for the dead.[27] Intense gaiety preceded a mimed death that occurred at a given musical signal. The mood of the dance would become somber as one of the male participants sank to the ground feigning death. The other female dancers would then take turns kissing the deceased back to life, whereupon all would celebrate in a general round dance. The make-believe scenario was then repeated with a female dancer feigning death on a certain cue and the male dancers in turn reviving her with kisses.[28] Naturally the kissing part of the dance was always popular, but the modern mind cringes at the thought of passing germs from mouth to mouth in times of plague. It is a jarring but interesting thought that this macabre practice of kissing the dead back to life is probably the original notion for the central moment in Petipa's grandest ballet, *The Sleeping Beauty*, when the prince revives his princess with a kiss.

The outcome of the medieval fascination with death was far-reaching. From superstition, lingering pagan beliefs, ignorance, and folklore, the peasants thought that the dead returned to lure the living into a dance of death, signifying that all classes of people really dance toward their deaths in the course of daily life. It is precisely the kernel of this ancient notion upon which Theophile Gautier built his scenario for the great nineteenth-century narrative ballet, *Giselle*. The ballet is based on a reconstruction of Germanic folklore by the poet, Heinrich Heine. Amidst a gathering of maidenly ghosts, Act II depicts Giselle's return to the real world to dance to death the lovesick hero whose duplicity had been the reason for her own demise.

Throughout the Middle Ages, the *danse macabre* provided a popular theme for literary and pictorial forms of expression, although it was rarely an actual type of dance.[29] The *danse macabre* is important in tracing dance's evolution because its various expressions are indicative of the Church-dominated medieval mentality. The concept of the *macabre* was rooted in the psychology of fear, and the Church seized upon it as a means of moral exhortation.[30] An imposing cultural idea until the concept wore itself out, it has lingered in symbols and inscriptions that are depicted in the skull and crossbones image and

12

the funeral epitaph *momento mori*. A sinister topic of medieval prose, the *danse macabre* often took on the form of a dialogue between its characters and a skeletal death figure. In chilling fashion, graphic works, wood cuts, and drawings depicted a parade of the living following a shrouded skeleton that wound along the walls of churches and covered bridges.[31] These literary and visual stories were meant to be stern warnings of humanity's worldly end and that death comes to Everyman regardless of loftiness of rank or station.

As the dawning sense of human equality pervaded the waning of the Middle Ages, the concept of personified "Death" stalking its prey was to the common mind a sweet revenge on the wealthy class.[32] Death leveled kings, bishops, and the poor alike, making all equal in the clutches of the grim reaper. The cult of death first appeared in the fourteenth century when the dominant idea of death had been the pious contemplation of the spiritual journey of the soul. In the fifteenth century, however, the ghoulish image of the rotting body attained greater significance for its ability to induce fear among the faithful.[33] Medieval death dances, as manifested in the forms of pictures and writing, were perhaps desperate statements reflecting the average person's growing disillusionment with the era's social, political, and religious climate.

Folk dance is not a dance form directly related to the theatrical performance of ballet. It has been discussed here for two basic reasons. First, folk or peasant dancing represents the continued human interest in dance as diversion and recreation even when it was not sanctioned by the the medieval Church. Second, after A.D. 1000, peasant dancing began to lend its own round and couple dance patterns to the developing courts of the feudal lords. During the pre-Lenten season, costumed and masked commoners, given a certain social license by carnival festivities, were allowed into the castles of the nobility for a celebration known as the Feast of Fools. After performing their songs and dances, peasants would be treated to refreshments and were allowed to mingle with the nobles. To continue the merriment, it was acceptable for the lords and ladies to parody the dancing of the peasants. Steps were not ordered or danced in a prescribed sequence by the nobles, who simply imitated what appealed to them. Thus, it was normal for dance movements to be performed without method or motivation, but according to the mood and imagination of the participants.

In due time and in keeping with the customs of chivalry,[34] hired minstrels attempted to refine and transform peasant dances for the well-to-do. However, without the craft of choreography and a body of codified technique at their disposal, minstrels achieved little that was permanent. Nonetheless, folk dancing found its way into the great stone fortresses of Christendom, influencing the development of medieval court dances that enjoyed a popular presence in the lives of the nobles. In addition, dance practiced by the upper class signified that it contained educational values and therefore transmitted ennobling characteristics. Thus, dance's courtly existence was assured of a firm and honored place in the houses of the mighty.

In the Middle Ages power of the sword was the only actual distinguishing mark between the common people and their lords. Organically, the feudal sys-

13

tem was a fighting body of upper and lower classes held together by socioeconomic bonds of mutual dependency necessary for survival.[35] Before the eleventh
century, medieval life boasted no luxuries, delicacies, or refinements that are
usually associated with good living.[36] The so-called nobles were as uncouth,
uneducated, and unpolished as their serfs. The overlord's primary concern was
to maintain the hierarchical structure of his feudal kingdom, to see it functioning well, and to keep his feudal neighbor from stealing it from him.[37]

As Doomsday passed in 1033 and the world did not come to an end as fore-
told, people's fears and uncertainties gave way to a more positive outlook
toward physical existence. After the millennium, greater political stability
allowed for the amassing of wealth among the nobility. Abetted by the development of a heavier breed of horse, improved agricultural techniques spurred population growth. The expansion of towns and the reawakening of the old Roman
cities escalated commercial traffic. Organized inland trade routes, as well as the
centrality of the Rhine River and its many tributaries, began the establishment
of a formidable economic force that would bring forth the modern concept of
continental Europe. The crisscrossing of Europe by throngs of pilgrims on their
way to holy shrines, like Santiago de Compostelo in the northwest of Spain,
generated great monetary activity, giving rise to a genuine bourgeois class.[38] As
a matter of pride and ambition, the overlord wished to improve and embellish
himself, his family, and his court, and he now possessed the wealth to accomplish this. Consequently, outsiders became attached to the feudal courts with
the responsibility of instructing the nobles and their children in the fundamentals of reading, writing, etiquette, comportment, music, poetry, and dance. The
most honored of these court attachés was the troubadour.

## TROUBADOURS AND MEDIEVAL COURT DANCE

At the end of the eleventh century, European cultural centers developed in an
area known as Provence, which extended from the south of France to northern
Italy and Spain. These centers resulted from a fortuitous combination of elements. Geographically, the areas included dry and craggy mountains as well as
the vast pastoral countrysides that were rich in the produce of grain and wines.
Blessed with a mild climate, the lands were owned by a leisurely, graceful upper
class who provided the basis for uniquely refined courts. Aristocratic men and
women enjoyed a way of life that valued the concept of ideal love that, in turn,
brought forth a gentility of manner, tempered according to the laws of chivalry.
The refined ambiance and patrician attitudes of the upper class were reflected
and glorified in the poetic renderings of the troubadour.[39] Conversely, the utter-
ances of the troubadours provided guides to the social and moral behavior of
those who read their poetry. Of aristocratic family background, troubadours
numbered over 400 and named some twenty women in their ranks.[40]

The troubadours of Provence were poets and songwriters who flourished
from 1100 to 1244 when the violent quelling of the Albigensian heresy

destroyed the Provençal way of life. Their passionate poetry had enormous social influence because it created around the ladies of the court an aura of cultivation that up to that time, nothing had approached. The vassalage of man to woman was the central metaphor of their love poetry, as Bernart de Ventadorn tells us, "Lady, for your love I join my hands and worship."[41] The troubadours were well-traveled, many having participated as soldiers in the Crusades. During their journeys they absorbed all kinds of information, including much of the classical learning from Byzantine scholars and other marks of civilization.[42] As serious court adjuncts, troubadours enjoyed deliberating the classical writers' views on education, and were accordingly judged as arbitrators of good taste and manners. Troubadours were engaged to arrange *fêtes* for baronial households and to act as social educators. Often, their duties included the long-term education of young boys and girls of noble birth. One of the loveliest legends to survive from the troubadour's pen was "Del Tumbleor Nostre Dame," (The Tumbler of Our Lady), which told the tale of an old street entertainer who paid ecstatic homage to the Mother of God by the only craft he knew—dancing. Falling exhausted before her image in a church, he was found the next morning sleeping in the statue's arms.

The earliest known and foremost of the Provençal poets was William of Poitiers,[43] the ninth overlord of a large area known as the Aquitaine. In his time, William enjoyed a particularly enthusiastic disposition toward the fair sex, which he celebrated in love songs that he fondly referred to as his *canzos*. During the first Crusade William had taken asylum at a friendly and luxurious court in Asia Minor. While there, he had the opportunity to steep himself in Moorish songs and absorb Islamic culture in general. This extraordinary experience, in a setting where Arab poets had been worshiping their ladies for at least 200 years, prompted him to shape his poetry the way he did. William's sung verses were a type of lyrical poetry that subtley focused on a set of amorous attitudes toward women that reflected concepts known as courtly love.[44]

The appreciation of woman emerged in Europe during this period and was augmented by the cult of the Blessed Virgin. One anonymous medieval writer explicitly stated the superiority of womanhood over man because Eve was made from Adam's rib, she was made in Paradise, a woman conceived God, and Christ first appeared to a woman after the resurrection. By transferring the intense medieval veneration of the Virgin Mary to the lady of one's choice, a married noble woman was extolled and desired by the poet for her graciousness and beauty. By the same token, he regretted she was unattainable due to her rigorous purity. Significantly, as non-physical forms of flattery, the poems of many an impecunious young troubadour were attractive passports to a powerful husband's favor.[45]

Among the earliest sources to elevate the *lengua d'oc*, or vernacular Provençal speech, to the status of a literary language, William's *canzos* were influential in the cultivated forms later developed in Italy by Dante Alighieri, Giovanni Boccaccio, and Francesco Petrarch. Inspiration for William's mellifluous songs and those of his admirers and imitators included a mixture of Latin

15

verse of the clergy, sonorous oriental influences from knightly encounters with Moors and Saracens, cadences of church music, and native popular songs of wandering minstrels. Centered on praising the beauty of women, the joy of love, and the pleasure of amorous pursuits, the *canzos* were always accompanied by dancing (*caroles*), which all the more served to heighten their emotional messages.

As part of the troubadour's entourage, entertainers known as minstrels and *joglars* (jugglers) were hired to accompany songs and to perform acrobatic dances.[46] The genealogy of the minstrels and *joglars* traces itself back to the Roman *pantomimi* when the technique of storytelling with gestures and body movement was perfected and became notable in Roman theater for its exquisite subtlety of expression. Eventually, however, like the crumbling of the Roman Empire itself in the fifth century, pantomime deteriorated into a broader fun-filled form of entertainment. Bowing to the demands of diminishing levels of taste, wandering mimes learned additional crowd-pleasing skills from other nomadic entertainers, and so playing musical instruments, performing acrobatic tricks, juggling, and joking became the order of the day for the next 600 years.

By the twelfth century performers who were associated with the courtly activities of the troubadours fell into two categories. Those who specialized in providing music and musical accompaniment for court functions were known as minstrels. Entertainers who had the skills of acrobats, stilt walkers, tight rope walkers, and other diverse amusements were known as *joglars*. Since dance in courtly society was much valued for its educational merits (having been sanctioned by its very presence in the earlier writings of the saints, John, Ambrose, Basil, etc.), minstrels and *joglars* gave instruction in dancing, music, and courtly manners as part of their profession. As knowledgeable men who composed music and poetry, troubadours were credited for developing rigid rules for the dance compositions arranged by their assistants, rules that much later would be reflected in the structure of the Renaissance court ballets.[47]

Over time and by their mutual activities, the troubadours, minstrels, and the *joglars* synthesized into the profession of the dancing master. In their fledgling roles as teachers, these gentlemen had quite a challenge in creating dances for their noble pupils. Assuming the duties of instructor, they borrowed the rowdy peasant dances as the rudiments for courtly versions so that the dances included the same indefinite floor patterns and footsteps as the peasant dances. However, these earliest dancing masters were confronted with redesigning movement for the interior of great stone fortresses.[48] Before they could make much headway in teaching the court their dances, they had to instruct the males how to behave in a mannerly way and even how to step in their *poulaines*,[49] shoes with curiously long and curled toes. Females had to be taught how to manipulate their trains and to securely wear their *hennins*, the unwieldly single or double conical-shaped headdresses favored by upperclass women. Refinement in all things became the objective of court life, and so dance activities developed more and more artifice. Due to the emphasis on refinement, the contrived elegance in the dancing tended to become stylized so that court dances became conventionalized and emotions were carefully contained.

Around 1100, the *branle*, a form of *carole*, emerged in northern European countries as the most common court dance. Here the dancers were aligned in a closed or semi-closed circular formation, male and female alternating in places. *Branles* were fairly simple dances emphasizing slow and quick rhythmic shifts of weight forward and backward and side to side. A second form of the *carole* characterizing the dances of southern European countries was the *farandole*.[50] By contrast, *farandoles* were linear dances in which dancers continuously moved forward. The simplest patterns were serpentine figures, curving, twisting, and turning at random according to the pleasure of the leader. More complex patterns involved snail-shaped configurations of linked dancers and the subsequent dissolution of the figure.

The *farandole*, like the *branle*, was danced to sung accompaniment, often out of doors. The beauty of this dance was further developed when arch-shaped figures were introduced. Now the dancers lifted their linked hands, allowing the leader to lead the line "under the arches."[51] At some point the arched formations created by uplifted arms disappeared from this dance form and it is thought that the explanation lies in the height of the fashionable but exaggerated *hennin*. While lifted arms remained a characteristic of the rowdy dances of the peasantry, raised arms were not seen again in court dancing until the early eighteenth century. In twentieth-century theatrical dance, the arch-shaped formations of the *farandole* reappeared as a choreographic device in the exquisitely poetic, lifted-arm patterns highlighting the choreography of Mikhail Fokine's masterpiece, *Les Sylphides*. A generation later, the same use of lifted arms emerged as the choreographic hallmark of the *corps de ballet* movement in George Balanchine's *Concerto Barocco*, *Symphony in C*, and *La Sonambula*.

## COURTLY COUPLE DANCING

Court dances had two chief functions: showing off oneself and courtship. The *branles* and *farandoles* certainly lent themselves to the first concern with their display of preening, parading, and posturing movements. Dancing had always been considered a group activity, until the rowdy mate-seeking dances of the peasants evolved and couple dances began to appear in the social activities of aristocrats. Couple dances were convenient and refined vehicles for purposes of courtship that introduce a question. How did Western dancers ever get themselves out of the *carole* line with its circles, arcs and serpentine meanderings? How did the notion of a single male dancing with a single female occur? The answer probably lies with the twelfth-century phenomenon known as the Courts of Love.

Organized and presided over by judges who were highborn ladies, Courts of Love tried and ruled on romantic matters according to the genteel tastes of the ruling class.[52] The subtleties of love were much discussed even by university scholars who took to praising their chosen ladies in poems.[53] Around 1150, a certain Court of Love concerned itself with the dilemma of whether it is better to love a clerk or a cavalier. The court session was opened by the ladies Elizabeth of Fauçon and Elizabeth of Granges who wore garlands of flowers and sang love songs. The trial concluded with the decision that it was better to love a discreet and courtly clerk than a swashbuckling knight who tended to boast of his amorous conquests.[54] The culmination of the trial was then celebrated with light refreshments and a novel form of dancing during which the participants paired off in couples in the *estampie*.

The concept of the courtly couple dance derives from a mixture of the troubadour-inspired love songs and the work of his clever underling, the fledgling dancing master. Significant also for couple dancing was an admiration for the upper-class female in society. This attitude was blended with the widespread cult of the Virgin Mary,[55] which intensified as hundreds of cathedrals were built in her name. Cherishing women was a notion that found its way into court dances as a reflection of a lifestyle that prized and imitated the loving mutual esteem of the Virgin Mary and Christ.

With reference to the pairing off of dancers who participated in the socializing at the Courts of Love, various theories suggest that during the popular *branles*, a dancing male and the female to his right would step forward from the line to dance several patterns moving forward and backward. This couple dance became known as the *estampie*, a dance for two performed by one couple at a time while the others in the *branle* line watched. Without the constraints of being in a linked circle or line, they danced freely and for their own pleasure, the male surely delighting in showing off the charms of his partner and she, in turn, flattered by his presentation of her to viewers. The *estampie* was momentous in the evolution of dance because it replaced the sung *carole* with instrumental music that had a beginning, a middle, and an end. The *estampie* further contrasted to a *carole* because it eventually found a frontal focal point; the *estampie* was directed to onlookers, whereas the *carole* circled or wandered indefinitely.

For the first time in centuries, dancing was displayed before a human presence such as the lord and lady of the castle. In this sense dance took on the aura of a ceremonial activity, the male dancer paying homage to the lord and chivalrously calling attention to his exquisite counterpart. Most important, however, is that the *estampie* was the seminal form of ballet as a Western theatrical dance. That is, its performance was directed toward appreciative viewers. Ballet has always been primarily performed for the delectation of others.

Court dancing was part of the life of chivalry insofar as the dances stressed elegance of bearing, precision of execution, and coquetry on the part of the ladies. The earliest court dance reconstructed in our time is the *basse danse* of the late Middle Ages. These dances, so called *basse* (low) because they involved stepping and gliding movements, were in the form of a processional of couples.

It is possible to observe a chain of kinship between our classical ballet *terre à terre* movements and their mannerly executed ancestral steps described by scholars who continue to research the characteristics of the *basse danse*. Although stately and ceremonial, the *basse danse* did not necessarily have a prescribed order of steps. Rather, it was necessary that the courtiers rely on memory to endlessly combine anew the individual steps.

Peasant dances continued to enrich the dancing of the upper class, especially in their high-spiritedness, which lent a lively air to the newly devised dances at court. In France these were termed *haute* (high) dances and incorporated jumping or leaping steps that might be considered the roots of ballet's *danse en l'air* steps of elevation. Due to the women's *hennins* and long trains, they generally left the performance of the *hautes danses* up to the men.

## *MORESQUES* AND RELIGIOUS PLAYS

In the twelfth century, there appeared a dance form called the *moresque* in France, or *morisco* and *moresco* in Italy and Spain, respectively. *Moresques* were danced stories that related the century-old religious and territorial struggles between the Moors and Christians.[56] Motivated by religious beliefs, the earliest type of the *moresque* was performed on festival days. Participants consisted of townspeople in addition to the ubiquitous jugglers, acrobats, and musicians playing the fife and drum. The ingredients of the *moresque* varied little. The dancers frequently tied bells to their wrists and ankles and they danced and pantomimed a reenactment of the black-faced Moor giving battle to Christian soldiers. The inevitable defeat of the Moor resulted in a jubilant finale. In time, the nature of these *moresques* changed by becoming less religiously inspired and more entertaining. Additional attractions such as interludes of group singing and dancing, satyrs, nymphs, savages, and the use of elaborate tableaux increased their sophistication and popularity, especially in the great northern Italian towns.

Besides the *moresques*, there existed as early as the tenth century morality, miracle, and mystery plays or "sacred representations"[57] as they were called in Italy. These were dramatic skits devised for the purpose of teaching a Christian code of behavior, Bible history, and Christian dogma to the illiterate masses. All three types of plays were elaborately performed with singing and simple dances, and were popular fare on religious feast days. Similar to the morality plays that provided role models for a pious lifestyle, miracle plays often took the form of processional dancing to commemorate the miracles that had been attributed to the holiness of particular saints. During celebrations, relics of the saints were devoutly paraded through the streets amidst much sacerdotal regalia. Leading the procession and cloaked in rich brocade woven with silver thread, priests and deacons bore the gold-encased relics in special wooden chests. Billows of incense, the Gregorian chanting of the clergy, and their

19

rhythmic stepping further contributed to this devout spectacle. The populace, including children, were encouraged to join in these processions. Due to the musical rhythms of the singing, a swaying-like dance was produced as the procession advanced through the streets from church to church.

Mystery plays illustrated in colorful pageantry the nonrational aspects of Christian dogma called "mysteries." Quite often the venues for these religious presentations were the great stone façades of the cathedrals. Huge Gothic doorways, heavily carved with religious figures, served as perfect settings for the faithful to view dramatizations of Christian teachings.[58] Thus, the sense of spectacle was still present in the lives of men, but in a religious guise. Anyone fortunate enough to witness the traditional Holy Week services in Seville to this day will gain an impression of the atmosphere and character that these medieval plays and processionals produced in their time.

## PAGEANTS

The medieval pageant brings us closer to the beginnings of the ballet. In fact, pageants contained many elements of Renaissance court entertainment and the seventeenth-century theatrical traditions that were firmly established by the court of Louis XIV. The pageant was an ambulant spectacle that retained certain aspects of the structure of the morality, miracle, and mystery plays, but in essence it was less genuinely religious. A pageant consisted of a parade of elaborate platforms constructed by the trade guilds of the town. The various guilds competed with each other in devising ornate, mobile scenes to pay homage to their patron saints and provide splendid advertising for themselves. Enlivened by dancers and singers who were guild members, elevated platforms displayed allegorical themes that were based on any and all aspects of medieval life, thus proclaiming something to please every onlooker. These floatlike constructions with their living *tableaux* were pulled through the streets, and as the pageant drew to a close, the participants would end their parading with some welcomed nourishment offered in the guildhalls. This culinary aspect of the event was an invitation to devise fantasies of a different nature so that pageants were eventually followed by elaborate guild-sponsored banquets. Contemporary descriptions of postpageant feasting, which preceded crusades or celebrated political alliances, suggest that the food itself was often obscured by its very embellishment.[59]

The pageant's most direct relationship to the ballet was that the richly festooned floats were the forerunners of theatrical scenery. Constructed with large, standing flats mounted on rolling wagons, these extravaganzas served to hide the façades of the city buildings and, in so doing, provided unique atmospheric effects.[60] From this juncture, it was but a small step for later artisans to explore design possibilities that led to the concept of stage decor.

# Summary

The ancestral roots of the ballet are inextricably related to the development of European civilization from ancient times through the sixteenth century. During its social, religious, political, and economic struggles, Europe was infused with the presence of dancing. From the classical age of Greek drama, followed by the Roman *pantomimi*, the troubadours, and folk and court dancers, various human purposes were served by dance so that diverse forms of it evolved to fit each need. When it was under the control of cautious prelates, dancing in the early Church was used to divert the proverbial Roman energies for revel and bacchanal toward group participation in pious religious ceremony. The troubadour served as poet, educator, and elitist entertainer while his associates, the wandering minstrels and *joglars*, facilitated the demand for dance instruction throughout Western Europe. When folk dancing and court dancing developed as social custom, the moresques, morality plays, miracle plays, mystery plays, and pageants brought with them ever-increasing elements of dance presented as spectacle.

# Chapter Notes

1. Maria-Gabriele Wosien, *Sacred Dance: Encounter with the Gods* (New York: Thames and Hudson, 1974), pp. 8–12.
2. Ibid.
3. Lillian B. Lawler, *The Dance in Ancient Greece* (Seattle: University of Washington Press, 1967), p. 11.
4. Ibid., p. 82.
5. Ibid., p. 87.
6. Sheldon Cheney, *The Theatre: Three Thousand Years of Drama, Acting and Stagecraft* (New York: Tudor Publishing Co., 1949), p. 82.
7. Ibid., p. 95.
8. Quintilian, *Institutes of Oratory: Loeb Classical Library* (Cambridge, MA: Cambridge Harvard University Press, 1958–1960), II, 9. 21.
9. Lawler, p. 139.
10. Ibid., pp. 139–140.
11. Ibid., p. 139.
12. Will Durant, *Caesar and Christ: A History of Roman Civilization and of Christianity from Their Beginnings to A.D. 325* (New York: Simon and Schuster), 1944, p. 380.
13. Lawler, pp. 143–4.
14. Lincoln Kirstein, *Dance: A Short History of Classical Theatrical Dancing* (Brooklyn, NY: Dance Horizons, 1969), p. 379.

15. Ibid., p. 127.
16. Anna Ivanova, *The Dance in Spain* (New York: Praeger Publishers, 1970) p. 90. Six boys danced originally, but by the twentieth century the number increased to ten.
17. Wosien, p. 104.
18. Joseph and Frances Gies, *Life in a Medieval City* (New York: HarperCollins Books, 1981), pp. 89–93.
19. Ibid.
20. Kirstein, *Dance*, p. 91.
21. Wosien, plate and caption, number 48.
22. Curt Sachs, *World History of the Dance* (New York: W. W. Norton & Company, 1963), pp. 95–102, 280–281.
23. Marjorie Rowling, *Life in Medieval Times* (New York: Paragon Books, 1979), p. 24.
24. Kirstein, *Dance*, pp. 88–9.
25. Rowling, p. 191.
26. Sachs, pp. 256–8.
27. Ibid., 252.
28. Kirstein, *Dance*, p. 86.
29. Johan Huizinga, *The Waning of the Middle Ages* (Garden City, NY: Doubleday & Co., 1945), p. 145. On one recorded occasion, the danse macabre was enacted in performance. In 1449, Philip III, Duke of Burgundy, had it staged in his mansion in Bruges.
30. Barbara Tuchman, *A Distant Mirror* (New York: Ballantine Books, 1978), pp. 508–9.
31. Wosien, p. 122, caption 65.
32. Kirstein, *Dance*, p. 85.
33. Tuchman, p. 506.
34. Kirstein, *Dance*, p. 101.
35. Huizinga, pp. 67–77.
36. Rowling, pp. 35–45.
37. Maurice Keen, *The Pelican History of Medieval Europe* (Middlesex, England: Penguin Books, 1987), p. 49.
38. Meg Bogin, *The Women Troubadours* (New York: W. W. Norton & Company, 1976), pp. 28–9.
39. Ibid., p. 37.
40. Ibid., pp. 8–36.
41. Ibid., p. 21.
42. Lawson, *A History of Ballet and Its Makers* (London: Dance Books, 1973), p. 9.
43. Marion Meade, *Eleanor of Aquitaine* (New York: Hawthorn Books, 1977), p. 13.
44. Denis de Rougemont, *Love in the Western World* (Greenwich, CT: Pantheon Books, 1956), p. 113. The European cultivation of passionate love began as a reaction to Christianity's doctrine on marriage by people whose spirit was still pagan, whether by nature or lifestyle. The earliest expressions of passionate love to come down to us from the Middle Ages were the love letters between Abélard and Héloise in 1118. By mid-century, the concept of passionate love was referred to as *cortezia* or courtly love.
45. Bogin, p. 53. Bogin has been quick to point out that scholars have disagreed regarding the interpretation of troubadorean love poetry, arguing respectively that it can be

read as platonic love, or a cover for adultery, or religious allegory. To varying degrees, all three were probably intended.

46. Ibid., p. 16.
47. Melusine Wood, *Historical Dances: 12th to 19th Century* (London: Boydell Press, 1984), pp. 7–8.
48. Ibid.
49. Permanent collection, Museum exhibit commentary. Bata Shoe Museum, Toronto, Canada. *Poulaines* originated around 1100 with the Duke of Anjou, Henry Plantagenet, who attempted to conceal a deformed toe. Becoming wildly fashionable by the mid-twelfth century, Edward III proclaimed that the legally permitted length of the shoe, which ranged from six to twenty-four inches when stuffed with moss to maintain its shape, was to be dictated by income and social standing. A prince of the blood, however, could have as long a shoe as he wished. By the fourteenth century, the clergy considered such shoes to be the work of the devil.
50. Wood, p. 12.
51. Ibid.
52. Rowling, p. 81.
53. Ibid.
54. Ibid., p. 82.
55. Ibid., p. 80.
56. Ibid., p. 133.
57. Ibid., p.127.
58. Rowling, p. 187.
59. Kirstein, *Dance*, pp. 111–113.
60. Ibid., p. 113.

23

# 2

# *Renaissance Spectacle in Italy*

For centuries, massive forces of superstition and ignorance in northern Europe were in conflict with the sensuous elements of the Byzantine world of the Eastern Roman Empire. Lying conveniently between these two areas and with a temperament braced by its Greco-Roman heritage, Italy was the ideal incubator for the birth of a new age. Medieval people had been God-centered with an eye turned toward the immaterial values of faith, hope, and love. Their lives were directed by a desire to escape from the darkness and harshness of a semi-barbarous world into a heavenly reward promised by the Christian creed. The progressive expansion of the human horizon, however, is the silver thread running through history and, in time, the Western world changed. A new era dawned, shaped by the reawakening of confidence in the ancient Greek notion of human potential. Rejuvenated creative energies joined with Roman material values of the here and now, resulting in what has become known as the Italian Renaissance. Not since the glory days of imperial Rome had Europe been so vibrant, so diversely productive, as with its renewed trust in people's abilities. In this new society dance figured prominently, dancing that would eventually evolve into classical ballet.

The Crusades had precipitated the revival of ancient learning that formed the Renaissance. Returning from the Holy Land, Crusaders carried home classical and Islamic ideas and attitudes. From 1100 onward, continued contact with Eastern civilization vastly extended the West's store of Greek, Roman, and Arabic mythology, philosophy, science, and art. The dedicated scholars of European monastic orders seized upon this precious material, reinterpreting it in their voluminous commentaries as an embellishment of Christian ideology. Slowly but surely, the thoughts of antiquity filtered into Western life.

Several centuries later, the Byzantine Empire, which was a bastion of Greek and Arabic culture, Roman traditions, and Christian religion, fell to the Ottoman Turks in 1453. The upheaval sent hundreds of scholars scurrying westward toward the shores of the Italian peninsula where they were welcomed in the spirit of the times. Possessing a treasure-house of ancient knowledge, Eastern men of learning provided the keystone for the European Renaissance by supplying new concepts of society. The unique worth and privileged place of the individual in the universe, the awakening desire for beauty, and the renewal of the pagan pursuit of happiness were paramount. Fortunately, the great wealth being acquired by Italian merchant families created a generous patronage to sponsor research in new ideas relating to all aspects of human activity.[1]

Present in this extraordinary period were elements of rebellion in the Western mind. The tide was turning against the iron fist of the Church, which had frequently caused the previous 500 years of human energy and curiosity to be used in the service of esoteric inquiries as bizarre as William of Occam's quest to determine how many angels could dance on the head of a pin. Church domination generally disallowed all scientific research and artistic discussions, considering them subversive. Hence, its staunchly held attitudes alienated the intellectually active, inadvertently fueling society's need to know.

# HUMANISM

Due to its growing wealth and its religious, political, and geographic circumstances, Italy first nurtured the new spirit of the times. After a thousand austere years, the heartland of the once-mighty Roman Empire became the cradle of a massive intellectual and cultural rebirth. The Papal libraries, having survived the fury of Visigoth invasions, were rich sources for investigations into the past. Universities intended as places where all the knowledge in the universe could be housed sprang up throughout northern Italy. So influential was the revitalization of classical literature that people's self-concept was reshaped, resulting in the notion of a people-centered, rather than God-centered, universe. Soon classical ideas were mingling with Christian values to produce a resounding awareness labeled by subsequent historians as Humanism. And so, two of the most cherished aspirations of the age were a richer, more civilized way of living and the pursuit of supreme artistic excellence with all its ennobling virtues.

Developing humanistic values called attention not only to a person's physical nature, but also to the pragmatic advantages of the physical over the spiritual half. Whereas a medieval Christian's greatest hope had been for a better life beyond the grave, Renaissance people held the conviction that earthly existence with its rich possibilities for living was significantly instrumental in helping them achieve heaven. This abrupt and dramatic change in thinking underscored the Renaissance's proclivity for the sensuous and a keen delight in the material aspects of daily life. Thus, dance in its fullness returned to the arena of special human events. The so-called *intermedii*, further developed by the French into the *entremets* of court ballet, were danced by the ruling class for the delec-

25

tation of their aristocratic peers at intervals during elaborate spectacles and feasts.

Concomitant with humanity's fresh self-image were numerous scientific discoveries, mechanical inventions, and geographical explorations that would ultimately shape the modern world. The development of the printing press by Johann Gutenberg in 1450 facilitated the rapid dissemination of old and new knowledge so that, after a dormancy of more than a millennium, important advancements were made in physics, archeology, medicine, pharmacology, and astronomy. The advent of the printing press encouraged liberal thinking while it also dispersed the written word as never before. This invention for a widespread communication of ideas also spawned the Protestant Reformation and its tortuous rift with the Roman Catholic Church. Military theory and style of warfare were radically altered by the development of gunpowder and cannon. Economic development was spurred on when the craft guilds learned to produce metals and textiles in large quantities. Shipbuilding was but one of many industries to mutually profit from the creative energies of society. Better-built seafaring vessels led to dynamic international trade and global exploration, which called for more sophisticated navigational principles, methods, and instruments. Indeed, no area of endeavor went untouched by Renaissance society's curiosity and ingenuity.

By orchestrating a major shift from religious to worldly matters, the Renaissance inspired humankind to do new work in the arts as well as in the sciences. At the waning of the Middle Ages, unusual forms of literature appeared, penned by the genius of Dante and Petrarch. Written in vernacular Italian rather than classical Latin or Greek, as was the literary tradition, their profoundly moving works served as codifying agents for everyday spoken Italian. Henceforth, literature, as well as other written matter, was removed from the exclusive domain of churchmen. It was only a matter of time before reading the native tongue became desirable for the nobility as well as for the emerging merchant class.

# ART IN THE RENAISSANCE

The times in which people are born influence how they use their talent and energies. When economic wealth flourishes and patronage is wisely disbursed, artists are induced to nurture their capabilities to bring forth great art. The Renaissance witnessed a remarkable coinciding of artistic genius with circumstance that made this extraordinary 150 years better than the world had ever known. The idea of self-culture or becoming educated by acquiring knowledge originated with Petrarch and was epitomized in the personage of Lorenzo de Medici (1449–1492), the prototype Renaissance man. Patronized by the Medici dynasty, Renaissance architecture, sculpture, and painting had an enormous impact on shaping the advancement of Western civilization.

Revived concepts of Aristotelian metaphysics such as cosmology and mathematics, in addition to principles of Roman government and architecture, celebrated the person and his worldly values. Architecture, according to sixteenth century artist and critic Giorgio Vasari, was the most universal, necessary, and useful of the human arts, and for whose service and adornment sculpture and painting existed. Drawing heavily on remnants of ancient temples, arenas, triumphal arches, and newly excavated classical sculpture, Renaissance artists conceived their marble, bronze, and granite inspirations with themes recovered from Greek and Roman mythology. The ancient buildings and statues served as blueprints for the fifteenth century's bold interpretation of human experience, which it reflected in its own architectural design.

The Renaissance artist was a particularly exciting synthesis of the exquisite spirituality of the medieval world and the intellectual and emotional disposition of the new era. The novel forces and ideas of this singularly complicated time period resulted in an outpouring of human energy and ambition. Stimulated by rediscovered Platonic ideas on universal order, Renaissance artists produced a fresh vision of the world. In particular, the Neoplatonic construct of universal harmony, formulated by Plotinus in his *Enneads* (c. 255), influenced artists and philosophers alike. Neoplatonism systematically ordered all levels of existence—from God to the heavenly bodies of the next level, down to the visible world. Humanity's challenge in this scheme was to rise up through the levels and become one with God.[2] From this line of thought would arise the Renaissance's rich concept of cosmic dance in which highly organized dancing at court functions symbolically reflected the harmony of the cosmos created by God, drawing His blessings to the earth. Cosmic dance was therefore understood as beneficial to society.

The advancement in painting went hand in hand with scientific endeavors. When artists finally mastered the techniques of modeling their subjects in light and shadow, intensely alive and dramatic works superseded the two-dimensional flatness of the medieval style of recording the human form. Giotto di Bondone (1276?–1337) had shown the way, painting his figures with expressive features and endowing their physical shape with the suggestion of movement.[3] The artist and architect Filippo Brunelleschi (1377–1446) uncovered the subtleties of linear-perspective construction.[4] Brunelleschi understood that parallel lines on the same plane appear to converge into a single vanishing point. The principle of the relationship between distance and the diminution of objects as they appear to recede in space allowed for paintings of astonishing realism. Artists, in using this idea on two-dimensional canvases, created illusions of three-dimensional space and tangible objects. Just so, Brunelleschi prepared the way for the connection between the relationship of geometry to the potential of human movement, i.e., choreography. Hence, the mathematical basis of massive spectacle was founded wherein the notion of choreographed theatrical dance would soon be defined.

By the twelfth century, secular music had evolved on various levels from the folk songs of common people to the refined *canzos* of courtly ladies and gentlemen. The Renaissance development of precision metal tools, in addition to experiments in Pythagorean mathematical theory and its relation to sound,[5] enabled artisans to devise and produce a large number of musical instruments of which the organ (c. 1400), the violin (c. 1500), double bass (c. 1500), and harpsichord (c. 1500) remain in current use. Renaissance music received an additional boost in 1501 when Ottaviano Petrucci invented a way to print musical notation with movable type. Now a plentiful supply of new music was available and less costly than that laboriously copied by hand. Printed music was also more accurate with the greatly reduced possibility of errors and variants in its reproduction. Most importantly, printed music encouraged extensive distribution and exchange among composers and musicians all over Europe.

Humanistic thinking, which espoused man as the measure of all things, was the foundation of the age's massive creativity in the sciences and the arts. The flood of original and recovered information had a direct influence on the Renaissance prince regarding his personal creative urges and his subsequent desire for entertainment on a spectacular scale. While public display employed in religious celebrations had been previously controlled by the Church, the Renaissance attitude was not only tolerant of spectacle, but also valued its use to promote political power and to flaunt private wealth.

One of the earliest Renaissance examples of meshing classical themes from antiquity with the Italian religious pageants or "sacred representations" was in the court of the mighty Medici family of Florence.[6] No one understood better than the Medici that beautiful things and events could overawe as effectively as prowess on the battlefield. The Medici were gifted opportunists who rose from the bourgeois ranks of money lenders to the status of popes and royal consorts. They eventually married into the courts of Northern European countries offering dowries ripe with the works of Raphael and Bronzino. Lorenzo de Medici (1449–1492) used his lofty station to patronize painting and sculpture, as well as establish an academy of learning devoted to the study of Greek and Roman literature. His academy's understanding of ancient philosophy, mythology, life, and theater, while not always accurate, did supply a wealth of inspiration for the "sacred representations" that Lorenzo ordered to be held for the general population at carnival time. Tinged with classical pagan literary themes, these presentations came to be known as *trionfi*, and were echoes of Roman triumphal parades. They resembled medieval pageants in the sense that they were religious spectacles mounted on chariots, but they incorporated the additional dimension of literature. The themes soon lost their religious purpose and the *trionfi* became increasingly filled with political flattery or exotic fantasy. The mythological connotations in many of these *trionfi* were well-suited to contemporary happenings at the Medici court. Social and political commentary could thereby be focused on current affairs with a clever use of allegory. In time, masked spectacles became standard fare for welcoming and impressing distinguished personages of foreign states, and history came full circle. The effect of the entire extravaganza was reminiscent of a visual re-enactment of pagan Rome welcoming home its victorious generals.[7]

28

Beginning with the earliest forms of public and private entertainments, Renaissance society demanded interludes of singing and dancing between scenes that presented mythology. Having little patience with a strict revival of Greek drama or the antique lore of gods, Renaissance nobles and their deeds were commemorated by having mythological themes recast in formulas, symbols, and metaphors to fit what was current in fifteenth-century experience. Emphasis was on the elaborate spectacle that included a variety of diversions and was thus pleasing in part to all those in attendance. In fact, no distinction clearly defined one form of entertainment from another. In keeping with the zeitgeist, the Church eventually encouraged these official public displays of pomp and wealth.

## THE DANCING MASTERS: DOMENICO DA PIACENZA, ANTONIO CORNAZANO, GUGLIELMO EBREO

Central to the development of the dance throughout the Renaissance was the professional dancing master. His work was considered a serious endeavor, and much time and effort were devoted to it so that dancing became an official part of upper-class life as well as a natural human pleasure. When the steps of favorite dances began to be recognized as individual movement patterns, that is, separate from the dance itself, the dancing master was able to assemble a composite of steps. Hence, a new methodology of dance appeared.

29

While the profession of dancing master was already seminal in the activities of the troubadours and minstrels of the late Middle Ages, the earliest practitioners identified by name lived in the fifteenth century. They were Domenico da Piacenza and his students, Antonio Cornazano and Guglielmo Ebreo. These men had been trained from youth so that their experience and knowledge of dance surely exceeded that of their earlier counterparts. Attached to powerful dynastic families in northern Italy, dancing masters were responsible for teaching and rehearsing resident nobles for courtly balls where they were expected to perform precisely executed steps prescribed for each dance. They arranged a great variety of dances to newly introduced musical forms, and the products of their efforts became the rage of the ruling class wishing to learn them.

Domenico da Piacenza, whose exact dates are unknown, was born in the late fourteenth century and left a treatise compiled by his pupils entitled *De arte saltandi et choreus ducendi* (1460, On the art of dancing and conducting dances). He poetically defined the Lombardy style of dance in northern Italy as an activity that reveals the sweet harmony created in our hearts by music. He goes on to say that being imprisoned within us, this sweetness and harmony struggle to get out and can only issue forth as beautiful patterns of movement. The treatise established that there was a body of independent ideas and codified dance steps that could be used in various contexts, and in this sense Domenico fostered the

development of choreography. The first part of his manuscript was devoted to the various movements of the body and elements that constitute the dance, such as rhythm, bearing, lightness, memory and, lastly, the mystic or inspiration of the dance that is required to keep it from becoming mere physical exercises. In the second part, Domenico enumerated basic steps of which nine are "natural" and three are "artificial."[8]

Domenico signed a number of *balli* (high, or jumping, dances), indicating that they and their music were his creations. *Balli* were figured dances and their keynote was variety; they had their music specially composed and could not be danced to any other. One example, *La Sobria*, called for a certain interplay of feelings between the performers, and was one of the earliest efforts in fashioning dramatic choreography. Celebrating fidelity, *La Sobria* was executed by a woman and five men wherein the course of the dance she accepted the attentions of one while successively rejecting the other four. In *Gelosia*, complex evolutions were followed by three couples with the men constantly changing partners. In a number of these dances the explanatory text was dramatically evocative and gives indications to the performer such as ". . . she regards him with an air of anger . . ." and ". . . he makes a gesture to touch her shoulder. . . ."[9]

Domenico stated that the *bassa danza*, which was a stately and slow dance, had a uniform rhythm throughout, while his *balli* had various rhythms, with at least four main ones. In all, he recorded seventeen *balli* but only four examples of *bassa danza*. This suggests that the latter's stately and gliding evolutions were losing favor to the *balli* with their change of rhythms and greater freedom of movement. *Balli*, sometimes referred to as *balletti*, had a spirited aspect about them, but within a very restrained framework. The dances became so popular that they eventually found their way into most Italian entertainments of the time. Antonio Cornazano (1431–1500), a student of Domenico, commented extensively on the execution and relative merits of the various *bassa danza* and *balli* in a manuscript entitled, *Libra dell'arte del danzar* (1465, Book on the art of dancing). So basic were these two categories of dances that, while time gradually altered and added to their character, examples of their descendants were the French *menuet* and the English jig.

Although there were numerous written descriptions of court dances, the fleeting nature of dance has made it often difficult to gain an exact idea of what they were really like. Long journeys between courts were not all that common, and until a reliable continental mail service was established by the Thurn und Taxis family at the end of the fifteenth century, transmission of information was limited. Lack of firsthand communication with the original creator of the dance could introduce errors. Interpretation of manuscript symbols was sometimes problematic so the recreation of others' dances was an obstacle for many Renaissance dancing masters. However, considerable interest and scholarly research in historical dance's stenography, musical notation, and preserved musical instruments are ongoing today, and have provided a growing understanding of the period's social dancing. As the result of much cross-examination of extant manuscripts, it is possible for specialists to reconstruct and perform early

30

dances with relative accuracy. The dancing manuals are thus an extremely important source for providing information about dances of the past.

A highly respected attaché at the court at Urbino, Guglielmo Ebreo (c. 1400), whose name translates into English as William the Jew, was active around 1460. He was widely praised for his ability as a dancer and for his musical understanding. It is thought that he descended in his profession from the Jewish *spiëlmann*. These men organized the proscribed ceremonial dances in the *tanzhäuser* of European ghettos where various sects of the Jewish religion chose to reside and practice their faith apart from the general population. Here, his skills would have involved the creation of appropriate steps and gestures for circle and line dances cited in the Old Testament. More important, he would have acquired the necessary organizational deftness to control large and enthusiastic crowds on the dance floor.[10]

Early in his career William was apprenticed to Domenico da Piacenza and afterward he became a familiar figure at the court of the Medici. He then served as dancing master to the royal children at the court of Naples where he taught the fashionable Milanese figured dancing known as *ballo lombardo*. He also spent some time teaching dancing at the formidable house of the Sforza dynasty in Milan. During this period, William dedicated his treatise, *De Praticha seu arte tripudii vulghare opusculum* (1463, On the Practice of the common art of dancing), to the ruling duke, Gian Galeazzo Sforza. Wandering the length of Italy, he continued to be warmly welcomed in the most advanced Italian circles. Duke Federigo da Montefeltro's court at Urbino was probably the most humanistic and accomplished in Italy and boasted a splendid library of books and manuscripts. Eventually, William settled in Urbino and put his theoretical and practical ideas to work as the duke's dancing master.

William's treatise made the earliest substantial contribution to Western theatrical dance. Widely read by dancing masters of the time, the treatise called for the strict application of rules in the service of beauty. It instructed its readers in the necessary qualifications for dancing that must be rooted in refined comportment. William's book was not meant to be solely a compilation of his dances and instructions for performing them. Rather, he strove to give a comprehensive and philosophical view of dance, and in so doing, he explained its nature. Drawing upon the era's popular Neoplatonic ideas of the universally ordered levels of existence, he drew an analogy for the power of dance. Emphasizing the harmony between the moving body, the inner spirit, the musical inspiration, and the intellect, William created a theoretical basis for dance that dignified its presence in social life and justified its educational ramifications henceforth.

In the course of his treatise, William stated the prerequisites for the artistic dancer. In regard to the necessary qualifications of a dancer, he based his ideas on those of his beloved teacher, Domenico. These include *misuro*, or the ability to keep time; *memoria*, the ability to precisely memorize the steps and their sequential ordering; *partire del terreno*, the skill to gauge the movement in its allotted space; *aiere*, the dexterity of the upward lift of the body with its corre-

31

sponding settling down; *maniera*, the connection of the footwork to the rise and fall of *aiere*; and lastly, *movemento corporeo*, the graceful, modest and sweet comportment of the dancer. With his theoretical contributions, William helped lay the foundations of a new style of dance.[11] By the middle of the fifteenth century, country dances were beginning to infiltrate the stately court dances and their more lively nature greatly accelerated the popularity of *balli*.

A sixteenth-century commentary on etiquette and social mores for the nobility was sketched by Count Baldassare Castiglione in *Libro del cortegiano* (1528, *The Courtier*). An incomparable literary and artistic achievement that inspired later writers like Spencer, Sidney, and Cervantes, the work was mandatory reading for the upper class. This book established a standard of behavior aimed toward achieving beauty and harmony in life. The author advises discretion, decorum, nonchalance, and gracefulness in all things.[12] As a practical version of the *canzos* of the troubadours, *The Courtier* exercised a profound influence on the evolution of European sensibilities and was a noted reference work for Renaissance dancing masters. Reading Castiglione's treatise provided the ideal image to which a nobleman should aspire. The book reconfirmed the dancing master's concepts of carriage, posture, and movement that were necessary in creating ballroom dances for high society.

# *T*HE *INTERMEDII* OF THE ITALIAN COURTS

Florence was the fifteenth-century cultural capital of Europe and its Academy, founded by Lorenzo de Medici, was one of the most emulated institutions of the Medici court. There, the highly valued ancient knowledge lay with the learned men of the Academy. With its fame extending far, the Medici court and its lifestyle were eagerly copied by other powerful nobles including the Sforzas of Milan, the Estes of Ferrara, and William's enlightened employer, Federigo Montefeltro of Urbino. All these gentlemen contended for similar greatness, copying the Florentine vogue in every way. Hence, one of the chief responsibilities of their Renaissance academies was to produce entertainments consisting of comic or tragic plays with danced interludes called *intermedii*. Scholars found their inspiration for *intermedii* in classical models of heroic behavior rather than in the Bible, which made them entirely secular in nature. Extraordinary in every detail, these grandiose and complex events celebrated weddings, birthdays, and state visits. They consisted of elaborate feasts juxtaposed to entertainment that presupposed of its guests a knowledge of antique myth and allegory.

Originally, court entertainments were dramatizations filled with much admired, erudite notions of Greek and Roman mythological themes that only a carefully educated class of people could appreciate. First, as lofty spectacles they served as powerful political propaganda for the ruling class throughout northern Italy. While gorgeous display of great wealth was certainly a deterrent to the

Renaissance court ball with dancers performing a moresque. Etching by Albrecht Dürer. (Courtesy of the Victoria & Albert Museum, London.)

aggression of a potential enemy, it also conferred an awesome dignity on the noble who paid for it all. Second, insofar as current events could always be found to have some half-hidden parallels in ancient literature, the entertainments and their danced interludes were vehicles for richly cloaked social and political commentary. Thus, spectacle served as a platform where checks and balances within the Renaissance ruling class were observed, weighed, and renewed.[13]

These intellectual extravaganzas were designed to serve as appropriate vehicles for the moral edification of the Renaissance courts. Human nature has always responded to sanctimonious sermonizing as tedious, but it became palatable when cloaked in the fanciful and sensual richness of mythology and allegory. While it pleased the scholars that the *intermedii* should employ the use of complex symbolism and allegory, the highly revered aspect of these events was probably not fully understood by well-to-do audiences of the time. Although the aristocratic courts clamored for sumptuous and ingenious display, they most likely possessed precious little critical faculty, having no basis for comparison.[14] Clearly, the impact of humanism had transformed the art of medieval religious festival and harnessed it to Renaissance government as an instrument of rule.

Lavish Italian productions with *intermedii* were held in the immense halls of princely palaces. The occasion usually followed the custom of the banquet taking place in one heavily ornate room and the entertainment in another. The hosts and guests of honor were seated on a dais at one end of the area with other guests placed at several tables spanning the length of the room. Tables were set with decorations of amazing intricacy and invention. Plates and wine goblets were commonly fashioned of gold, silver, and rock crystal. Exquisite two-pronged forks and stiletto-like knives of silver and ivory replaced eating with one's fingers. Each guest arrived and departed with a personal set of dining utensils contained in a little velvet pouch attached to the owner's belt. In keeping with the Renaissance lust for life, it was not uncommon for over one hundred kinds of dishes to be served in numerous courses by an army of servants. On record is a report of an interminable evening of festivities and food offered in 1493 by the Doge of Venice. The party featured for dessert a staggering variety of cakes, along with an entire population of candy figures. These miniature spun sugar confections reproduced the allegorical figures that had just danced in the evening's *intermedii*, as well as presented detailed depictions of the host, the pope, several cardinals, and a number of distinguished members of the Sforza family.[15]

After the feasting, guests usually moved to a similarly ornamented hall or ballroom arranged for the entertainment. Here, noble amateurs coached by the resident dancing master performed in an assigned area. The true focal point of the entertainment was the chief dignitary or guest of honor, not the performers who occupied the center portion of the floor. While the honored guest was centrally seated at one end of the hall, other guests observed from the sides and overhanging galleries. In principle, the *intermedii* boasted a more weighty intellectual basis than the outdoor *trionfi*. Often arranged by artists like Leonardo da Vinci, Sandro Botticelli, and Giorgio Vasari, these social functions were further enhanced by luxuriously decorated areas of Renaissance palaces. Potted forests of greenery, splashing fountains, mechanical heavens, and rocky grottos were dispersed throughout the performing space so that the dramatic action moved from one area to another. Richly costumed dancers selected from the court nobility had to be reasonably skilled and disciplined to perform the exacting geometric floor patterns choreographed by those who masterminded the spectacle. An actual historical account of an *intermedii* honoring the Sforza ruler is recorded in the following:

> The apogee of these arrangements for eating and dancing occurred in Milan in 1489, and has been sometimes referred to as the "first" Ballet. More truthfully, it was a banquet-hall, but all the entremets [danced interludes] were related to one another in a consistent pattern, and the *fête* was designed as an artistic entity, though the dramatic action was fragmentary and any expression of emotion merely a literary device for seemly display.[16]

34

# $\mathcal{S}$UMMARY

The Renaissance opened up a new and radical discussion of the scientific method. The study of human anatomy, plants and animals, physics and medicine changed the world forever. Through its great literature, Renaissance discourse on the human condition and moral behavior occupied a central place in a society bursting with self-assertion and curiosity. Insatiable energies for sensory pleasure—for every self-indulgence, for building, for making war, love, and hate—consumed the lives of the ruling class.

The rapid evolution of new technology and the growth of trade, stemming from the opening-up of the new world, rendered life better for more people than ever before. With the weakening of the medieval Church and the ensuing Reformation, the concept of a national state took hold and established the face of modern Europe.

The Renaissance *trionfi* superseded the profound spectacle of the medieval Mass, followed by the splendid Italian entertainments and their danced *intermedii*, the highest form of celebration. Biblical symbolism, which was mandatory during the medieval times, was replaced with singing and dancing in a style larger than life. A mixture of tragedy and fantasy was the basis of a theatrical form that was a metaphor for man's mortality and possibility. Founded on a complex lifestyle and begun by the rekindling of human centrality in the world, *intermedii* were constructed from recovered ancient knowledge as well as fifteenth-century inventions in science and art.

A variety of stately and sprightly social dances designed by the period's most famous theorists and practitioners Domenico da Piacenza and Guglielmo Ebreo contributed to the danced portions of the entertainments. The overall coordination of activities was assigned to people expert in organizing and producing events like these; hence, the designated profession of the dancing master emerged. As teacher, choreographer, and social arbitrator *par excellence*, his position was integral to Renaissance society and made possible the establishment of dance as an art form in Western culture.

35

## $\mathcal{C}hapter\ \mathcal{N}otes$

1. David Fox Scott, *Mediterranean Heritage* (Boston: Routledge & Kegan Paul, 1978), pp. 5–44.
2. Plotinus, *Enneads* (London: Penguin Books, 1991), V. 1.
3. Giorgio Vasari, *Lives of the Artists*, trans. George Bull (Baltimore, MD: Penguin Books, 1965), pp. 70–71.
4. Will Durant, *The Life of Greece* (New York: Simon and Schuster, 1966), p. 163.
5. Ibid., p. 164.
6. Kirstein, *Dance*, p. 127.

7. Roy Strong, *Art and Power: Renaissance Festivals 1450–1650* (London: Boydell Press, 1984), p. 44.
8. Wood, *Historical Dances*, p. 30–31.
9. Germaine Prudhommeau, *Histoire de la Danse* (Paris: Editions Amphora, 1989), pp. 34–35.
10. Walter Sorell, *Dance in Its Time: The Emergence of an Art Form* (Garden City, NY: Anchor Press/Doubleday, 1981), pp. 36–37.
11. Otto Kinkeldey, *A Jewish Dancing Master of the Renaissance: Guglielmo Ebreo* (Brooklyn, NY: Dance Horizons, 1972), pp. 22–23.
12. Baldesar Castiglione, *The Courtier* (Harmondsworth, Middlesex, England: Penguin Books, 1984), pp. 61–69.
13. Strong, pp. 65–74.
14. Kirstein, *Dance*, p. 134.
15. Michael Ennis, *Duchess of Milan* (New York: Viking Penguin, 1992), pp. 294–98. While scholarly accounts of Renaissance celebrations abound, Ennis provides a colorful rendition of a party attended by Isabella of Aragon in 1493. The author engagingly brings to life the historical event by recreating the atmosphere and visualizing for the reader a plethora of descriptive detail.
16. Kirstein, *Dance*, p. 133.

36

# 3

# *The Ballet de Cour in France*

The newly founded and powerful Sforza dynasty heralded a period of great prosperity in Milan in 1450. Bolstered with the acquisition of enormous wealth produced by the introduction of the rice, wool, and silk industries, the city state flourished. Following the example of the Medici patronage of artists and scholars in Florence, the Sforza dukes embellished the duchy of Milan in Italy's northern Lombardy region. The family became well known for its lavish support of painters, musicians, dancing masters, architects, and scholars. At one point, their court was the most splendid in Europe, partly due to the fame of its magnificent celebrations that culminated in Baldassare di Belgiojoso's *Paradiso* of 1490. Amplified by the elegance of the Sforza lifestyle, the Italian Renaissance reached its pinnacle.

When Charles VIII of France passed menacingly through Lombardy in 1494, he and his entourage were amazed at the wealth of dancing in the Milanese court entertainments.[1] No expense was spared for these grand occasions and their renown spread far beyond the borders of the state. One presentation boasted the participation of nearly 100 dancers, while another had costumes and scenic effects designed by Leonardo da Vinci. At century's end Milan had become Europe's most important dance center, with dancing itself the favored form of entertainment. Milan's development of figured dancing was fashionable and in such demand that it was known in various European courts as the *ballo lombardo*.

## FRENCH ASSIMILATION OF ITALIAN CULTURE

As supremely confident as the sixteenth-century princes were in their grandeur and cultivated style, they were also violent, cunning, and dangerous. For years the French had been leading forays onto Italian soil. The newly crowned and soaringly ambitious Valois heir, Francis I, looked south with envy at the great

Italian palaces and their gardens, the sumptuous Church properties, and the rich and verdant Sforza countryside. He had heard of the family's dazzling court surrounded with beauty and genius. Francis was flooded with impressions, and he saw the area and its culture in terms of his own country; somehow all this had to be acquired for France. In the course of events resulting from generations of territorial disputes, convoluted politics, and ever-changing loyalties, Francis overwhelmed the Duchy of Milan in 1515 at the bloody battle of Marignano.[2] Perhaps the most important long-range effect of this struggle was that Italian Renaissance culture began its movement northward on a large scale. The French assimilation of Italian culture was to have far-reaching consequences for the development of ballet.

Since the thirteenth century the French had enjoyed their own seignoirial versions of stately dances, mingling them with elements of masquerading. French dances followed a minimum set format and were essentially a means of revelry for the upper class. The *Bal des Ardens* (1393, Masque of the Wild Men) was a long-remembered event because of its disastrous climax, and could have been rightly called a kind of *danse macabre*. A masquerade was given at the Hall of St. Pol in Paris to celebrate the wedding of a court lady who had been twice widowed. According to tradition, remarriages were occasions for mockery, involving all sorts of license, disguises, and the blaring of discordant music. To partake in the irreverent fun, six nobles, including King Charles VI, were disguised as wood savages. They were dressed in linen body suits soaked in resinous wax to hold frazzled pieces of rope which gave the revelers a shaggy, hairy look. Because of the obvious danger to the performers wearing the inflammable disguises, torches had been banned from the hall. The dancers entered the ballroom chained together and began their capers, indecent howls, and obscene gestures to the great amusement of the other guests. The king excused himself from the group of dancers to momentarily tease and flirt with the Duchess of Berry. A drunken and late-arriving guest, Louis d'Orléans, entered the ballroom with torch in hand despite the ban. In order to discover the identity of the players, and perhaps to purposely court danger, the tipsy Orléans held his torch above the savages and a spark fell. One by one the chained dancers were set afire. The Duchess threw her skirts over the king and saved his life, but only one other dancer, the Sire de Nantouillet, survived by hurling himself into a large winecooler filled with water.[3]

French interest in dance theory and notation began to appear in conjunction with the popularity of masquerades and revels. An unsigned and undated writing of the late 1400s, *Le Manuscrit des Basses Danses de la Bibliothèque de Bourgogne* (Stately Dances of the Library of Bourgogne), consists of twenty-five pages of general instructions followed by descriptions, rules for execution, notation, and music for fifty-nine long-remembered *basses danses*. It discusses four elementary steps, *pas simple*, *pas double*, *branle*, and *démarche*, in addition to the necessary bow or *révérence*. The manuscript is not didactic, and is thought to have been prepared as a memory aid for its first owner by a well-meaning dancing master.[4] Also surviving is a similar work, *L'Art et Instruction de bien Danser* (l496, The Art and Instruction of Dancing Well), edited in Paris by Michel Toulouze, one of the first music publishers. It gives a text with explication for forty-one named *basses danses* found in the Bourgogne manuscript and seven new dances in which men and women dance different movements. The music for each dance, along with its number of notes and measures and the dance's notation, is specified. One of the dances *La Beaulté de Castille* (The Beauty of Castile) introduces a significant innovation in that it is a dance for three, although there is no indication as to the male-female makeup of the trio or any call for dramatic rapport among the dancers.[5] In 1521, Robert Coplande published an English translation of Toulouze's work that included instructions for dancing new dances "after the manner of France," and several variants of earlier ones.[6] Antonius de Arena recorded some fifty-eight *basses danses* in 1529 similar to those in the Bourgogne manuscript that are expressed in an unusual mixture of Latin grammar incorporating French, Provençal, and Italian words.[7] While the choreography is given for *tordions*, *branles*, and *saltarellas*, the musical accompaniment is not. From the first appearance of the Italian dancing masters at the French court, dances began to take on more complexity and refinement, which sowed the seeds for the French court ballet.

## CATHERINE DE MEDICI AND *L'ACADÉMIE DE POÉSIE ET MUSIQUE*

Catherine de Medici (1519–1589), great-granddaughter of Lorenzo the Magnificent and scion of the Florentine banking family, married into the ruling Valois house of France as part of a dynastic alliance in 1533.[8] Fourteen years and seven children later, she became the French queen when her husband ascended the throne as Henry II. From childhood, Catherine had been imbued with the physical beauties prized by the Renaissance, being nurtured on the Italian *intermedii* that were patronized by her sophisticated, gifted, and enormously rich relatives. She naturally grew to understand that the very ballets she herself loved to dance in, carried significant social and political uses.[9] True to the art-loving heritage of her ancestors, Catherine proceeded to subsidize the literary and musical institutions in her new country. Later, as regent and as the Queen Mother, she made her Italian legacy of court ballet and their *intermedii* a permanent part of French culture.

With Catherine's encouragement, a number of dancing masters from Milan's cradle of choreographers were enticed to Paris by the Maréchal de Brissac in 1554. Leading the group was the theoretician and foremost dancer of his day, Cesare Negri (1536–c. 1604). With him came the skills of figured dancing that eventually culminated in the lively fashion of Italianate dancing and the splendid court ballets of Catherine de Medici's regency. Included in Negri's entourage was his influential and talented colleague, Pompeo Diobono, famous as a teacher and soon to become instructor to Catherine's four sons. He was assisted in his efforts by the dancer and choreographer Tettoni Bernardo, and later by Virgilio Bracesco and Palvello Ludovico whose performing gifts were widely acclaimed. Known for developing strength, skill, and grace in his pupils, Giovan Gallino was appointed as the king's personal dancing master, but soon extended his lessons to the young nobles. As a result of these visiting gentlemen, an intensive period of instruction in figured dancing began in earnest, and the French court proved to be eager learners.

*L'Académie de Poésie et Musique* (The Academy of Poetry and Music) was a famous Parisian school sponsored by Catherine's son, Charles IX, and headed by Jean Antoine de Baïf[10] (1532–1589), a major scholar of the classics who was greatly influenced by the theories and practices of the Italians at the French court. Charles IX believed that when music is disordered, morals become depraved, but when music is well ordered, men are morally disciplined. His intention in supporting the Academy was thus far-reaching, encompassing religion and ethics as well as music.[11] Adopting Baïf's ideas on song, verse, and dance, the Academy synthesized and produced his concepts in lavish entertainments, looking to models of classical heroic behavior rather than the Bible for its inspiration. Baïf's central theory, which was a major contribution to the ongoing development of ballet into the twentieth century, proposed that the segments of dance, music, and spoken phrase should dovetail to form a harmonious and pleasing organism of artistic expression.[12] While Baïf's aesthetic concept of unity was novel in sixteenth-century court circles, he intended it to re-establish and epitomize fundamental notions of classical Greek art as they related to the spectacles that were masterminded for the Valois court.[13] Although short-lived itself, the ideas and intentions of the Academy persisted after its royal subsidy was discontinued.[14] Moreover, the very existence of the Academy as an official institution set an important precedent in the growth of French art and culture.

Before 1550 there had been little regard for the relationship between declaimed verses and the melodic line. In founding *L'Académie de Poésie et Musique* in 1570, Baïf hoped to achieve a literary and musical reformation by educating practitioners and the public alike. Instrumentalists were encouraged to compose music that would coincide with the rhythms in metrical verse. Following the same rule, the length of dance steps had to closely fit the duration of musical notes. Baïf believed the ancient Greek playwrights perfectly translated the complex rhythms of their prose into plastic form. It was his desire that the Academy rediscover this balance of music, verse, and dance.

## BEAUJOYEULX AND THE *MAGNIFIQUES*

Arriving from Italy as a virtuoso violinist around 1555, Baldassare da Belgiojoso, who later gallicized his name to Balthasar de Beaujoyeulx (d. 1587), was engaged by Catherine de Medici as court dancing master in charge of training dancers, and organizing and producing royal entertainments. Thus, the Valois court continued the sponsorship of Italianate dancing, which Beaujoyeulx cleverly wedded to the French penchant for glittering masquerades. These spectacular hybrids were called *magnifiques*[15] and were the precursors of the French *ballet de cour*, the ballet of the court in which the dancing style was indistinguishable from popular social dances of the day. The costly displays were used to celebrate great occasions, but underneath they mediated religious quarrels and served to legitimize the monarchy with their splendor. They were also designed to demonstrate to foreigners that France was not totally ruined because of past wars, internal politics, and religious conflicts.[16] As an essential part of *magnifiques*, the social dances of the court were theatrically applied to dramatic and philosophical purposes. Although the same nobles participated in both dance forms, the purpose changed from dance as a personal activity to dance presented for extraordinary entertainment in the *ballet de cour*.

Many examples of Beaujoyeulx's *ballet de cour* were produced during Catherine de Medici's lifetime,[17] but only a handful have survived in any detailed description. One of these *magnifiques*, *Le Paradis d'Amour* (1572, The Paradise of Love), celebrated the marriage between Margaret, daughter of Catholic Catherine and Henry, to the Protestant Huguenot leader, Henry of Navarre, who would become King Henry IV. Catherine claimed to use the celebration as a way of establishing peace among Catholics and Protestants, the two squabbling Christian factions within her realm. For some time, religious wars had been convulsing France. In 1517 Martin Luther had publicly challenged the dogma and practices of the Roman Catholic Church, giving rise to the Protestant Reformation that spread across the European continent in many interpretations. The Huguenots were French Protestants who followed the teachings of John Calvin, which opposed traditional Christian theology. Calvin proffered the notion that redemption was by predestination and not by the exercising of free will in doing good works. Although the crown regularly persecuted Huguenots, they persisted in their beliefs, causing ongoing chaos and bloodshed.

Permeating Renaissance thinking was the neoplatonic construct of universal harmony formulated by Plotinus in the *Enneads*. According to the philosopher, celestial motion is circular, and when it is imitated reality is experienced as order surrounding a center, a cosmic dance. Plotinus alluded to this experience of center by comparing it to a Greek chorus harmoniously dancing and singing around a leader. Because this activity is inspired by truth, he believed that the dance reveals "the sources of life and intelligence, the principle of existence, the cause of goodness and the origin of the soul."[18]

Catherine de Medici adopted the popular Renaissance notion of cosmic dance and proposed that spectacles designed to reflect the workings of heavenly bodies would bring peace to volatile France. The Valois court embraced the Pythagorian-Plotonic astrological belief that the number harmony of the universe decidedly influences all human endeavor and the outer world of nature. The concept of number harmony was intricately applied in the construction of

41

her multifaceted productions, particularly in regard to the geometric configurations of dancers in the danced interludes. *Le Paradis d'Amour* presented thematic material through allegory and symbols that thinly disguised the religious turmoil between Catholics and Huguenots in France.[19] Hence, religious conflict itself was the pretense for engaging the feuding religious factions in theatrical spectacle to portray the forces of good, represented by the Catholics, and of evil, represented by the Protestants. The Renaissance mind believed music and dance were aural and visual images of concord and had the power to put oneself at peace, thereby creating peace with one's neighbor. At the ballet's conclusion, therefore, all obstacles were overcome in a grand danced segment, and together the participants in the ballet entered the gates of paradise.[20]

Unfortunately, Catherine de Medici's seemingly good intentions only resulted in more anguish when a few days later, a Catholic killed a Huguenot noble, giving rise to fresh rancor nationwide. The St. Bartholomew's Day Massacre (1572) ensued, leaving hundreds dead on both sides. History has traditionally linked Catherine to the bloody affair, although the full truth behind the terrible fray will probably never be uncovered. It has been noted that the horrific massacre obscured the central theme of Catherine's life, and cost her a place in history as a creative genius in the art of festival.[21]

A year later, Catherine celebrated the election of her second son to the Polish throne by commissioning the poet Pierre Ronsard, current leader of the *Pleiade*, a literary academy, and the composer Roland de Lassus, to collaborate on an appropriate *magnifique*. Entitled *Le Ballet de Polonais* (1573, The Polish Ballet), it focused on impressing its elite audience of French courtiers and Polish diplomats. Allegorical French verses were set to music depicting "truth disguised under a mantle of fable."[22] Amateur court dancers were instructed by Beaujoyeulx, who used the medieval dance device of *estampie* to direct all their action toward the honored guests. It was probably this production that earned Catherine's dancing master the title of "founder of French court ballet."

By all accounts, the most memorable part of *Le Ballet de Polonais* was the final grand ballet with sixteen nymphs seated on a silver rock representing the sixteen provinces of France. Descending onto the floor space, the ladies were reported to have flawlessly performed ingenious figures comprised of interlacing movement patterns designed by Beaujoyeulx. This dance form, so novel to the Polish guests, was the figured dancing inspired by the Italian influence at the French court. It involved static positions, patterned movement, and patternless flux between figures. The much-admired performance introduced dancers, who portrayed pure and elevated beings, gliding through some forty or more such complex geometric figures. Each pattern represented a moral virtue or an eternal truth echoing the spiritual side of man. The audience was expected to decipher the meanings of each with the aid of librettos provided beforehand. Transitions between the figures could be abrupt, moving swiftly from serious to playful qualities. The geometric figures, one after the other, forming, breaking, and reforming, symbolized the endless succession of birth and death in the transmutation of the elements and the change of the seasons.[23]

The spectacular danced segment usually came at the end of the performance. While no written notation of the choreography for figures in *Le Ballet de Polonais* has been uncovered, sparse phrases and the reflections of theorists give some idea as to the "look" of the event. The single most descriptive passage that does exist is from Jean Dorat's libretto for the Polish Ballet, part of which follows:

> Once the song was finished the dance began
> Of the Nymphs moving in certain ways like troops
> And their rhythmical gestures gave witness to their joy . . .
> They blend a thousand flights with a thousand pauses of the feet
> Now they stitch through one another like bees by clasping hands
> Now they form a point like a flock of voiceless cranes.
> Now they draw close intertwining with one another
> Creating an entangled hedge like a kind of bramble bush.
> Now this one and now that switches to a flat figure
> Which describes many letters without a tablet.[24]

Visual evidence for the Valois *magnifiques* is evoked in six drawings and eight tapestries now in the Uffizi Gallery in Florence. While they are marvelous depictions of the events and give tremendous atmosphere, examination of them alongside written documentary reveals a general discrepancy between what one sees and what one reads. However, their existence as tangible objects confirms the increasing importance that the upper class attached to fleeting beauty as the sixteenth century progressed.[25]

For a generation, the codified ballroom steps dating back to Domenico da Piacenza had been brought north by Milanese dancing masters.[26] The actual steps leading the dancers through one figure to the next were taken from popular ballroom steps along with courtly gestures and strict etiquette adapted to theatrical use. There was apparently no attempt at virtuosity in Beaujoyeulx's dance language, which emphasized stately elegance of the vertical body. At the end of the *magnifique*, Catherine requested that the aristocratic cast descend into the spectator area of the hall to invite the audience to join in *branles* and other forms of social dancing, putting a convivial conclusion to an extraordinary evening.

The success of *Le Ballet de Polonais* was due to the pleasing geometric configurations that continued to develop according to French taste. This single presentation was, therefore, a turning point establishing French dance as Europe's dominant school. In the end, it was the music for *Le Ballet de Polonais*, with its universal Italian terminology and its potential for vocal drama, that supplied the foundations for opera and left the future of dance to France. Although it would be 150 years before dance disengaged itself from spoken declamation and sung recitation altogether, the interim allowed French dancing masters to busy themselves with creating a dance form that was essentially French in taste, style, and terminology. From these lengthy efforts dance eventually emerged as an autonomous art.

# *LE BALLET COMIQUE DE LA REINE:* ART, POWER, AND THE DIVINE RIGHT TO RULE

The year 1581 witnessed the presentation of what historians generally consider the first authentic ballet because of its highly structural integration of music, dance, verse, and decor. Under the general title of *Le Ballet Comique de la Reine* (The Dramatic Ballet of the Queen), the production was presented on the occasion of the Duc de Joyeux's marriage to Marguerite of Lorraine. Although less than a third of the musical score was specifically marked for dancing, Beaujoyeulx held central responsibility for the entire performance. Under his guidance, the development of figured dancing as a spectacular dance form reached its peak, constituting the most successful European experiment with the human body in theatrical space up to that time. Aside from its profusion of symbolism and references to current religious and political turmoil, the *Ballet Comique*'s sheer artistic appeal was one of overriding power.[27] In realizing Baïf's ideas on aligning the components of music, dance, and verse into a unified whole, and by attempting to render the plot choreographically, Beaujoyeulx brought the *ballet de cour* into full flower. A political, philosophical, and ethical mirror of its day, the *Ballet Comique* was a premier example of a new genre.[28]

The spectacle's thematic material was the classical tale of the evil enchantress, Circe, who with "unrivaled grace," mischievously interacted with gods, goddesses, and gentlemen whom she transformed into beasts, satyrs, dryads, and naiads—all of whom were presented in a number of *intermedii* or *entremets*, as they were called in France. Circe was eventually overcome by Jupiter's thunderbolt, and in the allegorical conclusion the gods happily paid homage to greater deities, the king and queen of France who were present in the audience. The *Ballet Comique* has been summed up as an original and unique mixture of French taste and Italian theories on classical drama. While the production resulted from ideas that had been fermenting for years, it took the skill of Beaujoyeulx to successfully harvest them.

The *Ballet Comique* did not resemble ballet as we know it today. Produced in a huge salon in the Petit-Bourbon palace within the Louvre complex, its performance space was three-quarters in-the-round with free-standing scenery dispersed about. The dramatic action was directed toward the royal party seated at one end of the room, while most of the audience viewed the ballet from double galleries temporarily constructed on the sides. Probably an exaggeration, it was estimated at the time that 9,000 to 10,000 spectators were in attendance.[29]

Beaujoyeulx left us only a glimpse of the way he manipulated his figures in the *Ballet Comique*. In the first of twelve patterns included in one *entrée*, there were six nymphs abreast in one line across the hall. Three more nymphs were positioned in front in a broad triangle with Queen Louise (Catherine's daughter-in-law) at the apex. Behind the line three others formed the same shape. As the music changed, they spiraled in and out among each other in a patternless flux, returning to their first position. Looking down on the floor space of the ball-room afforded the viewers clear impressions of the constantly changing danced figures woven by well-drilled courtiers. The six-hour-long spectacle culminated with a grand ballet of sixteen dancers divided into four groups distinguished by the color of their costumes. They worked their way through numerous configu-rations laden with beauty and meaning that was represented and expressed in squares, circles, spirals, and triangles. No sooner did one group break out of a pattern, than an arriving group formed a new one, creating a visual and kinetic interplay of movement.[30] The heart of Baïf's theory, based on the Pythagorean-Plotonic philosophy that all things are related to number, produced in the preci-sion of the measured dancing one of its most perfect artistic expressions.[31]

A novelty developed in Italy that became a theatrical feature of the *Ballet Comique* was the pastoral, a special literary interlude inspired by Torquato Tasso's sixteenth-century drama, *Aminta* (1573). The nymphs and satyrs in *Aminta* provided a contrast to the deities of antique lore. Rustic in nature, their presence contributed a bucolic note to the drama. Tasso intended the pastoral element to emphasize the common desire for peace, pleasure, and love benefi-cial to society.[32] On a more subtle level, he used the device as a thinly veiled criticism of the Machiavellian pragmatism within the Italian court.[33] Adapted to French tastes, Beaujoyeulx's inclusion of Tasso's arcadian nymphs and satyrs in the *Ballet Comique* completed what he considered to be authentic classical Greek drama. The tone of the pastoral form greatly enhanced the contrived magnificence of the production, and surely pleased the audience with its infer-ences for a becalmed France.

One year after the presentation of the *Ballet Comique*, Catherine de Medici ordered a beautiful publication that recorded a description of the spectacle. She directed that its stated purpose was to enable those who were not present to savor the event and to grasp its import from afar. In truth, all festival literature, including Catherine's, significantly described the subtle interaction between art and power. With his great wealth, the Renaissance prince patronized the cre-ation of art, which in turn, reflected his grandeur, his liberality, and his taste, and hence, reinforced his God-given right to rule.[34] For some time to come, com-memorative books on court ballets established themselves as a literary genre meant to be passed on to posterity as monuments to princely magnificence.

The commemorative text, engraved frontpiece, and musical score of the *Ballet Comique* give an idea of the handsomely danced figures with their appro-priate poses and gestures that gratified eyes, ears, and mind. Several hundred copies of the printed *Ballet Comique* were presented to European courts and wealthy families. This revelation of French court ballet incited widespread imi-tation, thus acknowledging France's cultural superiority on the Continent and England. Other contemporary accounts of the *Ballet Comique* also attested to its splendor. However, even though magnificence was seen as a virtue necessary to a ruling family, France had incurred large debts at home and abroad. The cost for this extravaganza was such that domestic and foreign opinion derided the prodigal expenditure and a reaction set in at court. Instead of sparking further

45

artistic experiment and research in French court ballet, the custom of the grand spectacle came to an abrupt halt. In 1589 Catherine died, and her *magnifiques*, ostensibly devoted to restoring peace, were seen no more.

For the next thirty years, noble amateurs and their hired dancing masters contented themselves with dance forms including *ballets burlesques*, and *ballets mascarades*, which were more amusing if less artful. Little documentation has survived regarding the period between 1581 and 1610, so it is difficult to form a clear idea of the genres and the evolution of court ballet during that time because the format was not yet fixed. However, the ballets immediately following the *Ballet Comique* have been established as being primarily of a literary and political nature.[35] Due to the depleted treasury, the further excesses of Catherine de Medici's last son, Henry III, and the traveling court of Henry IV, the productions had neither elaborate settings, rich costumes, nor permanent places for performance.

The court ballets between 1610 and 1620 became heavily poetic and musical, lampooning the content of dramatic and lyrical works. Played out in a theatrical setting, they were the scene of a magnified but subtle power struggle between the noble as a royal subject and the emerging concept of the king as the embodiment of the nation. While French political aspirations had been the predominant expression of Valois spectacles, from 1620 to 1636 satirical and erotic *ballets burlesques* became their own object, reveling in notions of political subversiveness, opposition to official culture, obscenities, and a hefty indulgence of the senses.[36] Consisting almost entirely of *entrées* or processions of a variety of characters who established their identities by dances, costumes, and subtle verbal references, the appearance of the dancers in what were really mini-masquerades became the chief objective. By diminishing the importance of narrative and scenery, *ballets burlesques* focused on choreographic autonomy of the individual and the occasion itself.[37] Some ballets were full of self-criticism and pointed lewdness, especially after 1624, and producing and dancing in them were akin to modifying court lifestyle.[38]

*Les Fées des forests de Saint Germain* (1625, The Fairies of the forests of Saint Germain) was a well-documented production in the burlesque style. The choreography introduced dance in a new theatrical context, presenting it as independent of the scenario and decor. The focus was on the individual dancer who was elaborately costumed in noble, grotesque, or allegorical attire. By conspicuously showing himself, a royal subject symbolically represented himself as a force of political resistance toward the established order of the realm. As a result of the growing social contraints he felt imposed on him, flagrant self-display was a noble's search for prestige, and even his very survival, via metaphor within a theatrical arena.[39] The burlesque form responded to the marked taste of the era for improvisation that imprinted a series of unrelated danced *entrées*. They were sometimes performed to singing, and in front of unchanging decor that depended on the varying dimensions of the dancing area. Professional mountebanks and buffoons were hired to perform the more difficult steps and acrobatics.[40]

To satisfy the upper class's demands for relatively inexpensive but entertaining diversion, special *ballets mascarades* were arranged by dancing masters who frequently produced impromptu parties and performances in smaller residences like Montmorency, Chevreuse, and Montbazon. The new ruler, Henry IV (1553–1610), delighted in watching these lively and often satirical shows that alluded to the personalities and happenings of the day.[41] *Entrées* from *ballets burlesques* were a part of masquerades, and comic characters were introduced along with grotesque and droll effects. Related dialogues and speeches, which were the foundation for a danced musical-drama like the great production of 1581, were abandoned. No special integration of music, dance, poetry, and decor was expected. While no set form dominated the event, a vogue for improvisation went hand in hand with the emphasis on dancing, fancy dress, and scenery. In the *ballets mascarades*, the atmosphere of a private party was enhanced when guests arrayed in their own evening clothes, masks, and amusing disguises performed popular social dances in their host's ballroom. The masquerade would end with a grand finale in which all would participate. Afterwards, minus their masks, the revelers socialized and danced until dawn.

While these less costly but fashionable evenings of masquerade balls and theatrical burlesques were devoid of dramatic interest and artistic expression, they warranted a lingering taste for dancing in high society. *Ballets burlesques* did not stage geometric figures; rather, they stressed the transitional movement between figures. Dancers were not called upon to make homogeneous groupings requiring keen attention and much practice, but instead, they twisted around the axis of their own bodies preferring the individual presence over the choreographed group. Most important, the popularity of burlesques and masquerades opened up the development of the *divertissement*, dancing for the pure sake of dancing, which emphasized bravura technique, often at the expense of a coherent plot.[42] Thus, the hiatus between grand French spectacles gave important incubation time to a wealth of previously generated dance ideas.

The political and religious strife of Henry IV's reign and his less-than-elegant personal tastes demanded a relative austerity at court, so full scale spectacles reappeared only after his death. A new king and new times instigated a revival of theatrical entertainments and their own innovations,[43] which gave a fresh start to the growth of dance. Louis XIII (1601–1643) was a devoted lover of court ballet like his royal predecessors beginning with his great-grandfather, Francis I. Louis's nobles were also accomplished in the art, and they not only performed in *ballets burlesques* devised for them by professional dancing masters and musicians, but occasionally repeated these performances outdoors for the inhabitants of Paris. Following the royal example, military officers as well as courtiers developed a passion for dancing. One famous recollection tells us that the Maréchal Françoise de Bassompierre was so enamored of the dance that when he was about to attack a stronghold, he turned to his aids with the battle cry: "The decor and the dancers are ready—let the ballet begin!"[44]

In the early seventeenth century, theaters began to appear in Paris, and their productions of *ballets mélodramatiques* were popular. These predominantly

47

—

*Ballet Comique de la Reine*

musical works presented mythological plots that included fantastic masquerades, danced *entrées*, singing, and pantomime. The grotesque elements and vulgarities of the burlesques helped attract the attention of the emerging bourgeoisie and widened the interest in public performances. The first important *ballet mélodramatique* was *Le Ballet de Monsieur de Vendôme* (1610, The Ballet of Monsieur Vendôme), which used dancers as a living alphabet to spell out words and phrases. It also combined the fanciful entrances of the *ballets burlesques* and *ballets mascarades* with dramatically related entrances to connect the action. A prime factor that helped popularize these productions was the recent development in music. The great Italian composer Giovanni Palestrina had opened up the complex mechanics of the dramatic diction of sung words hitherto considered lost in antiquity. Knowledge of his researches on vocal techniques had an effect on the sung verses that advanced the dramatic action in a production. So significant was Palestrina's impact on composers like Claudio Monteverdi that it took only a few generations for music to pursue its own course on Italian soil, and from early sung dramatizations came full-blown opera. As a result, the dance in Italy stagnated and assumed its secondary role as a decorative incidental to operatic production.

## *LE DÉLIVERANCE DE RENAUD*: LOUIS XIII AS DEMIGOD

Thirty-six years after the extravagant *Ballet Comique*, *Le Déliverance de Renaud* (1617, The Liberation of Renaud) appeared. The ballet was a political statement exalting the new monarch Louis XIII as the annointed and, thus, supreme royal power in France.[45] It was the first time that the young king showed his will to become independent of his mother and her minister, Armand Jean du Plessis, Cardinal Richelieu. Richelieu had been developing the concept of the divine right ruler (which would be exploited to the fullest under Louis XIV). The Valois dynasty had been discredited for its ineffectiveness during the religious wars. Richelieu's policy was to bolster the crown by replacing weakness with strength at the expense of liberty. He thereby established the monarchy into a tyrannical and absolutist form of government in the name of Louis XIII.[46]

As a matter of royal education, Louis XIII studied dancing, and most notably, chose the mythical tale of *Renaud* to make his coming-of-age appearance.[47] Richelieu was largely responsible for using court ballet to establish the sixteen-year-old's divine-like status in the eyes of the people and to confirm his authority over those who contested it.[48] The plot of *Renaud* was coherently expressed through mime and sung words, and served as a pretext for numerous danced *entrées*, some of which featured grotesque elements. The work ended with the prerequisite grand ballet in which the entire cast took part.[49] After the singular performance of the resplendent *Ballet Comique de la Reine*, the French love of expressive dancing had been satisfied with social masquerades and burlesques for over thirty years. *Renaud*, therefore, was a welcomed advancement in court ballet because its elements related to a cohesive dramatic action presented on a large scale.

In the production of *Renaud*, Louis XIII danced the role of a demigod, the Demon of Fire, an illusion to the concept of a divine right ruler. The metaphorically cloaked scenario portrayed the king introducing order to his land in triumph over anarchy, a theme that reflected his intentions of quelling civil war and establishing a peaceful and prosperous France.[50] An ulterior motive for the opulent production was to assure the foreign diplomats at court that all was well with the king's marriage in spite of his poor health and his shy and withdrawn personality; Louis would not produce an heir for another twenty years.[51]

The king's talented favorite Duke of Luynes, Charles d'Albert, who danced alongside Louis in the title role of *Renaud*, was the Superintendent of Court Pleasures and a trusted advisor. Thanks to de Luynes and his assistant, the poet Durand, the *ballet mélodramatique* received a brilliant but ephemeral development between 1615 and 1621.[52] Nobles performed with professionals such as

DANSE GENERALE, ET DERNIERE.

12. BALLET DE LA DÉLIVRANCE DE RENAUD

The finale of *Le Déliverance de Renaud* featured Louis XIII in the role of a demigod. (Courtesy of the Victoria & Albert Museum, London.)

49

the incomparable Marais, a famous mime, singer, and musician. Dancers assumed several roles in each ballet. All were expected to have a good ear, a quick and faithful memory, lightness, and a good constitution. With few exceptions, women did not participate; their roles were performed by masked males *en travesti*,[53] a term describing those who took female roles and dressed accordingly.

The high style of the late Renaissance drew on accumulated theatrical knowledge while adding novelties of its own time. By now, singing had replaced declamation. Vocal content contended with a greater emphasis on dancing because Louis XIII was an excellent dancer. For the first time, choreography took precedence over the decor in a major production because of the king's central place in this ballet. What made *Le Déliverance de Renaud* also remarkable was its use of shifting scenery enclosed by a proscenium arch, sky borders, and backdrop in a temporary setting, the Louvre's *Grand Salle*. In this production, the elevated stage action occurred at one end of the hall, claiming focus for itself while still directing its theatrical impact toward the guest of honor.[54] It was the custom for various groups of dancers in the production to descend onto the main floor space of the ballroom, which, at this date, was still reserved for performers. Use of the additional space increased the physical dimensions of the spectacle and allowed for greater numbers of participants in an expanded performance area. In keeping with the lofty subject matter, the danced figures in *Renaud* were formal, consisting of stately processionals, facile turns, glides, and reverences. According to court ballet tradition, the evening concluded with social dancing occurring among performers and audience.

50

The nineteenth-century Renaissance ballet historian Henry Prunières simplified the many different forms that spectacles took over the years, reducing them to three major categories.[55] He specified works, which in their time were essentially dominated by spoken lines, the *ballets comiques*, and the *ballets tragiques*. Spectacles that largely consisted of musical elements, Prunières designated as *ballets mélodramatiques*. Lastly, he considered varied court spectacles of loosely related, highly theatrical improvised scenes to be *ballets mascarades*. These were most to the French taste and became very popular. *Ballets mascarades* were social affairs and could be performed in private residences. The various forms were further distinguished by the fact that the comic and tragic ballets primarily had intellectual appeal while the musical and masquerade forms were predominantly visual. By the end of the Renaissance, all three forms merged into the highest flowering of court ballet, becoming *ballets à entrées*.[55]

# BALLETS À ENTRÉES

Danced masquerades and burlesques appeared in theaters open to the general public around 1630. Thinly structured on the mythological and pastoral themes dictated by the literary men at court, these works acquired some internal cohesion and were known as *ballets à entrées* for their many and varied entrances.[56]

The prime concern of *ballets à entrées* was to produce the effect of a continuously changing visual display. The courtly amateurs who danced in these ballets were of widely uneven technical skills, but they looked on participation in the performances as part of their aristocratic birthright. Due to an increased use of the dance element in spectacles, court dancing masters were beginning to assign French names to steps and devise choreographic rules specifying how steps should best be used. As a result, the foundation for the future standards of academic dance was further enforced with the codification of these techniques. Between 1581 and 1635, well over 800 performances of the various forms of court ballet were given all over France. Information on many of the productions was disseminated across Europe, but what has survived is sparse.

The clearest description of the structure and values of the *ballets à entrées* was penned by Nicolas Saint-Hubert in *La Manière de composer et faire réussir les ballets* (1641, The Manner of composing and making successful ballets).[57] Based on his personal experience, he stated that as long as a ballet was well made, it would be successful whether it was in the serious or comic vain. Saint-Hubert addressed a number of points in his formula for creating good *ballets à entrées*. The theme or subject supporting the *entrées* should be appropriate for dancing and they, in turn, should be pertinent and relevant to each other. The balanced use of the serious and grotesque *entrées*, along with fresh subject matter and original costumes, makes a ballet all the more interesting. Prior to the performance, a poetic description of the ballet for the viewers is advised, thereby increasing the audience's pleasure. The music should be composed only after the subject matter and *entrées* are carefully planned so that it follows what the dancers do and represent.

Of the dancing itself, Saint-Hubert thought that the movement of the dancers should reflect the characters they portray, whether nobles, villagers, soldiers, or even lame persons. Because ballet is silent play, its elements of figures, steps, actions, costumes, and properties should be used in a way that clarifies what is being represented. Dancers ought only be given steps that they can perform well with the identifying properties that they are required to carry. Sufficient rehearsal time must be allotted to ballets according to their length since improvisation is never successful. Costumes, above all, must be beautiful, well made, and suitable. Regarding stage machinery, he thought it brought great embellishment to ballets when it is well designed and skillfully handled. Finally, Saint-Hubert insisted on the necessity of a *mâitre d'ordre* (similar to a twentieth-century combination of *régisseur* and artistic director) to oversee all aspects of production.[58]

51

# EQUESTRIAN BALLET

Along with the elegant pastiche of the *ballet à entrée*, other grand forms of spectacle proliferated the Renaissance princely life. Perhaps the most costly were equestrian ballets devised to emulate ancient Greek military games. More than displays of brute strength and violent competition, the complex nature of equestrian ballets elevated the medieval tournament to a *pas d'arms* wherein a show of skill with weapons and horses was raised to an art. Originating in Italy and imported by Catherine de Medici, equestrian ballets found favor among French nobility and came to be called *carousels*, which were the foundation of the equine art of *dressage* during seventeenth and eighteenth centuries. In *carousels*, the pageantry and excitement of the medieval tournament were combined with the visual design and musical grace of the court ballet.

As outdoor displays, equestrian ballets provided a form of entertainment that adapted perfectly to military practice fields and the large square courtyards of Renaissance palaces. These regal affairs filled the desire for lavish display left void after Catherine's final ballet production. On the practical side, it was imperative that the king's cavalrymen ride daily during times of peace to maintain their skills as a fighting force. *Carousels* were time-consuming for the dancing master who also had to be competent as a riding and fencing master. The horses and their riders were drilled in military fashion to fit the various four-

*Carousel for Ferdinand II.* The picture records the complex configurations of an equestrian ballet performed in the outdoor theater of the Grand Duke of Tuscany in 1637. It represents the development of the intrinsic relationship between art, political power, and choreography under the Renaissance prince. Etching by Stefano Della Bella. (Courtesy of the Art Institute of Chicago.)

52

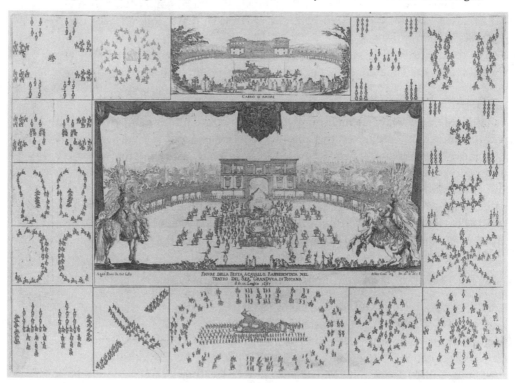

footed moves to the music that guided the participants in playing out the spectacle. Invariably, the gorgeously arrayed riders on their equally decorated mounts acted out (to the accompaniment of singing) dramatic situations modeled on the themes of the contemporary court poets Tasso and Ariosto.

Beginning with the reign of Henry IV, equestrian ballets afforded a show of military skill and might under the guise of spectacle that was beautiful to behold. Images of cosmic harmony brought down from heaven to earth were echoed in the movements of horses and their riders in accordance with the obsessive preoccupation of the Renaissance court *fête*.[59] Countless illustrations of their ground patterns remain to assure us of their entertainment value. Not only were graphic renditions of these ballets recorded with special notation (since horses have four legs), but the vocabulary of the steps such as jumps, cabrioles, gallops, and turns were shown to relate to the musical accompaniment. Actors and singers outlined the general plot before the spectacle began. The dancing horses were trained to follow complex cosmic patterns and rhythms that underscored their relationship to ballet. These dancing segments were interspersed with mounted duels, chases, and mock battles that lent bravura to the proceedings, but more importantly, kept the king's soldiers in fighting form.[60] It was recorded that Henry's son, Louis XIII, periodically took the field to join in his cavalry's equestrian ballet. Just as Renaissance court ballets ended with a grand ballet, so did the equestrian entertainment end with a magnificently staged finale in the form of a grand battle. French interest in *carousels* eventually subsided due to their exorbitant cost, the opening of public theaters, and the popularity of opera.

53

# $\mathcal{M}$ASKS AND DANCERS *EN TRAVESTI*

Throughout the Renaissance, masks were a prerequisite for extending the allegorical fantasy in court ballet and equestrian spectacle, and were used well into the eighteenth century. Since the dawn of humankind, wearing masks had been a favorite device for heightening events that ranged from divine worship to public celebrations to theatrical productions. Some authorities believe that masks originally appeared as a result of tribal aspiration to a divine countenance, while others claim that it evolved from a desire to astonish, terrify, or simply change the human appearance. In the vast Greek and Roman theaters, masks were probably developed to project the work of actors across a great distance and were shaped to express tragic, comic, and satirical expressions. The tradition of mask-wearing in Europe was carried over from antiquity into the medieval religious plays via the ubiquitous *pantomimi*. Made of wood or leather with painted detail, the masks of the *commedia dell'arte* did not express a specific emotion. They wore an indefinable expression as full of possibilities as of impossibilities, which every epoch "read" differently. Although the *commedia* masks were devoid of specific emotion, each had a unique shape or look, giving the illusion of permanency to favorite characters played thousands of times by generations of actors.[61]

Following the Renaissance desire to recover the principles in the art of antique theater, masks were worn in sixteenth- and seventeenth-century ballets to create the illusion of transcending the human condition by those who took the roles of divinities and other mythical creatures. The mask's indefinable expression meant that the communication of ideas had to come primarily through the body, the refined movement of the head, and to a lesser degree, elements of costuming and the properties they carried. Successful use of the mask demanded a constant and perfected play of the body and head that required thorough study. If the body was subtle in its play, the mask became a far more effective means of expression than facial muscles.[62]

When mask-wearing was adapted to social customs, a courtier following the formality of a disguise could leave the stuffy atmosphere of the court balls and descend to the street to dance and carouse with the high-spirited townsfolk. From London to Paris and Venice, mask-wearing was also part and parcel of illicit sexual license, peaking during pre-Lenten revelry. Masks were useful for individuals in prolonging the intrigue and coquetry at court masquerades as well as public venues of amusement. On these occasions, women did participate in the festivities, and masks were considered a necessary part of female apparel. In court ballets, masks were worn by all, including men *en travesti* who specialized in dancing female roles. While males commonly danced *en travesti* in the Renaissance, by the nineteenth century, due to changing tastes and a lack of male dancers, the custom was reversed with women costumed for the role of the ballerina's male counterpart.

## Sixteenth-Century Writings on Ballet

The Renaissance left many detailed literary and pictorial descriptions of its dances. In addition to publications that recorded French court entertainment from the *Ballet Comique* onward, theorists produced a considerable amount of commentary. Three of the best-known authors on the dance were practitioners themselves and their writings provide special insight into the evolution of ballet. The Florentine, Fabritio Caroso (b. 1553) was one of the most experienced dancing masters to lend his expertise to Valois ambitions. In 1581, Caroso's *Il Ballerino* (The Dancer) was published, substantiating the fact that Italy had an established style of dancing with a glossary of terms and rules for executing steps. The book records instructions for over one hundred dances that indicate considerable technical progress since the time of Guglielmo Ebreo in the previous century.

Some years later, Cesare Negri, an Italian contemporary of Caroso who spent an active career in Milan and Paris, penned *Nuove Inventioni de Balli* (1604, New Inventions in Dancing), which described social dances, their steps and etiquette required in performance. Negri's book set down in a logical fashion the foundation of classical ballet. It included general advice about dancing, fifty-five technical comments, and his directives for a large number of dances. Both the manuals of Caroso and Negri attest to the gradual technical development of dance. They confirm that virtuosity, inherent in beats and turns, existed and was the domain of the male dancer. Negri's treatise contains the earliest mention of the "bend of the knee," which was given as advice for the proper preparation of jumps and *capriolles*.

Thoinot Arbeau's (1519–1596) *Orchésographie* (1588, *Orchesography*) appeared in the form of an engaging treatise written as a dialogue between the author and his dance pupil, Capriol. The book was to have a long-term influence on the evolution of dance, its impact being equal to the performance of the *Ballet Comique*. *Orchésographie* was chiefly concerned with discussions of dance steps and notated rhythms like the *pavane, allemande, gaillarde, courante, gavotte*, and twenty-three versions of the *branle*. While these were originally social dance forms in the sense that Arbeau and young Capriol discuss them, their steps and rhythms were absorbed into theatrical dance as the forms continued to develop. Many practical hints for solving technical difficulties were incorporated into Arbeau's precise instructions for executing the steps, positions, and dances. For instance, the book's illustrations complemented his ideas on basic positions of the body, the transference of weight from one leg to the other, and the use of the arms.

An important tangible heritage of sixteenth-century dancing, the *Orchésographie's* significance cannot be overemphasized. By the year of its publication, the French had become preeminent in the development of dance. Up to this time the clever and charming Italians were the dancing masters sought after for their great knowledge and tradition. But by the end of the sixteenth century, Italianate know-how was assimilated with French taste. Creativity in the arts burgeoned under the aegis of an increasingly powerful and centralized monarchy, establishing France as the breeding ground during ballet's infancy.

# RENAISSANCE COURT THEATERS

A momentous concept that the Renaissance took from antiquity was that of a special place for entertainment—a theater. Romans had been the last to build public arenas. When the early Church banned all theatrical activities, the notion of a specific performing site was nearly lost. Compared to the relatively sophisticated level of Renaissance music, the state of theatrical dance was fragmentary and often incidental in nature. The most important factor explaining this discrepancy in its growth was the lack of a permanent home for dance. Since there was no specific location for court ballets, every spectacle called for original plans, a special place, and the appropriate personnel. Every performance had to assume a new creation structured from all the necessary elements, and it required the temporary adaptation and adornment of a palatial hall for the performance. The existence of ballet entertainments was fleeting, for after the performance, all was disassembled and lost except for its memory. Therefore, the move from ballroom to theater had enormous implications for the development of dance.

When certain occasions called for a very large area, the courtyards of Renaissance palaces provided generous spaces. Water spectacles were also given outdoors and made use of existing rivers, canals, and lakes. First introduced by the Medici family, *naumachia* were modeled on a festival form of classical antiquity. Extraordinary and comparatively rare, they depicted realistic sea battles. A familiar ingredient of Valois family festivals was the flooded palace courtyard. Through sophisticated engineering, the space was filled with approximately five feet of water and various kinds of floating vessels engaged in mock fighting, while the aristocratic audience peered down from windows and balconies of the surrounding palace. A Valois *naumachia* of 1589 portrayed eighteen galleys manned by a Christian force that overcame a band of Moorish ships to the cheering audience's satisfaction. The cast of a *naumachia* consisted of a select few nobles who commandeered their diminutive warring fleets with great bravura, urging their servant-sailors to fight to the end in an effort to create excitement and make the battle realistic.[63]

The gardens of Renaissance palaces were also adapted to theatrical use during pleasant weather. The *balletti* that were produced for outdoor entertainments were similar to those given indoors in their use of myth, music, and danced configurations. Gardens consisted of a wide variety of designs that were characteristically ingenious and altogether enchanting. Plans preserved in Italian archives have provided excellent illustrations of the similarity that existed between garden-planning and theatrical design in the Renaissance. Both could be abundantly grandiose and complex in detail. Gardens offered splendid settings for lavish entertainment, the celebration of aristocratic marriages, and other great events. While stone architectural facades of arches, columns, fountains, and terraces furnished a form of theatrical scenery, the developing art of topiary also contributed to the atmosphere. Boxwood and other kinds of densely growing plants were clipped into architectural shapes as well as fanciful forms of animals and an array of purely geometrical shapes that are still maintained at the garden theater of the Villa Rizzardi near Valpolicella.

The reappearance of an ancient manuscript, *De Architectura* (first century B.C., *On Architecture*) by the Roman builder Marcus Vitrivius Pollio, heralded its first of many printings in 1486. It proffered directives that led to the construction of permanent performing places, Renaissance theaters. The old concepts were swiftly adapted and incorporated into the building plans of many a fifteenth-century noble. Leonardo da Vinci was praised for a spectacle he devised in 1493 that featured seven gyrating planets. Entitled *Il Paradiso*, it was one of the first court entertainments totally enclosed in a specially created and permanent environment where an aristocratic audience was presented with calculated visual and aural delights. Generally, the earliest Renaissance theaters had floor plans that were similar to the rectangular halls, ballrooms, courtyards, and even tennis courts that they were meant to replace. They were only distinguished by a permanent wooden platform at one end of the space.

*De Architectura* received a monumental commentary by Sebastiano Serlio around 1560, and subsequent theater architects used this information as a guideline for the next 150 years.[64] One design scheme added by Serlio was the use of artificial perspective invented by Brunelleschi in the previous century. He adapted his plan of illusory three-dimensional stage space to fit into Vitruvius' simpler structure. In so doing, he produced a new idea in scenic design that symbolized an individual perception of external reality.[65] Serlio's theater called for rectangular walls covered by a roof, a raised stage on one side of the rectangle, graded semicircular seating arrangements for the audience on the opposite side, and typical Roman vomitoriums that were exit and entrance ways to channel the flow of spectators in an orderly fashion.

The Renaissance desire for an illusion of spatial depth in a limited stage area required precisely constructed sight lines. Many of these late sixteenth-century theaters presented a single vanishing point to the audience.[66] Andrea Palladio's Teatro Olimpico in Vincenza, which was begun in 1580, incorporated his most important concepts published in *I Quattro Libri dell' architettura* (1570, Four Books on Architecture). The beautiful theater is noted for three openings in the permanent stage wall that frame streets that recede in accelerated perspective to three separate vanishing points. The Olimpico incorporated permanent wood and plaster architectural scenery, decorating the stage wall behind the rather shallow stage floor.

The completion of the Farnese family's theater in 1619, which was designed by Giovanni Baptista Aleotti at Parma, heralded the first modern venue for entertainment. The theater incorporated a small, permanent proscenium arch meant to hide stage machinery, and featured a movable curtain that was opened and closed relative to the dramatic action. Still considered a ballroom theater, the Farnese *intermedii* used the stage and the ballroom floor. The building provided permanent arena seating for the palace playhouse. This arrangement was necessary as long as entertainments were still mixed in with social dancing.

By 1638, Niccolo Sabattini had made many improvements in the theater designs of Serlio. Following the rules of perspective, more elaborate buildings, statues, and forests were painted on large flats to give the illusion of vast three-dimensional objects. Mechanical conventions with origins dating back to the ancient Greek theater were powerful elements in Renaissance productions. Sabattini was responsible for improving crane-like structures for flying both actors and large set pieces, including chariots and billowing heavens. A purely Florentine invention, and one that Brunelleschi had worked on two centuries before Sabattini's improvements, were the much loved *nuvola*. Cloth-covered wooden frames that suggested clouds were devices meant to bring the heavens to earth. So popular were *nuvola* that they continued to be used and perfected well into the eighteenth century. A contraption known as the *deus ex machina* (god from the machine) was imperative for effecting abrupt or dramatic endings. When the intricacies of plot called for swift and authoritative solutions, the god Zeus as a *deus ex machina* might arrive in his chariot down through the *nuvola* to judge or decree. Having solved the human predicament, he would then ascend to his heavenly haunt.

From decade to decade, concepts of theater buildings grew and changed. Most of these early seventeenth-century theaters had backdrops and borders to mask lanterns used for illumination and to obscure the flies, a term referring to the space above the stage area. Wings or side panels parallel to the proscenium were introduced to keep backstage commotions hidden. One of the most influential minds working at the time was Giacomo Torelli (1608–1678), whose skill at creating magical effects seemed endless. Just a few of his new inventions and refined versions of earlier ones included a revolving stage and raked floors that sloped downward toward the spectators to increase the illusion of depth. He built devices to simulate burning cities, churning seas, moving clouds, and shifting rocks. Torelli perfected the use of trap doors and machines for lifting and lowering performers as well as scenery. He was able to arrange for palaces and ships to arrive on stage at climatic moments. His system of wheels and rollers allowed one technician to change scenery in less than a minute.

During the Renaissance, there was no seating in what is today called the orchestra area or stalls so that the more action-filled parts of the production easily lent themselves to this space. Italian innovations for constructing theaters and devising the stagecraft for presenting entertainments grew in importance when they were adopted by French architects. Renaissance stages were comparatively small, being designed primarily to house the performance of actors. They were not built to hold the large spectacles that comprised the court ballets. The only dances performed on them were the interludes for dancers appearing between the acts of a drama. The Renaissance concept of stage space exerted considerable influence on dancing masters who arranged the choreography. They essentially directed the action of the dancers from the elevated stage toward the seating area. Dance configurations had to be arranged so that a pleasing design on stage would be seen by the audience facing it. Dancing masters also had to rethink the most effective presentation of a solo performer as seen from an elevated proscenium stage instead of the three-quarter view of a ballroom.

# *T*HE ADVENT OF PUBLIC THEATERS

In the seventeenth-century growing merchant class, tastes invited the presence of public theaters, which, in turn, encouraged the promotion of theatrical development. During Louis XIII's reign his brilliant and crafty minister, Cardinal Richelieu, built the most advanced theater of the time in Paris at the Palais Royal in 1637. This theater, designed by Lemercier, had two houses. The smaller one seated 600 spectators and was used for plays. The second theater held 3,000 and was used for musical productions that required large amounts of scenery and heavy machinery for creating spectacular effects.[67] The Palais Royal was eventually turned over for public use, which meant that for the price of a ticket, anyone could attend plays and operas laced with dancing interludes. Whereas the action of the ballet had previously extended into the house, by 1645 it was permanently confined to the stage area. The proscenium arch, originally intended to hide machinery and lighting equipment, once and for all separated performers from the audience. By the end of his life, Richelieu had commissioned a number of well-equipped auditoriums for the growing Paris audiences.

Succeeding Richelieu, another great minister, Jules Mazarin, wished to bring to France the musical predominance of the court ballets of his native Italy. He greatly encouraged the production of operas to be given for the court and in public theaters for the increasingly supportive Parisian public. Consequently, the regency of Louis XIV witnessed an emphasis on the musical or melodramatic ballet in which expressive singing replaced spoken verse and the dancing element was minimized. A splendid opera with danced interludes, *La Finta Pazza* (1645, The Maiden Feigning Madness) was realized on the large stage of the Salle du Petit Bourbon in the Louvre. Torelli was brought to France to collaborate with ballet master Giovanni Balbi, whose dances were characteristic of regional and occupational themes reinforced by appropriate costumes and

The figured dancing of the ballroom was adjusted to theatrical purposes in these moments from *La Finta Pazza*. (Courtesy of Jerome Robbins Dance Division, The New York Public Library for the Performing Arts, Astor, Lenox and Tilden Foundations.)

59

props. The magnificence of Torelli's set designs, however, completely overshadowed all the other elements of the production including the dance, and his flamboyant decor set standards for the next one hundred years.

An added challenge for choreographers resulted from productions in French theaters. Because of the proscenium arch and the elevated stage, the dance's spatial orientation acquired a new aspect. It became imperative for the dancers to move sideways with the greatest possible skill, giving impetus to the functional necessity for turned-out legs. The important fifteenth-century qualifications of *aiere* in the dancer's manner of comporting himself led to a greater refinement of jumping steps. When performed on a raised stage, jumps emphasized the vertical dimension of movement, eventually starting the vogue for elevation steps. Furthermore, the proscenium provided a definite separation of performers from the audience, thus the spectacle became more theatrical and less of a social affair.

Masks were still prerequisite in the new theaters just as they had been in the ballrooms because productions were still concerned with ancient Greek theatrical principles and subject matter. Masks proclaimed the identity of the characters to the audience and gave fuller expression to performers on stages that were at considerable distances from the audience. Stage makeup with its paint and powders was still in the future, and for dancers and singers who were illuminated for the most part in the softness of thousands of candles, masks were necessary to convey meaning.

60

# Summary

In discovering the origins of ballet, history looks to sixteenth-century Italy and France. The revival of learning, which was the hallmark of the Renaissance, also revived the human spirit. The new learning, or Humanism as it was to be called, gave people a concept of self-esteem. It embraced any attitude that exalted man's relationship to God, his free will, and his superiority over nature. Philosophically, humanism made man the measure of all things. Society recognized its desire to enjoy the physicality of life and the living of it. In a human-centered world that the new knowledge confirmed, the creative psyche flourished, exploiting numerous avenues of expression.

Over time, the Renaissance prince skillfully worked out the complex relationship between art and power, which resulted in the divine right of kings to rule. With his wealth, the Renaissance prince patronized the creation of art, which, in turn, reflected his grandeur, his liberality, his taste, and therefore, his God-given right to rule. Expensive theatrical display became a formidable political tool and toy of the absolute monarchies of the future; their class would subsidize the best of ballet and opera in the centuries to come.

Renaissance culture spread northward, and with it came a flurry of Italian dancing masters engaged to plant their splendid court entertainments onto French soil. Renaissance society desired and relished all forms of spectacle. Italianate French court productions were highly complex creations involving dance, myth, poetry, and song that were assembled by skilled artisans under the direction of court scholars. These dramatic performances with danced interludes were indoor entertainments that were confined in terms of space, but exceeded outdoor entertainments in their quality of conception and refinement of production. Thus, France succeeded Italy as the center of theatrical dance, having assimilated the precious Italian know-how with its own inimitable taste and style.

The most celebrated example of the court ballets occurred at the Louvre in 1581. The *Ballet Comique de la Reine* presented the ancient tale of Circe in splendid allegory to celebrate a royal marriage. One after another, complicated floor patterns with symbolic meanings were traced by carefully rehearsed aristocrats under the direction of Balthasar de Beaujoyeulx. No expense or detail was spared to prepare this sumptuous feast and gorgeous entertainment. While the *Ballet Comique* was a huge success, its great cost kept it from being repeated. This ballet stands alone as the most influential and first-rate example of a Renaissance dance and music production, beautifully realizing the ideals of cohesion, harmony, and balance set by Jean Antoine de Baïf and the *Académie de Poésie et Musique*.

The Renaissance, with its fresh view of the human condition as the pivotal force in the universe, was the turning point in dance's evolution. The power and might of wealthy Italian and French dynastic families were reflected in the danced interludes of classic tragedies and comedies performed in palacial ballrooms, and even in the popular equestrian ballets. The generous patronage of great families became a political necessity. In addition to the court ballet, the Renaissance craze for building encouraged the growth of dance as an indispensable part of life by constructing the first theaters to be built since antiquity. In time, these theaters provided a permanent home to house the practice and performance of theatrical dance. Thus, the Renaissance not only gave new life to the notion of dance as social tradition, but demonstrated that it was an important means of entertainment. The international art form called classical ballet sprang from this fertile soil during the reign of Louis XIV.

61

# *Chapter Notes*

1. Ivor Guest, *The Dancer's Heritage* (Baltimore, MD: Penguin Books, 1962), p. 15.
2. Francis Hackett, *Francis the First* (New York: The Literary Guild, 1935), pp. 164–66.
3. Tuchman, pp. 503–6.
4. Prudhommeau, p. 15.

5.  Ibid., p. 20.
6.  Ibid., p. 21.
7.  Ibid., p. 22.
8.  Lydia Joel, "Catherine de Medici, Part I: The Early Years" (*Dance Magazine*, April, 1990), pp. 50–54.
9.  Frances A. Yates, *The French Academies of the Sixteenth Century* (Nendeln, Liechtenstein: Kraus Reprint, 1968), p. 251.
10. Marie-Francoise Christout, *Le Ballet de Cour de Louis XIV: 1643–1672* (Paris: Éditions A. et J. Picard, 1967), pp. 16–17.
11. Yates, p. 19.
12. Ibid., p. 23.
13. Ibid., p. 21–23.
14. Ibid., p. 30.
15. Strong, pp. 21–22. Strong provides an illuminating exposition of the term *magnifique* and all it came to represent in Renaissance culture.
16. Ibid., p. 99.
17. Catherine was widowed in 1559, and while she officially became a dowager queen, she continued to exert enormous influence at court (especially in regard to her *magnifiques*) during the successive reigns of her surviving sons, Charles IX and Henry III.
18. Wosien, p. 20.
19. Yates, pp. 256–58.
20. Ibid., p. 256. Whether the meaning of *Paradis d'Amour* was intended as a wedding celebration or as a warning to Protestants, Yates opines that "the charging of court entertainment with the dynamism of contemporary theology and politics must have reached a terrific intensity."
21. Strong, pp. 124–25.
22. Lincoln Kirstein, *Movement and Metaphor: Four Centuries of Ballet* (London: Pitman Publishing, 1971), p. 51.
23. Joel, "Catherine de Medici, Part IV: A Bitter End, A Joyous Legacy" (*Dance Magazine*, July, 1990), p. 44.
24. Mark Franko, *Dance As Text: Politics of the Baroque Body* (Cambridge: University of Cambridge Press, 1993), p. 23.
25. Strong, p. 101. Strong cautions that the Valois drawings and tapestries should be taken only as a general impression of *magnifiques* because they give an aesthetic unity to the festive occasions that they probably never had in reality.
26. Mark Franko, pp. 27–28.
27. Yates, p. 259.
28. Margaret McGowan, *L'Art du Ballet de Cour en France* (Paris: Éditions du Centre National de la Recherche Scientifique, 1963), p. 247.
29. Henry Prunières, *Le Ballet du Cour en France avant Benserade et Lully* (Paris: H. Laurens, 1914), p. 134.
30. Franko, pp. 41–42.
31. Yates, pp. 248–49.
32. Kirstein, *Dance*, p. 152.
33. Will Durant, *The Renaissance: A History of Civilization in Italy from the Birth of*

    *Petrarch to the Death of Titian, 1304–1576* (New York: Simon and Schuster, 1953),
    pp. 555–67.

34. Strong, p. 144.
35. McGowan, p. 49; pp. 56–60.
36. Franko, p. 69.
37. Ibid., p. 79.
38. Ibid., p. 69.
39. Ibid., p. 2.
40. McGowan, pp. 138–39.
41. *Larousse Encyclopedia of Music*, ed. Geoffrey Hindley, 1977, "French Music before
    the Age of Lully" (Secaucus, NJ: Chartwell Books, 1977), p. 186.
42. Sorell, pp. 82–83.
43. Yates, pp. 276–77.
44. Françoise de Bassompierre, *Mémoires contenant l'Histoire de sa vie* (Cologne: 1665),
    tome III, p. 266. Bassompierre participated in and witnessed hundreds of court
    ballets; and his memories provide numerous details of performances and the
    atmosphere surrounding them.
45. McGowan, p. 108.
46. Yates, p. 291.
47. McGowan, p. 104.
48. Ibid., pp. 176–77.
49. Ibid., p. 108.
50. Ibid.
51. Ibid., pp. 108–10.
52. Christout, p. 11.
53. Ibid., pp. 17–18. Masquerade balls and burlesque ballets costumed *en travesti* were
    exceedingly popular in the court of the last Valois King, Henry III, and had become
    a convention by the reign of Louis XIII.
54. McGowan, p. 105.
55. Prunières, pp. 110–40.
56. Prudhommeau, pp. 131–38.
57. Christout, pp. 26–28.
58. Nicolas Saint-Hubert, *La Manière de composer et faire reussir les ballets* (Paris: chez
    François Targa), 1641.
59. Strong, pp. 56–57.
60. Ibid.
61. Pierre Louis Duchartre, *The Italian Comedy* (New York: Dover Publications, 1966),
    pp. 41–44.
62. Ibid.
63. Cheney, pp. 101–2. The *naumachia* originated in ancient Rome when watertight
    amphitheaters were designed for naval fights. Two decorative fleets manned by sea
    warriors (Roman slaves) were set to fight against each other to the great amusement
    of the public. It is known from reports of the day that later, when the temporary sea
    was drained out of the arena, the pavement was strewn with valiant servants slain in
    the game of battle. They were then unceremoniously dragged away to the lion's den.
    Julius Caesar hosted *naumachiae* that were played on a long natural lake surrounded

with spectator seating. On at least one occasion, fifty ships engaged in a bloody fray intended as a mock battle.

64. Kenneth M. Cameron and Theodore J. Hoffman, *A Guide to Theatre Study*, 2nd ed. (New York: Macmillan Publishing Co., 1974), pp. 90–92.
65. Ibid., p. 92.
66. Luigi Squarzina, *Teatri e Scenografie* (Milan: Touring Club Italiano, 1976), p. 73. Vincenzo Scamozzi's design for the ducal theatre of Vespasiano Gonzaga at Sabbioneta has survived as an example of the numerous architectural experiments with perspective occurring at the time.
67. Christout, p. 34, ff. 50.

# 4

# *Baroque Ballet*

In the theater arts of France's great classical period, the baroque style of ballet revealed itself by incorporating lofty subject matter arranged with the intention of praising the qualities of the sovereign and his rule. The dramatic material was allegorical in nature, a persistent element in entertainments that dated back to the Renaissance's emulation of ancient mythology. From the moment of ballet's origin, conceived from the inspired ideals supporting Jean Antoine de Baïf's *Ballet Comique*, its defining characteristic had been a coherent plot put forth in a unification of visual and aural components. In the baroque ballet, balanced and integrated presentations of myth, fable, music, song, poetry, dance, costumes, and machinery for creating effects were underscored with a distinctive voluptuousness of form, color, and texture.

The richly dramatic style of the baroque era resulted from a reaction to the religious, social, and aesthetic strictures of the Protestant Reformation. Fueled by the educational mission of the Jesuit fathers, the baroque style emphasized an expressive art. It rigorously embellished the order and symmetry adhered to by artisans of the Renaissance with twisting, spiraling, and fluttering forms in its architecture and sculpture. The favored form of baroque ballet at court was a combination of the *ballet mélodramatique* and *ballet masquerade*. In these predominantly lyrical and visual presentations, successive scenes consisting of fables were held together by skilled fusion of thematic, vocal, and choreographic elements. At its most elegant state, the style embodied a perfected form of the *ballets à entrées*, similar to the directives set forth by Saint-Hubert in 1641. From the early 1650s onward, ballets were engineered by a fabulous assemblage of talented collaborators and royal patronage. Baroque ballet commenced with the lengthy rule of Louis XIV, and by the end of his kingship dance was firmly established as a theatrical form in the care of professionals. The counterculture of the *ballets burlesques* had finally run its course. Louis undertook to expand the propaganda potential that had been inherent in Catherine de Medici's *ballets de cour* in order to aggrandize his position. With the lifelong efforts of the king and his uniquely gifted artists, the development of ballet peaked and became the province of the French.

# $\mathcal{T}$HE COURT OF LOUIS XIV: FROM THE *FRONDES* TO VERSAILLES

As a child, Louis and his widowed mother had lived under dire threats to his life and throne during civil rebellions known as the *Frondes*. Uprisings were first instigated by the Parlement of Paris, the French courts of law, that decried the heavy taxation crippling the peasantry and the middle class while the aristocracy was exempt. Compounding the danger, several rich and powerful nobles who were close relatives of Louis believed they had rightful claims to the throne and aggressively plotted against the boy-king. Above all, hatred of the foreign advisor to the regent queen, the Italian Jules Mazarin, fueled the rioting. After five years, the persistent civic unrest was finally put down by the government in 1653. The monarchy was still intact and Louis, having come of age, assumed the reins of power from his mother.

The *Frondes*, with their barricades and municipal chaos, had left a mark on Louis that was never to be erased. The memory of those dangerous times was traumatic and the men responsible were still around, some in positions of power and capable of inciting new disturbances. The experience had taught Louis that treachery lurked everywhere. From then on he mistrusted everyone from his ministers of state to the Parisians. His future strength would be founded on the monarchy's absolute political control and reinforced by his soldiers, a standing army of 400,000 who made up the most powerful military machine France had ever known.

Having inherited a genuine affection for the ballet, Louis XIV also understood its ideological potential and used the dance as an instrument to help stabilize and centralize his restless country. Despite strong punishments, the crown had been unable to subdue dissident nobles who had instigated eleven civil wars in forty years. The king judged that in its fullest flower, ballet could be an auspicious means for reducing factional, domestic strife and building national prestige. Ballets had always been the strongest venue for social interaction among the nobility. Thus, in order to get control over his court, Louis understood he needed to control the dance. To accomplish this, he confiscated the ballet for his own use by institutionalizing it and, as a result, all organization and performance of ballet was subject to his authority.

To achieve his ends, Louis built the stupendous palace of Versailles away from the perils of the city and its inhabitants, the majority of whom he viewed as a smoldering mob. Versailles housed his family and his court of several thousand aristocrats lured from all over France. Rich ceremony and elaborate etiquette were part of Louis XIV's design that encouraged the cultivation of a

36. BALLET ROYAL DE LA NUIT. LE ROY EN SOLEIL

The youthful Louis XIV costumed for his role as the Sun in *Le Ballet de la Nuit*. (Courtesy of Jerome Robbins Dance Division, The New York Public Library for the Performing Arts, Astor, Lenox and Tilden Foundations.)

protocol-laden atmosphere that tightly regulated human behavior in royal circles. Because the destinies of the courtiers were dependent on their capacity to please the king, they wholeheartedly embraced their new lifestyle. Their wealth and energy were devoted to myriad pleasures, not the least being the court ballet. Living off the King's bounty, encouraged to enjoy such diversions as the chase, cards, cuisine, boudoir, and ballet, the nobles neglected their distant estates, leaving them in the hands of managers. With their private lives corrupted and their political power so painlessly sapped, serious intrigue against the crown was dissipated and Louis emerged as the supreme monarch. One of the mottos traditionally attributed to Louis, *"L'état c'est moi"*[1] ("I am the state"), equates his very being with the French nation, and he spent his long life actualizing the royal watchword.

Everyone who has left a verbal picture of Louis XIV as a young king was impressed by his healthy constitution, dignified bearing, and his handsome and youthful appearance. Wishing to manifest his majesty by dancing himself, Louis's personal participation proceeded to endow ballet with a magical grandeur that it has retained for over 300 years. In addition to being a keen ballet patron and practitioner who took daily lessons, the king was surrounded by a cluster of artists whose varied talents were responsible for the development of ballet. His entire court was concerned with the elaborate and lengthy entertainments, whence the aristocracy basked in the proximity of their dancing king. Subsequently, the years of Louis's reign witnessed intense activity in theatrical dance.

Young Louis appeared in numerous ballets, including *Les Noces de Pélée et de Thétis* (1654, The Marriage of Pélée and Thétis), *Le Ballet des plaisirs* (1655, The Ballet of pleasures), and *Le Ballet et de Psyché* (1656, The Ballet of Psyche). Historically, his most important role was as Apollo in *Le Ballet de la Nuit* (1653, The Ballet of the Night), which is said to have lasted half a day. A true *ballet à entrée*, diverse elements of nighttime were the connecting theme for forty-five entrances of danced configurations, logically staged with a clever mixture of contemporary political statement, ornate myth expressed in the poetry of Issac de Benserade, extravagant costumes, and the complex machinery of Torelli. The work was divided into four integrated parts, each three hours in length and ending with a grand finale. Resplendently costumed as the rising sun, Louis was the central figure in the last segment of the ballet when he was called forth by the goddess of dawn and her attendants representing the twelve hours of daylight. Amidst great pomp, the sun was praised by the spirits of love, honor, grace, and peace. Just as Egyptian rulers of antiquity had identified themselves with the sun, so, too, from this time on Louis embraced the idea that he was "*Le roi soleil*," the Sun King who was the light, the center, the energy source of France.

# ℱRENCH ACADEMIES

Louis's politically driven desire to put the ballet totally under his domain by removing it from noble competitors called for its institutionalization within an official framework. This coincided with the ambitions of Jean Baptiste Colbert, Louis's great financial minister, whose intention was to further enhance the king's growing prestige. Various academies had already been founded for this purpose, but they also served to organize artists and direct their energies into appropriate channels under the surveillance of the crown. Cardinal Richelieu's establishments for drama, painting, and sculpture, *L'Académie Française* (1635) and *L'Académie de Peinture et Sculpture* (1643), were strong precedents and models for creating an institution of dancing. Consequently, Letters Patent were drawn up with twelve articles of directives for *L'Académie Royale de Danse* (1661).

The document's preamble explained that the young king equated the importance of the dance with that of the military. In wartime, nobles were in the service of the king's army, but in times of peace they were in the service of his ballet. The physical exercise of dancing benefited the physical requirements needed in battle as they benefited the grace and well-being of an aristocratic performer. During the disorders and confusion of the *Frondes*, however, a great number of abuses introduced through ignorance and incompetency were causing the king's ballet irreparable harm. While there was no direct reference to his father's reign or the capricious *ballets burlesques* that characterized it, the Letters Patent blamed the nobles for the laxness in dancing, noting that there were not many capable of performing in the king's ballets. The document went on to say that it was astonishing to find so *few* properly trained people capable of teaching correct dancing. Although the *ballets burlesques* had called attention to the individual dancer, they were of an era that lacked the pedagogical infrastructure to train and perfect participants and so abuses remained. Hence, the problem was approached on two practical fronts: the dance itself as a subject to be studied was singled out from its context within spectacle, and greater attention to training dancers was addressed.[2]

Thirteen dancing masters were announced by Colbert as members of the Royal Academy of Dance to accomplish its aims and to enforce precise rules for maintaining high standards. The members, along with their apprentice sons, were expected to teach dancing as well as perform old and new dances weekly. They were also directed to act as a licensing bureau, to examine, approve, and register all aspiring dancing masters.[3] Although on paper the Royal Academy's document was a fine instrument for reorganizing and upgrading dance at court, its good intentions produced negligible results, and its existence was ultimately ineffectual. As called for in the statues of the the Letters Patent, the Academy was to meet regularly in a place where they could deliberate, correct, and perfect dancing. Instead, the group usually preferred to convene at the *Cabaret de l'Epée de Bois*, the Wooden Sword tavern, where, it was said, they discussed everything but dancing. It seems that they achieved little more than socializing, having left no concrete record to the contrary. However, *L' Académie Royale de Danse* continued to exist, finally disappearing around 1780.

The Royal Academy of 1661 drew criticism for what was occasionally attempted during its first ten years. Since 1334, a powerful musicians' guild, the *Confréries de St. Julian* (Fraternity of St. Julian), had been the official body for licensing, teaching, notating, and making dances. The guild had always viewed dance as a function of the profession of music, not as an independent and autonomous activity. Although Louis XIV had granted this group renewed status with Letters Patent in 1658, Colbert left the musicians out of his new Royal Academy of Dance that, in effect, finally gave dance its desired freedom from being in the service of music. The leader of the *Confréries*, Guillaume du Manoir, was outraged at this turn of events and criticized the new academicians in his pamphlet *Le Mariage de la Musique avec la Danse* (1664, The Marriage of Music with Dance)[4] for their own inadequate preparation to do the work at hand. He questioned the dancing masters' technical competency as practitioners and accused them of trying to monopolize dance.[5] The most serious charge du Manoir leveled was their lack of musical understanding, citing an instance when the new academy presented a *menuet* to the music of a *sarabande* because both forms had the same time signatures. He was emphatic that a dance was always composed to an air and not vice versa. He also complained that the dancing masters had interchanged a *gavotte* with a *bourrée*. This, he stated, broke the art of dance from its true framework of music in which, for him, alone had meaning.[6]

Since the sixteenth century, the nobility had been the dancers in the performances at court, and while most relished the task, some were ill at ease. In his *Mémoires*, the Duc de Saint-Simon gave an account of the debates on etiquette, behavior, and rules of precedence in court ballets. Strict protocol pertaining to the order of their appearance applied to the fifteen families of the Royal House of France down through those of foreign nobles at court, marshals of France, dukes, and counts. Inevitably, the demands of the more exalted over the less illustrious often interfered with balance and internal logic of a production, flawing the ballet.[7] In wintertime, one to three ballets a week were put on, and all who could participated in what must have been a daunting challenge of logistics and diplomacy for the dancing masters.

At Louis's court, the popularity of ballets reached an all time high, considerably adding to the number of participants. Written and pictorial descriptions of earlier ballets indicate that groups of sixteen to twenty carefully drilled dancers executed predetermined dances. In a strictly regulated order, they also performed individually or one couple at a time. Now, the cast was often increased fourfold, which taxed the time and patience of those in charge. On occasion, careless observance of the dancing master's directions in performing transitions between danced figures created confusion. Insufficient rehearsal time frequently led to faulty execution of steps, and the ineptness of some of the aristocrats stained the king's ballet. Clearly, there was need for regulation, and deliberations on the subject persisted throughout the period. As guardians of French civilization, aestheticians and writers of *L'Académie Française* rekindled the desire to discover the art of the ancients. They reread Aristotle's emphasis on art as meaningful imitation of nature. For these French intellectuals, the Aristotelian notion defined the vast range of human experience that they felt was expressible in poetry, music, and movement. Art, according to the Greek philosopher, was a distillation of life expressed in a harmonious and unified manner. How then, some wondered, did the marred performances and poorly conceived entertainments currently being presented relate to the meaning of art?

The theoretician Abbé Michel de Pure wrote in a publication, *Idées des Spectacles Anciens et Nouveau* (1668, Thoughts on Old and New Entertainments), that the dancing masters were embarrassed by the inadequacy of certain nobles with whom they had to work. These amateurs could not correctly execute the steps they had been taught, making it impossible for dancing masters to carry out their ideas.[8] In comparing new productions with those of Louis's earlier court ballets, de Pure gives us his impression of the level to which theatrical purpose and taste had sometimes fallen.

. . . luxury having prevailed over intelligence, greater stress was laid on expense
than on perfection, on showiness than on solidity and on accessories than on
the principal. Little regard now came to be had for the various talents of the
dancers, the originality of the steps was despised, and, worst of all, it was
desired to please the Court and the Ladies, who are the two rocks on which
common sense is wrecked and are the evil destinies of fine works. The scene
was packed with people of quality who were shamelessly sought out that a part
of the expense might be unloaded on them and who accepted out of vanity. All
that the intelligent professionals, who found themselves burdened not only
with this large number of people of quality, but also with their clumsy, pre-
sumptuous and, therefore, incorrigible efforts, were able to do was to compli-
cate the *entrées* by a large number of figures and mask as best they could by
these various changes the faults of these great nobles, who were either badly
made or poor dancers.[9]

As to the productions themselves, de Pure notes that they often lacked suitable
subject matter that was expressive and without cumbersome irrelevancies. The
*entrées*, he cautioned, should naturally spring from the subject matter, employing clarity of meaning and balance in their composition; music should be suited
to the characters represented just as masks and costumes should be appropriate.
When these requisites were absent the king's ballet was diminished.

Another commentator on the ballets of the period, the well-traveled Dutch
philologist Isaac Vossius noted that danced spectacles in general emphasized
their form and eye-appealing display while the gestures of the dances were
devoid of meaning.[10] By 1660 there may have been as many as two hundred
schools of dance in Paris. Vossius maintained that they had not done a good job
since not even the professional dancers were adequately trained to make their
movements meaningful. Therefore, it remained that a strong controlling body and
an organized setting would benefit the dance in the long run, just as academies
had proved effective in the maintenance of French literature, architecture,
music, painting, and sculpture.

## L'ACADÉMIE ROYALE DE MUSIQUE ET DANSE

Increasingly occupied with affairs of state, Louis retired from dancing in 1670
long before age deprived him of the grace and vigor to do it well. A line from
Racine's *Britannicus*, which intimated that the ancient Romans disdained their
emperor for playing in theatricals,[11] may have given Louis pause concerning his
active involvement in ballets even though he enjoyed it very much.
Furthermore, royal productions were beginning to demand a level of competency from the court that was sometimes more than even accomplished amateurs could achieve and still maintain their dignity. Fortunately for ballet and in
accordance with court protocol, the courtiers retired along with the king.
However, Louis reasserted his aims to ensure that ballet, which had long been

considered a unique part of French culture, would maintain its importance despite the retirement of the courtiers as its principal performers.

In a renewed effort to overhaul the ballet, Louis XIV called for the revitalization of the intentions of the original body of the Royal Academy of Dance (1661). He directed that the ideas for protecting the dance be absorbed into the *Académie Royale de Musique* (1669), which produced operas. This expanded body, *L'Académie Royale de Musique et Danse* (1672), was essentially a theatrical enterprise meant to develop the musical arts as one of the most significant ornaments of state. The Academy was successful at achieving its goals and still exists today as France's national theater, the Paris Opera. Under the directives of a formal charter, the creation of ballet performances for the court was henceforth entrusted to hired dancing masters. Their private students who became professional dancers, along with musicians, designers, and librettists, worked within the Royal Academy of Music that now included "Dance" in its title. Thus, under the law of the land, the profession of ballet replaced performing as an elegant pastime for noble dilettantes. The Royal Academy of Dance of 1661, as ineffectual as it was, survived for over 100 years. When it finally disappeared around 1780, it listed in its membership many famous dancers, including Gaëtan Vestris. It should not be confused with the Royal Academy of Music, which added dancing to its responsibilities when Pierre Beauchamp became its chief ballet master in 1673.

From childhood onward, Louis XIV had grown up obsessed with his greatness and desired that the world should see him that way. Accordingly, he insisted that first-rate talents work to enhance the magnificence of his reign. Upon his retirement as a dancer, there still remained his inspired and competent professional dancing masters, composers, designers, and librettists to keep the king's ballet alive. Duly absorbed into the Royal Academy of Music and Dance, dancing masters and their collaborators flourished within the institutional security of a permanent home. Alas, the court ballet was dead and the profession of ballet began its journey to the present. Becoming the career of professionals, ballet's creative talents would be largely freed from the amateur whims of court life.

# JEAN-BAPTISTE LULLY

Music had always been closely linked with all aspects of Renaissance entertainment, but never before did it occupy the significant place that it held in the baroque era. The composer Jean-Baptiste Lully (1632–1687) was the consummate artistic personality serving the reign of Louis XIV, and he was most responsible for the general direction that the ballet would take in its first hundred years. Not primarily a dancer, though he apparently danced and performed well, he was a clever, altogether unscrupulous,[12] and abundantly talented musician. As a native Italian in the French court, Lully brilliantly used his extensive gifts as artistic creator and producer in conjunction with his political astuteness and boon companionship with Louis XIV. The composer was not only genuinely admired by Louis as an outstanding musical master, but throughout Lully's life the king supported and favored the artist's prodigious work. Lully wholeheartedly involved Louis in his numerous ballets as the king was not only a great supporter of the arts, but was a competent performer as well. In return for the unfailing patronage, Lully's deliberate and authoritative melodies mirrored and honored the mighty monarch's long reign. It was through their joint participation in one of Lully's early dance productions, *Ballet de la Nuit* (1653), that Louis XIV earned forever the title of "The Sun King," a part he is said to have danced exceedingly well. Lully's music ensured that the king's interpretation of the "sun" perfectly reflected his extraordinary role in life in which no ruler before or after him has surpassed.[13]

Lully is remembered for his intimate knowledge of the problems of composing music for ballet. As an experienced dancer, he understood the body's natural rhythmic flow and how its phrasing could most successfully be accomplished with similar musical phrasing. Lully saw to it that his ballet music was precise and without undue ornamentation. His compositions reflected a melodic lushness in their very structure so that secondary embellishments were unnecessary. Following the ancient principles of harmony and unity, his music was classical in the purist sense while it was full of lyrical airs sustained by simple counterpoint. Departing from the Renaissance's prevailing use of 4/4 meter, Lully encouraged the baroque trend toward 3/4 time and its variants of 6/4, 3/8, and 6/8 tempos in his compositions. After 1671 Lully wrote primarily serious *tragédies-ballets* based on the texts of Philippe Quinault. They were of an intellectual bent using the noble genre of movement, and involved five acts with a prologue. In these works Lully softened the manner of the Italian recitative to the French taste. He evolved the musical equivalent for the declamation of French dramatic verse. In recitative, he used musical intervals for expressive and symbolic purposes, and thereby transmitted the meaning of the text through music.[14]

It has been said that a comprehensive discussion of the *menuet* would necessitate compiling two centuries of French social history, including its ceremonies, manners, customs, art, and music, as well as the many dance steps invented on its behalf. It is believed that the *menuet* was derived from a sprightly folk dance of Western France called the *branle de Poitou*. It was Lully who introduced it at court in 1653. Arriving as a climax in the ballroom dancing at court, its tempo was tamed for aristocratic use. It proceeded to thrive in the late seventeenth- and eighteenth-century ballets and ballrooms as a symbol of ceremonial attitude characteristic of a feudal society. A perfect expression of the artifice surrounding luxurious palace life, the *menuet* was replete with refined and mincing steps that became slower as the century wore on. Spontaneity and energetic movement were present, although controlled in keeping with good manners. Couples in order of their social importance performed versions of the dance strictly taught by dancing masters. The *menuet*, like all social dance forms, was prefaced with bows to partners as well as to spectators. The general shape traced by the dancers was a figure eight and later the letter "Z." Early on, the English upper class joined in the craze for the *menuet*, and it was duly noted that in addition to much practice, the requisite for dancing it well was "a languishing eye, a smiling mouth, an impressive carriage, innocent hands and ambitious feet."[15]

The musical scores for Lully's ballets followed a set format wherein the dance forms reflected the compositional structure. That is, the *allemandes*, *pavanes*, *menuets*, and *courantes* were always set in between the solemn musical introductions and triumphant finales. Lully's music was the perfect complement for the quality of movement emerging from the newly evolving ballet steps of which he himself had firsthand practice. Lully not only implemented his own ideas on the sensitive unification between music and movement, but he also saw the necessity for creating productions that had the coherence of one choreographer, one composer, one designer, and one dramatist. Lully's insistence on unified collaboration was novel in France since it had previously been the custom for many composers, poets, and dancing masters to work on one production. Up to this time, too many collaborators had often spoiled the results of their efforts. It was a tribute to Lully's leadership that he forbade such top-heavy arrangements that produced, at best, mediocre entertainments. Among his many ballets composed and produced over the years were *La Puissance de l'amour* (1656, The Power of love), *Psyche* (1671), *Les Festes de l'Amour et de Bacchus* (1672, The Festivals of Love and Bacchus), and *Le Triomphe de l'amour* (1681, The Triumph of love).

Lully and the great French playwright Molière joined their artistic efforts on a number of theatrical projects, including what was perhaps their greatest collaboration, the *comédie-ballet*, *Le Bourgeois Gentilhomme* (1670).[16] Eventually the two assimilated elements of the *commedia dell'arte* into their joint work. The *commedia dell'arte* style of theater originated in Italy and had come to France in the sixteenth century. More recently, its popularity was revived when Jules Mazarin encouraged Italian theater companies in Paris. The *commedia*'s standardized characters of Harlequin, Scaramouche, Brighella, and Colombina, with their improvised comic bits known as *lazzi*, provided a goldmine of comic devices for the sublimely satirical Molière to shape and adapt for his scripts. Molière was further able to offer Lully a special kind of inspiration that springs from brilliant collaboration because the playwright was also an experienced dancer. Accordingly, Molière directed his characters to move in a style that reflected their zany lines. Lully, in turn, stylized his music to support the antics of Molière's individual characterization.[17] Thus was born a new level of artistic oneness that would in time contribute to our contemporary concept of ballet.

While Lully's most profound contribution to the development of ballet centered on his dance-sensitive musical compositions, he also served as the Royal Academy of Music and Dance's first director. When the King authorized his well-loved musician to take over the Royal Academy of Music in 1672 and add to its scope equal attention to dancing, Lully naturally relied on Pierre Beauchamp. His experience and knowledge as the Superintendent of the King's

74

Ballets was vital in taking charge of dance performance and pedagogy. Together, Lully and Beauchamp envisioned the principles and methods necessary to produce dance for the world's first ballet company.

# PIERRE BEAUCHAMP

The artistic gifts of Pierre Beauchamp[18] (1631–c. 1705) figured significantly in the rapid development of seventeenth-century dance. He was born into a family whose profession had been court violinists, and their name was associated with the most important artists of the era. Beauchamp was the twelfth of fourteen children, and was trained as a musician as well as a dancer according to the regulations of the time. Beauchamp debuted professionally in 1648 and soon developed his specialty for comic roles. He was considered to be a masterful choreographer and dancer who excelled in the execution of *pirouettes*. In developing the earliest forms of academic turning, Beauchamp also experimented with the *tour en l'air*, or air turn. He was still dancing with vigor in 1701. A daily newsleaf, the *Mercure de France*, reported that the Spanish ambassador was stupefied on learning of Beauchamp's advanced age, which was not apparent while watching him dance even without a mask. Historians generally credit Beauchamp with new concepts in ballet composition, perhaps his weightiest contribution. When asked about the seemingly endless variations of choreographic ideas in his ballets, Beauchamp replied that his inspiration derived from the patterns formed by pigeons as they scurried after the grain he flung to them.[19]

Beauchamp had the good fortune to collaborate with Molière in 1661. The renowned comic playwright was preparing *Les Fâcheux* (The Bores) for a grand reception at the newly opened and magnificent Vaux-le-Vicomte to which Louis XIV was invited. Their collaboration resulted in the invention of the *comédie-ballet*, which was the most important advance in baroque dance since the development of Renaissance geometric figures and the non-figured *ballet burlesque*.[20] Beauchamp was assigned to compose the music and to choreograph a separate ballet for insertion into Molière's comedy piece about various kinds of dull personages. But there were very few competent dancers available since the training school of the Royal Academy was not yet in existence. Bearing this difficulty in mind, Beauchamp and Molière agreed that the dancing should relate to and extend the plot of the play, thus providing a structure that would allow for an unprecedented amount of dance and dramatic amalgamation. Using elements of the burlesque, they grafted *entrées* onto the scenario, binding dance within the textual meaning. Hence, the small number of dancers at their disposal were woven into the plot, and their dancing was meaningfully merged with the play's dialogue into a very successful whole.[21]

While *ballet burlesque* had invoked the importance of the individual and subversive politics at court, the *comédie-ballet* with its integrated structure was a metaphor for the unified body of France under the monarch. This put an official end to the *Frondes* and to the political satire and criticism in court ballet; the potentially autonomous aristocrat was reduced to an impotent courtier. By building the splendid Vaux-le-Vicomte, Nicolas Fouquet had announced his autonomy to Louis XIV. The beauty of the chateau and the gorgeous reception had been a public statement of competition for glory with his royal guest. Two weeks later, Louis had Fouquet thrown into prison where he languished for nineteen years, although his wife was allowed to remain in the superb dwelling. Consequently, by erasing the counterculture of the court, so blatantly evident in Foquet's actions and the *ballets burlesques*, Louis, Beauchamp, and Molière maximized the promotion of the king's supreme authority,[22] which would be reflected in the perfection of the *tragédies-ballets* of his reign.

Beauchamp's efforts resulted in numerous advancements in the creation and production of ballet. The cornerstone of French dance of this period lay in the classical ideals of clarity, harmony, and balance. While the formations of the danced figures and ballroom steps were still of uppermost importance as when Renaissance audiences sat around three sides or viewed ballets from overhead galleries, change was in the air. Beauchamp encouraged the development of the aesthetic of the vertical line of the individual dancer's body with its complementary carriage of the arms and partially turned-out legs.[23]

The richness of the human body's design potential became more apparent when framed by a proscenium arch. Spectators marveled at the visual effects of composed body shapes set in deep perspective that was created by tracks of diminishing flats of scenery in the receding stage area. Set designers, influenced by French architectural calculations that were based on Italian views of perspective, provided the ballet with a type of decor where the eye, undisturbed by excessive detail, was drawn toward the spacious, centered dancing area.

Under the aegis of Pierre Beauchamp, the presence of adequate and deep stage space, as well as the growing emphasis on technical nuance, once and for all eliminated the need for the ballet to descend into the house for effectiveness. The separation of stage from audience allowed for the creation of genuine illusion, establishing dance as a theatrical entity rather than merely a vehicle for social amusement. Also, due to Beauchamp's influence, interest in the body's design potential recalled the Renaissance notion of *aiere* by extending the dancer's uplift and verticality with the use of jumping movement. A major breakthrough, *la danse par haut* (the dance of elevation) would in time evolve into *petit* and *grand allégro* steps, characteristics of the balletic idiom.

Cardinal Richelieu had built the Palais Royal in 1637, a magnificent galleried hall for theatrical presentations.[24] Louis XIV gave it to the drama school, *L'Académie Française*, and Molière presented plays in it for the Parisian populace. When Molière died in 1673, Lully took over the theater, and it was on its elevated stage that Beauchamp worked out the special problems of early classical ballet choreography as seen from the audience's focal point. Until 1687, Lully and Beauchamp created works of unsurpassed baroque elegance along with costume designer the elder Jean Bérain, librettist Isaac de Bensarade, and chief machinist Carlo Vigarani. The professional dancers appearing in these

76

ballets, most notably Pierre Beauchamp, Louis Pécourt, Claude Balon, and Beauchamp's nephew Michel Blondy, were dancing masters themselves. Additional dancers were found among private students of Lully and Beauchamp and skilled commoners who had danced in court ballets prior to Louis's retirement.

In 1681, the Academy granted women the right to perform professionally. Lully had gotten the idea when several great ladies of the court, including the dauphine, were much applauded in his *Triomphe de l'amour*. After the event, Lully was determined to introduce professional female dancers on the stage of the Palais Royal, and in so doing, Mlle. Lafontaine became history's earliest professional ballerina. She appeared in rightfully claimed female roles that had been performed by men *en travesti* since 1672, thereby initiating a welcome and meaningful reform in the ballet. She was followed by Marie-Thérèse Subligny who was the first professional ballerina to perform in England where she learned the jig and may have later introduced it to the French stage as the *gigue*. Little by little, the popularity of male dancers came to be shared with women until the astonishing debut of Auguste Vestris in 1752.

From the time of Beauchamp's appointment as principal ballet master in 1672, the Royal Academy of Music and Dance under the general direction of Lully was the official and active body in regard to the theory and production of ballets. Although dancers working under ballet masters daily maintained their technical skills, a training school was founded at the order of Louis XIV and added to the Academy in 1713. Not until 1780 was a children's school established where three classes a week were given to impoverished but promising boys and girls between the ages of six and ten, whereupon they graduated at eighteen.

When Beauchamp retired from his position as Superintendent of the King's Ballet and principal ballet master at the Academy in 1687, he was succeeded by his former student, Louis Pécourt (1653–1729).[25] Pécourt's appointment as principal ballet master insured the perpetuation of the excellent standards previously set. As a well-known dancer, his light and precise dance technique was said to have exceeded that of Beauchamp's. His most famous role was in Lully's *Triomphe de l'amour*. Directing the work of the Academy for six years, Pécourt continued to add to his credit the choreography for numerous ballets, revivals of works by Lully, and a large number of dances that were outstanding for their variety and charm. One of his greatest successes was in collaboration with André Campra who composed the music for *Les Festes Venitiennes* (1710) from which the score and several of his dances survive.[26] His many creations were duly edited and preserved in notation by Raoul Feuillet.

# *T*HE *DANSE D'ÉCOLE*

The establishment of a model institution for dance within the *L' Académie Royale de Musique* in 1672 invested all aspects of the king's ballet with great refinement. Owing to Beauchamp's interest in the development of the individual's dance technique, the concept of *danse d'école* emerged from an accumulation of dance ideas going back to medieval and Renaissance times. *Danse d'école* is defined as schooled dancing that follows time-honored and strict rules for executing specific poses and steps. The term is known in the English language as classical ballet. The Academy oversaw the formal adoption of the five classical positions of the legs, mandatory use of the ninety degree turnout of the legs for maximum balance, and the development and codification of old and new ballet steps.

Under the auspices of the Academy, the danced figures of the *ballet de cour* were blended with the technical nuances of the *danse d'école*. Academic steps consisted of moving from foot position to foot position in movements that were straight forward, open, round, serpentine, and beaten. The introduction of a precise manner of dancing these steps required exact instruction for the performers. There were specified poses and positions to be studied along with their special terminology and rules for correct execution.

The nomenclature of a common dance language was in place, having been cast into the French language by the Academy. Steps were categorized into *courantes, coupés, demi-coupés, pas de bourrées* or *fleurets, contretemps, jetés, chassés, sissonnes, pirouettes, cabrioles, entrechats,* and *balancés*. The steps were numerous, and it is recorded that the *pas de bourrée*, by way of example, had no fewer than ninety-four variations.[27] Innumerable methods for accomplishing *pirouettes*, which were now divided into *en dehors* and *en dedans*, were set forth, and even a form of *tour en l'air* was stipulated. The seeds of the *danse de l'éléva-tion* were planted for a forthcoming conquest of space. Lully's insistence on *pas d'expression* gave new vitality to the dance. Complementing details, such as the frequent use of castanets, evoked an ethnic flavor to the dancing while adding to the overall richness of texture in the dance.[28]

Stylized arm movements and the bearing of the upper torso, called *port de bras* and *épaulment*, were also part of the body of material to be systematically mastered by all dancers working under Beauchamp. Broad gestures and acting poses were developed to clarify the dramatic intentions of the dancer and to intensify the impact of the singer's declamation. In ballroom dances, the development of arm movement, regulated by specified positions, was less evident due to the manner in which sleeves were set into garments. The arms could only move forward without some restriction. However, the hands were free and they were emphasized with inward and outward rotation of the wrists and the natural placement of the fingers.[29]

As for the dances themselves, they were numerous. Earlier dances were preserved while ballet masters invented new ones. *Branles, courantes, pavanes, gaillards, gavottes, sarabandes, gigues,* and hundreds of variants of the *menuet* were popular. While these dances were those of social dancing in the ballroom, they were also found in ballets. The difference was only one of degree. The professionals performed more embellished steps than the amateurs, although as Germaine Prudhommeau points out, their level of intricacy and virtuosity did not exceed those of the kind described by the sixteenth-century Italian masters Coroso and Negri.

Inherited from the rational climate of Renaissance court dance was the ancient Greek classification of the dancers into three types. As addressed by the Royal Academy, the concept of these fundamental categories received further definition in the baroque ballet. The individual's perfectly proportioned physiognomy and beauty marked him as a *danseur noble,* or heroic dancer, of which the Adonis-like, young Louis XIV was the magnificent archetype. The opposite of this was the *danseur comique,* or comical grotesque dancer, modeled after the dancers of the Italian acrobatic companies and the raucous *commedia dell'arte.* A combination of certain elements in each of these provided a category of middle ground, the *demi-caractère* type who was attractive, but whose dancing style displayed a skilled vigor. Each of the three categories at the Academy was exclusively the domain of the dancers who fit the classification and interchange of roles was rarely permitted. Furthermore, the Academy assigned which steps belonged to what category. The three categories of performers danced in the manner that was common to the characteristic comportment of their roles whether they played gods or villains. The dancers were further identified with appropriate costumes and the particular props they carried.

# EIGHTEENTH-CENTURY WRITINGS ON THE BALLET

The lifelong work of Claude-Françoise Ménéstrier (1631–1705) figured in the perfecting of the *comédie-ballet* and the *tragédie-lyrique* genres of the baroque period. Ménéstrier was a Jesuit priest who chronicled and theorized on public celebrations and even staged important events himself. His activities were motivated by the Catholic clergy's rigorous mission to recall its dissident members to the Church of Rome. As a major part of their activities, the Jesuit order developed a form of theater at the Parisian College of Clermont/Louis le Grand that was a force in Counter-Reformation humanism. The Jesuits held that nonliturgical theatrical displays were good if put to good uses, and that human beings do have free will to make good moral decisions. The ballets that were created by the Jesuit theater (1660–1761) were thoroughly professional and preserved the lavish stagings of Louis XIV's court ballets. They served as an important part of the city's network of communication in framing the policies of the king and the moral attitude of the court regarding the Counter-Reformation.[30]

Ménéstrier had become an expert in producing equestrian ballets in keeping with the educational goals of the Jesuits, and his first publication was devoted to their rules of procedure. In 1658 Ménéstrier was assigned the duty of preparing a ballet for a reception welcoming Louis XIV to Lyons, and in researching the project, collected every ballet scenario he could find. The success of the *fête* made the priest's reputation, and from then on he was in demand for his theoretical expertise, which was integral in the preparation of Jesuit dramas all over France, and in particular, in the wealthy court of Turin in Northern Italy.

Ménéstrier's fame led to a second book, *Des Ballets anciens et modernes selon les rèles du théâtre* (1682, Ancient and modern ballets according to the rules of the theater), in which he described the various genres of court ballet and recorded their themes, serving choreographers with ideas right up to the nineteenth-century Romantic ballet. He discussed what was appropriate subject matter for ballets, giving a range from pure caprice to history and mythology. He concluded that a libretto that combined myth with history was most effective because it intertwined heaven and earth, lending a certain grandeur to the ballet not found in mere history. Ménéstrier was faithful to his period in thinking that productions should be a combination of poetry, singing choruses, and choreographed figures. By their very nature he considered that ballets could not be treated as plays or dramatic works, but were strictly imitations of nature.[31]

The most important technical writing to emerge from the first years of professional dance was done in 1700 by the dancing master Roaul Feuillet (1675–1710), who had previously served as grammarian in Beauchamp's school. Feuillet's book, *Chorégraphie ou l'art de décire la danse par caractères, figures et signes démonstratifs* (Choreography or the Art of Recording the Dance through Types, Figures and Demonstrative Signs), brought the reputation and status of French dancing masters to a level accorded to the great Italian masters of the Renaissance. His work was widely disseminated, being translated and published in 1706 by the English dancer John Weaver under the title *Orchesography or the Art of Dancing*. The same year, another English translation by P. Siris appeared with the title of *The Art of Dancing*. Eleven years later, Gottfried Taubert translated Feuillet's system into German under the title *Rechtschaffener Tanzmeister* (1717, The Worthy Dancing Master), greatly extending the French influence on European dance. The English dancing master Kellom Tomlinson used its various English translations as reference and to notate his own collection of dances in *The Art of Dancing Explained by Reading and Figures* (1724).

Feuillet's writing was essentially a technical manual. As written information, it served to stabilize the French ballet terminology; it systematically arranged existing ballet steps, which was done in a complex and probing analysis; and it defined the five classic positions, although these were in part reminiscent of those presented in Arbeau's *Orchesography* a century earlier. In *Chorégraphie*, Feuillet developed a system of dance notation claimed by Beauchamp to have been his own invention twenty-five years earlier.[32] Regardless of authorship, both the technical manual and the dance notation, which recorded nine dances devised by Louis Pécourt and fifteen by Feuillet himself to illustrate the use of notation, were concerned with steps as they related to ballroom dance, as well as to theatrical forms of dance.[33]

Dance notation, accompanying scores, and graphic renderings of seventeenth- and eighteenth-century theatrical and social dances were published just as sheet music is today. It required skill to interpret these beautifully drawn dance notations that included a considerable amount of information. For instance, Feuillet's recording of Pécourt's dances indicated the nature of the steps, which were a variety of intricate running, springing, and beaten movements along with their accompanying rhythms. The spatial design of the dance was conveyed by drawing the path or track that the dancer followed, signifying the overall patterns created in the dance. Special symbols were used to mark the movement for a bow, turn, jump, rise, or fall. What is not stressed in the notation is the carriage of the head and body. With exacting detail, however, eighteenth-century treatises dealt with the carriage of the head and placement of the body. Comportment for the ballroom differed little from that of theatrical dances because all, including men, wore corsets. This highly schooled posture was absorbed into the *grande promenade*, a walk in very high style that commenced all social dances at court balls.

A quarter of a century after Feuillet's publication and its various translations, Pierre Rameau's important book, *Le Maître à Danser* (1725, *The Dancing Master*) appeared. Louis XIV had raised his obsession with personal dignity to one of public grandeur and, after he died in 1715, his heirs slavishly perpetuated the established protocol and behavior at court. Fittingly, Rameau set down detailed instructions in his book for a courteous demeanor at royal balls, the correct order of the proceedings, and the required politeness and reverence between ladies and gentlemen. The abundance of contrived artifice called for a studied way of moving the body. Specifically, the foot was thrust somewhat forward to show off the diamond buckles on one's shoe. This was accompanied by maintaining a slight bend of the knee while the head and shoulders were held erect. From across the channel, Lord Chesterfield wrote letters to his son, admonishing the young man to seriously approach his dancing lessons, noting that all things should be done in the stately minuet time as the true mark of a gentleman.

Rameau's instructions surely had in mind a courtier approaching the glittering rooms of Versailles, attired in brocade, jewels, and powdered wig. Even the sumptuous staircases that one descended and doorways through which one passed had not an unadorned square meter of space as part of its design. One's feet touched floors of the most exquisite inlay of colored woods or precious needlepoint carpets. Only those of highest birth might sit in the presence of Louis XV and then only on backless chairs called *taborets*. All gestures and greetings were in accordance with the prescribed court etiquette. And so, the intimate language of the body developed its own expression, reinforced by the magnificence of its surroundings and a strict code of behavior, all duly reflected in the ballroom.

While Rameau's book was concerned with social dances, it also referred to stage dancing of the day. By commenting on timely examples of leading ballet dancers, he carefully explained the movement style of the ballroom dances that are discussed. As an illustration, when Françoise Prévost became the principal ballerina of the Royal Academy, Rameau referred to her as one who displayed to perfection the *danse d'école* training. He noted that she put all the rules into

81

*Le Menuet* was the domi-
nant dance form for 140
years after Lully intro-
duced it into French
court ballet. Etching by
Auguste Danse.
(Courtesy of the
author.)

practice with such grace, correctness, and energy that she could be looked upon
as a prodigy of her kind. Rameau discussed quality of movement in dancing
based on his impressions of performers and acknowledgement of his association
with the great dancing masters of the time.

Rameau's treatise considered in detail the proper forms of etiquette, social
gesture, and court protocol, as well as their relation to dancing the opening
*branle* followed by *gavottes* and *menuets*. He expounded on the five positions of
the legs, the use of the *demi-coupée* and such steps as the *balancé, jeté, pirouette,
entrechat,* and *sissonne,* which were often similar to those we perform today by
the same names. Rameau followed the ideas of Beauchamp in discussing *port de
bras* at length. He was the foremost dance writer of his day to examine the
notion of oppositional movement of the limbs, the coordinate workings of the
right arm with the left leg and vice versa. First, he regarded opposition as giving

the body a more interesting appearance, being necessary to the harmonious design of the body. Second, he emphasized that oppositional movement aids in balance and technical accomplishment because it is a natural and organic characteristic of the human body.[34]

It is clear from the accounts of Feuillet and Rameau that the structure of a ballet technique had evolved.[35] As one looks back over three centuries of ballet's growth, there is a persistent development. Yet the dancers, teachers, and choreographers who lived through these years experienced the gamut of emotional trauma in their work. Glorious times led by genuine talent predictably fell into periods of less creative activity. Efforts to change dry but honorable tradition often caused riot, scandal, and sometimes fisticuffs. Emphasis on virtuoso technique was inevitably at war with artistic expressiveness, as it continues to be. The decades that followed the splendid artistry of Lully and Beauchamp coincided with the dimming of the long reign of the Sun King. According to the cyclical nature of art, creative forces recede only to regroup and regenerate in the succeeding generation, synthesizing past experience into new artistic life.

At the beginning of the eighteenth century, a set formula had been established and adhered to for the creating of theatrical ballets, so revered and influential had been the impact of Lully's work. There were still the themes from Greek and Roman mythology that symbolically and allegorically related to the particular occasion for a production; there were still the sung and spoken sections interspersed with dancing. From the theoretical work of the Academy, the pedagogical system of the *danse d'école* allowed dancers to maintain the technical standards of excellence set by their masters. But often, the most inspirational aspects of the works of Lully and Beauchamp gave way to the less taxing formula of the earlier, predominantly visual *ballets à entrées*. As the times changed, so did the taste of Paris, and the paying public set the trend.

# Summary

The ballet enjoyed a spectacular rush of development in the first twenty years of Louis XIV's reign. The period witnessed the formal inception of what is known theatrically and pedagogically as classical ballet. Upon the monarch's retirement from his own amateur career, the dance moved from the domain of an elegant pastime to that of a serious profession. Louis XIV characteristically stimulated the emergence of great talents at Versailles and surrounded the early development of the art of the dance with men of genius, Lully and Beauchamp being the most celebrated of their generation. Within the Royal Academy of Music and Dance, Lully acted as composer, dancer, and visionary who oversaw the creation of ballets that were unified and interrelated wholes, supported on the plinth of unsurpassed elegance and taste. Beauchamp was most notably active in choreographing Lully's music and in overseeing the foundation of the *danse d'école* wherein ballet instruction was based on codified steps and formal posi-

83

tions of the arms and legs that were duly recorded. Fortunately, a large number of Pécourt's dances were notated by Feuillet, underscoring the variety and ricness of the steps, and these remain as testimony to the level of ballet's development.

By the time of Beauchamp's retirement and Lully's death in 1687, the most innovative period was over although its royal patron lived on to 1715. During this time, the formalized *ballet à entrée* remained immensely popular at court and in the several existing public theaters. Theatrical dancing in whatever form it took was still a major source of entertainment.

## Chapter Notes

1. *Hutchinson Dictionary of World History* (Oxford, England: Helicon, 1993, p. 361).
2. Mark Franko, *Dance As Text: Ideologies of the Baroque Body* (Cambridge: Cambridge University Press, 1993), pp. 109–12.
3. Ibid., p. 166–75. *Lettres patentes du roy, pour l'establissement de l'Academie royale de danse en la ville de Paris*. The most experienced dancing masters were called to serve, and while thirteen were announced, only twelve actually participated: François Galand, Jean Renauld, Thomas Le Vacher (who died and was replaced by Bernard de Manthe), Hilaire d'Olivet, the brothers Jean and Guillaume Reynal, Guillaume Queru, Nicolas de l'Orge, Jean-François Piquet, Jean Grigny, Florent Galand, and Guillaume Renauld.
4. Guillaume Du Manoir, *Le mariage de la musique avec la danse* (Paris: Guillaume de Luyne, 1664). This pamphlet contains a rebuttal to the "pretentions" of the thirteen dancing masters regarding their work in the Royal Academy of Dance of 1661.
5. Ibid.
6. Ibid.
7. Louis de Rouvray, Duc de Saint-Simon, *Mémoires of Louis XIV and the Regency* (Washington: 1901), Vol 3.
8. Christout, pp. 137–40.
9. Michel de Pure, *Idées des Spectacles Anciens et Nouveaux* (Paris: n.p., 1668, Chapter XI), p. 235–36.
10. Sorell, p. 149.
11. John B. Wolf, *Louis XIV* (New York: W. W. Norton, 1968), p. 276. Racine's play was based on Tacitus's *Annals XIV*, 308. Louis may have gotten the idea from Racine's play or from reading a translation of Tacitus. Whatever the reason, Louis retired from the ballet stage when he was only thirty-three years old, but remained its devoted patron and spectator for the rest of his life.
12. The Letters Patent for the Royal Academy of Music was granted to Pierre Perrin on June 28, 1669 (the Paris Opera's birth date). On March 19, 1671, it opened its doors with a production of the opera *Pomone*, which played successfully for eight months. By clever intrigue and his friendship with the king, chief court composer Jean-Baptiste Lully forced Perrin to sell his privilege or official authorization to produce opera. By December of 1671, Lully was in full control, and for the rest of his career he used and abused his monopoly to present only his own music at the Opera.

13. Christopher Hogwood, *Music at Court* (London: The Folio Society, 1977), pp. 50–61.
14. Hindley, pp. 220–22.
15. Louis Horst, *Pre-Classic Dance Forms* (Brooklyn, NY: Dance Horizons Republication, 1968), p. 65.
16. Maurice Pellisson, *Comédies-Ballets de Molière* (Paris: Éditions d'aujourd'hui, 1914), pp. 83–84.
17. Ibid.
18. Pierre Beauchamp has sometimes been incorrectly referred to as Charles-Louis, an older relative of the ballet master who played in the king's string orchestra of twenty-four violins.
19. Kirstein, *Dance*, p. 187.
20. Franko, p. 11.
21. Pellisson, pp. 59–61.
22. Franko, pp. 11–12.
23. Kirstein, *Dance*, p. 186.
24. André Lejeune et Stéphane Wolff, *Les Quinze Salles de L' Opéra de Paris* (Paris: Librairie Theatrale, 1955), p. 18.
25. Wendy Hilton, *Dance of Court & Theater: The French Noble Style, 1690–1725* (Princeton, NJ: Princeton Book Co., 1981), p. 30.
26. Ibid., p. 32.
27. Ibid., p. 47.
28. Prudhommeau, p. 154.
29. Ibid.
30. Judith Rock, *Terpsichore at Louis Le Grand: Baroque Dance on a Jesuit Stage in Paris* (St. Louis: Institute of Jesuit Sources), 1996.
31. Marian Hannah Winter, *The Pre-Romantic Ballet* (London: Pitman Publishing, 1974), p. 10.
32. Ibid., p. 45. According to Winter, Beauchamp circulated a non-copyrighted manuscript of his highly detailed notation system, and that it was widely known during his lifetime that he was the author while Feuillet and his own publication was its popularizer. In *Histoire de la Danse* (p. 148), Prudhommeau states that after Feuillet published his dance treatise in 1700, Beauchamp filed a lawsuit contending that thirty years earlier the king had commanded him to invent a notation system to record his choreography. Beauchamp had already composed five volumes of notated dances with their symbols. This he circulated among his colleagues, but had failed to sign and date his work. In spite of the testimony of twenty-five Parisian dancing masters who were witness to Beauchamp's legal claims, he lost the case in 1704. The shock was too much; Beauchamp took to his bed with a fever and died the following winter.
33. Hilton, p. 47.
34. Kirstein, *Dance*, pp. 194–99.
35. Hilton. See Chapters 3 and 4.

# 5

# The Advancement of Professional Ballet

The activities of the Royal Academy of Music and Dance in the early eighteenth century prepared the way for the introduction of a new style of ballet and for the technical development of the professional dancer. After Jean-Baptiste Lully's death, the balance of poetry, music, and dancing was upset, giving way to a revival of the simple dance *divertissements* of the *ballet à entrée*. Having no expressive mimicry or dramatic content of their own, numerous dances were arbitrarily inserted into operas and were often interchangeable in the general repertory.

## OPÉRA BALLET AND GALANT MUSIC

The use of *divertissements* eventually led to the invention of a new genre of theatrical dance,[1] the emphatically visual and musical *opéra-ballet*, which became immensely popular. The format for *opéra-ballet* was a prologue, three to five unrelated *entrées*, and an epilogue. Each part had its own internal logic, but the parts were not related to each other in terms of time, place, or idea, although a vague theme stated in the prologue might reappear in the epilogue.[2] The plot was sung at the beginning of each *entrée*, after which a ballet was danced. It is noteworthy that French librettists assigned an integral place to the ballet segment so as not to break the story line, a practice that foreshadowed dance's eventual break with the spoken and sung word. The first appearance of an *opéra-ballet* at the Royal Academy was *Les Saisons* (1695, The Seasons) for which a disciple of Lully, Jean-Louis Lully et Colasse, composed the music to a theme by Abbé Pic. This was followed by André Campra's musical score for *L'Europe Galante* (1697, Gallant Europe), wherein the genre became fully developed with numerous dances by Pécourt, marking a drift away from sustained drama. The cynical Campra was said to have commented that the only way to increase interest in the *opéra-ballet* form was "to lengthen the dances and shorten the skirts."[3] By 1730 both suggestions were realized.

The *opéra-ballet* form found its apogee with the dramatic and musical collaborative efforts of the writer Claude Pierre Fuselier and the composer Jean-Philippe Rameau. Their joint labors resulted in *Les Indes Galantes* (1735, The Gallant Indies), which concerned itself with four different love stories in four different countries. Fuselier had taken his libretto from the French Orientalist Antoine Galland, who translated *The Arabian Nights*. Characterized by its heroic splendor, *Les Indes Galantes* presented numerous changing and contrasting scenes enhanced with hundreds of costumes aglow in the light of thousands of candles. Theatricality was underscored with a stormy sea and shipwreck, a fire and several volcanic eruptions. The ballerina Marie Sallé danced "The Rose" in the Persian-styled third love story, during which perfume was sprayed over the audience for added effect.[4] The dancing segments choreographed by one of

LA VÉRITÉ
Personnage allégorique

*La Vérité*. A dancer of the Royal Academy of Music and Dance portrays the allegorical character, Truth, in an *opéra-ballet* of 1720. The grandeur of his costume, the mirror and the lance symbolically reinforce his role. (Courtesy of the author.)

87

Beauchamp's successors, Louis Dupré, were duly praised. In the next production, Voltaire's *La Princesse de Navarre* (1745, The Princess of Navarre), the dancing was again arranged by Dupré, and was said to have triumphed over the other elements due to its colorful musical underpinnings. Popular *opéra-ballets* continued to be created until 1773, and many of their *entrées* were maintained and repeated with success up to the French Revolution.

Jean-Philippe Rameau (1683–1764) greatly influenced the development of music written specifically for theatrical dance. Working in the prevalent *galant* style, which corresponded to Enlightenment aesthetic principles of logical order and clarity, Rameau's music featured simple harmonies that were organized and balanced with easily grasped melodic phrases.[5] The composer instinctively understood how the kinetic propulsion of the body was served by a strong orchestral pulse. In his score for *Les Indes Galantes*, Rameau added novel rhythms, articulate melodies, and a variety of instrumentation that reflected emotional nuances in the libretto. For pastoral scenes he used bagpipes, tambourines, recorders, and hunting horns to provide a bucolic contrast to palace and town scenes. Departing from the stately, four-square patterns of Lully's style, Rameau's music was dynamic, freer, lighter, and with more elaborate orchestration, which invited a choreographic outpouring of jumps, beats, and turns.

Ballet's stately *terre à terre* movement, which had been the predominant style of Lully and Beauchamp, began to defer to the *danse en l'air*. The practice of adapting ballroom dances for theatrical use with their emphasis on danced figures or floor patterns was minimized when efforts to improve execution of *pirouettes*, *entrechat quatres*, *sissonnes*, and *cabrioles* redirected the focus of the classroom and of choreography. Driven by the delights of *galant* music, all manner of beaten steps and leaps were in demand, so much so that those who favored the old days, critically remarked that ". . . once there were dances; now only jumps."[6]

## $\mathcal{C}$OMMEDIA DELL'ARTE AND PROFESSIONAL BALLET

Rapid technical development was primarily due to the recently acquired professional status of ballet. Toward the end of the seventeenth century, a nucleus of personnel consisting of ten women dancers, twelve male dancers, a ballet master, and a costumer staffed the Royal Academy. The ballet master arranged dances out of previously existing choreographic ideas, as well as invented new ones. The strict academic exercises of the classroom transformed ballroom steps as they were used on stage. No longer minions of the court, the dancers mingled more freely than ever with popular theatrical culture in Paris. Since one of the objectives of those trained in the *danse d'école* was to entertain, they continued to borrow from the amazing and popular Italian performers of *grotteschi* companies and the *commedia dell'arte* who frequently appeared in Parisian theaters.

Over time the Italian players enriched ballet with the spirit of their spontaneous stage presence. They did not rely on virtuosity alone. While the Italians performed at court like other traveling entertainers, they also frequented public theaters where a freer type of skit, not dependent on words, was more in demand by ordinary people. Normally, the eye is quicker to seize on the meaning of a gesture than the ear catches the meaning of a word. Although it is difficult to say precisely to what degree the Italian players affected theatrical dance, their nimble stunts and balances, as well as their great vitality and telling gestures, were familiar to ballet masters ever in search of new ideas. Moreover, the *grotteschi* and the *commedia* borrowed from the Royal Academy, inventing new steps to add to their own repertories of virtuosity that served their highly skilled art form of comedy and pantomime. Indeed, the Italian Theater of Paris, which housed these players, was the humanizing force that altered the strict formalism of the academic *danse d'école*.[7] With their traditions of gestural meaning and humor, the Italians urged the Academy toward creating ballets that were more understandable to its viewers.

Changing tastes of the audience and novel themes in ballets and operas allowed for modifications in what was considered to be suitable movement for dancers (many of whom were still of the noble class) to perform. The Italian theatrical presence in France continued to be a motivating force in the development of academic elevation steps, which were influenced by the stage movements of the entertaining *grotteschi*. The professional ballet was not blind to the buoyant acrobatics of Italian players who frequented theaters, fairgrounds, and city squares. Once the idea of jumping movement was accepted as an appropriate direction to be explored, acrobatic dancing came to terms with art. At this juncture, Beauchamp's successors had only to look, select, and refine the movement of acrobats as an additional reservoir of possibilities in laying the basis for *allégro* movement.

Along with the burgeoning technical growth, a quaint and charming style of ballet emerged in the new profession. Referred to as pastorals, the format was so adored by the rising middle-class that it endured throughout the century. The pastoral tradition, recalled from the Renaissance literary source of Tasso's *Aminta*, found a danced form in the artless rusticity of the rococo aesthetic. These extremely popular presentations featured graceful idylls peopled with shepherds and milkmaids, and were based on themes of Arcadian country life that were expressed by the *danse d'école* rules of movement and gesture. A highly transitional period, the era evolved a choreographic approach where ballet steps of the *danse d'école* were reinforced with lengthy amounts of expressive gesture to convey meaning. Choreography included *pas de deux* work, but the male did not yet elevate his partner although they danced side by side, face to face, and back to back. *Demi-pointe* was called for, implying the slight lift of the heel as well as the three-quarter foot position in present use.[8] The pastoral format eventually perfected itself into the so-called anacreontic ballet, a style named for the Greek lyric poet Anacreon (582–485 B.C.) whose mellow and simple verse celebrated the pursuit of bucolic pleasures.

89

During the first half of the eighteenth century, theatrical dance activity was intense not only at the Royal Academy, but at the other Parisian theaters, most notably the Opera Comique and the Italian Theater. Various court theaters of Louis XV and his nobles were also active; Madame de Pompadour's well-organized theater within her living quarters at Versailles was in continuous production. Of the many theatrical works presented at this time, it is difficult to discern how many were *ballets sans paroles*,[9] that is, ballets without words. However, by mid-century certain pioneering ballet masters began to champion the wordless *ballet d'action*.

There were also dance performances at muncipal fairs like the *Foire Saint-Laurent* and *Foire Saint-Germain* that became the true breeding ground for theatrical innovation. The entire history of the fair theaters reveals a continuing struggle between the royal academies that held the exclusive privileges for performing, and the unlicensed entertainers who worked the fairgrounds. Forbidden to enact the kinds of plays and ballets of the academies, street performers begged the question by creating pantomines, amusing ballads, comic dances, and monologues. Time and again, the fair theaters were demolished only to miraculously reappear. The fairs' myriad activities drew great crowds of people from every station of life. The air rang with sounds of fights, disputes, laughter, and songs. Rogues fooled the gullible with loaded dice, and tooth-extractors blew horns to announce their services. The public thronged to the fairs to shop for cakes, cheeses, soap, wine, and hats. They were entertained by acrobats, marionettes, parades, and *commedia dell'arte* skits, and they themselves could dance the *rigaudon*. At the *Foire Saint-Germain* in Paris, a particular favorite was Gertrude Boon, called *La Belle Tourneuse* for her thrilling sword dance. In the long run, the significance of the fairgrounds for the development of ballet was that in order to side-step the academies, unlicensed dance makers were forced to experiment.[10]

With the great surge of development in the dancer's technique, the winds of change began to focus once again on logic and reason in theatrical work. Louis de Cahusac (1700–1759) was a French librettist and dance historian who collaborated with Jean-Philippe Rameau on a number of *opéra-ballets* performed at the Royal Academy. Over the years, Cahusac had been in a position to closely observe the state of ballet, and he understood that its growing lexicon of technique was but a means to an end. He frequently complained of the antipathy that plagued dancers who stubbornly refused to give meaningful expression to their steps. In 1754 he published a three-volume opus, *La danse ancienne et moderne, ou traité historique sur la danse* (Ancient and modern dance, or historical treatise on dance) in which he passionately argued for the dramatic aims of expressive dance. He emphasized the significance of single gestures as the "bearers of the soul's emotions."[11] Thus, he figures as one of the earliest champions of the forthcoming *ballet d'action*, i.e., narrative ballet in which expressive gesture and pantomime replace words to advance its story.

While the growth of ballet during these years was centralized in Paris, it was never cut off from foreign influences. The proximity of London and the special English character encouraged an interest in French ballet. During the sixteenth century, the growing French taste for pageantry and masquerading moved north to the English court where the tradition evolved into Christmastide revels or mummings and, later on, masques. Tudor England, desiring its full share of European Humanism, had included elements of dancing along with speeches and singing in its Renaissance masques sooner than other northern countries.

During the reign of Henry VIII (1509–47), masques came to be organized by the Master of Revels, Thomas Cawarden. The earliest masques resembled a cross between an *entremet* and a *ballet de cour*. The great ennobled men and women of the land, including the royal family, participated in the events and were ceremoniously rolled into the ballroom on large, ornate chariots. In 1585 English ambassadors were solemnly received in Paris and assisted in several evenings of *ballet de cour* in private residences. This occasion marked a transmission of various elements of French court ballets to the English form of spectacular entertainment and the masque became a veritable *grand ballet de cour*. Although coherent dramatic elements were present in masques, what the English upper class most desired were colorful costumes, lavish decorations, and a generous amount of dancing. Ballroom dance and pantomime had been popular forms of entertainment since the days of the Tudor kings, Henry VII and Henry VIII, so it was natural for the masques to absorb and elevate social dance and mime. Somewhat later, the tradition of masques, as well as the dancing associated with them, greatly benefited from the dilettantism of Elizabeth I.[12]

Under the Stuart rule, the masque reached its zenith in the care of the court poet Ben Jonson (1572–1637), and became England's unique contribution to the early development of musical theater. Jonson's erudite scripts endowed the genre with profound literary and social force. Court masques featured rich allegorical verse, elaborate machines for moving scenery, and gorgeous costumes. The climax of a masque occurred midway when masked and disguised nobles entered to perform a specially prepared dance. The dancing itself included the Anglicized *moresque*, or morris dance, amplified with French and Italian styled geometric figures. Performers had bells tied to their legs and often were dressed to dramatize characters in English folklore. Masques were the favored activity for celebrating marriages, flattering royal hosts, and impressing foreigners with a display of costly entertainment.

Between 1605 and 1634 Ben Jonson and the scenic artist Inigo Jones (1573–1652) collaborated on many excellent examples of the masque, including *Twelfth Night: A Masque of Blackness* (1605). Their partnership of unique and

91

complementary talents raised the unsubstantial and fleeting masque to a form that approached a grandeur unseen anywhere in Europe.[13] Jones visited Florence in 1613 and rigorously studied the development of scenic perspective and the extraordinary stage machines and devices conceived by Italian artist-engineers. Their theatrical splendors inspired the English master designer to new heights in devising British court entertainments that integrated the full glory of the late Italian Renaissance.

In 1609, Ben Jonson and Inigo Jones increased their historical impact by inventing the antimasque following a detailed suggestion made by Queen Anne. This new genre served to relieve the audience from the uniform solemnity of the masque, and by being noticeably different, strengthened the purpose of the main event. The antimasque presented more than one danced entry and introduced wildly humorous and grotesque elements into the proceedings as direct contrasts to the tremendous elegance of its counterpart. *The Masques of Queens* (1609) represented a finely tuned integration of masque and antimasque, and the form was enormously popular with the courtiers.[14] In time, the demand for dazzling display replaced the preeminent place of Jonson's poetry. During the country's Civil War, masques disappeared when the oligarchy was deposed and supplanted by Oliver Cromwell's dictatorship. Although the masque form never revived,[15] its emphasis on visual beauty affected the evolution of ballet.

London life had long supported a tradition of diverse theatrical activity. While the beloved masques belonged exclusively to the elite realm of the British aristocracy, the taste of the common people reflected itself in a broad spectrum on the English stage. British theater became noted for its wide variety of entertainment, even on a single program. Catering to a paying public, Shakespeare centered his plays around the dramatic action of real human experience while thematic symbolism was secondary. There was also a simpler dimension of amusing performances in the city's bustling life, and variety acts of mimes, comedians, popular singers, jugglers, and acrobats were always available at a small price.

Centuries ago the arts in England did not have the institutionalized patronage of the monarchy as they presently enjoy. Thus, the lack of official direction and control happily allowed artists the freedom to experiment. By the same token, Britain's heritage of public theaters shaped an audience tolerant of innovation. As to the ballet, however, there had never been the opportunity for it to develop as it had in France under the sponsorship of the opulent Bourbon coffers. Consequently, native English theatrical dance grew on a smaller scale, but its public was ever eager for the visits of dancers from abroad.

# JOHN WEAVER

The restoration of the crown after the English Civil War and the Cromwellian rule brought back a vibrant theater to London life. The glorious music of Henry Purcell enchanted the court of Charles II, while William Congreve's comedy of manners received its share of public enthusiasm. The Englishman John Weaver (1673–1760) stands out as the dominant British figure in the dance profession by the turn of the century. The son of a dancing master licensed by Oxford University, Weaver worked in London from 1702 to 1733 as a dancer, teacher, and choreographer. He published his translation of Feuillet's treatise *Chorégraphie* in 1706,[16] giving the English the benefit of Beauchamp's systematized technical knowledge along with the codified French terminology. Weaver knew and worked with visiting French dancers so there was continuous artistic exchange, and undoubtedly his ideas made an impression on them.

During his busy career as a choreographer, Weaver found time to write about dance theory and history. Perhaps his most important writing was *Anatomical and Mechanical Lectures* (1721), the first scientific treatise to relate the kinetic workings of the human body to a technical analysis of classical ballet positions and steps. Weaver's *Lectures*, influenced by the physiological research of English surgeons at Oxford, identified four categories of dance movement, i.e., bending, stretching, turning, and jumping, noting that they "are to Dance as Light and Shade are to Painting."[17] Since Weaver's students were some of the first to take over ballet from amateur courtiers, he rightly understood that they were in need of anatomical knowledge. He also discussed the early baroque classification of dancers according to their physical build, thereby introducing to English readers the concept of the *danseur noble*, *demi-caractère*, and *grotesque* categories.

In Weaver's publication *Essay Towards a History of Dancing* (1712), he frequently alluded to the necessity for meaningful gestures to permeate the body's movement. In attempting to imitate classical models he felt strongly that dance was an expressive medium and that virtuosity should support characterization rather than exist for its own sake. The idea that a story could be related in mime and movement without sung or spoken explanation was taken from classical notions and revived by Renaissance commentators. But this was only an idea, for it had not yet been successfully achieved until Weaver's most famous work, *The Loves of Mars and Venus* (1717), demonstrated his theories on the dramatic potential of ballet. His was the original, if imperfect, *ballet d'action* wherein the dancers conveyed the dramatic plot during distinct sections of dance based on conventional steps and a robust amount of pantomime and gesture. *The Loves of Mars and Venus* broke new ground in the making of a full-length professional ballet by incorporating action and gesture to advance the story line instead of having to rely on sung or spoken recitation of verse.

Prior to Weaver's experiment with *ballet d'action* for the English stage, an unusual segment of dance was presented in France in 1714 as part of *Les Grandes Nuits*.[18] These were highly festive entertainments given during the long summer nights in the palace park of Sceaux. At one performance a dramatic duet was featured that focused attention on a narrative revealed solely by bodily gesture. The short piece was arranged as an interlude for one of a series of parties given by Louis XIV's daughter-in-law, Louise, the Duchess of Maine. She commissioned Jean Joseph Mouret to set music to dramatic verse penned by

Houdart de la Motte, but had the lines mimed by two professional dancers rather than spoken by actors. Contemporary accounts of the evening recorded that the well-known dancers Claude Balon and Françoise Prévost were skilled and expressive enough to bring tears to the eyes of each other as well as their audience.[19] Although the duet was a great success at the party, the idea of a danced story failed to find fertile ground in the professional ballet world of the Royal Academy where it might have flourished. Rather, it was an isolated artistic event born before its time. The *Grandes Nuits* ceased in May of 1715 due to the deteriorating health and subsequent death of Louis XIV.

In addition to John Weaver, there were lesser precursors of the *ballet d'action* who worked not altogether independently of each other in various parts of Europe. By way of certain productions in Paris, some of the English style crept into the French capital while the influence of French ballet masters after the restoration of Charles II in 1660 was felt wherever they traveled.[20] French dancers visiting London were intrigued by British dramatic art that dealt primarily with the complexities of the human condition and not Greek gods with Bourbon counterparts. Naturalness and lack of affectation in English dancers had always been noteworthy for many a continental viewer. Lacking institutionalized direction, the English stage was fresh and vital. These elements present in London's theaters influenced the practices of French dancers and choreographers. As a consequence of much artistic channel crossing, the Paris Opera occasionally presented primitive forms of *ballet d'action*, but these productions were considered so unusual that they were often announced to the public at curtain times as ballets played in mute scenes.

94

# Seven Early Professionals

A number of performers during this period emerged to catch the public's notice and are remembered today for their unique contributions to the developing art form. One of the most extraordinary male dancers of the time was the six-foot-tall Louis Dupré (1697–1774), the finest *danseur noble* of his day. The inimitable Dupré, as Casanova wrote of him, was still dancing in his fifties, and was duly famous for performing the figured *terre à terre* movement of Beauchamp's generation with enormous dignity and gravity of manner. Affectionately named Le Grand Dupré by his adoring public, he had spent time in England and had danced in Weaver's *Loves of Mars and Venus*. In his many years as a dancer and ballet master at the Royal Academy, he experimented with improvisation in order to seek out the relationship between dance steps and their musicality.[21] Undoubtedly, this led him to add to the variety and richness of ballet steps as well as ascertain their most economic means of execution. He also succeeded as a choreographer, creating *opéra-ballets*, most notably *Les Indes galantes*. Dupré's illustrious pupils Jean Georges Noverre and Gaëtan Vestris, whose contributions to ballet reach well into the twentieth century, attested to his reputation as a discerning teacher.

Françoise Prévost (1680–1741), a protegé of Lully and Beauchamp, was one of the earliest professional female dancers. Debuting in Lully's *Atys* in 1699, she remained the foremost French ballerina for thirty years. Prévost was probably the first female choreographer, creating for herself a collection of solos based on twelve commonly known ballroom dances of the period. The work was first known as *Les Caractères de la danse* (1715, The Characters of the dance)[22] and remained popular for decades. The choreography was established on instrumentation in the orchestra. Jean Frey Rebel's descriptive score identified and distinguished the solos by giving them a recognizable melodic line. Each solo presented a charming anecdote of a pastoral theme reflective of its musical form. For example, the grave *sarabande* was dramatized by a deceived lover who complains and seeks advice from the gods. The lively *gigue* was interpreted as a giddy girl who asks the gods of love to send her a simple shepherd who will not tire of dancing with her. Although masked, Prévost's great expressiveness in her imaginative dance composition was due to the meaningful gestures and subtle body language that she used to convey the various themes. Dancer, choreographer, and teacher, her contributions place her among the very earliest developers of *ballet d'action*, and as the most important ballerina of her generation.

Marie Sallé (1707–1756), a pupil of Mlle. Prévost, was extremely interested in the expressive nature of dance. Although she spent much of her career working in Paris, she found a greater creative freedom outside the official shackles of the Paris Opera. As a child prodigy, Sallé had achieved enormous success in London. Later she returned to triumph there in 1734 in her own dramatic ballet, *Pygmalion*. At this time she discarded the *panier* worn by all female dancers and appeared in a simple draped dress with her hair loose about her shoulders. Sallé was said to command an extensive range of emotions while dancing in her many roles. Among her greatest achievements were her interpretations of roles in the comedies of Lully and Molière, and her participation in Campra's *opéra-ballets*. Sallé, whose contributions to dramatic dancing equaled those of Rameau's eminently danceable *galant* scores, was highly praised when she appeared in *Les Indes galantes*. It is an everlasting compliment to her honored place in dance history that the great composer George Frederick Handel frequently paid verbal tribute to her musical sensitivity.

While Marie Sallé possessed a strong technique, she was also a supreme actress. As a child she had learned pantomime from the French and Italian players at street fairs and later studied with England's most famous Harlequin, John Rich. She was imaginative in her interpretation of dances and creative in her poses, and it was noted that her gestures were transformed into heartfelt emotion. In effect, Sallé was a living example of those artistic notions of Lully that signaled the importance of unity and expressiveness in dance. She was particularly deft at creating her own *pas de deux* that included supported poses, and her duets were said to be true conversations in movement.

Although virtuoso partnering and intricately supported poses were not yet in vogue, the meaningful interchange of danced movement and gesture between Sallé and her better partners gained appreciable attention from the public. As a very young dancer, Sallé was known to have performed Prévost's *Les Caractères de la danse*. She later refined this work by turning it into an exceedingly poetic *pas de deux* with Antoine Laval.[23] To heighten the effect of the presentation, she arranged for costumes of Grecian design to substitute for contemporary eighteenth-century dress and even omitted masks. For thirty years Sallé pleased an international public with her collection of love duets retitled *Caractères de l'Amour*. The relationship between the experiment at Sceaux, where Prévost and Balon had emotionally touched their audiences, and Sallé's twelve *pas de deux* was a logical step forward in charging choreography with greater expressiveness.[24]

Marie-Anne de Cupis de Camargo's (1710–1770) vivacious personality and technique helped carve the prototype of the ballerina. Remembered simply as La Camargo, she exhibited a fiery brilliance in her dancing that was attributed to her Spanish-Italian ancestry. Her expertise no doubt related to her *danse d'école* training with the celebrated Prévost. Legend has it that in a fit of jealousy over La Camargo's public acclamation, Prévost refused to teach her further. Undaunted, the feisty dancer sought lessons with Dupré as well as Blondy and the elderly Pécourt.[25] These gentlemen perfected her penchant for sparkling footwork and soon she seriously rivaled the great male dancers of the age. One evening a male dancer missed his cue to enter the stage and Camargo was said to have seized the moment. Rushing to his position, she proceeded to dance his variation to perfection. Shortly thereafter, Madame Prévost retired from theater life.

Credited as an inventor of new steps and a developer of old ones, La Camargo could manage with ease all the virtuoso jumps and beats that were the domain of male dancing. While deeming the *gargoulliade* an inappropriate step for herself, she was one of only two dancers who were able to perform the *saut de basque*.[26] La Camargo became the rage of Paris when she caused a scandal by shortening her skirts to ankle length in order to display consecutive *entrechat quatres*. Although moralists agonized over this impropriety of costume, the shorter skirts remained and enabled new advances in female technique. History has recorded that La Camargo had many physical defects as a dancer; it is a tribute to her as an artist that she knew how to avert attention from her faults by emphasizing her liveliness and charm.

The contemporary and popular rival of La Camargo was Marie Sallé. However, their styles and hallmarks were at opposite ends. While Camargo was highly regarded for her technical ability, Sallé was revered as a ballerina with a formidable acting talent. Already, in the early days of the profession the conflict between dazzling virtuosity and expressive spirituality was typified by the contrasting artistry of Camargo and Sallé. Audiences of the day, fierce in their contentions and preferences, were passionately devoted to one dancer or the other. While such ardent interest was healthy for theatrical dance in general, it fore-

96

shadowed a trend that has haunted the art to the present day. The perennial struggle for dominance between form and content in art is ongoing. Emphasis on dance technique for its own sake ignores expression and creativity. At the same time, emotionality and invention are empty as communicators of meaning without the framework of a highly developed technical system. When Voltaire was asked to comment on the two ladies, he diplomatically averted outcry from their respective fans and scripted the comparison in the following: "Ah Camargo how brilliant you are! But, great gods, how ravishing is also Sallé! Just as your steps are light, hers are soft! You are inimitable, but she is something new: The nymphs jump like you, but the graces dance like her."[27]

Barbara Campanini (1721–1799) exhibited an energetic technique acquired from the classes of Rinaldi Fossano, but the impression she gave was also reminiscent of the expressiveness of Marie Sallé. It was said that her dancing style combined Italian virtuosity, French grace, and English dramatic flair.[28] She was famous for her *pirouettes* and mastered the *entrechat huit*, a virtuoso jump characterized by the legs crossing eight times. Along with her richly faceted talent, a new dimension of personal expression was sanctioned as part of the ballerina's domain. La Barbarina, as she was known to her admirers, projected a natural flair for comedy, thereby greatly extending her range and popularity in addition to expanding the scope of early professional ballet. On the personal side, she was notorious for carrying on numerous affairs with aristocratic admirers, most notably the Rhineland ruler, Prince Carl Theodore, and she ended her life as a wealthy countess and generous philanthropist.

Jean Baptiste de Hesse (1705–1779), the son of French actors, was already a seasoned performer when his comic and grotesque style of dancing earned him a strong reputation. Named ballet master at Versailles in 1747, he created *L'Opérateur Chinoise* (The Chinese Operator), which was considered a ballet-pantomime wherein six amusing scenes were enhanced with dances that wordlessly told the story. This work was soon mounted at the Italian Theater in Paris, confirming his importance as a skilled professional. In the following ten years, de Hesse made fifty-eight more ballet-pantomimes using the same format for presenting successive and vividly comic scenes without words. De Hesse was much respected by his contemporaries and was Europe's most prolific ballet master up to this time. Unfortunately, he left no written accounts of his theories or his ballets, and barely misses being consigned to oblivion in dance history. His memory is saved by a charming pictorial record of *Divertissement pantomime, la Guinguette* engraved by the artist Gabriel St. Aubin.[29]

De Hesse was not alone in his pioneering for he was soon joined by a collaborator, Antoine Pitrot (c. 1720–c. 1792), who went on to independently create wordless ballets for the Italian Theater in Paris. In his program notes for the pantomime ballet *Ulysse dans l'île de Circée* (1764, Ulysses on the isle of Circe), Pitrot apologized to the audience for his dancers who lacked the dramatic skills to meaningfully perform their mime scenes.[30] While not a choreographer of great individuality, Pitrot is regarded as a pioneer of *ballet d'action* because he readily absorbed the innovations of his more inventive colleagues. His great aplomb, strong technique, handsome features, and ebullient personality made him a popular performer and *bon vivant*. Police records, citing Pitrot's scandalous female entanglements, tavern brawling, and dueling in a number of European cities, give an accurate account of his whereabouts and confirm that he traveled widely, being in constant demand across the Continent as a dancer and choreographer.

# $\mathcal{T}$HE BALLET IN VIENNA

Franz Hilverding (1710–1768) was an Austrian dancer and choreographer who returned to his native Vienna after a sojourn of further study with Blondy in Paris. A man of exceptional culture, Hilverding created pantomime ballets and pastorals based on the works of Racine and Voltaire that were also notable for their musical scores by Joseph Starzer. Some idea of Hilverding's choreographic style is revealed in a collection of etchings and drawings assembled by Count Durazzo.[31] There is a noticable difference between Hilverding's staging and that which is depicted in previous iconography. Dynamic motion of the individual dancers and the use of asymmetry in group scenes indicate that he called for emotion rendered by the entire body rather than just by face and arms. He eventually designed ballets in which the dancers carried the entire dramatic line, reinforcing the story with meaningful gesture. Some of his productions were examples of the ever-growing trend to rid ballet of its superfluous conventions such as helmets, masks, wigs, and *tonnelets* for "noble dancing," which were costumes reminiscent of Roman armor.

In 1757 Hilverding accepted an invitation from the Empress Elizabeth to work in Russia. Accordingly, his favorite pupil, Gaspero Angiolini (1731–1803), assumed his duties at court and in various theaters in Vienna. Angiolini's innovative ballets were not unlike those of his master. He used scenes from everyday life as well as ethnic and national themes in designing his scenarios. His conception of ballets also appears to have emphasized and accented the dancing itself, while relying on elaborate theatrical gesture to spell out the action. His successes led him to produce a danced version of Molière's *Don Juan* in which the story line was logically rendered and enhanced by Christopher Gluck's (1714–1787) superb score.[32]

The collaboration between Angiolini and Gluck was a momentous occasion. Continuing the trend begun by the French *galant* composers toward assigning specific melodic themes to characterization, Gluck was a musician of the highest caliber who understood the needs of dramatic ballet. Gluck also had firsthand knowledge of the academic dance, having studied and performed it at the Viennese court in conjunction with his musical education. He wrote a score for *Don Juan* that matched the compelling emotional content of the plot. Whereas Lully's music always framed its thematic material in the preclassic dance forms employing *menuets*, *gigues*, *passepieds*, and *courantes*, Gluck's composition underscored and logically meshed with the rise and fall of the histrionic action.[33] As a result, the descriptive power of Gluck's music alleviated the need for a sung explanation of the dramatic sequences.

Important for the quality of future ballet music was the fact that Gluck did not compose a series of dance numbers as typified by Lullian standards. Instead, his music followed the dynamics of the danced drama. Angiolini and the composer mutually benefited from their joint efforts, and again collaborated on Gluck's magnificent opera, *Orpheus et Eurydice* (1762) and on the ballets *Sémiramis* (1765) and *Alessandro* (1766). Interestingly, it was largely due to the work of Gluck that, in time, the term "opera" would once and for all come to replace the word "ballet" that had been loosely used to connote any work of music and dance.[34] And so, the direction of ballet turned one more corner in its journey into the future.

With the example of the Royal Academy firmly established to produce ballets and skilled dancers, other European cities began erecting theaters at the turn of the century. One after the other, great public institutions modeled on the Paris Opera were founded, and their ballet schools ensured a constant flow of new dancers to participate in the productions of opera and ballet. The construction of London's Haymarket (1705), the Royal Danish Opera (1726), Covent Garden (1732), the Vienna Burgtheater (1748), the Royal Swedish Opera (1773), the Bolshoi Theater in Moscow (1776), La Scala in Milan (1778), the Grand Théâtre in Bordeaux (1780), the Bolshoi Theater in St. Petersburg (1783), and the Estates Theater in Prague (1784), provided permanent homes for theatrical productions. Countless superb court theaters such as the baroque theater at Versailles appeared, a wedding gift for Marie Antoinette. Also erected were the Württemberg family theaters at Stuttgart and Ludwigsburg Palace, the exquisite Curvilles Theater in Munich, the Hermitage in St. Petersburg, and the Drottningholm Theater at the summer palace near Stockholm. The ballet schools and companies associated with these houses were subsidized by government monies, with the intention of assuring national prestige as well as high technical standards of training and performance.

99

# Summary

Professional ballet was built out of decades of high artistic and technical creativity. When the French ballet receded into post-Lullian formalism, a new format, the *opéra-ballet*, appeared, accompanied by the highly danceable *galant* musical style. The voluptuous orchestration of Jean-Philippe Rameau's colorful melodies was matched by a greater physicality in dance movement—an indication of dance's future autonomy. John Weaver experimented in London with the wordless, expressive *ballet d'action*. His counterparts, Franz Hilverding and Gaspero Angiolini, working a generation later at the Viennese court, continued to pioneer the notion of a danced and mimed story.

In the early part of the eighteenth century, a considerable number of talented professional dancers were already being applauded for their unique achievements. The famous rivalry between Marie Sallé and Marie-Anne de Cupis de Camargo (La Camargo) contributed to the novel concept of the "ballerina" as a sensitive interpreter of the human condition as well as a virtuoso. Many dancers and ballet masters, notably Sallé and Hilverding, actively urged reforms in theatrical customs and costumes. Schools created a demand for dancers to serve as teachers for the multitude of students flocking to their doors. Additional theaters were built in European cities to house a paying public made up of the growing merchant class. All that the ballet seemed to be wanting was the central component of genuine artistic leadership and superior ability to provide new vision and to function as a consolidator of several generations of accumulated knowledge and expertise.

## Chapter Notes

1. Hilton, p. 31.
2. Prudhommeau, p. 159.
3. Cyril Beaumont, *A Miscellany for Dancers* (London: C. W. Beaumont, 1954), p. 134. According to Castil-Blaze, *Arethuse*, an opéra-ballet created by Danchet and Campra, received a lukewarm reception and means were discussed for improving the *mise en scene*. "I can think of only one way, . . . etc." said Campra. *Histoire de l'Académie Imperiale de Musique* (Paris, 1855).
4. Kirstein, *Dance*, p. 210.
5. Hindley, pp. 224–25.
6. Kirstein, *Dance*, p. 207.
7. Ferdinando Reyna, *A Concise History of Ballet* (New York: Grosset & Dunlap, 1964), p. 54.
8. Winter, pp. 68–82. See illustrations.
9. Prudhommeau, p. 164.
10. Pierre Louis Duchartre, *The Italian Comedy: The Improvisation, Scenarios, Lives, Attributes, Portraits and Masks of the Illustrious Characters of the Commedia dell'Arte* (New York: Dover Publications, 1966), pp. 109–13.
11. Sorell, p. 263.
12. Kirstein, *Dance*, p. 170.
13. Anne Daye, "The Sun King Eclips'd," *Proceedings, Society of Dance History Scholars* (Society of Dance History Scholars, 1997), pp. 58–60.
14. Kirstein, *Dance*, p. 174.
15. Daye, p. 65. Popular heir to the English crown and the embodiment of the perfect prince, Henry Stuart was an excellent dancer, having a genius for sponsoring and participating in festivals. Daye suggests that if he had not died of typhoid in 1612 at the age of nineteen, Prince Henry might well have established a dance culture in Britain, and a generation earlier occupied Louis XIV's unique place in shaping the

history of the art form. Daye also notes that if masques had returned to royal life along with the restoration of the monarchy, a fresh tradition of court ballet might have developed, but Parliament had put too many constraints on Charles II to allow him to resume the luxurious celebrations.

16. Hilton, p. 51.
17. Lawson, p. 30.
18. W. H. Lewis, *The Sunset of the Splendid Century* (Garden City, NY: Anchor Books, Doubleday, 1963), pp. 190–210. Lewis gives a detailed account of court life, amusements, and customs surrounding theatrical performances at Sceaux, emphasizing the enthusiasm with which the nobility embraced the seven deadly sins.
19. Winter, p. 49.
20. Hilton, p. 50.
21. Lawson, p. 31.
22. Winter, *The Pre-Romantic Ballet*, pp. 50–51.
23. Parmenia Miguel, *The Ballerinas: From the Court of Louis XIV to Pavlova* (New York: The Macmillan Co., 1972), p. 19.
24. Winter, p. 51.
25. Prudhommeau, p. 173.
26. Winter, p. 162.
27. Beaumont, p. 170. Author's translation in the text for the following: "Ah! Camargo, que vous êtes brillante, Mais que Sallé, grands dieux, est ravissante! Que vos pas sont légers et que les siens sont doux! Elle est inimitable et vous êtes nouvelle: Les Nymphes sautent comme vous, Mais les Grâces dansent comme elle." Voltaire. (*Mercure de France*, January, 1732.)
28. Winter, p. 63.
29. Winter, p. 87.
30. Ivor Guest, *The Ballet of the Enlightenment: The Establishment of the Ballet d'Action in France, 1770–1793* (London: Dance Books, 1996), p. 5.
31. Winter, pp. 94–95. See illustrations.
32. Ibid., pp. 132–34.
33. Hindley, p. 234.
34. Ibid.

101

# 6

# Growth and Refinement of Classical Ballet

Professional ballet persisted as a major form of French artistic expression for decades after Lully and Beauchamp launched its initial brilliance. While chore-ographers were continuing to stage ballets reminiscent of those of their great forebears, *galant* music and the *opéra-ballet* brought about a considerable expansion of technique. Although dancers were rapidly improving their *pirouettes* and jumps in an effort to dazzle, laments were beginning to issue from the pens of men like Jean Jacques Rousseau who pleaded for greater expression in the arts. Writers were begging the Paris Opera (Royal Academy) to adapt to new forms of expression while this was already happening outside the house. The English actress-ballerina Heather Santlow, who had created the role of Venus in Weaver's *Loves of Mars and Venus*, was being praised for her powerful performances exhibiting new forms of expression. The encyclopedist, playwright, and philosopher of theater Denis Diderot gave a glimpse of what he thought about the distractions present in contemporary eighteenth-century productions at the Opera. Diderot had a character in his play *Le Fils naturel* plead with artists to:

> . . . forget the sensational; seek for a picture; get close to real life and first of all leave room for the exercise of pantomime to the fullest extent. . . . I really believe that neither the poets, musicians, decor artists, nor dancers, have as yet a true conception of their theatre. Is it prostituting philosophy, poetry, music, painting and dancing to busy them with an obscurity? Each of these arts in particular has for aim the imitation of nature. . . . The dance awaits still a man of genius; it is everywhere bad because it is barely suspected that it is an expressive art. . . .[1]

Time has acknowledged the advanced work of professional talent credited to Sallé and de Hesse, the dramatic innovations of Prévost and Balon at Sceaux, and Weaver's experimental *ballet d'action, The Loves of Mars and Venus*. But theirs were lone voices crying in the night of a hundred years. By mid-eighteenth century, all large French cities had ballet companies modeled after Paris, just as the courts and capitals of Europe had entertainment copied from that of Versailles. However, in common with their archetype, they too suffered from a formalized dance that lacked inspired direction and begged for renewal. The contributions to the emerging realism of the *ballet d'action* by Hilverding were remarkable, but often limited to the far-away Viennese and Russian audiences. Angiolini was distinguishing himself for his ability as a composer by turning out various examples of *ballet d'action* that manifested a close relationship between the music and choreography. He also commissioned from Gluck dynamic dance music for the choreography of *Don Juan*, but in spite of the quality and success of his ballet, outdated elements in costuming marred its originality. Although Angiolini made engaging use of national dances and Slavic folk steps that he acquired during the years he lived in Russia, standard conventions in ballet-making and the eclectic *opéra-ballet* form endured.

The work of a dozen or so dance personalities during the early eighteenth century represented isolated attempts to introduce new ideas in a period that was finding its way toward a very special reformation. At one time, mime and meaningful gesture replaced sung verse, as in Weaver's *Loves of Mars and Venus*; at another time real people in comic and exotic plots were preferred to mythological figures, as in de Hesse's *L'Opérateur Chinoise*. Occasionally masks and wigs were put aside by Hilverding and Sallé just as skirts were shortened by La Camargo to show her mastery of foot work and the potential of the female technical range. Advances in theatrical production also enhanced ballet performances by incorporating reasonable usage of stage machinery. Stage lighting was improved when oil lamps began replacing the hundreds of candles required to light the scene, allowing for greater control of illumination, as well as reduced fire hazards.

103

But what was needed most to elevate the dance to a new level of glory equal to its recent developments in technique and production was a centralizing force that would emerge from a consistent and logical philosophy of art. The man to accomplish this, Diderot's man of genius, whose vision would synthesize all of theatrical dance's finest characteristics and previous contributions, finally appeared. A true son of the Enlightenment, Jean Georges Noverre would bring about the ascendancy of the choreographer. Only then, with the choreographer at the vital center, could the needed reformation occur, pointing the way for ballet of the future. Accordingly, Noverre's life-work embodied the transition from the early years of the profession to the dawn of Romanticism.

# *C*HE FATHER OF MODERN BALLET

Jean Georges Noverre (1727–1810) entered the popular *Opéra Comique* around 1743 as a professional dancer during the administration of Jean Monnet, one of the most remarkable impresarios of his day. There, under the tutelage of Le

Grand Dupré and Rameau, who dared to break away from the set musical forms of Lully, Noverre was profoundly influenced. The presence of François Boucher, the famous court artist who designed sets and costumes for Monnet; Charles Favart, the poet and playwright who developed novel theatrical scenarios; and the great actor Préville immeasurably enriched the young dancer's development. Noverre's close association with the expressive and untraditional ballerina Marie Sallé, who took a hand in choreographing dances for the company of fourteen, also had a lasting impact on him.[2]

At the Royal Academy the laws governing ballet were inviolate. The conceptions that Lully, Beauchamp, and the costumer, Jean Bérain, had formulated were now devoid of fresh inspiration but were slavishly copied. The Royal Academy had been founded to preserve the dance as a uniquely French art, and it held the exclusive privilege of authorizing all dance productions in state-owned theaters. It thereby strictly enforced its own traditions and conventions of *opéra-ballet* in all the most important French theaters. The Royal Academy jealously guarded its national treasure, an established institution of dance where the tenets of its schooling and its art were sacrosanct by law. Only those who grew up in the Academy's confines had a right to inherit its governance. As a result, theatrical trends occurring elsewhere had limited entrée into its halls, while its own choreographers and teachers looked to the formulas of past successes for their productions.

By 1760 ballets everywhere had become disjointed medleys of entertainment, often lacking general organization and internal logic. Dramatic plots were minimized, logical sequence often became irrelevant, and music merely served the decorative dancing with a beat instead of merging with expressive movement to form an artistic whole. Ballet titles like *Loves of . . .* or *Fêtes of . . .* provided generic frames in which *divertissements*, as dances in theatrical productions came to be called, had some thread holding them together, but now they lost even that element of cohesion. This fragmentation of creative effort actually came to be called *Fragments of . . .* whatever theme or composer happened to lend bits and pieces to a production. All the leading dancers in every *opéra-ballet* at the Academy or theater under its auspices performed their specialties with the most skilled virtuoso among them concluding the choreographic sequence, whether or not this format related to the thin thematic action of the piece. Dancers in a number of Paris theaters frequently made up for the laxness in artistic direction by exhibiting their special technical abilities when the dramatic indications should have led them to the contrary.

Superb dancers, such as the Vestris family, the Gardel brothers, and the Dauberval couple, were often kept from giving their best performances so weighted down were they with *tonnelets*, plumed helmets, leather masks, and thick heels.[3] Around 1675 heels had been contrived and added to boots to keep feet firmly fixed in stirrups. Shortly thereafter, they became enormously fashionable, adding height and grandness to both men and women. In this way, heeled shoes entered the ballroom for court dancing. Under Louis XIV red heels could only be worn at court; with this restriction, the custom implied the wearer's elite status.[4] By another account the *tonnelets* and breastplates for Bérain's mythical warriors, as well as the ballerinas' heavily boned bodices, were still perquisite stage attire, despite the fact that they impeded the dancers to the point of absurdity.[5]

In an atmosphere lacking the Lullian genius for rich collaboration, the young Noverre witnessed composers, choreographers, and designers working independently of each other's ideas, indifferent to their common goal. When it came to assessing theatrical dance around him, Noverre was both acerbic and undiplomatic. As yet unscathed by the tumultuous ups and downs of the profession, his early years attested to the fact that he was an eighteenth-century "angry young man." His reformist obsession, keen intelligence, and innate good taste caused him to voice his indignation more often than not, making his career a succession of short-lived engagements and numerous petty enemies. Noverre departed the *Opéra Comique* for a position as a dancer at the court in Berlin, but soon accepted an invitation to compose his first ballet in Marseilles. He next moved to Lyons where, in addition to creating ballets, he partnered La Camargo. While there, Noverre received acclaim for his first ballet without words, *Les Fêtes Chinoises* (Chinese Festivals) in 1755.[6]

By the time David Garrick (1717–1779), the great English actor and manager, arrived on the theatrical scene in Georgian England, the role of dance as an essential component of all sorts of theatrical presentations had been heartily enforced. Garrick invited Noverre to re-create his Chinese ballet renamed *The Chinese Metamorphosis* for British audiences, a work that reflected the current rococo rage in Europe for all things oriental. Noverre's acquaintance with Garrick resulted in mutual respect and a lasting friendship, but most of all, the famed Shakespearean's theatrical knowledge and the dramatic power of his performance had an indelible influence on the young ballet master's artistic formation. Unfortunately, the Chinese ballet fared less well. It opened on the eve of the Seven Years War, and the public was outraged that a French ballet was playing in London. Garrick tried to assuage the matter by announcing to the audience that Noverre was actually Swiss and had engaged many English dancers in the company, but it was to no avail. At its sixth performance, riots broke out in the theater between the common people and the nobility as to whether or not the ballet should be allowed to proceed. In the end Noverre's ballet was forcibly removed from the stage and Garrick paid his young friend compensation for the time remaining in his contract.[7]

## NOVERRE'S INTERNATIONAL INFLUENCE

In 1760 Noverre moved to the Stuttgart court of Karl Eugene, Duke of Württemberg, who was renowned as a patron of the theater. The duke had recently sold off part of his army as mercenaries, dismissed his chief advisors, divorced his wife, and felt free to invest his wealth in what he most favored,

*The Father of Modern Ballet*

theatrical production at his court.[8] When Noverre was engaged as ballet master, the extravagant duke made available to him every consideration, including the services of the Neapolitan composer Niccolò Jomelli, the master costumer Simon Boquet, and the illustrious scenic designer and machinist Jérôme Servandoni.

Noverre enjoyed the eager cooperation of the most famous dancers of the time because of the duke's celebrated reputation for providing an artistic haven. Gaëtan Vestris was a frequent guest artist; Jean Dauberval danced there under Noverre's direction for nearly two years. Noverre discovered the great talent of Charles Le Picq at this time, elevating him from the *corps de ballet* for special training.[9] Together, the two men worked out a new school of virtuoso dancing made feasible only when heavy costumes were relinquished on occasion. Le Picq's versatile style (it was often said that he was "always in the air") called greater attention to the possibilities of the *danse par haute*, giving a unique aerial dimension to the art. Commending the French on the precision that the dancing of the day had achieved, the Italian ballet master Gennaro Magri cited Le Picq as an example and was in awe of the dancer's mastery of *ambuettes*.[10] Noverre, as a pedagogue and theorist, and Le Picq as a dancer with physical attributes naturally suited to the rules of *danse d'école*, elevated the lesser category of *demi-caractère* to such a degree that it preceded that of the traditionally superior *danse noble*. A description of the dancer at this date takes note of his charming features, slender body, and light-but-spirited elastic movements. Above all, the exquisite finish of his execution and his grace and airiness in *demi-caractère* dancing triumphed, showing audiences a more flamboyant manner of male dancing.

Other dancers, many of them well known from Noverre's London days, were engaged to form a company of fifteen principals and a *corps* of twenty-three men and twenty-one women.[11] Both ballet itself and Noverre prospered in this idyllic setting. Noverre's production of *Médée und Jason* (1763, Medea and Jason) was a great triumph, featuring Mademoiselle Nency, whom he had trained in London. Nency's style recalled the earlier expressiveness of Sallé yet represented a new combination in a ballerina. She was said to possess an amazing dance talent, but, in addition, demonstrated an acting ability reminiscent of the dramatic manner of the incomparable Garrick.

While in Stuttgart, Noverre profited from the court's artistic climate and produced many other ballets, including *Le Mort d'Hercule* (1762, Death of Hercules), *Orpheus und Eurydice* (1762, Orpheus and Eurydice), and *Antoine et Cléopâtre* (1765, Antony and Cleopatra). The potency of ancient Greek and Roman dramas, and its application to dance, engrossed Noverre. Through the association with his friend Garrick, Noverre appreciated the possibilities for stunning dramatic action in tragic and violent love stories where the hero or heroine must die at the hands of fate. Since the Renaissance *intermedii*, the darker aspects of ancient Greek and Roman culture had never been considered appropriate subject matter for dance performances. But so successful was Noverre's conception of danced tragedy in heroic ballets filled with humanity

106

and feeling that some thirty of his numerous works ended on a calamitous note.[12]

As Noverre matured, his penetrating thought and terse criticisms on dance found an unrivaled and permanent outlet in *Les Lettres sur La Danse et Les Ballets* (1760, *Letters on Dancing and Ballets*), which he had begun in London after the fiasco of *The Chinese Metamorphosis*. Practicing what he preached in print, Noverre's finest choreography contributed largely to the emancipation of dance from its post-Lullian position as mere decorative diversion. In a number of his ballets he replaced mythological deities with real people as central characters. Credit for this shift in plot preference can again be traced to the influence of Garrick and the realism of British theater.[13] Noverre's approach signaled the right for choreographers to place human destiny with all its trials and tribulations at the heart of the ballet. During this period, Noverre's reputation grew to such lengths that he even earned the esteem of Voltaire. Along with Garrick and a few others of his calibre, these men were perhaps the only people who fully appreciated the comprehensiveness of Noverre's philosophy of art during his lifetime.

Due to internal politics and a near-bankrupt treasury, Noverre's contract at the Württemberg court was terminated in 1767 although he retained the respect of the duke and his entourage.[14] Noverre immediately journeyed to Vienna where his life would begin a new series of events, all of which would further his ambition to be associated with the Royal Academy, the Paris Opera. In Vienna he was appointed ballet master at the Burgtheater and dancing teacher to the young Archduchess Marie Antoinette. Hilverding and Angiolini had both preceded Noverre in the Austrian capital before Empress Marie Theresa had sent them, each in turn, to the imperial house of Russia. Because of his two predecessors' commendable work in upgrading the technical capacities of Viennese dancers and their experiments with realism in choreography, Noverre encountered a ballet company of considerable ability. His reputation acclaimed him in Austria by way of the dancers he had worked with in London and Stuttgart, and by his famous colleague Gaëtan Vestris, who had revised the master's ballets for the Viennese audience.

Noverre collaborated with Christopher Gluck on several productions at the Viennese court. This brief association worked to their mutual advantage and pleasure, but also benefited ballet immeasurably. According to a contemporary account, Noverre was able to solve a major staging problem in Gluck's *Orpheus* by placing the singing chorus offstage and allowing dancers to mime the choral work.[15] So expressive was his choreography for the *corps de ballet* that the audience believed the dancers were singing.[16] Noverre's commitment to the idea of internal cohesion within a work strongly influenced Gluck, who once and for all gave ballet its autonomy. Gluck purposely removed unrelated intervals of dancing between the acts of an opera, which had been the format of the durable *opéra-ballet* style. Instead of ballet languishing in the service of opera, he directed that it be given its special evenings where it could develop according to its own nature. This independence from the dominant needs of music hastened dance's growth and resulted in perfected forms of tragic, heroic, and anacreontic ballet.

Noverre set down his own precise guidelines for anacreontic ballets in a revision of his *Lettres* in 1807.[17] The anacreontic ballet, he stated, calls for pleasant situations shown in varied and picturesque scenes. Sentiment, love, and grace must dominate the stage while lightheartedness should underscore the depiction of delicate pleasures and artless love. For example, Cupid might toy with the fates of blissfully carefree characters, only to restore peace and balance at the ballet's end. Noverre had experimented with anacreontic choreography in creating *La Fontaine de Jouvence* (1754, The Fountain of Youth), *Les Réjouissances Flamandes* (1755, Flemish Merry-Making), *Les Grâces* (1768, The Muses), and many others. After 1760, however, he concentrated on more serious subject matter although the anacreontic form remained popular well into the early nineteenth century.

In 1773 Angiolini returned from Russia and witnessed Noverre's work in Vienna. The two men engaged in a bitter literary struggle when Angiolini claimed Noverre had usurped Hilverding's theories on the inherent dramatic possibilities in ballet. Angiolini wished to protect Hilverding's place in history as an innovator, but Noverre had claimed himself to be the originator of reforms in ballet. Hilverding had already staged *ballets d'actions* and had dispensed with crude, comic productions. Some years earlier he had also on occasion abandoned conventionally elaborate costumes and masks. A second point of contention between the two men was that Noverre thought that ballets should not be governed by the same rules as drama. Angiolini attacked Noverre's works on the basis that they ignored the unities of time, place, and action, which meant that only one story should occur, in a single locale, within twenty-four hours. He claimed the subplots of Noverre's multiaction scenarios confused the audience.[18] Noverre's battles with his talented contemporary were long and tiresome. However, these three pre-Romantic ballet masters were very close to one another in their fresh approaches to choreography. They were all genuine creators of *ballet d'action*, formulating and often borrowing each others' ideas for their work. If Noverre appears to overshadow them, it is mainly due to the magnificence of his written legacy. Disheartened by the much-publicized row and unpleasant atmosphere that his ongoing confrontation with Angiolini produced, Noverre left Vienna to work at the Royal Theater in Milan.

By 1776 Noverre's ideas and ubiquitous activities were influencing ballet in most of the capitals in Europe, but he longed for the coveted appointment of ballet master at the Royal Academy. It had always been his greatest desire to work at the very heart of the ballet. This ambition was finally realized through the intercession of his former pupil Marie Antoinette, now queen of France. His appointment to the Academy was acclaimed by newspapers and bulletins as the arrival of a great composer of ballets. Writing for *Mercure de France* in 1777, the respected journalist La Harpe commented that Noverre was "a worthy rival of Pylades and Bathyllus in the art of speaking to the eyes with gesture and movements."[19] Noverre was soon to find that working there was not the haven of Stuttgart where he had been in full control.

Noverre's directorship turned out to be one of his less creative periods, although his dances for Gluck's opera *Iphigénie en Tauride* (1779, Iphigenia in Tauris) were acclaimed a great success. He was gratified to show off his dazzling former student to the court and the Paris Opera when Le Picq guested in a hastily revived *Les Caprices de Galatée* (1776, The Whims of Galatea). Of this one-act duet, which also featured the reigning ballerina, Marie Guimard, the *Mercure de France* noted that there was only one choreographer alive with the multifaceted ability to make something so good out of something so slight.[20]

Noverre befriended and sought out the collaboration of the relatively unknown Mozart on *Les Petits Riens* (1778, Bagatelles). The young composer claimed to have written twelve sections of the ballet including the overture and the *contredanse* although his name does not appear on the manuscript. To these, Noverre added six old French airs. This enraged Mozart who complained in a letter to his father that Noverre's audacity amounted to musical insensitivity. The ballet received several performances, but Mozart was neither paid or given credit for the music.[21]

From the very start, Noverre's tenure at the Royal Academy was fraught with a network of enemies conspiring to undermine his artistic conceptions. While envious colleagues fostered bitter controversy over his appointment, old methods of running the institution often tied his hands. The unpopular queen's intervention in obtaining his directorial position was viewed as more of her political meddling since Maximilien Gardel and Jean Dauberval had been in line for the post that went to Noverre.[22] Furthermore, Noverre's reformist ideas, previously published in his writings, threatened the reactionaries within the Academy. From the hierarchical position of Marie Guimard, who had been a friend and colleague, down to the humblest opera employee, the ballet master was viewed as an upstart foreigner from the provinces.

Noverre's wish to emend choreography, production, and teaching methods, as well as his ideas on musical selection, costuming, and scenic design, shook those who clung to the traditions and the security provided by the conservative establishment.[23] From within the Academy, intrigue piled upon intrigue while the press continually aired Noverre's complaints. None of his creations satisfied the dancers or the management, and his ballets were subject to an unceasing flow of petty criticisms from those with whom he worked. Written accounts from outside the house, however, attested to the excellent quality of the ballets and their creator.

Under pressure from the administration, a hastily arranged production of the major tragedy *Les Horaces* (1777) drew acute criticism, suggesting that the Paris audiences were not ready to accept profoundly emotional subject matter expressed in dance and mime. The irascible Noverre attempted to compromise whenever he deemed it possible in accordance with his artistic standards. But by 1780, the man was completely disillusioned in his position as director.[24]

109

After three and a half years he tendered his resignation in a seventeen-page letter, noting that he had not received his promised pay or any other satisfaction. His departure was a final action that proved to be tainted with the unsavory machinations and breach of promises by Maximilien Gardel regarding Noverre's rightful pension and lodgings.

Upon leaving Paris, Noverre once again contracted to work in London where his ballets were received in triumph during the 1781–82 season. He continued to choreograph, alternating his time between London and Lyons. When the King's Theatre in London burned down, he retired to his home outside Paris. However, because of the dangers produced by the French Revolution due to the fact that Noverre was a former employee of the doomed king and queen, he returned to the safety of London when the King's Theatre was reopened. Noverre's successes there resumed, and the British press noted that his ballets displayed such powers of taste and imagination that he was truly a poet.

When Noverre returned to France in 1795, he was ill, with his savings, property, and pension greatly reduced by the Revolution. The last fifteen years of his life were devoted to revising the *Lettres* and writing about the theater, a subject on which he displayed deep knowledge and insight into artistic as well as technical problems. The retired ballet master attended performances and rehearsals at the Academy and followed the careers of young artists. He deplored the shortage of male dancers due to the massive military conscription of Frenchmen during Napoleon's rule. He was deeply saddened to see the pompous and dull spectacles still presented at the theater, his own efforts toward change being ignored. Noverre was particularly pained to see the way the young Auguste Vestris was allowed to waste his enormous talent because of his personal lack of taste and the incompetent artistic direction in power.[25] At the same time, Noverre's greatest ballets continued to be revived, even in far-off Russia, by his former students Charles Le Picq and Charles-Louis Didelot. New editions and translations of the *Lettres* were continually spreading his message so that at his death in 1810, his fame and influence were stronger than ever. Noverre's work lives on today in every dancer in the classroom or on the stage, and in every choreographer the world over, a living tribute to a great artist.

## NOVERRE'S WRITINGS: *THE LETTERS ON DANCING AND BALLETS*

The chief source of information on Noverre's accomplishments in the development of ballet is his monumental legacy, *Les Lettres sur la Danse et Les Ballets*. Penned in 1760 as a series of letters to an imaginary friend, Noverre was following a format much favored in eighteenth-century literature for expounding complex ideas. Contributing also to an appreciation of Noverre's work were the professional activities of his pupils. They spread his ideas over the face of Europe, and they saw to it that his concepts were handed down through generations of dancers. Noverre loved the pure dance born of natural movement and expressive of the passions, one that was stripped of mannerisms and false grace.[26]

According to his philosophy of art as expressed in the *Lettres*, Noverre strove to represent a more naturalistic style by making his ballets a creative synthesis of what was essential in nature, as opposed to merely copying it along with its abundant details. To accomplish this objective, Noverre specifically dealt with seven major points:

1. Regarding the training of dancers, he emphasized that correctness in dance technique as laid down by Beauchamp and others must be tethered with sensitivity to the individual's anatomy.
2. Of prime concern, the pedagogical consideration of the dancer's personality and style is prerequisite to artistic development.
3. He stressed that the validity and sincerity of gestural expression within dramatic context are of the upmost importance in creating a ballet.
4. Noverre called for the logical development of plots that must be thematically integrated, and the omission of all superfluous solos and irrelevant dance techniques.
5. Noverre was adamant that music be appropriately suited to the dramatic development of the plot.
6. He insisted that costumes, decor, and lighting be compatible with the introduction, plot, and climax of each act within the ballet.
7. With the disappearance of masks in his own ballets, Noverre pronounced his advanced ideas on stage make-up for dancers.[27]

The *ballet d'action*, so prominent in Noverre's work, was still an uncommon theatrical style for the time, one that fortified dancing with heroic gesture that strove to develop and extend the dramatic action. To give force to his ideas, he theorized that the work of the choreographer centered on three components: the dance, in general, is the pictorial element of graceful poses and the movements that link them; the ballet component is rendered by the danced figures and the technical nuances of the *danse d'école*; and the pantomime component expresses emotion and the "states of the soul" in gestures.[28]

Noverre did not single-handedly create the *ballet d'action*. In fact, the term first appeared in a theory book of Père Ménéstrier as far back as 1682. More recently, Louis de Cahusac had written extensively on his own concept of *ballet en action*. Rather, Noverre's work was the product of decades of evolving ideas and practices. Although he never acknowledged their efforts, certainly the contributions of Sallé, Weaver, Hilverding, Angiolini, and de Hesse figured in the early conception and formation of narrative ballet. Noverre's merit, in fact, reached beyond the scope of the *ballet d'action* because he gleaned, refined, and actualized the most elite aesthetic ideas of the time into his choreography. More often than not, he worked in unsympathetic circumstances while producing over 100 examples of *ballet d'action*.

Noverre's procedural methods for composing choreography were evolved from his many years of experience.[29] First, he sought a plot and worked out the moment-by-moment sequential action, paying special attention to its internal logic. He then created dance movement and gesture suitable to the plot. At this point he would engage a composer to write a musical score to fit the structure of the ballet as outlined. Noverre built the main story line and subplots of his ballets with highly constructed heroic gestures. He, therefore, had to rely on extensive program notes to fully illuminate the action, a practice that became the basis for the famous quarrel he carried on with Angiolini. Angiolini, who worked at the less-restricted Vienna Court Opera, felt that program notes were inadequate devices and that the dancing and mime themselves should convey the plot.[30] In this regard, some of Angiolini's works were more advanced because the masterful dramatic structure of Gluck's scores enhanced the intent of Angiolini's choreography and the emotional clarity of his pantomime.

Another remarkable aspect of Noverre's thought expressed in his *Lettres* was his extraordinary insight into the artistry necessary to the role of the teacher. His advanced ideas of what should enter into the education and nurturing of dance artists and choreographers are as true today as they were then. So enormous was Noverre's philosophical and practical impact on ballet that his presence is ever with us. While his influence was great at the time of his death, years later his ideas on dramatic-ballet were still being implemented in the work of a long procession of choreographers, including Jules Perrot, Mikhail Fokine, Leonide Lavrovsky, and more recently, Antony Tudor, Agnes de Mille, and Kenneth Macmillan.

## OTHER EIGHTEENTH-CENTURY CHOREOGRAPHERS

Although Noverre stands out as the visionary giant of his age, the times were replete with other talented choreographers who were also wonderful dancers, and each in their own way contributed to the development of dance art.

### JEAN DAUBERVAL

An esteemed younger contemporary of Noverre, Jean Dauberval (1742–1806) was trained at the Royal Academy, becoming in turn a superb dancer, teacher, and choreographer. While there, he was greatly influenced by Noverre's theories on *ballet d'action* as they pertained to his own choreographic efforts.[31] He returned to his native southern France in midlife with his beloved wife, the ballerina Magdeleine Théodore. For over seven years the two artists helped establish a vibrant dance center in Bordeaux, frequented by the performances of the finest dancers of the day. There, in a magnificent new theater, Dauberval had a mandate to create ballets and the freedom to experiment with innovative ideas not tolerated at the Royal Academy.[32] During Dauberval's directorship, his student, colleague, and friend, Eugène Hus, established the theater's first ballet school in 1790. Dauberval was perhaps the most influential and revered teacher of the entire period, listing among his pupils Antoine Bournonville, Charles Didelot, Salvatore Viganò, and Jean Aumer.

Dauberval is remembered for perfecting the comedy ballet that first began to appear in the early eighteenth century. Like Angiolini, Dauberval also used scenes from daily life as his inspiration. His emphasis on bucolic and comic elements in the ballet's action contributed to the development of character dancing. Taking various steps from traditional folk dances, he exaggerated the movements for stage purposes. Because folk dance is a visual contrast to the highly refined look of the *danse d'école*, employing both styles in the choreography enriched the total effect of a ballet. Dauberval treated the normal human predicaments of his central characters with farcical humor based on plots he devised or borrowed from drama and literature. At the last minute, imminent catastrophe in the story line was always averted by some lighthearted resolution. Silly people with humorous names and behavior operated within a funny situation to the audience's delight.

Dauberval's most famous work, *La Fille mal gardée* (1789, The Unchaperoned Daughter), celebrated the goodness and the common sense of ordinary people just thirteen days before the storming of the Bastille that signaled the start of the French Revolution. Some years before, the French writer Pierre Beaumarchais had skillfully attacked the pretensions of the nobility and the established order in his censored plays. One of the most successful was *The Barber of Seville*. By making the barber smarter than his noble master, Beaumarchais found the fuse to the social and political cataclysm that exploded in 1789. The sequel to the play, *The Marriage of Figaro*, which the very modern Mozart had adapted to opera in 1786, was even more pointed in its subversive criticisms of the privileged and was banned by the crown for its slurs on the aristocracy. But the public's curiosity had been whetted by private readings and widespread hearsay, and it was only a matter of time until the most offensive passages were toned down and the play was produced with enormous success.

The time was ripe for Dauberval's rollicking ballet statement of a socially classless atmosphere, one sympathetic to the common people of France's long-suffering Third Estate. The choreographer, however, was careful to avoid the problems that had beset Beaumarchais' plays.[33] Dauberval conceived his rustic comedy with elements of innocence, optimism, and good humor, and devoid of politics, satire, and irony. The ballet's action was so clearly constructed that no explanation beyond the dancers' mime was needed, and no artificial theatrical effects marred its naturalness.

Ballet and politics are frequent bed partners. Shortly after the premiere of *Fille*, the news arrived from Paris that the clergy and aristocracy had agreed to join the Third Estate in the self-proclaimed National Assembly to determine urgently needed social reforms. To wild applause, Eugène Hus, who was dancing the leading male role on the night of July 3, interrupted the ballet's harvest scene. Moving to the edge of the stage, he raised a glass to honor the jubilant audience of commoners whose delegates in Paris had won the vital concession

113

Jean Dauberval's *La Fille mal gardée* introduced real people and commonplace situations into the subject matter of ballets. (Courtesy of the author.)

from the upper class.[34] The dark aftermath of Hus's joyful toast during a ballet recalls an earlier performance when Catherine de Medici's elegant *Paradis d'Amour* was followed by the St. Bartholomew's Day Massacre. On the day of *Fille's* fourth performance, the Bastille was taken and six years of civil bloodletting had begun.

*La Fille mal gardée* has been continuously revised by ballet companies worldwide. It has been present in Russian repertory since its St. Petersburg premiere in 1818. In the West *Fille* was recreated in 1960 by Frederick Ashton for the Royal Ballet and later set on American Ballet Theatre. Although Dauberval's choreography has been lost and the original score, consisting of old French songs and airs that he himself had put together, is rarely used, the ballet's heartwarming plot has ensured its place among the classics.

Present understanding of the nature of eighteenth-century works like *La Fille mal gardée* is made possible by preserved *livrets*, which were program notes of the day. Because dramatic pantomime dominated most eighteenth-century ballets, a story that was well-chosen and put in written form was important for the fullest possible comprehension of the audience and the success of a ballet. The availability of *livrets* was also a means of advertising a ballet. Although *Fille* was wonderfully free of any obscurities, many, including Noverre's tragic and heroic works, were not, and needed commentary. *Livrets* were written by the choreographer to clarify his on-stage intentions to the audience. Lengthy in their plot descriptions that varied from eight to forty pages, they are invaluable to specialists today because they illuminate attempts at modern reconstruction of lost ballets. Moreover, *livrets* as authentic records are excellent indicators of the gradual changes in theatrical tastes, emphasis, and style.[35]

## SALVATORE VIGANÒ AND THE ITALIAN *COREODRAMMA*

The innovative contributions of Salvatore Viganò (1769–1821) to the pre-Romantic era placed him among the foremost theatrical successes of his time. Geographically removed from the rampage of the French Revolution, Viganò emerged as a unique, creative artist. His background could not have better pre-pared him for his career as a choreographer. He came from a well-off family of Italian dancers, musicians, and intellectuals who provided him with the ideal professional education called for in Noverre's *Lettres*. One of his earliest teachers was his uncle, the composer Luigi Boccherini, with whom he studied music the-ory. In his student days Viganò's gifts had greatly impressed Jean Dauberval. The Frenchman saw to it that the budding young Italian learned the entire inheri-tance of the *danse d'école* that, by that time, was tempered with the critical writ-ten words of Noverre.[36] An astute observer with the financial means for travel, Viganò made lengthy studies of the Vatican's collection of classical statuary. The effectiveness of Antonio Canova's flowing marble creations that glorified the human form was not lost on the choreographer. As a result, the plasticity of Viganò's future ballets profoundly reflected the personal influence of the greatest Italian sculptor of the period.

Viganò fulfilled engagements in Venice, Vienna, and Milan at the beginning of his performing career. He met and married the beautiful Maria Medina of Spanish heritage, and the dancing couple enjoyed public acclaim for the yield-ing quality of movement displayed in their duets. Accepting work at the Burgtheater in Vienna, he collaborated with his family friend Ludwig van Beethoven to create *Die Geschöpfe des Prometheus* (1801, The Creatures of Prometheus), an epic study of humanity's struggle with good and evil impulses. With this exceptional work, Viganò's artistic direction solidified. Leaving virtu-osity and the mimed equivalent of spoken words behind, he directed his con-ception of dramatic dance toward expressive gesture, which he envisioned minutely set to music. In 1813 he was installed as principal choreographer at La Scala. He referred to the form of dance art that he perfected while there as his *coreodramma*.[37] It was an unusual idiom that employed movement and music in a subtle and complex manner.

Coreodramma was characterized by its realistic settings, while genuine pantomime was used to supplant conventionalized gesture. The dance movement in the coreodramma was intended to be a combination of expressive, naturalistic gesture and traditional dance perfectly cadenced in its subordination to the music. His intent was to fuse designed movement into fluid sequential actions. Viganò dispensed with the large corps de ballet performing gestures in unison. Instead, each dancer retained individuality within picturesque groupings in which the choreographer set specific movements to the music. Wishing to emphasize the totally expressive effect of the dancers, he often dressed them in tunic-styled costumes of softly draped fabric. Sandal-styled shoes called cothurns were frequently used by Viganò's dancers since their heel-less sole contributed to a more lyrical flow of movement.[38]

Viganò was probably the first choreographer to come close to achieving the ancient ideal of a perfect synthesis of music, dance, and mime. His ballet La Vestale (1818, The Vestal Virgin) for La Scala was on a large scale with an even larger budget, providing a huge orchestra and ensuring the best designers. He spent vast amounts of time developing and putting together his ballets, which resulted in a less prolific output than his famous contemporaries. His special talent for creating a highly expressive form of dance lay in his predilection for painstaking detail. Viganò's approach to choreography was to begin with a large plastic group design and then, little by little, add detail after detail until he was satisfied with the effect.[39] So ingenious in its precision was Viganò's coordination of dance, mime, and music that he died without disciples or imitators to carry on the coreodramma, for there was no one of his stature who could produce such complex dance innovations.[40]

Although Viganò made an impact on the ballet of his time, his rhythmic pantomime, finely subordinated to music, would probably seem less like dancing to our modern eye just as it did to some of his critics. The old preference for virtuoso display over expressiveness found devoted followers among those who disliked the coreodramma. Viganò's work, while differing from that of Dauberval's in style, nevertheless emphasized the expressive possibilities inherent in dance movement. Although both gentlemen were genuine precursors of the Romantic era, during his lifetime Viganò was able to show the art world a fresh, if not permanent, conception of the ballet.

## GENNARO MAGRI

His dates are unknown, but Gennaro Magri lived and worked as a successful choreographer and dancer in many public and court theaters of northern Italy, and in Austria's imperial cities in the latter half of the eighteenth century. His Trattato Teoretico-Practtico di Ballo (1779, Theoretical Treatise of the Art of Dancing) remains the most complete source of written information on the techniques of theater dance and the grotesque style. Included in the treatise is a lengthy explanation of the ballet positions, steps of the era, their relationship to

116

the music, and those steps that are exclusive to the *grotteschi* category. The second part deals with the duties of and advice to dancing masters, instructions on noble behavior and etiquette, a detailed commentary on the minuet and contredances, as well as an explanation of his notation. It affords the contemporary reader a rich appreciation of the crossover and exchange between the strict academic dance and more popular forms of entertainment once ballet was in the care of professionals. Magri recorded an invaluable amount of facts, details, and advice.[41] He explicitly discussed various approaches for accomplishing types of *pas de bourrée* and *pirola* (*pirouette*), and emphasized that all require exceptional balance. He greatly admired the elder Vestris's command of the *pirouette*, Le Picq's mastery of *ambuettès*, and Pitrot's *aplomb*, and on occasion referred to Noverre's theories to give weight to his own thoughts.[42] He also expressed his knowledge and ardent desire to pass on the technical information to future generations. Magri's work is a major key to understanding the evolution of ballet technique, and gives a strong impression of ballet teaching during the period.

## THE GARDEL BROTHERS

In the pre-Romantic ballet some three hundred dance dynasties dominated the stage.[43] As it was the family tradition to follow in the footsteps of one's forefathers, dancing masters produced a dancing progeny. Among those most remembered were the brothers Maximilien and Pierre Gardel, sons of a French ballet master at the Polish court. Maximilien (1741–1787) claimed he was the first dancer to appear at the Royal Academy without a mask since he wished to be recognized as himself on an occasion when he replaced an ailing colleague. It is also recorded that he was was admired for accomplishing the triple *pirouette* in heeled shoes. During his comparatively brief life,[44] Maximilien served as ballet master at the Academy and pioneered the development of ballet pantomime. He pleased the public with anacreontic ballets that were in vogue for their appealing simplicity and idyllic settings.

117

Pierre Gardel (1758–1840) followed in his brother's footsteps at the Academy as a *danseur noble*, as ballet master, choreographer, and director of the ballet school. Upon his brother's death, Pierre assumed control of the ballet that coincided with the beginning of the French Revolution, and, being the political weathercock that he was, survived nine different regimes. His authoritarian manner determined dance's development in Paris for the next three decades. As skilled in social and political manipulation as at choreography, Gardel managed to be productive, clever, and entrenched in his position. No doubt he maintained the treacherous post of chief ballet master at the Academy by borrowing some of the very tactics of the tyrannical revolutionaries around him.[45]

Gardel's successful ballets were based on ancient myths according to the conventions of the time, but they also incorporated realistic elements of romance, adventure, and passion.[46] A former pupil of Noverre, he had learned from the master the craft of formulating theatrical excitement. The emotional intensity in his characters pleased critics and thrilled audiences who often witnessed the real-life drama of the guillotine. By contrast, his lighter anacreontic ballets, danced by the cream of the Royal Academy's talent, provided the public some respite from the stress of dangerous times.

# REVOLUTIONARY BALLETS

*Fêtes Révolutionnaires* formed a new category of dance that spread throughout France after 1789.[47] Revolutionary ballets took shape as outdoor festivals that were designed to assemble the masses for the purpose of commemorating the virtues of the newly acclaimed Republic. Indeed, public spectacles became classrooms for instilling in people behavior and attitudes deemed appropriate by Charles Maurice de Talleyrand, one of the most devious and enigmatic characters running the Revolution. The impact of these odd events was intensely felt by anxiety-ridden participants as a way of turning inner fears into outer elation.[48] Under the new French Republic, the Committee of Public Safety was established to protect public morals. In fact, however, it served as a spying agency while it protected the bloodthirsty radicals then in power. Censorship in all matters, including the arts, was its major activity. Ballet was the least affected since its nonverbal nature made it harder to detect the airing of dissident viewpoints.[49]

118

At the height of the Revolution, public theatrics were recognized as powerful instruments of political propaganda, necessary for fueling revolutionary sentiment among the French. As called for by the Committee of Public Safety, tens of thousands of National Guardsmen were the organizing force behind festivals that were gigantic processionals with spectacular elements. All over France these day-long affairs replaced the celebration of Christian holidays under the country's newly declared atheism. Comprised of huge tableaux, revolutionary ballets featured specially constructed, monumental earthworks dug by unemployed actors and dancers wishing to be politically correct. Here, the public, handled by out-of-work ballet masters, danced dances to celebrate the victory of the people in their struggle against tyranny. By the same token they marched and chanted slogans to honor the ideals of the usurpers of monarchial power. Fireworks, as well as the significant force of National Guardsmen, were always included to ensure the presence of enthusiastic crowds.[50]

The ambitious Pierre Gardel presented himself as an adamant revolutionary, espousing the cause by repeatedly appearing in the danced sections of these events. Gardel was among those choreographers frequently designated to orchestrate the *Fêtes* since only someone trained in the skill of dealing with crowds could establish any organization among thousands of people. Hoards of citizens were enlisted on the sites of the recently dug earthworks to engage in speechmaking, toasting of current heroes, singing the "Marseillaise," and dancing. As prologue and epilogue, they paraded through the cities pulling floats

*The Hat of Freedom.* Townsfolk celebrating changes brought about by the French Revolution, dance around the hat of freedom, a symbol that ultimately brought a new form of tyranny. (Courtesy of the author.)

that glorified liberty, equality, and fraternity. Among Gardel's revolutionary ballets were *Hommage à la Liberté* (1792, Offering to Liberty), *Le Triomphe de la République* (1793, Triumph of the Republic), and *La Fête de l'Être Suprême* (1794, Festival of the Supreme Being). Altered versions of these daytime shows and processionals often received evening performances in theaters. Theatrical performances had never been so effectively used in arousing emotions in times of national crisis.[51] Absurd as these spectacles were in retrospect, involvement in them probably seemed a small price for Gardel, who managed to retain both his lofty position at the Academy and his head.[52]

Despite the highly inferior nature of revolutionary-style ballets, they did a great service to dance in the long run. By attending them, republican audiences were brought closer than ever before to theaters, and they developed the habit of frequenting performances.[53] Equality and brotherhood threw open theater doors to everyone. Formerly in the employ of royalty, professional dancers were now seen as citizens of France like everyone else. In this way ordinary people learned to support theatrical dancing, thereby creating a demand for more productions and adequate venues to house them. One of Gardel's best anacreontic ballets during this period, according to the *Gazette National*, was *Le Jugement de*

*Paris* (1793, The Judgment of Paris), which the new audiences admired for its luxury, voluptuousness, and freedom from political overtones.[54] That same year, the ballet master Sébastien Gallet introduced a one-act patriotic *divertissement*, *La Fête Civique* (Civic Festival), and Noverre's pupil, Coindé, rearranged choreography for an opera under the title *La Liberté des Negres* (Liberty of the Negroes).[55]

The political and social shifts brought about by the Revolution ultimately achieved a dramatic change in the conventions of stage apparel. Finally, the time had come when the archaic traditions of masks, wigs, helmets, heels, *tonnelets*, and *paniers* were once and for all abolished. While severe criticism of theatrical dress by Noverre and others was ongoing, real change was not seen in their day.

Perhaps the greatest painter of his turbulent times, Jacques-Louis David (1748–1825), who had designed many of the *Fêtes Révolutionnaires*, was asked to create a new style of clothing that would express the proper dignity of true republicans of France. Always agreeable toward requests of the powerful, the artist set about his new challenge with pleasure and inspiration.

David had been greatly impressed with a performance of Noverre's much-criticized ballet *Les Horaces* (The Horaces), which he had attended in 1777 at the Paris Opera. In fact, Noverre's ballet had proved to be the motivation for David's dramatic painting, *The Oath of the Horatii*, completed in 1785.[56] Intended as a manifesto of the coming new age, the picture exulted personal sacrifice, patriotism, and virtue in reaction to rococo indulgence. Its composition consisted of four emboldened male figures in Roman military togas and sandals contrasted with four trembling, barefoot females fluidly draped in lighter fabrics. Based on the idealized garments of ancient Greek and Roman heroes, who were prized by the leaders of the Revolution, the artist had his point of departure and a paradigm for the new French fashion.

David emphasized simplicity and the natural shape of the body. He produced high-waisted dresses that took on the look of Grecian columns.[57] The new silhouette featured cascading drapings that echoed the movement of the legs and torso. For men, David designed elegant short jackets and added flowing cravats and slim trousers to substitute for the brash red bonnets and striped pants that had been the mark of the pugnacious *sans-culotte*,[58] as the new republicans called themselves. Heeled shoes formally worn by men and women of the old regime fell from fashion because the Revolution had taught that all people stand on the same level. Despite the frequency of fatal pneumonia,[59] *cothurns* and pretty silk slippers were worn by everyone who could make them. Both sexes wore hairstyles arranged or cut close to the head, particularly flattering in revealing the female neck and shoulders. In due course the new trend in fashion radically influenced costume design. The lighter, freer styles opened up new possibilities for expanded movement of the entire body, facilitating the work of the choreographer and benefiting the effect, effort, and beauty of the dancer.[60]

120

O Chute épouvantable et digne de mémoire!

*La Danse*. Post-revolutionary fashion transformed stage apparel. The lighter costumes and heel-less shoes allowed for an extended range of movement. (Courtesy of the Victoria & Albert Museum, London.)

# POST-REVOLUTIONARY BALLET AND THE WALTZ

After the Reign of Terror, when this especially bloody period of the French Revolution exhausted itself, Pierre Gardel was as secure as ever in his post. Mention must be made of his lengthy career as ballet director when France made its governmental transition from monarchy to republic. No longer "Royal," the Academy became the national theater of France, and to this day, is known as the Paris Opera. That the ballet survived[61] at all and then went on to flourish in the Romantic age, we must give credit to Gardel's tenacity as well as his knowledge. So violent was the political upheaval that it could have abolished all royal institutions just as it murdered the royals themselves. Gardel managed to preserve the treasure house of ballet's academic tradition although he did little to help it adjust to changing times.

The grandiose *Fêtes* gradually ceased so that Gardel could revise some of his earlier ballets, including the ever popular *Télémaque* (1790, Telemachus) and *Psyché* (1790, Psyche). Not until the turn of the century, however, did the recovering economy allow for new ballets. Returning to the business of art, Gardel, in a move away from the *ballet d'action* style, created *La Dansomanie* (1800, Dancemania),[62] dispelling accusations that the years he spent working on revolutionary spectacles left him artistically sterile. The light comedy that Gardel termed a fantasy proved to be an extraordinary success, and was often used for benefits, which were the fund-raisers of the day.

Structured on an amusing tale of an aristocrat with a mania for dancing, *La Dansomanie* broadly satirized the old regime and its various forms and styles of dance. Noverre found the ballet insulting to the serious ballet tradition,[63] but it was extremely popular with the public. It is noteworthy in the evolution of theatrical dance that *La Dansomanie* was the first ballet to have the subject of dancing itself for the central theme.[64] As an indication of progress, new steps in the *livret* of the ballet were mentioned, such as the *temps de flèche, pirouette sur le cou-de-pied*, and the earliest appearance of the term *arabesque*, to describe an elegant pose of the body.[65] It was also one of the first ballets to incorporate into its scenario the new ballroom waltz that became a symbolic expression of the French middle class. Nothing like *La Dansomanie* had ever been seen, and the bourgeois audiences devoured its frolicsome fun.

In republican France, change was nowhere more strikingly evident than in the public and private ballrooms where the new voguish passion for waltzing obliterated the *menuet*. The authors of the Age of Enlightenment—Rousseau, Diderot, and Voltaire—had espoused the pursuit of personal happiness. They sanctioned the courage of defiance against the restraining bounds of feudalism and emphasized the natural state of humanity as opposed to the superficiality of the rococo lifestyle. By 1800 the emotional appeal of these novel ideas found expression everywhere in European society, but never more so than in the expansive 3/4 rhythm of the waltz that mirrored the new mood. The waltz's rapid turning steps and its general effect of unbridled whirling was akin to the euphoria of the political liberation experienced by republican audiences. For anyone practiced in waltzing, even today, the emphasis on the first beat of the measure might be considered a metaphor for the individual's assertion of "I." After centuries of oppression that was forcibly removed by the French Revolution, common people assumed an importance heretofore not dreamed of.

Waltzing became wildly popular on and off stage all over Europe. Although the waltz received its share of condemnation from the old guard, which cited its excessive exuberance and the close proximity of partners as immoral, the dance has survived more than two hundred years as an expression of the middle class. Originally a ballroom form in 3/4 or 3/8 time, the waltz derived from the Ländler danced by Austrian and German peasants for centuries. In the 1770s waltzes were being notated and published in France. The form first appeared in a theatrical context on the Viennese stage in Martin Solar's opera *La Cosa Rara* in 1786,[66] and Mozart later included it in the ballet music for his operas. By

122

adapting the waltz to his ballet in *La Dansomanie*, Gardel bowed to the spirit of the times in a stunning departure from his establishment classicism. In so doing, he opened the way for enormous enrichment in theatrical dance, although he himself failed to pursue that direction.

When France finally settled down, Gardel was able to reopen the repository doors of the rich heritage established by Beauchamp and Lully. Unfortunately, in preserving the security of his executive position, the steadfast director categorically refused new talent at the Opera. Faithful Louis Milon, who had worked alongside of Gardel as his chief assistant for twenty-seven years and was considered an excellent choreographer, posed no threat. Unlike other European opera houses, where yearly contracts controlled the flow and fate of personnel, no changes in ballet masters occurred at the Paris Opera unless death or retirement decreed it. The house became essentially a self-contained empire. As a result, at the dawning of Romantic ballet, the superiority of France's academic establishment was still considered the loftiest, but none of the new era's greatest stars would be from the Opera. Romantic choreographers would come from the lesser theatrical houses of the Paris boulevards while others were foreigners. In the end, Gardel left to posterity a magnificent empty shell.

*Tom and Jerry "Sporting a Toe."* As the middle class prospered, rollicking quadrilles, polkas, and the pleasures of the waltz outmoded the stately *menuet*. The incorporation of ballroom steps and rhythms was noticeable in the expanding vocabulary of nineteenth-century choreographers. (Courtesy of the author.)

123

HIGHEST LIFE IN LONDON. *Tom & Jerry "Sporting a Toe," among the Corinthians, at Almacks in the West*

# ᲒHE VESTRIS FAMILY

The illustrious Vestris family were all dancers of the first order over a period of several generations. Teresa, Angiolo, and Gaëtan were three of seven Italian-born children who trained in France and danced throughout Europe. Teresa Vestris (1726–1808) was already an established artist in 1746 when she appeared at the Paris Opera and helped pave the way for her younger brothers. Trained by Dupré, Angiolo (1730–1809) was Noverre's leading male dancer during the choreographer's Stuttgart period. Gaëtan Vestris (1728–1808), also a pupil of Dupré, became the glory of the Paris Opera, displaying the grand and stately manner of his great teacher. In 1751 he was made *premier danseur*, and enjoyed many triumphs in Paris and in other European cities.

Gaëtan Vestris's gifts were concentrated in his *danseur noble* style, but he gave more freedom to elegant poses than was previously seen. It was said that his performances were masterpieces of nobility and grace, and that the quality of his *pirouettes* exceeded all others. He had danced under Noverre's direction at Stuttgart and had high regard for the choreographer's innovations. Gaëtan himself was acclaimed as the most modern dancer of his time. Confident in his extreme good looks, he danced without a mask in Noverre's *Médée und Jason*, astounding audiences with the dramatic force of his expressive acting and noble gestures.[67] While he was without doubt a fine technician and a very great interpretive artist, he was only mildly successful as a choreographer. After retiring in 1782 he spent his later years managing the career of his promising offspring and running the Paris Opera's ballet school. Commenting on his life he boasted that there were only three great men in Europe, the King of Prussia, Voltaire, and himself.

Auguste Vestris (1760–1842), Gaëtan's son by his mistress, Marie Allard, inherited his father's popular title "God of the Dance," and he reigned supreme during his own long career. A child prodigy taught by his adoring parents, he was first seen by an unbelieving public at the age of twelve. The *Mercure de France* waxed glowingly: "Strength, precision, brilliance of execution, graceful build, finished technique, beautiful stance, intelligence—every advantage of a sunny personality and a consummate talent are combined in this child."[68] Auguste set a new pattern of dancer; in mastering and blending the *noble*, *demi-caractère*, and *grotesque* categories he became the complete dancer. When time dimmed his technical powers, his expressive skills emerged and even Noverre noted that his miming seemed to join silent speech to his movements.[69] Auguste's extraordinary virtuosity exceeded his father's fame as a *danseur noble*, and once again emphasis on technique overshadowed the significance of artistry. Auguste's sensational elevation was remarkable for the time; his beats were considered almost miraculous, making him the most eminent dancer in Europe. When he and his father jointly appeared in London in 1781, they were so successful that Parliament interrupted its sessions to attend their performance. More technically adaptable than his exalted father, Auguste's amazing facility for endless *pirouettes* prompted a popular doggerel that circulated at the time and described him as a dancer ". . . who on one leg could do What erst no mortal could achieve on two."[70]

The undisputed star of the era, Auguste developed into an adroit and much sought-after teacher in his middle age. The exhilaration of freedom felt everywhere after 1789 loosened and expanded the rules of the *danse d'école*, facilitating the standardization of a heightened style of technique. Based on the intimate understanding of his own gifts, Auguste the teacher envisioned to what limits the dancer's body could be pushed, and his methodology raised technical levels beyond all previous expectations. He also taught elegance and the art of seductively capturing the audience. He encouraged his students to show an alluring freedom, to be charming and coquettish with the spectators.[71] In training the dancers who were the founders of the Romantic ballet he passed on his knowledge of turns, jumps, and beaten steps to the next generation.[72]

Considered temperamental and difficult in his youth, Auguste Vestris relied on his amazing facility for dancing to carry him with the general public. Noverre greatly admired his passionate approach to dramatic parts and worked with him in London where both men had fled the Revolution. Yet Vestris was

Auguste Vestris in his prime. He combined virtuosity with elegance to become the first "complete dancer." (Courtesy of the Victoria & Albert Museum, London.)

Eliza Bartholozzi (Madame Vestris) accompanying herself with a mandolin at the height of her career. (Courtesy of the author.)

often guilty of gross artistic indiscretion in his interpretation of roles, and his general inattention to meaningful detail gained considerable criticism. One news pamphlet remarked that ". . . the height to which the young Vestris has carried the dance lowers the art in elevating the artist."[73] It would seem that egomania was a family trait, for an amusing anecdote relates the elder Vestris publicly acknowledging that only his son Auguste was his superior as a dancer, noting that, "Gaëtan Vestris is his father, an advantage which nature has denied me." Auguste's son, Armand Vestris (1786–1825), also became a dancer and choreographer. He studied with his father and grandfather from the age of four and then worked in Italy, Portugal, and at the King's Theatre in London. Armand married dancer, vocalist, and actress Eliza Bartholozzi who became the famous Madame Vestris of English theater history.

# FOUR BALLERINAS

Greatly admired among the many celebrated ballerinas of the period, Marie Allard (1742–1802) excelled in comic and character parts. Her sparkling personality, feminine form, and buoyant dance style earned her extensive praise from theatrical commentators and the public alike. She had the distinction of appearing in the premiere of the Noverre-Mozart collaboration, *Les Petits Riens*. However, as mistress of the renowned Gaëtan Vestris, perhaps her most important claim to history was in becoming the mother of Auguste, genetically endowing him with a natural affinity for the air.[74]

Marie Guimard (1743–1816) began her career at the Comédie Française, and by 1763 she was the leading ballerina at the Paris Opera, dancing in the ballets of Gardel and Noverre. She was an excellent actress, full of natural sweetness and charm, and an exponent of the stately style of the *danse d'école*. Because of her social connections at court, she was one of the most formidable powers in French theatrical life, wielding enormous influence in the administration of the Opera. In the course of her long career, she acquired great fame and a fortune to match. She named her elegant house, designed and decorated by the city's most celebrated artists, the Temple of Terpsichore. It had a theater that served as a place for elite performances and a meeting point for the most important dancers, singers, and actors in Paris.[75]

Another exceptional woman was the German dancer Anna Heinel (1753–1808), a pupil of Noverre when he was in the employment of the Duke

Marie Guimard's shortened skirt showed her footwork which was still limited by heeled shoes. (Courtesy of the author.)

127

of Württemberg. In addition to her height and remarkable poise, she possessed exceptional virtuosity and accomplished the *pirouette à la seconde*, a feat that was facilitated by heel-less shoes that, it is said, she herself designed. Heinel's skill at slowly revolving on one leg in a second position extension while holding perfect balance was always cause for audience amazement. She was much admired by Noverre who regarded her as a great tragedienne. After enjoying considerable success in Paris and London, she retired at twenty-nine, married the famous Gaëtan Vestris, and settled down to raise their son, Adolphe Vestris, who did not follow the family profession.[76]

Giovanna Baccelli (1753–1801) was an Italian dancer who worked in London with great success in Noverre's ballets. In 1782 she was allowed five performances at the Paris Opera where she danced with the virtuoso Charles Le Picq, and was toasted as Auguste Vestris's most beautiful partner. An interesting description of her very musical dancing reported that she was seen balancing, alighting, and turning on the toes of her shoes.[77] Sir Joshua Reynolds and Thomas Gainsborough immortalized her seductive charms on canvas during the years that she was the notorious lady-friend of the Duke of Dorset.

# CHILDREN'S BALLET COMPANIES

An overview of pre-Romantic ballet must make mention of the presence of *kinderballett*, which were children's dance companies. One of the earliest was Franz Sebastiani's group that was famous for its pantomimes and very active in Germany between 1756 and 1770. Another *kinderballett*, specializing in harlequinades that demanded extensive acrobatic training in the preparation of the children, was run by the Viennese ballet master Felix Berner. At the beginning of his enterprise in 1761 Berner established a preparatory school to train youth, which became a source for renewing his company's personnel as young charges outgrew their positions.[78]

One of the most prolific personalities that directed *kinderballett* was Friedrich Horschelt (1793–1876).[79] Born of an extensive and influential dance dynasty, Horschelt conducted most of his activities in Austria and Germany. Dancer, director, and teacher, he was skilled at creating ballets for children ranging in age from four to twelve years. Among his outstanding pupils who went on to adult celebrity were Therese Heberle and Anton Stuhlmüller. Horschelt's frequently copied training methods included quasi-military drill work that was always the favored part of his ballets. He was known to have used as many as 180 young performers in a given ballet, and from all accounts, his works were as difficult as they were disciplined and effective. The *corps de ballet's* remarkable precision in the formation of parallel lines, squares, circles, and diagonals of choreographic evolutions gave them the appearance of moving as one and became the basis for the company's fame.

Not only was *kinderballett* extremely popular with court and public audiences for its diminutive charm, but the children's companies were perfectly logical institutions to provide schooling, internship, and stage experience in a single setting. The offspring of dancers could be trained and maintained in a meaningful manner while their performing parents sought employment in the courts, theaters, and fairgrounds across Europe.[80] Horschelt's *kinderballett* was dissolved in 1821 by royal decree so that a scandal could be squelched before it became public knowledge. Overly ambitious stage mothers were suspected of procuring their dancing daughters for Prince Alois Kaunitz-Rittberg whose "fondness for nymphets" was well known.[81] The talented Horschelt was entirely innocent of the matter, subsequently being appointed ballet master for the Munich Opera. Prince Kaunitz, on the other hand, was quietly removed from court and exiled to a country retreat.

More enduring was Josephine Weiss's ballet school for girls from five to twelve years old. In 1845 she took her *kinderballett* to the Paris Opera where thirty-six little girls and one boy performed with such professionalism that reviewers held them up as models for the spoiled and unruly Opera *corps de ballet*. Weiss's troupe went on to appear in fourteen different ballets and short *pas* at Her Majesty's Theatre in London, followed by highly acclaimed performances in Canada and the United States.

# Summary

Ballet was flourishing as a profession by the middle of the eighteenth century. The engaging works of Angiolini, Dauberval, and de Hesse were widely recognized and appreciated, as were a number of stellar performers, but much in the dance profession remained in need of artistic guidance. The great reformer of the age was Jean Georges Noverre, father of modern ballet. The literary summation of his lifework, the *Lettres* centered around identifying all of the most expressive elements of the art of dance as he knew them, and casting them afresh into a vital conception of the *ballet d'action*. Noverre dealt with the molding of the individual dancer as a performing artist, and in so doing, caused a major advancement in the dancer's technique. He also raised the art of choreography to new heights of expressive possibilities by examining the nature of human experience in relation to theatrical dance itself. His greatest pupils— Dauberval, Didelot, and Viganò showed the unmistakable imprint of his ideas on their work. The careers of a number of other celebrated dancers and choreographers bridged the periods before and after the French Revolution. In particular, members of the Gardel and Vestris families survived the dangerous times of civil war and preserved the organizational and technical foundations of academic ballet for the Romantic era. Highly influenced by Noverre's extensive artistic activities and his luminous writings, European ballet experienced a forceful rebirth which, in many instances, is ongoing in current ballet and modern dance.

The French Revolution, cataclysmic as it was, had a positive effect on theatrical dance because it brought ballet to a larger segment of the public. After a few years of dismal pseudo-propagandistic, revolutionary spectacles, the ballet at the Paris Opera opened its doors to a liberated nation. Under the new laws, all Frenchmen had access to what was French, and French ballet, in turn, responded with a new beginning. While Gardel kept the ballet infertile at the Paris Opera, other ballet masters freely enjoyed the opportunities afforded by the new times. They incorporated the energetic and colorful folk dance steps of the common man into their choreography for the boulevard theaters, thereby expanding the previous repertory of steps and poses. In creating the seedbed of the forthcoming Golden Age of Romantic ballet, France renewed its status as a dance mecca.

# Chapter Notes

1. Denis Diderot, *Oeuvres complètes*, ed. J. Assezat (Paris: 1875–1877), VII, p. 157–58. The phrase, "imitation of nature," is taken to mean a poetic and natural presentation of reality, devoid of mannerisms and artifice.
2. Deryck Lynham, *The Chevalier Noverre: Father of Modern Ballet* (London: Dance Books, 1972), pp. 14–15.
3. Winter, p. 109. In *l'Art du Théâtre* (1750) François Riccoboni had criticized corsets and Roman breastplates, not as outdated conventions, but because they impeded movement and, hence, expressiveness.
4. Permenent collection, Exhibit commentary, Bata Shoe Museum, Toronto, Canada.
5. Lynham, pp. 134–36.
6. Ibid., p. 20.
7. Ibid., pp. 36–39.
8. Ibid., p. 57.
9. Ibid., p. 58.
10. Gennaro Magri, *Theoretical and Practical Treatise on Dancing*, trans. Mary Skeaping, Naples, 1779 (London: Dance Books, 1988), p. 123.
11. Lynham, p. 58.
12. Ibid., p. 142.
13. Ibid., p. 141.
14. Ibid., p. 64.
15. Lawson, p. 39.
16. Hindley, p. 234.
17. Jean Georges Noverre, *Lettres sur la Danse et les Arts Imitateurs*, Paris, 1807 (Paris: Editions Lieutier, 1952), p. 277.
18. *Enciclopedia dello Spettacolo* (Rome, 1952–1958). Entry: Gaspare Angiolini, "Lettere di Gaspare Angiolini a monsieur Noverre sopra i balli pantomimi" (Milan, 1773).
19. Guest, *The Ballet of the Enlightenment*, p. 101.
20. Ibid., p. 99.

21. Emily Anderson, trans., *Mozart's Letters* (Boston: A Bulfinch Press Book, Little, Brown, and Co., 1990), pp. 85, 91.
22. Guest, *The Ballet of the Enlightment*, pp. 85–88.
23. Ibid., p. 157.
24. Ibid., pp. 156–60.
25. Lawson, p. 40. Ivan Valberkh, a visiting Russian ballet master, wrote after seeing Vestris perform in 1802 that "he danced paying no attention to his arms, turns like a mad person and occasionally sticks his tongue out." A famous etching depicting this last bit of stage impropriety survives in the picture collection of the Bibliothèque Nationale in Paris.
26. Lynham, p. 159.
27. Jean Georges Noverre, *Letters on Dancing and Ballets* (Brooklyn, NY: Dance Horizons, 1975).
28. Winter, p. 121.
29. Lynham, pp. 146–57.
30. Guest, *The Ballet of the Enlightenment*, p. 68.
31. Lynham, p. 158.
32. Guest, *The Ballet of the Enlightenment*, p. 259. Dauberval was considered to be a strong candidate to lead the Paris Opera, but became embittered by the internal politics surrounding the post and subsequently moved to Bordeaux. In a letter to an unidentified friend, he revealed his sentiments regarding the Opera. "We try not to follow all the nonsense of the Académie Royal de Musique, for the artistes there (as you know) are furiously persecuted by all the fools who direct it, and I thank my lucky stars that I am a long way away from a dump where bogus talent continues to be protected."
33. Ibid., p. 367.
34. Ibid., p. 389.
35. Judith Chazin-Bennahum, *Dance in the Shadow of the Guillotine* (Carbondale: Southern Illinois University Press, 1988), pp. 3–9.
36. Gianfranco D'Aronco, *Storia della Danza* (Firenze: Casa Editrice, S.P.A., 1962), p. 211.
37. Giannandrea Poesio, "Galop, Gender and Politics in the Italian Ballo Grande," *Reflecting our Past; Reflecting on our Future* (University of California, Riverside: Proceedings, Society of Dance History Scholars, 1997), p. 151.
38. Winter, p. 180. See Illustration 126, p. 188.
39. Ibid., p. 190.
40. Poesio, p. 151.
41. Magri, pp. 66–68.
42. Winter, p. 150.
43. Ibid., p. v.
44. Like Lully, Maximilien Gardel died from a foot wound that turned gangrenous. Lully had accidently struck his foot with his conductor's baton, perhaps in a state of rehearsal anger or during the passion of performance. Gardel, on alighting from his carriage in a typical, filth-strewn street of the times, stepped on a chicken bone that pierced his shoe and fatally infected his foot.
45. Winter, p. 167.
46. John V. Chapman, "Auguste Vestris and the Expansion of Technique" (*Dance Research Journal*, 19/1, Summer, 1987), p. 17, footnote 23. Gardel's ballets emphasized dancing at a time when Noverre was urging ballet masters to include more

131

silent acting in their works. Chapman notes that one of Gardel's most important contributions ". . . was to give dancers such as Vestris an opportunity to display their tours de force as well as their mimic talents."

47. Chazin-Bennahum, p. 82.
48. Simon Schama, *Citizens: A Chronicle of the French Revolution* (New York: Alfred A. Knopf, l989), p. 504.
49. Chazin-Bennahum, pp. 70–71.
50. Schama, pp. 503–8.
51. Guest, *The Ballet of the Enlightenment*, p. 340.
52. Chazin-Bennahum, p. 89.
53. Ibid., p. 130.
54. Guest, *The Ballet of the Enlightenment*, p. 341.
55. Nègre is the French word used during the eighteenth century to denote Africans or peoples of the Caribbean.
56. Winter, p. 181.
57. See Illustration on page 4.
58. Schama, p. 830.
59. Exhibit commentary, Bata Shoe Museum, Toronto, Canada.
60. Judith Chazin-Bennahum, "Women of Faint Heart and Steel Toes," *Rethinking the Sylph: New Perspectives of the Romantic Ballet*, ed. Lynn Garafola (Hanover, NH: University Press of New England, 1997), pp. 121–30.
61. Guest, *The Ballet of the Enlightenment*, p. 355.
62. Prudhommeau, p. 185.
63. Chazin-Bennahum, *Dance in the Shadow of the Guillotine*, p. 155.
64. Prudhommeau, p. 185.
65. Ibid.
66. Horst Koegler, *The Concise Oxford Dictionary of Ballet* (New York: Oxford University Press, 1987), p. 442.
67. Noverre, *Letters on Dancing and Ballets*, p. 91.
68. Guest, *The Ballet of the Enlightenment*, p. 55.
69. Chapman, p. 14.
70. Alexander Bland and John Percival, *Men Dancing* (New York: Macmillan Publishing, 1984), p. 98.
71. Cyril Beaumont, *A Miscellany for Dancers* (London: Love & Brydone, 1954), pp. 29–30. From the memoirs of Dr. Véron.
72. Chapman, p. 15.
73. Ibid., p. 12.
74. Miguel, pp. 50–58.
75. Ibid., pp. 71–89.
76. Ibid., pp. 59–64.
77. Guest, *The Ballet of the Enlightenment*, p. 206. Guest points out that Baccelli's feat on her toes, surely achieved in heeled shoes, was not indicative of early pointe work, but did presage the ballerina's eternal desire for the ultimate illusion of lightness.
78. Winter, p. 145.
79. Ibid., pp. 247–53.
80. Ibid., p. 145.
81. Ibid., p. 251.

# 7

# The Foundations of Romantic Ballet

Romanticism refers to the nineteenth-century European artistic movement during which the values of emotion and individualism were in opposition to the rational ideals expounded by the classicism of the previous age. Romanticism's quixotic style of theatrical dance was the most glamorously visible product of a multitude of the period's historical manifestations. A new generation of European artists gave vent to their imaginations, lyrically expressing themselves in a return to nature, in the exaltation of feelings, and in a desire to transcend the human condition. The special vision and yearning of the Romantic spirit were wonderfully conveyed in dance productions, particularly through the participation of the Romantic hero and a unique and perfect creation—the Romantic ballerina.

The chief venues for Romantic ballet were the stages of Paris and London. A unique dance style was initiated from outside the Paris Opera establishment by French and Italian ballet masters whose inspiration and skills were allowed free rein to create a new style of theater art. Paramount among the trends in ballet were the preference for a more personal means of expression, a liberation from the traditional restraints imposed by eighteenth-century formulas for dance-making, and an emphasis on cultural diversity emerging from the spirit of nationalism. Writing at the end of the century, the German philosopher Johann von Herder had promoted the notion of the inherent value of diverse peoples and their unique folk traditions as being a fundamental state of humanity. In so doing, Herder honored all religions, languages and mores, instilling pride for one's own cultural expressions while encouraging a fascination with foreign ways.

Napoleon had swept away the last remnants of the *ancient régime* and all it stood for. Following his exploits, republican ideas that expounded human rights spread throughout the Continent altering European life in countless ways. In a critical milestone for ballet, the dances of the common people—folk dances— were pulled into the ballrooms frequented by the middle class, as a result of the tolerance for pluralism that accompanies universal pride in nationhood. *Tarantellas* from Italy, the *jota, sardana, seguidilla, bolero,* and *cachucha* from Spain, the French *cancan,* the German *ländler* and its derivative *valse* or waltz, the English *hornpipe,* the Hungarian *czardas,* and the Slavic *polka, mazurka,* and *hopák* compose but a short list of folk dances that crossed frontiers and heightened the pleasures of bourgeois society. Enjoyed for their freedom, passion, color, rhythms, and high energy, these dances were soon absorbed into the *danse d'école* where they lent their uniquely rich elements to an expanding repertory of ballet movements. National and ethnic dances thus played a prominent role in the creation of Romantic ballets.[1] Refined, codified, and named, the ballet steps of Magri and others were newly worked out by men such as Auguste Vestris, Jean Coulon, Jean Petipa, Filippo Taglioni, and Carlo Blasis to form the technical material of Romantic ballet.

Like most advances in aesthetic development of people, the Romantic era's art forms resulted from a violent reaction to factors philosophical, political, social, and economic. Thoughts and attitudes underwent radical modifications paralleling the momentous changes in the human condition. The Enlightenment, followed by its unexpected brainchild, the French Revolution and its immediate aftermath, had shown Europeans that they could, by force if necessary, determine their political fate. Coupled with this newly emancipated mentality was an equal amount of individual responsibility that the recently altered class structure was not yet equipped to handle, resulting in further political upheaval supplanted by more civil wars.

134

The horrors of the Industrial Revolution fueled broad social change and rapid (and thus complex) economic growth. These changes soon blanketed con-

The dawning sense of political freedom encouraged a vogue for social dancing all over Europe. The mood of an early nineteenth-century bourgeois ball is wittily captured in Ehrensward's drawing. (Courtesy of the author.)

tinental Europe and England with an avalanche of evils that rivaled the deposed monarchy and the Napoleonic Wars. Factories belching soot clouded and despoiled the horizons so that townspeople longed to escape to natural landscapes. Large-scale manufacturing resulted in a shift of population that created overcrowded cities, rampant child labor in the absence of restricting laws, and living conditions disastrous to the health of the general population. Subsequently, the waning agrarian life left farms dangerously underproductive, contributing to major socioeconomic problems affecting the greater part of society.

## THE AESTHETIC SHAPING OF THE ROMANTIC BALLET

The Romantic period, in terms of its own spiritualism, picked up where the Middle Ages left off. The imagery evoked by medieval literature, artifacts, and eccentric notions served as the font of the Romantic's artistic conceptions. It was a preoccupation of many French, German, and English scholars to collect and preserve the heritage of legendary deeds of the Crusaders in the age of chivalry. Great interest was aroused in the folkloric tradition still in evidence in the nineteenth century. Just as artists of the Renaissance had an insatiable curiosity for the archaeological fragments of antiquity, so did the Romantics dreamily contemplate the disintegrating Gothic ruins, long-ignored medieval manuscripts, and folktales recalling sinister legends of death dances.

Much of the substance of the Romantic ballet style was derived from Gothic folklore, the remnant of old superstitions and corruptions of historical fact. Legends were an inexhaustible source of inspiration for Romantic choreographers in so far as they were endowed with allegorical meaning that gave a tinge of poetry to everyday life. Characteristic of the era was a craving for the mysterious aura of all things medieval, which were duly romanticized in nineteenth-century novels and melodramas.

With the predominance of Christianity in the Middle Ages, the devil had taken center stage as the antiChrist and was fitted with all the most evil aspects of the human personality. Thus, a sinister and powerful dark side was part of Gothic legends, and figured in the new taste in ballets, one that would contribute heavily to the public's enthrallment with the weird and grotesque. Witches and vampires were bizarre personifications of demonic elements in Romantic ballet; they functioned similarly to the Renaissance *deus ex machina* as a convenient means of instigating or solving human predicaments. Essential to Romantic ballets was the appearance of satanic creatures, often cloaked in beauty and grace, to change the course of events and play havoc with the lives of human beings.

For centuries folktales had passed down through the generations and their ghosts and goblins never stopped haunting people and literature. From St. Petersburg to the south of Spain, the old lore was cast into the tales of Krylov, Pushkin, Andersen, La Fontaine, Perrault, Hoffman, Cervantes, and Bécquer. Good and bad fairies, trolls, elves, and mermaids were all part of the stories that unfolded in the benevolent features of some supernatural creatures or the foreboding horror of others as they entered into human experience. Of the numerous varieties of fantastic creatures, the sylphs and wilis became the favored spirits of Romantic ballet.

The sylph was envisioned three hundred years earlier by an alchemist in Salzburg, Austria. A dreamer and a romantic from another era, Theophrastus Bombastus von Hohenheim, who called himself Dr. Paracelsus, believed in the existence of sylphs who, he said, were extracts of previously living people. They were mortals, but without souls. Inhabiting the air, they were able to transmute back and forth between states of being and non-being.[2] Wilis were comparable woodland creatures, young women who had arrived at their current vampire state by dying on the eve of their weddings.

The sentiment contained in poetic songs composed by the medieval troubadours broadly contributed to European culture[3] and therefore to the emotional content of Romantic ballet. That is to say, human feelings framed in musical form presented the key component in shaping the magical formula underlying the period's best repertory. Furthermore, the medieval world of chivalry, reflected and guided by the sentiments of its troubadours, did more than any other organized body, including the Catholic Church, to raise the status of women, by celebrating over and over again their feminine qualities. A closer look at this link, discussed in Chapter 1, reveals just how significant the Middle Ages were in influencing the spiritual aspects of a ballet style. Delicate feelings and poetic hyperbole in Romantic ballet were ancestral remnants of the lifestyles of the medieval French nobility.

Channeled by the work of philosophers and artists, colossal forces overwhelming human life realigned themselves to forge a new era rooted in a distant past. During the creative high point of Romantic ballet (1830–1845), it was not the medieval court dances that influenced the development of this golden age of dance. Rather, it was the poetic sentiments originally contained in the *canzos* or songs of the troubadours that the creators of Romantic ballet identified with and that satisfied the emotional yearnings of nineteenth-century audiences. The *canzos* produced a legacy that continued to determine a good portion of the Western world's concept of feeling as it entered folklore and literature.[4] On the heels of troubadorean love songs, Dante through his Beatrice proclaimed love to be the supreme experience of life. From then on, the pursuit of love became a major topic for Western literature, as Christian society was encouraged to defer to the female as the weaker, purer, and more virtuous sex to be cherished above all things.

The legendary themes of ghostly nuns in the moonlight, a sylph's power over a mortal being, and Giselle's sublime and purifying love still potent from her grave were irresistible to the nineteenth-century audiences. At a time in history when a war-weary Europe hungered for escape from new horrors of the Industrial Revolution, the Romantic ballet rediscovered, embellished, and presented anew medieval ideals. Chivalry, spiritual love, and its transcendental notions of man's destiny were offset by dark elements of superstition and

136

unknown fear, and this juxtaposition was the favored subject matter for ballets.

The earliest stirrings of what was essential in Romantic art appeared in the themes of a superb body of poetry penned by Arabian poets. As early as the ninth century there occurred a blending of Manichaeism, Neoplatonism, and Mohammedanism, and the fusion was mirrored in a religious poetry that used erotic metaphors similar to those of courtly troubadourean rhetoric. In the twelfth century the chief authors of this poetic style were al Hallaj, al Gazali, and Suhrawardi of Aleppo, all poets of supreme love. Their conception of the *Veiled Idea* was presented as a beloved object as well as a symbol of longing for the divine.[5] In Islamic culture, religious representational art was forbidden since it was thought to encourage idolatry (i.e., the worship of idols that rivaled Allah, the Islamic god). According to Islamic beliefs, religious art was not allowed to represent any aspect of humanity; it could only be ornamental. By using the literary device of hyperbole or exaggeration, however, poets were able to hint at stark reality without breaking Islamic laws. Because poetry consists of the fruits of rich imagination, it created a borderline attitude between the real and unreal. Islamic lyric and panegyric poetry produced a kind of mystical effect so that it was difficult to tell if the poet was speaking of carnal or ideal love. Therefore, images of thinly veiled allusion, delicacy of expression, and languorous beauty were at the heart of Arabian poetry.

Around the end of the seventeenth century a professional writer, Antoine Galland, became fascinated with Arabian literature while traveling in the East.[6] He prepared a French translation of *A Thousand and One Nights* that was subsequently published in all European languages. The voluptuous stories became the preferred reading matter of the time and contributed to the oriental elements in the arts and crafts of the eighteenth-century rococo style. The ballet master Jean-Georges Noverre was following the popular taste when he endowed *The Chinese Metamorphosis* with oriental atmosphere. The trend begun by Galland reached the nineteenth-century ballet stage with Joseph Mazilier's production of Lord Byron's poem *The Corsair*.

Shaped by an intense interest in Near Eastern and Oriental cultures, the zeitgeist of the Romantic epoch manifested itself through evocations of mysterious and sensuous elements that readily fit popular tastes and trends and so Romantic art was born. Romanticism was characterized by a passionate striving to discover meaning in human events, an effort that was uniquely reflected in all of the Romantic arts, but most perfectly in its ballet.

# EXPRESSIVENESS IN THE BALLET

Romanticism first took hold in the early nineteenth century as a literary movement rooted in the Eastern philosophy of transcendentalism.[7] It espoused the supremacy of intuition, over sense–perception and reason, as its aesthetic principle. Transcendental ideas influenced all art forms of the period by imparting to them rich dramatic underpinnings. The European literary establishment responded to the trying post-Napoleonic years with artistic concepts based on escapism and, in so doing, the stories of the German writers Novalis, Brentano, and E.T.A. Hoffman launched Romanticism. Poets from Goethe to Schiller, Balzac, de Musset, Byron, and the Shelleys, to name a few, were awash in the inspiration they found in Eastern mysticism, medieval poetry, and folklore. Because much of life was dismal and sordid, it seemed preferable that the poetry, novels, and ballet scenarios should aspire to represent expressions of imaginary worlds filled with poetic love, delicate feelings, and exotic places enhanced with eerie creatures. In developing the emotional aspect of Romantic literature, therefore, writers were revolting against the previous age of reason when excessive attention was placed on the formal structure of artwork as opposed to the expression of human feelings.

In the interim between the peak of Noverre's neoclassic dance and the advent of Romantic ballet, it was considered heretical to suggest change, especially at the Paris Opera where the aged Pierre Gardel still controlled dance production. Between 1789 and 1815, France had experienced wrenching social and political changes that created a nationwide imbalance hardly conducive to the flourishing of art. As we have seen, prior to 1825 the ballet had deteriorated. Instead of being a vehicle for the depiction of human experience, it comprised, at its worst, a showcase for ceaseless pirouetting and other acrobatic tricks devoid of meaning. The reformist ideas of Noverre's classicism had become conventionalized or ignored, and what had been so commendable in his ballets and in those of his contemporaries developed into a formalized, frozen, and threadbare tradition.

Albeit, as time passed, the momentum for change built up until resistance was no longer possible. The choreographers and writers of the Romantic age sought to de-emphasize stylized form and accentuate content characterized by lyrical and dramatic narrative. For ballet, this change in approach materialized in the shaping of fascinating plots, revealed through a splendid display of stage magic. Themes based on the miraculous, darkly mysterious, and touchingly morbid became the rage.

The significance of the Romantic ballets was their appealing and often profound emotional content. Ballet makers discovered the key to ballet's popularity—that dancing, by its very nature, was uniquely suited to transmitting the ideas of the Romantic movement. Because ballet production incorporated transcendentalist literary ideas, reinforced by visual and aural forces, theatrical dance was rendered a powerful medium of expression. The combined elements of plot, decor, and music were made wonderfully vivid by choreography purposely devised to convey the dramatic content through the work of dancers.

The spirit of the times, with all its positive as well as negative factors, spawned audiences who were in need of emotional catharsis. Romantic ballet was noted for its emphasis on escape into a fantasy world where the increasingly large middle class audiences could empathize with the alternately intense

Johannes Jelgerhuis' drawings of gestural and pantomimic techniques illustrate the influence of the expressive *commedia dell'arte* and *grotteschi* performers on the developing ballet. (Courtesy of the Collection Theater Instituut Nederland.)

and delicate emotions of human beings interacting with phantom creatures. The intriguing story lines of Romantic ballets were most often female-centered; a woman's tragic love was shadowed with villains or spirits. Ballet makers of the day understood that this kind of thematic material was the consummate psychological instrument that both relieved overwhelming social stress and offered a means of spiritual cleansing to the public.

In the eighteenth century, most choreographers had devised their plots around antiquarian myths. In 1827, however, the choreographer Jean Aumer managed to engage France's most successful playwright, Eugène Scribe, to put his ideas for *La Somnambule* (The Sleepwalker) into literary form. A direct inspiration in the formulation of Romantic ballets, melodrama had been widely popular in Europe for several generations and Scribe's expertise in the genre began a long line of unique ballet scenarios. His plays reflected the values and dreams of the hard-working middle class, which had a limited capacity for heroic idealism, being immersed in the tasks of daily commerce and bourgeois family life.

Melodrama had its roots in the popular Gothic novel, which expressed its fanciful images of the Middle Ages in scenes filled with gloom, violence, and terror. Melodramas provided an added thrill when audiences saw their stories vividly enacted in plays.[8] The genre also drew on simplistic stock characters in plots that pushed the limits of reality. The theme was stereotyped; good people suffer terribly at the hands of the wicked, but the virtuous triumph and all ends happily. After forty years of this type of dramatic fare, theatergoers were conditioned to accept the irrational as normal. Therefore, when Romantic-style ballet began to take hold, with its love of all things mysterious, audiences were prepared to revel in its implausible conceptual and visual format. The well-published Scribe produced a strong dramatic scenario for Aumer's choreography. Beguiled by the notion of a beautiful woman's unconscious state controlling her destiny as she perilously walks on the edge of a building in her sleep, press and public wildly applauded *La Somnambule*. Thus, Romantic-style ballets took shape.

In the two greatest Romantic ballets of the era, *La Sylphide* (1832, The Sylph) and *Giselle* (1841), the librettos juxtaposed the realism of rustic settings

The ninth scene in a series of illustrations depicting the dramatic action in a Viennese production of *Der Zauberschleier* (1840, The Magic Shawl). (Courtesy of the author.)

140

IX Abtheilung
Der Zauberschleier.

with the enigmatic spheres of iridescent creatures. Not only did this dual aspect of different worlds create interest provided by the very element of contrast, but it also enriched the dance's store of thematic content. The real and unreal worlds demanded contrasting choreographic idioms. For example, the realistic or local color portions of *La Sylphide* and *Giselle* used the *terre à terre* steps of the *danses d'école* as well as national folk dances and *demi-caractère* styles. The supernatural scenes of the ballets called for a greater development of the aerial aspects of the *danse d'école*. That is, *ballon*, or the quality of lightness in a dancer's movement, signified the epitome of her achievement as an interpreter of the ethereal. Jumping steps of all kinds were refined and perfected for the meaning they could impart to the characterization of chilling specters. Because these fleeting spirits were "powerfully present and dangerous" in the story, they provided the creative thrust for the ballet.[9]

The artistic incorporation of *pointe* work was the most important innovation in molding the non-real scenes in Romantic ballets. In his treatise of 1779, Gennaro Magri noted with pleasure that Antoine Pitrot raised his "whole body on the tip of his big toe, and extends all the joints so perfectly, that the whole thigh, leg and foot itself fall into one perpendicular line."[10] Two generations later, the practice of putting women on *pointe* was possibly encouraged by the occasional use of dancers suspended from wires. The effect of defying gravity was so desirable that females began to imitate the feat, using their own foot strength. As early as 1822, it was reported in the Italian theater journal, *I Teatri Drammatico Musicale e Coreografico*, that Amalia Brugnoli did extraordinary things on the points of her toes and that she had learned the feat from Armand Vestris,[11] grandson and son of the formidable Gaëtan and Auguste. *Pointe* work became mandatory for all principal female dancers since it provided the ultimate suggestion of weightlessness proper to the nature of the creatures that she portrayed. The first *pointe* shoes were heel-less, square-tipped, satin slippers that were part of the fashion of the times.[12] Also, they were similar to the slippers worn by acrobats and tightrope walkers. Ballerinas constantly tried to improve their *pointe* work by contriving a variety of aids. Silk shoes for stage use were reinforced around the leather sole and toe with extra stitching. Starched muslin, felt, or cardboard wrapped around the foot, added to the shoe's strength, while long ribbons tightly wound around the ankle gave extra foot support.[13] Not until circa 1880 were the first commercial blocked shoes introduced so that for a considerable time the Romantic dancer had to depend on her ingenuity to supplement her natural strength.

The masters of Romantic ballet intuitively developed a special body language that helped shape the development of theatrical dance. Expressive of the poetic sentiments evoked in the *canzos* and expanded by Romantic ballet, the *pas de deux* succeeded in reflecting the twelfth-century phenomenon of chivalry. Where else in art or life is the female treated with a similar degree of metaphoric courtesy and adoration as in the choreographic effect of supported *adagio* movement, with its soaring leaps and sublimely suspended lifts initiated by the ballerina's partner? The proximity of male and female as worked out in the

Scarves and floral wreaths gave added design to early *pas de deux* choreography as shown in Jelgerhuis' 1812 drawings of members of the Kobbler family. One of the sketches is the earliest to record *pointe* work. (Courtesy of the Collection Theater Instituut Nederland.)

142

Romantic *pas de deux* was, however, as much a result of practicality as chivalry. The ballerina's increasing use of her *pointes* made her balance more precarious and required highly attentive partnering. The artistic impression of this technical advancement was that of a great tenderness between dancers. While partnering reached a level of genuine complexity, it also demonstrated heightened powers of communication.

The unique quality of the academic *danse d'école* style was evidenced in the gentility of ballet body language. Romantic ballets called for their own style of *port de bras*, characterized by softness in the line of wrist and elbow and complemented by sloping shoulders and a slight inclination of the head. The novelty of female *pointe* work developed a subtle and poetic use of the ballerina's foot.[14] It enhanced the dancer's ability to defy gravity, to be the ethereal, never-to-be-attained ideal woman of the troubadour's passionate song or the fleeting, soulless creature of the forest.

The Romantic ballerina enjoyed an artistic position of great prestige thanks to the grooming she was given by her male teachers and choreographers.[15] Indeed, for the first time in the history of dance, the female presence superseded that of the male. The long-term effect that the adored Romantic ballerina had on the public's imagination proved for all time that a female in professional dance could survive, as well as genuinely contribute, to a growing art form. The greatest of the Romantic ballerinas were among the most admired, famous, and notorious women of their times. In the course of their long lives they were financially independent, they supported and doted on their illegitimate offspring, and they bravely survived the disapproval of bourgeois society.

Painting, like music, had for centuries been developing its potential as an instrument of theatrical expression. Since the late Renaissance, painted flats had provided background atmosphere for court entertainment in ballrooms. Soon the concept of shifting scenes was perfected, and by the year 1700, entire set changes could be made in seconds with the use of imbedded tracks for sliding decorative panels on- and off-stage. The emotional nineteenth-century paintings of Blake, Turner, Constable, Delacroix, and David impacted the coloration produced by the Romantic scenarists. Designers for the ballet partook of the tremendous excitement of the new times and enhanced Romantic ballets with impressive realistic settings offset by mist-laden landscapes of the unknown. Painted backdrops, awash in varied light intensities, contributed handsomely to the entire effort of ballet-making. Earlier experiments done by the pioneer photographer, Louis-Jacques Daguerre,[16] had indicated the extent to which light could enhance theatrical productions. It was as if the music evoked light, color, and visual atmosphere, wherein all was given life through the movement of the dance.

In Romantic ballet, rustic scenery was designed to be realistic in an effort to recall the beauty of nature. By the same token were the mandatory machines designed to fly dancers short distances, thus heightening the magical effects of the ballet. As the technical skills for flying objects and people developed, wires were used to suspend dancers on the tips of their shoes. Immediately before ascending in a flight of fancy, the dancer, perched on the point of a toe, appeared weightless and the mastery of *pointe* dancing became more desirable than ever. Trap doors, a carry-over from the baroque theaters, were a major feature in Romantic ballet, in that they made it possible for evil creatures to disappear into a fiery abyss. Ships rolling in tempestuous seas across the backdrop

143

Amalia Brugnoli, an early exponent of *pointe* work, is partnered by her husband, Paolo Samengo, in *L'Anneau Magique* (1832, The Magic Ring). (Courtesy of the Victoria & Albert Museum, London.)

intensified many dramatic moments. Audiences thrilled to the occasional hero-ine hurling herself over a cliff while many a ballet was enhanced by splashing fountains illuminated by stage lighting.

Music assumed a new importance in the Romantic ballet because it was asked to evoke the contrasting atmospheres of the real and unreal elements of the ballet. Before 1820, a handful of great composers, namely Lully, Rameau, Mozart, Gluck, and Beethoven, had been associated with ballet, but with the exception of Lully, not exclusively. Now change was in the air. In less than three weeks, Adolphe Adam composed the score for *Giselle*, which was so sensitively related to the scenario, choreography, and decor that ballet music attained a new importance. For the most part, however, Romantic ballet scores continued to be highly serviceable but marginal in quality, providing a beat to keep the *corps de ballet* together and emphasizing the ballerina's jumps and turns. The emotionally charged music of Chopin, Schubert, Liszt, Mendelsson, and Berlioz was not used for ballet until years later, because it was not considered to be "ballet music" by its own culture in its own time. Adam's composition had made an important breakthrough, but significant change in the emotional range of ballet music took full effect only years after the Romantic period had faded.

Technical improvements in the theater itself aided the development of the Romantic stage setting. The use of gas lighting increased the potential for atmospheric fantasy so that scene designers were able to achieve effects of breathtaking illusion unheard of prior to this time. Gas illumination made grad-ual variations in light intensity possible and dependable, thereby more closely fusing the visual effect of a painted backdrop to the emotional shadings of dra-matic content. One of the earliest lighting innovations was designed for the bal-let scene in the Meyerbeer opera, *Robert le Diable* (1831, Robert the Devil). The scenarist, Pierre-Luc Ciceri, envisioned the tombs of dead nuns in a convent cloister aglow in moonlight. Newly installed gas lighting was put to excellent use and the designer achieved ghostly shadows mingling with moon-beams.[17] Moreover, house lights were now dimmed during the performance, whereas in the previous century, the entire stage and house areas were continuously lit by several thousand candles. For nineteenth-century ballet productions, it became the custom to lower the house curtain between acts so that scenic surprises could be arranged.

In Romantic ballet, women reigned supreme for the first and only time in history because of the female-centered thematic material that always dominated the scenario. Although there were outstanding male dancers, most notably Jules Perrot, Arthur Saint-Léon, Lucien Petipa, and Joseph Mazilier, men were used to porter the idolized ballerina around the stage. Not only were they ignored and even scorned by critics of the time, but eventually they participated mostly as teachers and choreographers, their dancing roles often assumed by women *en travesti*. By the mid-nineteenth century, comparatively few male dancers were enrolled in France's professional ballet schools.

Although the lack of significant participation of the male dancer in the Romantic ballet was deplorable, the situation was not a totally negative one

144

because the emphasis on the female dancer allowed for enormous strides in the development of the ballerina's technique. Whereas bulky *paniers* and weighty skirts had impeded experimentation with the eighteenth-century dancer's physical potential, simpler costuming influenced by David's populist street wear revealed the workings of her physiognomy.[18] With more attention paid to their training, women became celebrated as performers. It was the inspiration of a number of ballet masters, in particular Blasis, Taglioni, Perrot, and Saint-Léon, that provided female dancers with the pedagogical and choreographic challenges on which their individual fame rested. Without these peerless male talents, there would have been no Romantic ballet and certainly not the bevy of Romantic ballerinas that crowned its presence. While the Romantic ballet's peak years were brief, they possessed a creative intensity that served to synthesize the cumulative results of well over a century of dance experience and experimentation into a veritable golden age.

# $\mathcal{T}$HE CREATORS

Paris was the primary locale of Romantic ballet and also represented the crucible of Europe's intellectual life. Composers, painters, writers, and dancers were drawn to the City of Light in search of the inspiration they needed for their work. These artists supported and nurtured one another, and their shared ideal was to produce art that would captivate their respective audiences without sacrificing the simplicity of their intensely personal expressions.

145

The institutional structure of the Paris Opera should have offered utopian working conditions to its artists, but the creative atmosphere had stagnated over the decades for lack of inspired leaders. The Opera's outmoded rules and conventions perpetuated by the classical establishment[19] continued to inhibit artistic expression. Thus it happened that freelance artists, independent of the Opera, pioneered the new age of theatrical dance.

Recently privatized, the Opera was currently being administered by the daring impresario Louis Véron. He was so impressed with the productions these outsiders were presenting elsewhere in Paris that he invited them to the great establishment's hallowed halls. A cluster of unique French talents from the freer boulevard theaters of Paris were joined by Italian ballet masters to work their theatrical magic under dance's most prestigious roof. Glamorous Italian and Austrian female stars were eager to unite with them to infuse ballet with renewed vitality.

## THÉOPHILE GAUTIER

The Romantic ballet's popularity and much of what we know of its dancing is due to the French author Théophile Gautier (1811–1872). He was not only a prolific and articulate critic of dance who commanded a lucid literary style, but he was also one of the finest poets of his age. As a member of an impassioned literary group that acknowledged Victor Hugo as its leader, Gautier was recognized for his mastery of words. Writing dramatic criticism for the newspaper *La Presse*, his reviews spoke of Romantic ballets through the vivid imagery of an accomplished poet. He was unchallenged at capturing in words the fleeting beauty of a movement, and his ability to pinpoint the uniqueness of a dancer's style informed and encouraged popular interest in ballet.

Gautier's fascination with dance led him to research and even create the scenarios for a number of ballets. That literary artists could provide choreographers with well-knit plots for their ballets greatly added to the quality of the final products. Furthermore, in the eyes of the cognoscenti, ballet's association with an illustrious literary figure like Gautier gave theatrical dance a distinction not previously enjoyed. While the Romantic ballet was formed by the accumulation of decades of technical knowledge, the art form triggered its unparalleled aesthetic synthesis by being grounded in the stimulating intellectual atmosphere of the epoch. Gautier himself commented that the Romantic movement was:

> . . . akin to the Renaissance. A sap of new life circulated impetuously. Everything sprouted, blossomed, burst out all at once. The air was intoxicating. We were mad with lyricism and art. It seemed as if the great lost secret had been discovered, and that was true. We had discovered the lost poetry.[20]

While Gautier was influential in his roles both as a poetic story-weaver and dance critic during the Romantic age, his interests were shared by a number of prominent contemporaries, namely Eugène Scribe, Jules-Henri Vernoy de Saint-Georges, Adolphe Nourrit, and Charles Nuitter. Together, these men and others of lesser fame produced ballet narratives that projected dream worlds and local color. Guided by a wealth of literary personalities, choreographers were able to stir emotions and ignite the imaginations of an audience as never before.

## CARLO BLASIS: THEORIST AND TEACHER

Carlo Blasis (1797–1878) was not only a central figure in the development of the Romantic ballet, but twentieth-century ballet, which is witness to the most incredible virtuoso feats, is greatly indebted to his pedagogic theories. Born in Milan and educated in the classics, painting, sculpture, and music, as well as dance, he had the best possible background for a choreographer and teacher. One of his students, Claudina Cucchi, remembered that he wanted his pupils to read extensively so that they would dance with genuine grace and elegance, something he thought was achieved only by a refined training of the soul and mind.[21] He studied in Bordeaux with Dauberval who rigorously instructed him in the precepts of Noverre. He attributed much of his technical development to the time-honored tradition upheld in the old French school of Pierre Gardel. He also trained in the classes of Auguste Vestris, from whom he learned the *pirouette* and that he later analyzed so meaningfully for his own students.

Blasis gave up performing at an early age due to a leg injury. During a stay in England, he published his magnum opus on dance, *The Code of Terpsichore* (1828), which became the standard for European ballet instruction and formed entire generations of dancers. Blasis's pedagogic method perfected the aerial and floating qualities of dancing called for in Romantic ballets. His book not only set forth the history and aesthetics of ballet, but also its technical theory, rooted in the *danse d'école*, expounded many of the same formulas still in use today. Blasis methodically applied the physical laws of equilibrium to the human body, and this approach gave rise to our current understanding of balance, placement, alignment, centeredness, and turnout. His geometrical interpretation of the body with respect to classical ballet positions developed in his students a sense of the same body placement and alignment that today's dancers strive to achieve. Blasis became the most important individual ballet teacher of the nineteenth century.

The structure of the twentieth-century ballet class stems from Blasis's three-part class. The *barre*[22] exercises develop the human instrument and progressively train the body to form the proscribed classical shapes. The exercises are then repeated without the support of the *barre*. In the final phase of the class, all the elements of the *barre* are transformed into dancing with the addition of jumping and turning movements. Blasis made a point of analyzing various body types and discussing how certain physical characteristics of a dancer related to his unique style and movement qualities. He reinforced his theories by illustrating the manual with fluid drawings that reflect the consummate grace, elegantly balanced poses, and well-placed torsos stipulated in current teaching methods.[23]

In 1837, Blasis was installed as the director of the *Accademia di Ballo*, the Imperial Academy of Dancing and Pantomime in Milan. Due to the introduction of his stringent methods into the Academy, Italy recovered its reputation as an important European dance center. From this citadel were developed dancers and teachers who spread his precepts across Europe, and in time, the world. At a point when the cult of the ballerina was in ascendancy, Blasis showed a favorable bias toward the instruction of the male dancer.[24] Discoursing on many of the pedagogical notions of the day, Blasis improved and enlarged the technique of Romantic ballet. He devised long combinations of steps known as *enchaînements* to develop lung capacity, leg strength, and stability so that the dancer could cope with the new complexities that choreographers were inventing. So swift was the technical development that only a generation earlier had a rich variety of individual steps been unheard of. A great artistic personality, Blasis's personal contacts and direct efforts extended to the ballet school in Moscow. Russia is indebted to him for instilling a tradition of revering precision and purity in technique regarding the schooling of its own dancers.[25] After Blasis's lifetime of solid contributions to ballet, his influence continued to be

147

felt. A generation later, Blasis's prize pupil, Giovanni Lepri, taught Enrico Cecchetti, who became in turn a teacher in Russia and the company teacher for that amazing Russian exodus of Diaghilev dancers.

## MARIE TAGLIONI: SYMBOL OF ROMANTIC BALLET'S GOLDEN AGE

The earliest and the most renowned of the Romantic ballerinas, Marie Taglioni (1804–1884) was trained by her father, Filippo Taglioni (1777–1871), an Italian ballet master at the Paris Opera who molded, coached, and choreographed for her. She also worked with her father's old friend and colleague, Jean-François Coulon (1764–1836), one of the most prominent teachers of the day. Marie Taglioni's effect on dance technique was both revolutionary and extensive. In the sense that she was the instrument of her father, Taglioni was one of the very few ballerinas ever to have assisted in creating a new style of dancing.[26] After the extraordinary debut of her art, novel for its effortless perfection and poetic transfiguration, all the dancers who saw her wished to "Taglionize" their own technique. It was said that no language could describe her motion and that "[s]he floats like a blush of light before our eyes . . . to distain the earth, and to deliberate her charming motions in the air."[27]

148

While Marie Taglioni did not originate dancing *en pointe*, she was the first ballerina to meaningfully incorporate the feat into her performances as the ultimate artistic expression of the unworldly aspects of Romantic ballets. *Pointe* work was simply an inseparable part of her style. Until then, dancers were known to display their strength by occasionally rising *en pointe*, but this was generally viewed as a trick and no precise techniques had yet been devised to teach its accomplishment. Prior to Taglioni, various written and graphic accounts indicate that when dancers were seen to rise *en pointe*, there were few examples that were not accompanied by bulging muscles and heaving shoulders. The one exception to this seems to be Magri's glowing description of Pitrot performing the *tordichamp en pointe*.[28] Under the relentless eye of her father, Taglioni presented the world with an effortless quality in her dancing accompanied by an artful use of the *pointes*. Thereafter, every principal female dancer was obliged to follow suit, and once the artistic and technical possibilities of dancing *en pointe* were understood, the ballerina became supreme, while the male was relegated to the demeaning role of her porter.

Despite a slight deformity in one shoulder and arms considered too long, Taglioni's stage presence transcended her defects. Her lightness was something that had been envisioned by her father and developed in her by his skill as a teacher. Various accounts tell how she religiously devoted two of her six hours of daily practice to foot exercises that made her soundless landings the sensation of Paris. Under Filippo's tyrannical eye and to the point of fainting, she worked at special exercises to maintain the pliability of her leg joints.[29] In preparing for her debut at the Paris Opera, she secretly rehearsed a solo to be inserted into the opera *Le Sicilien*. Coulon, who was coaching her, observed that

Marie Taglioni, symbol of the Romantic ballet. Her unique artistry placed the female at the heart of theatrical dance. (Courtesy of the author.)

the wonderful spirituality of her dancing style would instill such jealousy among the Opera's regulars that they might maliciously prevent her from dancing. Consequently, on the day of the performance, only the conductor saw her dance in a rehearsal specifically called to set tempos.

Taglioni's art was the product of her father's visionary objectives as well as her own enormous effort and submission to his demanding methods. It is unfortunate that Filippo did not leave a written legacy, for surely he was a most gifted pedagogue and could have had a more fully accredited impact on posterity if we knew him better. What is certain, however, is that behind every great dancer in history there is at least one predominant and driving personality responsible for shaping the artist, regardless of the physical and emotional trauma that may occur. In view of Marie's epic career, Filippo himself certainly exemplified the concept of an outstanding artist-teacher.

Filippo Taglioni had a significant role in establishing Romantic ballet. He achieved his greatest creative work in devising ballets to display his daughter's unique qualities. His most famous composition was *La Sylphide* (1832), a benchmark in ballet history.[30] The libretto was written by Adolphe Nourrit, a tenor at the Paris Opera, and it had an original score by Jean-Madeleine Schneitzhoeffer. The ballet reflected a dramatic duality, "a radical opposition of love, sexuality, and matrimony,"[31] concerning real characters that must contend with otherworldly affection in the transcendental regions of sylphs. The story skillfully combined a rustic Scottish setting contrasted with the presence of a woodland inhabited by sylphs. Besides providing his daughter with a superlative vehicle for her talent, the production introduced the first artistic use of *pointe* work to Europe. Also new in this production was the utterly simple white costume known as the forerunner of the Romantic tutu. Reflecting the layered and full-skirted fashion of the time, the Romantic tutu evolved from women's everyday apparel and was well adapted to supernatural creatures. Gauze was slightly stiffened to produce a wispy concoction that gave the illusion under stage lighting of a transparent being. Framed within the well-thought-out story, these innovations contributed to a combination of elements that depicted Romantic ballet at its best.

A major breakthrough was made in the evolution of the *port de bras* in *La Sylphide*. Taglioni wished to bring out the contrasting effect of the gossamer sylphs in the midst of sturdy Scottish highlanders. The choreographer did so by devising exquisitely delicate arm movements in such a way that the sylphs appeared to be weightlessly responding to the pressure of the air. While the *port de bras* was derived from the strict *danse d'école* positions, the particular quality of the movement that Marie Taglioni produced was pure art. Likewise, the style of footwork reflected the differences of the real and unreal worlds. Exuberant folk dance steps of the highlanders were a marked contrast to the quality of the Sylph's ethereal *pointe* work and soundless *ballon*. *La Sylphide* contained the right balance of reality and the supernatural, which caught and held the audience's imagination by means of ingenious new production techniques.

150

Taglioni's tailored choreography, coupled with the scenario by Nourrit, enjoyed success that established the pattern of form and taste that Romantic ballets would follow from then on. *La Sylphide* is the story of James, a Scotsman about to marry his childhood sweetheart when he falls in love with a woodland sylph who appears in his house. Torn between the real and the ideal woman, the young man chooses to leave his fiancée and pursue the air-like creature. He accepts an enchanted scarf from a witch he had insulted earlier in the ballet. When he innocently places the scarf around the sylph, her wings fall off, she dies, and more sylphs appear to bear her aloft to a spirit haven. Catering to the tastes of the time, the production was an enormous artistic revelation as well as a public triumph. It was often observed, however, that every ballet that Filippo created and Marie danced in thereafter was *La Sylphide* all over again. Be that as it may, their conception, production, and interpretation of *La Sylphide* represented a perfect achievement.

The last five years of Marie Taglioni's performing career were spent with her father in Russia. Not only was her dancing received with great enthusiasm, but also her unique artistry was a bewitching novelty for theatergoers. She took an interest in the training activities of the Imperial Ballet School and singled out the talent of the future Russian ballerina, Marfa Muravieva. It was to the Taglionis' personal regret that their contracts came to an end.

Marie Taglioni formally retired in 1847, but fifteen years later she returned to the profession, as a teacher of the most promising students at the Paris

Marie Taglioni and Joseph Mazilier in the opening scene of *La Sylphide*. The portrait illustrates the contrasts in plot, choreographic style, and costuming that defined ballets of the Romantic era. (Courtesy of Jerome Robbins Dance Division, The New York Public Library for the Performing Arts, Astor, Lenox and Tilden Foundations.)

Opera. She choreographed her only ballet, *Le Papillon* (1860, The Butterfly), for her protegé Emma Livry. Taglioni also initiated the system of examinations which was still in partial use at the beginning of the twentieth century. Due to her father's mismanagement of her considerable estate, the frail ballerina lost her fortune in the 1870 war and was obliged to emigrate to London where she taught deportment and ballroom dancing to select students. Among her English pupils was the future Queen Mary.

## JULES PERROT: MASTER CHOREOGRAPHER OF THE ROMANTIC BALLET

Jules Perrot (1810–1894) was a brilliant virtuoso dancer in a time when his abilities were not in demand. Having been taught by Auguste Vestris, he commanded all the great tradition of the ballet. He had gained considerable success in his youth dancing in the boulevard theaters of Paris, namely the Porte-Saint-Martin, the Théâtre de la Gaîté, and the opera houses of London, Milan, and Vienna. Gautier, who did not care for male dancing, admitted that Perrot's art made him momentarily lose his prejudice. Rich theatrical experiences during a freewheeling apprenticeship were the foundation of Perrot's remarkable career. Recognized as the outstanding choreographer of the day, his ballets were from beginning to end entirely products of his prodigious imagination. Because he was an outsider at the Paris Opera, he responded unfettered to the undercurrents of the Romantic movement and produced a veritable outpouring of ballets.

Perrot established himself as artist equal to the greatest exponents in music and drama. His dynamic choreographic style demonstrated a heightened fusion of dance and story line that dispensed with long and tedious passages of mime. Dating from the glowing success of *Giselle* in 1841, Perrot turned out his finely conceived ballets in London, Milan, and St. Petersburg. He was a master at creating *pas d'action* in which the dance steps themselves advanced the drama. Complex ballet narratives derived from serious literature, such as *Esmeralda* (1844), *Catarina* (1846), and *Faust* (1848), unfolded exciting events that were projected by innovative choreography for soloists and *corps de ballet* alike. His extraordinary ability to set the stage in movement and breathe life into large scenes deepened the meaning and intensified the atmosphere of his ballets. Often he borrowed the groupings of pictorial artists to give his own scenic canvases greater realism and interest.[32] In longer passages of pure dance, his choreography displayed an uncanny sensitivity in utilizing the essence of a dancer's style and technical potential. Unquestionably, Perrot was the most influential choreographer of Romantic ballet, and his consummate mastery achieved unequivocal autonomy for the art of choreography.

Perrot was a true descendent of Noverre whose writings he revered and carefully annotated for his personal satisfaction. Many of Noverre's principles were valid in the context of the Romantic ballet, and Perrot's talent and imagination were fed by the ideas and discoveries of his illustrious predecessor. Both choreographers were appalled with the bad taste and bad habits so long a part of ballet making; both were expert in skillfully breaking the rules of strict symmetry to obtain greater realism on the stage; both were masters at interlocking dance and pantomime; and both excelled in arousing the audience's emotions to the maximum. They shared a preference for dancers who simply and naturally expressed themselves and for choreographers who exhibited perfect taste. Perrot, so passionate in regard to his art, would have agreed with Noverre, who venomously commented that, were these things achieved in ballet, many bad dancers and choreographers would be freed for more useful work in factories and workshops![33]

## CARLOTTA GRISI: ROMANTIC MUSE

Throughout the Romantic period, vibrant creative intensity continued to enlarge the scope and popularity of the female in theatrical dance. Carlotta Grisi (1819–1899) was an Italian-trained dancer who came from an Austrian family of famous and theatrically well-connected opera singers. Although Grisi had studied ballet from the time she was a small child, she was greatly encouraged to develop her equally impressive vocal talents. At the age of sixteen she was dancing on tour in Italy when she met Jules Perrot, who was enchanted by her potential as well as her beauty and charm. On Grisi's arrival in the French capital a few years later, she became his student. With concentrated devotion, he proceeded to finesse her technique. Through sheer hard work, Perrot gave strength to her grace and tempered her natural vivacity with precision. He instilled elegance and clarity of pose into her movement style, the secrets to which Gautier said Perrot revealed solely to Carlotta.[34] Before long, she was dancing at the Paris Opera, and her special ability was noticed by press and public alike. Gautier, whose lifelong love and muse was Carlotta Grisi, wrote that she possessed strength, lightness, suppleness, and originality that placed her between Taglioni and the sensuous Fanny Elssler. It is generally thought that Grisi was the first ballerina to dance in boxed *pointe* slippers,[35] although the shoes would not be commercially produced for several decades.

## *C*HE CREATIVE HIGH POINT: *GISELLE*

In 1835, the German poet, Heinrich Heine, published *De l'Allemagne*, a collection of ancient Slavic folktales. On reading Heine's book six years later, Gautier found the perfect inspiration for a ballet that was finely shaped into a scenario by the experienced stage writer Jules-Henri Vernoy de Saint-George. Adolphe Adam extemporized the graceful and melancholy music in a week and Pierre Ciceri imbued his scenery with mystery and magic. *Giselle*, a work that came to epitomize Romantic ballet, was the artistic high point of the period because of its remarkable synthesis of scenario, choreography, music, decor, and lighting.

153

While *Giselle* was being created, *La Sylphide* was not yet ten years old, and in the evolving nature of ballet, many of the 1832 innovations were borrowed and grew into conventions. For example, the Romantics' obsession with the fragility and decay of feminine beauty was startlingly effective when expressed in the medium of dance. The concept of the heroine as a chimerical creature, superior to the man she loves, found renewed potency in the second act of *Giselle*, as well as later ballets. Another similarity to the production of *La Sylphide* was the style of costuming. Colorful peasant clothing matched the rustic settings in the first acts of both ballets while tight bodices, wings, and pale bell-shaped skirts were worn by the phantom creatures who appeared in the forests during the second acts of each ballet.

Enflamed by the excitement of the Romantic movement, Gautier and Perrot were convinced of Grisi's potential to realize their inspiration. According to his own account, Gautier had been thinking of the lovely Grisi when his idea for *Giselle* first took shape. Both men, eager to produce the new project, devised the heroine in their ballet collaboration with Grisi in mind. As a happy consequence, the role of Giselle became Carlotta's triumphant vehicle for the next eight years and its interpretation was her most significant contribution to the

Carlotta Grisi and Lucien Petipa in the *pas de deux* from *Giselle*, Act I. (Courtesy of Jerome Robbins Dance Division, The New York Public Library for the Performing Arts, Astor, Lenox and Tilden Foundations.)

154

profession. For the premiere, Grisi was partnered by Lucien Petipa, the Opera's handsome leading male dancer. Jean Coralli, ballet master of the Opera, was listed as the official choreographer for the ballet, although it appears certain that Perrot created the choreography for all the scenes in which Grisi and Petipa danced. Since Perrot was not an official member of the Paris Opera, he could not collect royalties for his work, nor could his name appear on the program. Writing about the ballet's poignant conclusion arranged by Perrot, Gautier remarked that many eyes prepared merely to gaze upon *ronds de jambes* and *pointes* were unexpectedly dimmed by tears. The choreographer's satisfaction was obtained, no doubt, from Carlotta's unparalleled success in the role, for by this time the two had become lovers.

The story of *Giselle* was rooted in Gothic legend, but theatrically sharpened by its authors. Gautier's initial inspiration foresaw the story's possibility as a danced version, while Saint-Georges' dramatic fine-tuning actualized the scenario. Giselle, a peasant girl, falls in love with a nobleman who keeps his aristocratic identity a secret. When Giselle discovers the truth, she succumbs to madness and kills herself with his sword. In the second act, the guilt-ridden prince carries lilies to Giselle's grave and is surrounded by wilis, the ghosts of young women who have died unrequited. Giselle has joined these will-o'-the-wisps and is commanded by their queen to dance her beloved to death. As the night wears thin, however, Giselle's intense and pure love, still powerful in death, spares the young man. In true Romantic spirit, he is remorseful but cleansed of his guilt, and she vanishes into her tomb.

Eight months after the premiere, the cause of Giselle's death was changed from a self-inflicted sword wound to that of a weak heart. Since the ballet was to be seen in London, it was felt that the story should be more to British tastes. Gautier advised Perrot that because *Giselle* was melodramatic and sentimental in essence, the English critics would not take kindly to misplaced histrionics of Shakespearean magnitude. The change in the cause of Giselle's death was made to a weak heart and the ballet was well received in the land of the Bard.[36]

*Giselle*, more than any other ballet of the era, was a milestone in establishing the choreography as the central means for communicating a narrative. In other words, the choreography was primarily conceived to present dancing for its own sake in a perfectly contrived dramatic frame. *Giselle's* story line was not relayed by formal pantomime, nor was the story meant to moralize. Rather a compositional device, termed the *leitmotiv*,[37] was introduced by Perrot. Various ballet steps and gestural motifs clearly associated with each character and corresponded to recurring orchestral passages. As the ballet progressed, these movement motifs and recurring musical themes accumulated, serving to act as visual and aural reminders of the characters passing from one situation to the next. In this way, *Giselle* exquisitely expressed a story through the dancing, while its musical structure underscored and reflected the meaning inherent in the choreography.

*Giselle* was not the first ballet to use the *leitmotiv*, but it is the earliest ballet to do so that is still in world repertory. The first act contains strong instances of this choreographic and musical procedure because it consists of a number of mime scenes necessary to establish the plot. One example of *leitmotiv* is the love theme for Giselle and Albrecht that is recalled in the mad scene as the first act nears the end and reappears in the second act. Another example is the pulsating, unharmonious theme associated with the jealous woodsman, Hilarion. Perrot used the *leitmotiv* effectively and with a certain freedom. Due to the unity of conception on the part of its talented creators, *Giselle* proved to be an artistic work capable of penetrating human sensitivities to a consummate degree.

155

# $\mathscr{T}$HE ASCENDANCY OF THE BALLERINA

One of the most memorable aspects of the Romantic ballet was its cultivation of the individual female dancer. The adulation of womanhood appeared as the central point in a new kind of theatrical dance. Ancient Persian poetry's cult of the sensuous-but-unattainable woman combined with the medieval cult of the Virgin Mary, and these dual elements were recreated in the Romantic ballerina. From the very first, the professional ballet had revered Louis Dupré, Gaëtan, and Auguste Vestris as its "gods." With the prestigious persona of Marie Taglioni, however, the Romantic era's ballerina became its centerpiece, demanding and receiving complete adoration in exchange for her art. Perhaps Gautier summed it up best: "She is the priestess of the chaste art; she prays with her legs."[38]

Numerous ballets were created in Paris, all attempting to emulate the success of *La Sylphide* and *Giselle*. Accordingly, with every new ballet the creator wished to acclaim a new star to follow in the footsteps of Taglioni or Grisi. Hand in hand with the ballerina phenomenon, ballet masters and teachers set about formulating the rapid growth of pedagogical innovations in classroom instruction. The new-styled *danseuse* inspired a large number of dramatic ballets built around a central female character. The negative aspect of this tendency to concentrate on training female artists resulted in so few male dancers being formed that, in time, it was necessary for women to take male roles. Although the male was scorned as a dancer, except for his respected position in Denmark and Russia, he did fill the vital roles of teacher, choreographer, and creator of the exquisite new ballerinas. We have already seen how Filippo Taglioni developed the genius of his daughter Marie, making her a legend in her own time, while Jules Perrot immortalized Carlotta Grisi in *Giselle*.

## FANNY ELSSLER: DRAMATIC DANCER

Shortly after Taglioni's historic appearance, the Austrian dancer Fanny Elssler (1810–1884) embarked on an equally distinguished career. A child prodigy, she possessed extraordinary dance qualities that were opposite those of the ethereal Marie. Elssler was an exuberant dancer, blessed with enormous powers of strength and flexibility, a brilliant command of *pointe* work, personal magnetism, and an instinctive theatrical flair. She was praised for her superb acting as well as her voluptuous style of movement with which, it was said, she drove audiences wild. All of this was capped by her enchanting personal beauty. Elssler had learned the folk dances of Spain, thus adding a colorful dimension to her work. She incorporated the lively spirit and rhythms of Spanish dances into her own staccato style of precise, quick steps on the points of her feet, called *tacquetée*.

From the moment of Fanny's debut at the Paris Opera, a spirited rivalry between Elssler and Taglioni was fueled by the Opera's director, Louis Véron, as part of a publicity campaign. The public, fascinated by the competitive ladies, was encouraged through literary commentary to join forces with the Taglionists or the Elsslerites. Before long, theatergoers were ardently supporting either the angelic floating of Taglioni or the ravishingly sensuous dancing of Elssler. As the enthralled Gautier put it, one worshipped either the Christian dancer or the pagan dancer.[39]

Elssler had been born into a family of musicians, her father and grandfather having worked in the service of Joseph Haydn. In humble circumstances, she and her older sister, Thérèse, began their dance training with Jean Aumer and Filippo Taglioni in Vienna. As children, it is thought that Fanny and Thérèse had been members of Horschelt's *kinderballett* company where they would have gained additional training and experience. From the start, Fanny was noticeably prettier and more talented, while Thérèse, who grew to be rather tall, often part-

Fanny Elssler performing "La Cachucha." The dance became her most requested solo during the two years she spent in America and Cuba. (Courtesy of the author.)

nered her in the early years of their careers. Thérèse was also to choreograph dances and re-set ballets for Fanny before the elder girl retired and subsequently married into the Prussian aristocracy.

Elssler's long career was to take her to the capitals of Europe, the United States and Cuba. So great was her success in attracting audiences that Congress adjourned for lack of a quorum on the day she performed in Washington, D.C. During her career, she danced in numerous good and bad ballets of the Romantic period while she excelled in comic and tragic masterpieces, notably *La Fille mal gardée* and *Esmeralda*. Perhaps her strongest roles, these two works showed to advantage her flair for character dancing. She mastered individual dances such as her renowned "Cachucha," which she choreographed and performed as a solo and, on many occasions, inserted into full-length ballets. Given her competition with Taglioni, Elssler insisted on performing *La Sylphide* but it was ill-advised because her physical style was not appropriate for the role of the Sylph.

Toward the end of her career, Elssler accepted engagements to dance in St. Petersburg. Like Taglioni before her, Elssler considered the opportunity to perform in Russia as the finest jewel in the crown of her professional life. Since the days of Angiolini and Le Picq, ballet had remained a very grand and honored showcase of Russian culture. Not only was Elssler fully appreciated there as a great artist, but she also felt renewed to work in the ideal circumstances offered by the Imperial Ballet. While in St. Petersburg, she collaborated with Perrot in reviving several of his ballets—to their mutual satisfaction and the public's delight. Although her physical powers were in decline, Elssler's supreme artistry as an actress made a lasting impression on the Russian public,[40] particularly in the title role of *Esmeralda*. In her private life, Elssler remained mild-mannered and serene in spite of her enormous successes. She gained considerable notoriety for her love affairs with aristocracy and wealthy bourgeoisie. In 1850, she retired and lived in Vienna until her demise in 1884. While Taglioni died forgotten and a pauper, Elssler aged in comfort and the good company of family, friends, and fortune she had acquired over many years on the stage.

## LUCILE GRAHN

Known as the "Taglioni of the North," Lucile Grahn's (1819–1907) dancing was described by Gautier as conveying melancholy, grace, abandon, and nonchalant lightness; he referred to her as a "Valkyrie walking on the snow." Ambitious and restless, she left the classroom of the ballet master August Bournonville and her native Denmark and went to Paris in 1837 to study with Jean-Baptiste Barrez, the renowned director of the Opera's ballet school. This move eventually estranged Grahn from Bournonville as well as Denmark.[41] From then on, she conquered the hearts of audiences from Paris to St. Petersburg, enjoying special successes in Germany.

Lucile Grahn became Fanny Elssler's replacement at the Paris Opera during the latter's sojourn in the United States. Elssler, who reigned at the Opera after Taglioni had gone to Russia, assumed the leading role in *La Sylphide*. Due to illness one day, Elssler was not able to appear. The director of the Opera chose Grahn to substitute in the role of the Sylph. Her aerial qualities proved her to be more suitable for the part than Elssler and thereafter the role remained, second only to that of Giselle, her most celebrated part. Lucile Grahn's career was not enlivened with the notoriety and emotional entanglements associated with the lives of other Romantic ballerinas. In 1856, she married an opera singer, settled in Germany, and in 1863 she retired from performing. At first she taught privately, but later became ballet mistress at the Hoftheatre in Munich from 1869 to 1875. Grahn assisted Richard Wagner with the staging of *Die Meistersinger von Nürnberg* and choreographed the "Bacchanale" from his opera, *Tannhäuser*. She was also responsible for the first Munich productions of *Coppélia* and *Sylvia*.

Lucile Grahn and
Lucien Petipa in
Mazilier's *Paquita*.
(Courtesy of the
Collection Theater
Instituut Nederland.)

## FANNY CERRITO

Fanny Cerrito (1817–1909) was one of a cluster of five extraordinary Romantic
ballerinas to grace the stages of Europe. While she introduced no innovative
techniques as did Taglioni and Elssler, she enjoyed a spectacular career as a
dancer. Born and trained in Naples, Cerrito became the darling of its San Carlo
Opera. After conquering the dance audiences in many Italian cities, her success
outside the country obtained for her the position of prima ballerina at La Scala
when she was only twenty-one years old. Fortunately for Cerrito, Carlo Blasis
had become the director of the Imperial Academy of Dancing and she was able
to profit from his pedagogic methods. It is well documented that *ballon* was one
of her strongest dance qualities. Cerrito's vivacious charm and stage presence
enhanced her public image in many of the now-forgotten ballets in which she
danced. Eventually, she successfully collaborated as dancer and choreographer
in several artistically interesting productions. In London, she worked with
Perrot and dazzled the public in his ballets, *Alma* and *Ondine*. In the latter
piece, which concerned itself with fanciful marine creatures, she herself devised
some of its loveliest choreography. Cerrito was so popular in England that the

press, changing the accent on her surname, adoringly dubbed her Miss "Cherry Toes."

Cerrito met and married the ballet master Arthur Saint-Léon, a virtuoso dancer, a remarkable choreographer, and an exceptional violinist. The couple's partnership produced some unusual ballets as well as considerable professional rivalry between themselves. As did all the Romantic ballerinas, the newlywed dancer continued to be pursued by the young gallants of the theater. Jealous of his adored wife and aware of his need to create, Saint-Léon chose to accept work in Russia while Cerrito continued her separate career.

Within a few years, Cerrito and Théophile Gautier collaborated on *Gemma* (1854), the first ballet to have hypnotism as its theme.[42] The ballerina not only choreographed the production, but also danced the leading role. By the time Cerrito received an invitation to appear in Russia, she was past her prime. Moreover, Russia was beginning to recognize and appreciate its native ballerinas, so that her success there was limited. Cerrito retired in 1856 and devoted herself to bringing up her daughter, born from one of her liaisons. Financially well off, she did not teach, although her keen interest in young dancers caused her to keep in touch with the dance world to the end of her life.

The era of the Romantic ballet was peopled with a host of many other good female dancers. Lisa Noblet, Pauline Duvernay, Adele Dumilâtre, and Amélie Legallois all had significant careers in Paris and London. While these dancers neither measured up to the greatest of the period nor contributed any unique additions to the art, they did their share in furthering the popularity and practice of theatrical dance. Many of them would be all but forgotten except through the tireless efforts of dance historians by whose research they live again for us in the flowery language and the faded prints of their era.

160

# Summary

Romantic ballet emerged in nineteenth-century Paris as an autonomous, full-blown artistic statement that brought audiences to laughter, tears, and exhilaration. Its distant roots ranged from the sentiments of Persian love poetry to Provençal *canzos* and to medieval folklore. Firmly embedded in the most powerful notions spawned by the Romantic movement, ballet achieved a unique significance in catering to the emotional needs of France's new middle class. The efforts of choreographers led them to discover new techniques for making movement profoundly meaningful. Hugely influenced by the passionate abandon of national folk dances that flourished in the wake of the French Revolution, choreographers uncovered a new level of the kinetic medium and joined it to their classical *danse d'école*. Like the arts of drama and music, dance fully expressed the gamut of human feelings.

Guided by the imaginations and the skill of the era's *literati*, choreographers produced marvelous theater, presenting ballets that they based on stories of human experience disturbed in its dreams and unsettled by supernatural beings. To interpret their new-style ballets, the Romantic choreographers drew from a stunning cluster of female dancers prepared for their tasks by visionary teachers. Epitomized by *pointe* technique, the ballerina's artistry was supported with greater attention to the preparation of musical scores and startlingly ambitious scenic devices, including the use of gaslight. Peaking with the creation of *Giselle*, Romantic ballet achieved landmark status in the history of the performing arts.

# Chapter Notes

1. Lisa C. Arkin and Marian Smith, "National Dance in the Romantic Ballet," *Rethinking the Sylph: New Perspectives on the Romantic Ballet*, ed. Lynn Garafola (Hanover, NH: University Press of New England, 1997), p. 12.
2. Sorell, p. 223. Centuries ago, the only explanation people had for illusory events often led to massive superstition and belief in supernatural creatures. The most realistic explanation regarding the sighting of beings like sylphs and wilis was one of a hysterical misinterpretation of nature. The combustion of gases under certain climatic conditions produced phosphorescent light on the marshy grounds of woods and cemeteries, giving rise to the sighting of phantoms.
3. Bogin, p. 10.
4. Rougemont, p. 78.
5. Ibid., p. 108.
6. Sorell, p. 177.
7. Rougemont, pp. 108–14.
8. Cheney, pp. 411–44.
9. Jody Brumer, "Redeeming Giselle," *Rethinking the Sylph*, p. 108.
10. Magri, p. 128.
11. Edwin Binney, III, *Longing for the Ideal: Images of Marie Taglioni in the Romantic Ballet* (Cambridge, MA: Harvard Theatre Collection, 1984), p. 11. Writing in her diary of Brugnoli's performance ". . . on the tips of her toes . . . ," Marie Taglioni commented that she did not find it graceful because in order to elevate herself, the dancer was obligated to make ". . . large pinwheeling efforts with her arms."
12. Special Exhibit "The Gentle Step," Summer 1996. Bata Shoe Museum, Toronto, Canada.
13. Ibid.
14. Ivor Guest, *The Romantic Ballet in Paris* (London: Sir Isaac Pitman and Sons, 1966), p. 18.
15. Ibid., p. 23.
16. Ibid., p. 43.
17. Ibid., p. 112.
18. Chazin-Bennahum, "Woman of Faint Heart and Steel Toes," *Rethinking the Sylph*, p. 123.

19. For over a quarter of a century, Pierre Gardel and his faithful minions had held the reins of the ballet at the Paris Opera, vigorously refusing change and progress in spite of the times.
20. Guest, p. 3. Gautier's use of the word "Renaissance" to describe the creative activity of the Romantics was intended to indicate the energetic spirit of the times rather than a *quattrocento* taste for antiquity. On the contrary, the Romantic period emerged from a reaction to the late eighteenth-century neoclassicism influenced by the Italian Renaissance.
21. Giannandrea Poesio, "Blasis, the Italian Ballo, and the Male Sylph," *Rethinking the Sylph*, p. 134.
22. The ancestry of the *barre* began with the sixteenth-century use of chair arms and sturdy table tops as mechanical supports to reinforce the dancer's balance. The *barre* in current usage is freestanding or affixed to classroom walls; it was introduced circa 1800. The device was derived from the bars used in the art of dressage. Eighteenth-century Austrian trainers at the *Hofreitschule* suspended show horses in slings supported by parallel bars for the purpose of teaching the animals footwork for equestrian performances. The art of ballet and the skills of dressage and fencing were highly refined in royal courts. Their proximity within palace walls allowed them to influence each other as well as borrow from each other whatever was deemed appropriate. All three activities shared certain characteristics, requiring superb coordination and excellent posture.
23. Sandra N. Hammond, *Letters on Dancing* (1831) (Princeton, NJ: Princeton Periodicals for Society of Dance History Scholars, 1990), pp. 1–6. E. A. Théleur produced an unorthodox treatise, *Letters on Dancing* (1831) that gives an idea of how widespread the interest in technique was with the period's ballet masters. His work is intriguing because it offers the reader additional insight into the style of dancers on the threshold of the Romantic ballet. Active in London, Amsterdam, and Paris in the first half of the nineteenth century, the obscureness of Théleur's career and his even more obscure writing appear to have been the result of derisive comments made by critical colleagues. Théleur took it upon himself to substitute the classical five positions of the feet for five "ground stations" and eleven "half aerial stations," claiming that while this may add complications, he wished to take into account all the richness of current developments in technique. He appears to be the first author to publish carefully drawn illustrations of dancers on full *pointe* and offers suggestions to increase foot strength in the fragile satin slippers of the day. His system of notation, which he called chirography, indicates that many eighteenth-century elements were still present in the technique, such as the *chassé* beginning in an open position and that *brisé*, did not imply a beaten step.
24. Poesio, p. 136.
25. Carlo Blasis, *An Elementary Treatise upon the Theory and Practice of the Art of Dancing* (1820), trans. Mary Stewart Evans (New York: Dover, 1968), pp. xi–xii.
26. Guest, p. 18.
27. Beaumont, p. 82. Quote from *The Monthly Chronicle*, 1838.
28. Magri, p. 128.
29. Erkki Tann, conversations (1995). In 1965, the Soviet ballerina, Ninel Kurgapkina, reconstructed Filippo Taglioni's grueling classes, which he gave to his daughter dur-

ing their years in Russia. The classes were based on the archival notebooks penned by Taglioni's Russian assistants, who documented the ballet master's methods and exercises in great detail. Kurgapkina's three-hour sessions were "set" on a selection of graduate students at Moscow's GITIS. Mr. Tann, an Estonian ballet master who participated in the project, explained that Taglioni's classes were found by the highly trained dancers to be so intense, repetitive, and debilitating that the project was discontinued after a few weeks.

30. Sally Banes and Noel Carroll, "Marriage and the Inhuman: *La Sylphide*'s Narratives of Domesticity and Community," *Rethinking the Sylph*, p. 91.

31. Ibid., p. 92.

32. Ivor Guest, *Jules Perrot: Master of the Romantic Ballet* (London: Dance Books, 1984), p. 258.

33. Ibid., p. 325.

34. Ibid., p. 34.

35. Parmenia Migel, *The Ballerinas: From the Court of Louis XIV to Pavlova* (New York: Macmillan, 1972), p. 207.

36. Mikhail Lavrovsky, conversation (1994).

37. Joan Lawson, *A History of Ballet and its Makers* (London: Dance Books, 1973), pp. 64–66.

38. Binney, *Longing for the Ideal* (Cambridge, MA: Harvard Theatre Collection, 1984), p. 7. Quote by Pierre Veron (*Le Monde Illustré*, 7 January 1882).

39. Guest, *Fanny Elssler* (London: Adam & Black, 1970), p. 81.

40. Ibid., p. 233.

41. Walter Terry, *The King's Ballet Master: A Biography of Denmark's August Bournonville* (New York: Dodd, Mead, and Co., 1979), p. 45.

42. Guest, *Fanny Cerrito: The Life of a Romantic Ballerina* (London: Dance Books, l974), pp. 142–43.

# 8

## The Romantic and Post-Romantic Ballet

The popularity of ballet with English audiences began to develop early in the 1700s with the activities of John Weaver and the frequent importation of foreign dancers and ballet masters. By century's end Noverre's many successes at the King's Theatre in London firmly established the tradition of a long and ardent appreciation of French dance. Having few proficient schools and no royally supported ballet during the Romantic era, London's vibrant public theaters relied on Paris for their continuous supply of choreographers and dancers. One of the best English ballet masters since the time of Weaver was the French-polished James Hervé D'Egville (c. 1770–c. 1837). He studied under Dauberval in France during the Revolution and, in his own words, became "a furious democrat." His successful productions for the King's Theatre, beginning in 1799, were revivals of Dauberval's action-packed ballets. With these works, D'Egville helped to bridge the gap on London stages between the time of Noverre and the imaginative creations of the Romantic age. He was also the proprietor of a dancing school and valiantly struggled to train British dancers. His efforts, however, met with unending criticism and his students only found work as *corps* dancers, supporting the foreign stars.

Throughout the Romantic era, it was French ballet artists who enhanced a variety of English theatrical enterprises. Whatever found success in Paris was soon to be seen in London. In fact, several of the finest examples of Romantic ballet were first produced on English soil by French and Italian ballet masters. It was simply an accepted practice to import French ballet to satisfy the considerable public demand. By and large, most native British dance activity was limited to ballroom dancing.

# ₽ERROT IN LONDON: *PAS DE QUATRE*

From the time of the successful London production of *Giselle*, Perrot worked steadily at Her Majesty's Theatre during its annual five-month season. He created numerous short pieces and a number of major dramatic works including *Alma* (1842), *Ondine* (1843), *Lalla Rookh* (1846), and *Odetta* (1847). Because of the brevity of his contract at Her Majesty's Theatre, he had to accept other choreographic assignments at the opera houses of Paris and Milan, and on occasion, performed in his own works. By all accounts, his professional reputation was in pace with his skill for making ballets.

In a discussion of the Romantic ballet in England, consideration of Jules Perrot's ballet *Pas de quatre* (1845, Quartet) is important. The ballet was a milestone in the development of choreography by successfully presenting dance for the sake of dance. At a time when narrative ballets filled with ethnic styles were the rage, a composition without folk elements or a story was unimaginable. With the theatrical acumen of the famous London impresario, Benjamin Lumley, *Pas de quatre* proved to be an amazing undertaking. Created as a highlight for the celebrations in honor of Queen Victoria's birthday, the choreographer was duly accorded the celebrity denied him in his own country.

Lumley conceived the idea of presenting four ballerinas together. Elssler and Cerrito had enjoyed huge success (even royal command performances) appearing in a duet in his theater two years earlier. While glittering solos by famous personalities were common, Lumley reasoned that a ballet with four of the era's greatest exponents of the art, each exhibiting her particular forte in superior choreography, would be unique. Working directly for the impresario and with all the ingenuity that his talent offered, Perrot arranged a group of exquisite variations presenting Taglioni, Grisi, Cerrito, and Grahn to an audience wild with expectations.[1] Squabbling had broken out between the spoiled Grisi and the spirited Cerrito during rehearsals in regard to who should have the privilege of dancing immediately before the revered Taglioni. Lumley advised the much harassed Perrot to decree that the more senior of the two would take the enviable place. Their diplomacy saved the day and aided in producing an extraordinary *coup de théâtre*. Gautier's eyewitness description of Perrot's work gives a colorful hint of the short *divertissement*, recalling the freshness of the choreography and its startling effect.

> The quartet commenced with an equally-balanced ensemble for the four, who had entered together simply, hand-in-hand. They then assumed posed groupings with Taglioni centered, as if paid homage by her juniors. "A quick traverse movement" led to a brisk solo by Grahn, followed by a *pas de deux* for Cerrito and Grisi, then a series of broad leaps all across the stage by Taglioni (her specialty). Each tour de force was greeted by rising applause, acknowledged by the individual dancer's curtsy. Grahn, in a brief allegro, turned on point "with dainty semi-circular hops." An andante for Grisi was all coquetry and spice.

165

This contrasted with the ensuing andantino for Taglioni and Grahn in a slower, more Romantic vein, which was interrupted by a brilliant series of turns, bounds, and balances by Cerrito. Taglioni followed in an allegro. The coda was a four-cornered contest. At the curtain call, Cerrito crowned Taglioni with a wreath of white roses while the public deluged the stage with bouquets.[2]

The set for *Pas de quatre* was a brightly lit garden landscape. The ballerinas wore bell-shaped Romantic-style costumes tinted a pale pink. Gone were the little mechanized fluttering wings of wilis and sylphs and instead the women were simply adorned with roses about their hair and on their dresses. Taglioni alone added her pearls. Although Cesare Pugni's music was not distinguished, its tuneful melodies served the purpose and has survived intact. The original cast of *Pas de quatre* gave only four performances in London although the piece continued to be danced for some years. Unfortunately, Perrot's choreography was lost, but Keith Lester created an adaptation in 1936, and Anton Dolin reconstructed the present version of the ballet in 1941. Supplying a lovely rendition of steps and poses based on A.E. Chalon's delicate prints, critical reviews, and the musical score, Dolin's work continues to be a favorite vignette of balletic art.[3]

Of major significance in the long run, *Pas de quatre* served to glorify the dance rather than the individual personality of the dancer. Perrot's choreography, contrived to show off the artistic and technical abilities of each of the brilliant artists, created a new and exciting dance form complete in and of itself. The most refined attributes of each dancer were blended with tasteful choreographic design to present virtuoso dancing for its own interest. As a result of Perrot's innovative composition, theatrical dance advanced because it demonstrated that ballet in its finest manifestation could survive without a story line and even without its original interpreters.

In the afterglow of *Pas de quatre*'s success, Perrot's last months in London were some of his most explorative. He choreographed two spectacular *grand divertissements* for Lumley's season at Her Majesty's Theatre. Perrot was breaking ground in preparing these new ballets. Springing from the experiments of storyless choreography that characterized *Pas de quatre*, *Les Eléments* (1847, The Elements), and *Les Quatre Saisons* (1848, The Four Seasons), they drew little on plot and much more on numerous dances unified by decorative themes.[4] Due to changing English tastes and different times, Perrot shifted his efforts away from the lengthy story ballets that marked his earlier efforts. Extremely popular for a few seasons, these pleasant works with their star-filled casts dominated the programming on ballet evenings.[5]

Critics were amazed that *Les Quatre Saisons*, consisting of fifty minutes of plotless dancing, could sustain audience interest. Prior to this time, choreography that demonstrated the power and the beauty of stage dancing performed for its own sake was rare. While the great works of Romantic ballet's Golden Age had been established on their melodramatic content, the gradual awareness of composing human movement for its sheer beauty took longer to dawn on choreographers.[6] Since ballet technique was making huge advancements, the

166

newness of complex *enchaînements* provided the eye with unprecedented impressions. Ultimately, Perrot's craftsmanship and his genius placed choreography on equal footing with man's other supreme artistic endeavors. Perrot left England at the end of the 1848 season, and with the absence of his talent, the salad days of London's Romantic ballet came to an end.

# BALLET IN DENMARK: AUGUST BOURNONVILLE

With the arrival in 1775 of the Florentine ballet master, Vincenzo Galeotti (1733–1816), ballet gained a foothold in Denmark and signaled the forthcoming Danish Romantic ballet. After years of working as a dancer and choreographer in Venice and London, Galeotti settled in the capital city of Copenhagen, laying the foundations of the Royal Danish Ballet. As a contemporary of Noverre and Angiolini, he was greatly influenced by their discoveries regarding the *ballet d'action*.[7] During forty years he created numerous ballets, introducing Romantic subject matter onto the Scandinavian stage. His most popular work was *The Whims of Cupid and the Ballet Master* (1786). A study in charming confusion, its story line consists of Cupid blindfolding lovers who have paid tribute to him, and then his mismatching the couples. According to the twentieth-century Danish ballet master, Hans Brenaa, *Whims of Cupid* is the oldest of all ballets to survive with its original choreography completely intact and is frequently performed in Denmark.

167

The titan of Danish ballet was August Bournonville (1805–1879) whose long career fostered an astonishing nucleus of dance activity. He had studied with his father Antoine, who was a French dancer and ballet master at the Royal Danish Opera House following the tenure of Galeotti. The elder Bournonville had been a student of Noverre in Vienna and thereby passed on the French master's precepts to his son. Later, he sent August to Paris[8] to study with Coulon and Vestris *fils*.[9] During his youth August performed widely, becoming noted for his spirited, joyful, and elegant style that has become the hallmark of today's dancing Danes. He achieved acclaim both in London and at the Paris Opera before accepting a contract in his native land in 1830 to dance, teach, and create a repertory for the Royal Danish Opera.

Bournonville was one of the most educated and cultivated theatrical personalities of his day.[10] Under his direction, ballet in Denmark flourished, becoming a national art in spite of its French origins. He was a man of high moral integrity and a strong social sense of duty. In developing Danish ballet to a new level of refinement, Bournonville's dancers came to be regarded as respectable citizens[11] while elsewhere female dancers were still blemished with the taint of the courtesan. During his career he recorded his thoughts on dance, memories of dancers, reflections on art, and accounts of his considerable travels in a triple-volume biography, *Mit TheatreLiv* (1848, 1865, 1877, My Theatre Life).

Not long after Paris acclaimed Marie Taglioni in *La Sylphide*, Bournonville created his own interpretation based on the many rehearsals and performances he had witnessed in France. The ballet was a vehicle for his promising student Lucile Grahn.[12] Having begun dancing in Denmark at the age when most children learn to walk, Lucile Grahn was an accomplished technician at sixteen. She had worked solely with Bournonville, and eventually he took her to France for further study and personal development. In addition to new choreography, the Danish *La Sylphide* (1836) boasted new music by the ballet master's countryman, Herman Lovenskjold.[13] Not wishing the ballet to be produced elsewhere and also to discourage Bournonville, the Paris Opera had asked a price for the Schneitzhoeffer score that exceeded the Dane's budget. Undeterred, he proceeded to commission an original composition when he returned to Denmark. Bournonville claimed that his version of the ballet was "completely different" from Taglioni's, having more dramatic merit, new dances and groupings, precision of execution, and greater national color that included Bournonville's taste for including regional dances in his ballets.[14] Because male dancing in Denmark did not suffer a stigma as it did in France, Bournonville was able to significantly strengthen the role of James. He was extremely critical of the Paris Opera's growing tendency to tolerate the male dancer as the ballerina's porter.

The Danish version of *La Sylphide* is lovingly preserved by the Royal Danish Ballet, and the numerous magical effects never cease to enchant the twentieth-century viewer just as they did well over 150 years ago. The Sylph still gently alights six feet from window ledge to floor without moving her legs; she still vanishes from an armchair when the Scotsman wishes to conceal her presence; she still disappears up a chimney in a wink of the eye. When the Sylph dies, she still floats diagonally upward through the stage space escorted by as many as ten beautifully grouped sylphs suspended from wires.

As Bournonville's performing days drew to a close, his creative forces produced thirty-five ballets in addition to *La Sylphide*, many of which are still in the Danish repertory. Bournonville's ballets were unusual for the Romantic period because they featured choreographically developed male roles; at one point, male students outnumbered females in his classes. Having been an accomplished dancer himself, he geared his teaching efforts toward the preparation of technically strong men who could fulfill his choreographic aspirations. In 1842 Bournonville composed *Napoli*[15] (Naples), which was inspired by a brief visit to Italy. As in most of his ballets, the Danish master interjected local color and the atmosphere of sunny foreign lands, an exotic element of Romanticism that particularly pleased his Nordic audiences.[16]

The dramatic aspect of Bournonville's ballets received his greatest attention. Not only was he painstaking with the pantomime in his choreography, but also he demanded its rigorous study by students in the ballet school. Bournonville used mimed scenes to link the situations and events in his ballet. Instead of conventional gestures, he created a chain of harmonious and picturesque poses and movements from nature or classical sculpture. His poses and movements were always in accord with the characters and their emotions, as well as time, place, and costume. The Bournonville style of mime was characterized by its clarity of meaning and its kinetic fullness; the entire body contributed to what was communicated.[17]

In 1849 Bournonville created *Konservatoriet*[18] (The Dancing School), an enchanting recollection of his student days in Paris when he attended the classes of Jean Coulon and the legendary Auguste Vestris. The two-act ballet depicted the disciplined life of the ballet students at the Paris Opera in contrast to the unrestrained hilarity of the *grisettes* of the music halls. On a deeper level, Bournonville wanted to pay tribute to his old teacher who had died a few years earlier. He incorporated an entire Vestris class in the first act; when analyzed, it proves to contain exactly the same *enchaînements* that he had learned from Vestris between 1826 and 1829 and recorded in his diaries. In addition, *Konservatoriet* included several of Perrot's male variations that were created when the two choreographers were under the tutelage of Vestris in the late 1820s. The preservation of this ballet's choreography is the most accurate account of what steps Vestris danced himself and of what he taught in the class-room.[19] Years later Bournonville again drew his inspiration from a trip to Italy and composed *Flower Festival in Genzano*[20] (1858); its charming *pas de deux* is frequently performed outside of Denmark. Once Bournonville was established at the Royal Danish Ballet, he made it a practice to use only Danish composers and employed the music of seven of his contemporaries.

Bournonville not only won high honors as an artist, but he was also widely admired as a solid Lutheran citizen and a good family man who deserved his bourgeois comforts. His personal values were reflected in his ballets, which were built on idealistic foundations. They were filled with ordinary people, the happiness of life, Christian symbols, and strong moralistic principles. Perhaps the most Danish of Bournonville ballets was *A Folk Tale*[21] (1854), which min-gled his middle class ethics with appealing whimsy in his interpretation of Romanticism. The old Danish legend tells of a nobleman's child who is switched with a troll. The child is brought up as a fairy while the troll is reared as an heiress, but all is set straight at ballet's end. As always in Bournonville ballets, emphasis was on the good traits in both human beings and imaginary creatures winning out over evil. He avoided the sinister and tragic side of Romantic fan-tasy and used goodness, purity, and justice to characterize people, supernatural beings, and situations.

The major portion of Bournonville's work celebrated the bourgeoisie stan-dards formulated by the authors of the French Revolution of 1789. That very year Dauberval had shown folksy characters in his ground-breaking comedy, *La Fille mal gardée*. Like a breath of spring air, the lives of real people were adapted to the ballet stage and were perceived to be far more fascinating than the mythological deities of old. As the naturalistic aspects of Romanticism's spiritual-versus-physical duality evolved, the door was opened wider for the entrance of the average person into ballet subject matter. Perrot employed intense realism in his great tragic *tableaux* and drew heavily on the plights of Everyman. *Giselle*,

169

*Faust*, and *Esmeralda* were rampant with notions of the injustice of the mighty toward the weak and the oppressed, who rise up against masters who clung to feudal customs. By contrast, Bournonville's body of work depicted a mission to uplift the spirit and refresh the senses. His home-loving and godly, family-man principles almost exclusively dominated the productions in what has been described as his Biedermeier style, which supported a commonly held social attitude that eroticism and the sinister endangered man's inner peace.[22]

## BOURNONVILLE'S WRITTEN LEGACY

During the course of Bournonville's career, he synthesized the most important discoveries of earlier masters in a manual written for the lifetime edification of his students. Entitled *Efterlade Skrifter* (1861, Choreographic Scriptures), it presented his theories, many of which were rooted in ideas of Noverre and Angiolini. By adapting the word "scriptures" to his purpose, the devout Lutheran elevated his solemn thoughts on dancing to a metaphysical level. The technical and artistic topics under discussion reflect Bournonville's sensitivity and wisdom as an artist-teacher. As put forth in the manual, his classes contained a variety of exercises and dance steps, although he did not emphasize the *barre* work, considering it merely to be a brief warm-up period.

The most substantial message found in *Efterlade Scrifter* is a comprehensive list of five major qualities and their subdivisions. Bournonville drew up a written guide for his pupils so they could check their own progress and hopes against his expectations. Under the general headings of the various qualities that a dancer must have, he expounded on the merits of each.

1. Regarding the physical qualities necessary for a successful dancer, Bournonville cited beauty of face and pleasing body proportions as essential. Developing a high level of musicality supports and defines these physical qualities of dance.
2. Bournonville noted that the development of intellectual qualities are learned over a period of time and are instrumental in the preparation of the dancer. Acquiring taste from careful observations of all aspects of dance as related to oneself implies artistic maturity.
3. In regard to all the important artistic qualities in a dancer, Bournonville felt that grace is foremost. While lightness is a prerequisite of the *danse d'école*, aplomb, or the manner of holding oneself well, must be present.
4. According to the Danish master, the most important quality necessary to the performer is a dynamic stage presence. Good facial projection is a reflection of inner character: the very window to the dance-artist's soul. The ability to communicate through gesture must be sensitive and clear.
5. Lastly, all these elements in a dancer can only come into being if they are rooted in the required technical qualities painstakingly described by

Bournonville. Proper head, shoulder, and hip placement over correctly turned-out legs give the body its unified solidity in space.[23]

Bournonville's classes demanded the acquisition of *ballon* and sparkling beats for the women as well as men. The tantalizing style developed in his students was distinguished by a fleetness of step that was not seen in the French or Italian schools of classical ballet training. Different approaches to elevation underlined the contrast between the masculine and feminine qualities of Danish dancing. While the men were noted for the strength and breadth of elevated movement, the women's *ballon* was characterized by lightness and delicacy crowned with lovely arm carriage.

Bournonville choreographed in such a fashion that there were no stylized interruptions in the flow of the movement. He never allowed the viewer's eye to rest on a dancer assuming a preparatory position or breaking the dance by walking to a new point of departure. When pauses occurred, they were lovely poses that he designed to be savored by the audience. He marked his style of *port de bras* with expansively defined classical positions, shaping arcs of movement that were clear, clean, and without ostentation.[24]

At the height of his creative powers, Bournonville spent a season at the Vienna Opera and from 1861 to 1864 he worked at the Opera House in Stockholm[25] before returning to Copenhagen. His personal influence in Europe was extensive while for many years his ideas were promulgated by his most celebrated students. In particular, Christian Johansson emigrated to St. Petersburg as premier dancer. Years later, at the invitation of Johansson, Bournonville journeyed to Russia where he readily exchanged ideas with the Frenchman Marius Petipa, who was actively engaged in shaping a new ballet style.[26] In old age, Johansson contributed to the artistic formation of Anna Pavlova, Vaslav Nijinsky, and the great twentieth-century pedagogue, Agrippina Vaganova.

171

# ℘OST-ROMANTICISM IN FRANCE

The courts and capital cities of Europe had slavishly followed the cultural lead of France since the style-setting reign of Louis XIV. During the halcyon days of the Romantic ballet's Golden Age, Europe still clamored for French glories. In demand were the ballet masters who reworked their wonderful creations for opera houses across the Continent. When not engaged at the Paris Opera, the great ballerinas eagerly accepted invitations to perform in Berlin, Stockholm, Brussels, Vienna, Warsaw, Madrid, St. Petersburg, and Moscow. Unfortunately, when the Golden Age's falling-off period began in Paris in the 1850s, its effects were felt far and wide. The profound seriousness of art gave way almost everywhere to a preference for lighthearted amusement. In dance halls all over Paris, the *cancan* of the untrained but adorable Jane Avril, and the equally untrained but deliciously coarse *danseuse*, "La Goulue," epitomized the diminishing taste glamourized by Parisian *grisettes*. The tragic Henri Toulouse-Lautrec recorded the extremity of the decadence in luminous chalk. A changing Europe was gearing itself up for the frenzied madness of the Belle Epoque that, in due course, came to a screaming halt at the start of World War I.

Considering the remarkable impact that the Romantic ballet exerted on the theater of its time, it is unexpected that it did not metamorphose into a new and even more splendid form of kinetic expression. As in all art, however, the Golden Age of Romantic ballet was followed by a decline in activity. Such times are necessary, for as Serge Lifar noted in commenting on the Romantic ballet, ". . . a continual exaltation would cause the heart to burst." Periodic lack of inspiration and innovation had always marked times of dormancy in the ballet until fresh vision appeared to ". . . chase away the shadows and let in the floods of light."[27]

In France, despite the fact that the ballet was housed and protected by the Paris Opera, a lack of significant new talent and public understanding of the art proved its undoing. The practical demands of a dancer's training were also ignored and contributed to a weakening of the Romantic ballet. During its creative peak, students at the Opera attended only three classes a week, which they had to pay for out of their own pockets. For some sixty boys and girls, ages six to eighteen, only two teachers were assigned to instruct all levels. Furthermore, classes in pantomime had not been taught for some time. Professional dancers studied at liberty in the "perfection classes" of the aged Vestris and Coulon who frequently taught at their private quarters, away from the theater.

Dance art declined to a shadow of its former presence although ballroom dancing occupied society as never before. Underlying the weakened state of ballet was the devastating sociopolitical fact that in less than a century, France had undergone five wars beginning with the Revolution, followed by Napoleon's continental rampage and defeat, and the downfall of three additional regimes. Indeed, the trauma to ballet art was too deep, its demise imminent. Post-Romantic ballet, the product of less talented choreographers and librettists, failed to measure up to the aesthetic feast rhapsodized about in the earlier writings of Gautier. When a worthy succession to Marie Taglioni was finally announced to the public, fate intervened. The promising Emma Livry died of burns when her costume caught fire during a dress rehearsal.[28] Remarkable as Caroline Rosati and Amalia Ferraris were, no young dancers emerging from the ranks could fill the slippers of Elssler and Grisi.

Art receded when backstage discipline floundered. More interesting were the anecdotes surrounding the ever present young swains who dallied with ravishing *danseuses* in the Opera's *Foyer de la Danse*. Missing were quality and integrity in new ballets offered at the Opera, the boulevard, and provincial theaters, for no choreographers were sufficiently developed to aspire to the lofty heights reached by Perrot. Many theaters throughout France, unable to compete with the showy extravaganzas in Paris, gave up presenting ballets altogether and closed their ballet schools.

*The Dancing School* by V. Palmaroli. The decline following the Golden Age of Romantic ballet was characterized by a lack of inspired artistic direction, creative energy, and discipline. (Courtesy of the author.)

Edgar Degas pictorially summed up the situation in numerous canvases. Of particular interest are those pictures portraying a white-haired and fragile Perrot trying to make something of a prettified collection of disinterested ladies of the ballet. In one canvas, the ballet master Louis Mérante maintains the dignity of his heritage in the *Foyer de la Danse* while encouraging his lackluster pupils to excel. Without exception Degas's ballet pictures noticeably lack male dancers. Thus, post-Romantic ballet in Western Europe was, for the most part, the anemic and crippled offspring of a giant.

## EMPIRE BALLET: ARTHUR SAINT-LÉON AND *COPPÉLIA*

The post-Romantic period in France (1850–1870) is known as the ballet of the Second Empire, referring to the presence of the Bonaparte dynasty on the Imperial throne of France. Except for a few singular choreographic ideas, no artistic innovation occurred in France from mid-century onward, although one very successful effort that played for years was Joseph Mazilier's ballet, *Le Diable à Quatre* (1845, The Devil to Pay) with music by Adam. Created around the humorous idea of mixed identities, the ballet succeeded in amusing the audience with its moralizing tone of illustrating a proverb that started a new, if minor, vogue in theatrical dance. The ballet's biggest drawing card, however, was Arthur Saint-Léon's appearance in the role of a violinist. Saint-Léon would cease dancing, and with the style and elegance of a Paganini, pick up his instrument and play at a given moment to the astonishment of the house.[29]

The one exceptional ballet of the Second Empire was Arthur Saint-Léon's brilliant comic success, *Coppélia, ou La Fille aux yeux d'émail* (1870, *Coppélia, or the Girl with Porcelain Eyes*), produced shortly before his death.[30] Based on an E.T.A. Hoffman story, the ballet combined a wild flight of imagination with a convincing examination of human psychology. Intermingling the magical sphere of automata[31] with a bourgeois setting, the ballet combined all of the best characteristics of the Romantic format. *Coppélia* stood alone as a superbly crafted example of various elements that comprised the repertory of the Golden Age thirty years earlier. Reasserting Romantic themes, the work offered a human heroine, realistic characters, and a village locale in contrast to enchanting mechanical dolls in a dark and eerie toy shop. *Coppélia's* concept drew on the much earlier tradition of comic ballet established by Dauberval's *La Fille mal gardée* in which, despite the absurd Widow Ragotte, young love wins out. Similarly, the befuddled doll maker Dr. Coppélius has a change of heart after being made a fool by the mischievous Franz and Swanhilda.

*Coppélia* had the benefit of Saint-Léon's distillation of elements of Hungarian, Polish, and Scottish national dances blended with the *danse d'école*, the superior score of Léo Delibes, and a charming use of novelty. No part of his ballet was subordinated to another and the expressiveness of the music related to the story as never before. The ballerina who interpreted the first *Coppélia*, Guiseppina Bozzacchi, had only danced the role eighteen times when Paris came under siege and all theatrical activity was suspended. Related to the hardships of the war, she contracted smallpox and died on her seventeenth birthday. And so, another promising talent and her great choreographer were lost to the dance world.

Symbolically reflecting the times, the automata in *Coppélia* suggested the dawning age of world mechanization and the sinister prospect of machines running amok. Not less significant, by 1870 the Renaissance's confident pronouncement of humanity as the center of the universe (an idea that had prevailed for three centuries) was ultimately shaken. *Coppélia* hinted at a veiled but no less real twentieth-century concept of anxiety that it revealed on the ballet stage. Under the grinding cogs and wheels of mechanical creatures in Act II, the distraught old Coppélius is utterly disoriented in the chaos created by his very own inventions.

What kept French ballet barely alive, although not healthy, was the institutionalization of a company and school within the structure of the Paris Opera. With the creation of ballets like Mazilier's *Paquita* (1846) and Saint-Léon's *Pâquerette* (1851), more and more themes tended to be repetitive. A falling off at the box office signaled a public grown saturated with the formula for making

174

Carlotta Zambelli at the Paris Opera. She stands to the left of her fellow dancers in rehearsal attire, Mademoiselles Boos, Vangaethen, and Piod. (Courtesy of the Victoria & Albert Museum, London.)

Romantic ballets. By the time the Second Empire fell in 1870, those who had ushered in, nourished, and sustained the Romantic ballet were either living in retirement, past their creative prime, or dead.

Not until the twentieth century did French ballet begin to regain its prestige as a national artistic force with the arrival of the Italian ballerina, Carlotta Zambelli. Gifted with virtuoso technique that audiences of the day were unused to seeing, her ability to display dazzling turns on *pointe* assured her supremacy. The charm and wit of her personality projected across the footlights, giving theatrical fullness to her interpretations of Giselle, Paquita, and Coppélia. After Zambelli's retirement in 1930, she continued to teach at the ballet school of the Paris Opera. Along with her French colleagues, Leo Staats and Albert Aveline as dancers, choreographers, and ballet masters, new life was breathed back into the birthplace of the profession.[32]

## ᴸUIGI MANZOTTI AND EXTRAVAGANZA: *EXCELSIOR*

In Italy the music-loving populace preferred the melodic operas of Rossini and Verdi to the shallow and lengthy ballet extravaganzas produced at La Scala. With the exceptional work of two younger choreographers, Pasquale Borri and

Guiseppe Rota, who staged powerful and compact dramatic works, Italian ballet was gradually losing public favor. However, Milan's excellent ballet academy continued to train strong dancers who practiced their art by dancing abroad as guest artists in St. Petersburg, London, and New York City. While Blasis's long-established teaching methods kept the school turning out accomplished ballerinas such as Pierina Legnani, Rita Sangalli, and Carlotta Zambelli, these dancers achieved their renown outside of Italy. Lastly, without the essential component of choreographic talent, the art of ballet stagnated in the country of its earliest origin.

Italy's post-Romantic years are memorable for a singular production entitled *Excelsior* (1881), assembled at La Scala and choreographed by Luigi Manzotti. The work focused on patriotic and historical subjects, reflecting a taste for dramatic ballet that had enjoyed a long tradition in the Italian theater.[33] *Excelsior* was an amazing mixture of theatrical show, and as an extravaganza of colossal dimensions it achieved a great success in Milan and in other countries where it toured. The spectacle portrayed the rise of civilization and the complex development of the machine age as a struggle between the Spirits of Darkness and Light. Once again, the impact of mechanization on European life found expression on the ballet stage by celebrating the invention of the telegraph, the use of electricity, the construction of the Suez Canal, and the digging of a tunnel through the Alps. An apotheosis of light and peace concluded the ballet with a "Grand Festival of Nations" that boasted a cast of five hundred people moving in precision formations.[34] Unusual for the time was the presence of some very good Italian-trained male dancers in *Excelsior*. Carlo Montanara not only took substantial dancing roles, but he also was cited for his masterful partnering. *Excelsior*'s choreographer, Manzotti, however, failed to achieve equal success in his later attempts at ballet making. Increasingly, his works became tedious repetitions of grandiose and empty presentations. The public responded with indifference to these costly reviews and critics rightly declared that such dance was not worth serious attention.

## FROM FROTHY BALLETS TO ENGLISH MUSIC HALL

In England the post-Romantic ballet, also referred to by historians as empire ballet, since it concurred with the British territorial amassment, was relegated to locales of light entertainment. The earlier recipients of many of the finest creations of Jules Perrot, London audiences sought to be amused with a variety of theatrical shows rather than elevated by art. Within a decade of the triumph of *Pas de quatre*, the ballet had descended to the popular music halls, sharing the stage with singers, comedians, and circus acts. Before that fall from grace, however, Perrot had been much in demand and appreciated by the British public for his incomparable dramatic ballets as well as his *divertissements*. Perrot's ballets of this later period never succeeded in reviving the glory of the golden years, but they did boast some achievements. While working in London, he opened the door to non-narrative ballet with *Pas de quatre*, *Les Eléments*, and *Les Quatre Saisons*, wherein the dancing itself was the prominent ingredient.

While waiting for a long-desired engagement at the Paris Opera to materialize, Perrot accepted an offer from Russia's Imperial Ballet in St. Petersburg in 1848. Fanny Elssler had engineered the invitation for him and he was attracted by the company's reputation for having an extraordinary artistic atmosphere. Russian audiences were clamoring for the highest caliber of ballet, and the Ministry of Culture had every visible means and intention of supporting it.[35] Facing the waning enthusiasm of English theatergoers for high art, Perrot left the London stage forever.

Empire-style ballet in London was dominated by the presence of Katty Lanner (1829–1908), choreographer, dancer, and daughter of the renowned Viennese waltz king. She emigrated to England where for many years she produced frothy ballets at the Empire Theatre. Included in the thirty-three ballets she set for British audiences were *The Sports of England* (1877), *Round the Town*

Adeline Genée during her years at the Empire Theatre. (Courtesy of the Victoria & Albert Museum, London.)

(1893), *On Brighton Pier* (1894), and *The Dancing Doll* (1905). Lanner's contribution to the era peaked when she engaged the Danish ballerina, Adeline Genée (1878–1970), as part of the national festivities in celebration of Victoria's fifty years as reigning Queen. So popular was Genée's stage charm that the dancer remained ten years to enchant her admiring public. In 1930 Genée had the distinction of serving as the first President of the British Royal Academy of Dance and was a founding member of the Camargo Society, England's seminal Royal Ballet.

The Alhambra was another London music hall that produced empire-style ballet. Due to its huge size, this theater specialized in ballets displaying large casts, spectacular effects, up-to-date topics and celebration themes. For its star material, ballerinas were generally engaged from the ballet school in Milan. The most famous personality to dance at the Alhambra was the pyrotechnical Pierina Legnani, whose extraordinary virtuoso feats ensured a thriving box office.

The Romantic ballet met a happier fate in Denmark. Fortunately, an artistic void in Danish ballet at that time provides present dance enthusiasts with what is perhaps the clearest picture of the lyrical quality of the Romantic dance. After Bournonville's death in 1879, his disciples regarded his life's work as sacred, and nothing of his pedagogy or choreography was allowed to change. The Bournonville ballets, their recognition of bourgeois values, style of movement, and remarkable use of pantomime were frozen in time. In that state of fortuitous preservation, they are performed today in the same manner as over a century ago.

178

# SUMMARY

A galaxy of individuals contributed to the Golden Age of ballet as it burst onto the stages of the Paris and London theaters. Not only did gifted ballet masters, teachers, and dancers shape the emerging dance art, but poets and composers also left their professional imprints. Once the artists involved in theatrical productions fully realized the possibilities opened up by their efforts, a whirlwind of creative activity enveloped them. Countless ballets replicating *La Sylphide* and *Giselle* were produced until the Romantic format exhausted itself.

It was during the Romantic period's soul-search for meaning that the ballet achieved a unique level of articulation as a communicator of emotions. The dancer's growing repertory of complex steps adapted from colorful national dances and the introduction of *pointe* work to the *danse d'école* lexicon provided additional material for the choreographer to blend with mime in the interest of storytelling. In the 1830s the dance achieved a new dimension in its potential for expressiveness when noted literary figures prepared ballet scenarios that clarified matters of the soul. In England numerous choreographic advances of Jules Perrot's *pas d'action* provided the blueprint for expressing deep feelings and high-minded ideals in dance. In Denmark, August Bournonville shaped his own interpretation of mid-nineteenth-century dance style, emphasizing the middle class desire for personal happiness to the exclusion of Romanticism's fascination with morbid and satanic elements. Maintaining the importance of the male role in his ballets, Bournonville and Danish dance avoided the decline suffered in Paris and elsewhere in Europe.

For a number of reasons, Romantic ballet ignited the public's imagination as never before. Romantic ballet arrived at a turning point when the cult of the individual ballerina began to give way to the emergence of dancing for the sake of dance, as shown in the choreographic structure of Jules Perrot's *Pas de quatre*. This brief storyless composition achieved the perfect blend of personality, technique, and choreographic design that exemplified the Romantic aesthetic: "art for art's sake."

The enthusiasm and vision on which Romantic ballet was established soon faded as its creators slipped into retirement. By 1850 the glory of the Romantic ballet's Golden Age had all but disappeared in Western Europe, burned out by the very flames that had caused its glow. Post-Romantic ballet in France and Italy languished in institutions barren of genius and passion. A new time was defining itself for Europe. Socialist author Emile Zola remarked that with the death of Victor Hugo, the great founder of nineteenth-century Romanticism, a whole civilization died: ". . . a civilization of pretty gestures, romance, artful lies, and subtle evasions . . . ," surely the quintessential elements of Romantic ballet.

# *Chapter Notes*

1. Guest, *Jules Perrot*, pp. 149–55.
2. Lincoln Kirstein, *Movement & Metaphor: Four Centuries of Ballet* (London: Pitman Publishing, 1971), pp. 158–59.
3. Koegler, pp. 318–19.
4. Guest, *Jules Perrot*, pp. 201, 221.
5. Ibid., pp. 201–2.
6. Ibid., p. 221.
7. August Bournonville, *My Theatre Life*, trans. Patricia N. McAndrew (Middleton, CT: Wesleyan University Press, 1977), p. 22.
8. Ibid., p. 27.
9. Terry, pp. 112–18. Vestris *fils* (son) refers to Auguste.
10. Koegler, p. 71.
11. Bournonville, p. 78.
12. Ibid.
13. Ibid., p. 79.
14. Ibid.
15. Ibid., pp. 88–95.

16. Ibid., pp. 88–90.
17. Terry, p. 153.
18. Bournonville, pp. 181–88.
19. Knud Arne Jürgensen, *The Bournonville Ballets: A Photographic Record, 1844–1933* (London: Dance Books, 1987), p. 57.
20. Bournonville, pp. 268–72.
21. Ibid., pp. 205–11.
22. Erik Aschengreen, "The Beautiful Danger: Facets of the Romantic Ballet," trans. Patricia N. McAndrew. *Dance Perspectives*, 58 (Summer 1974), p. 46.
23. Bournonville, *Études chorégraphiques dediées è mes élèves et mes collègues* (Copenhagen, 1861). The same year that *Efterlade Skrifter* was published in Danish, a version of the book appeared in French, parts of which were paraphrased for this volume.
24. Hans Brenaa, Conversation. 1980.
25. Bournonville, pp. 513–29.
26. Ibid., pp. 574–83.
27. Guest, *The Ballet of the Second Empire: 1858–1870* (London: Adam & Charles Black, 1953), p. v.
28. Ibid., pp. 30–38. Guest gives a touching account of one of ballet history's saddest human tragedies.
29. Guest, *The Ballet of the Second Empire: 1847–1858* (London: Adam and Charles Black, 1955), p. 44.
30. Guest, *Second Empire, 1858–1870*, pp. 107–31.
31. Kirstein, *Movement & Metaphor*, p. 170. A favorite, and usually successful, device on the ballet stage for creating illusion and fantasy, automata are metaphors for the unguessed possibilities in raw materials whether they be machines or humans.
32. Guest, "Carlotta Zambelli: Part Two," *Dance Magazine* (March 1974), pp. 44–56.
33. Poesio, "Blasis, the Italian Ballo, and the Male Sylph," *Rethinking the Sylph*, p. 133.
34. Margot Fonteyn, *The Magic of Dance* (London: British Broadcasting Corporation, 1980), pp. 83–85. See illustrations.
35. Guest, *Jules Perrot*, pp. 224–29.

# 9

# *The Evolution of Ballet in Russia*

While the Revolution of 1789 had disrupted theater arts in France, it promoted a vigorous acceleration to the growth of the ballet elsewhere. Many dancers at the Paris Opera fled the country to find employment and opportunity in England, Scandinavia, and other parts of Europe. Thus, the composite of knowledge embodied in the technique of the *danse d'école* and the story telling of *ballet d'action* as amplified by Noverre and his contemporaries was widely disseminated by French dance artists. Since the ballet was still subjected to Gardel's old-guard conservatism entrenched in the Paris Opera, France relinquished its position as the mecca of theatrical dance. Recently aroused from its primordial sleep, Russia was to become the country that championed the progress of ballet.

From earliest times, Russian folk dance flourished as one of the most colorful human activities indigenous to that vast and remote land. The most noteworthy characteristic of all Russian folk dance was an intimate connection between the movement and the melodic line. The extreme musicality particular to Russian dancing is quite natural, reinforcing the notion that Russians have always displayed a national genius for the art of movement. The earliest known forms of Russian dances were spontaneous circle-and-line patterns called *khorovod* that, in part, stemmed from heathen religious rites. They were performed solely by women, as was the custom of the Muslim Tartars, to unaccompanied folk songs as part and parcel of an evolving Slavic culture. Enriched by the steps and rhythms of exotic influences from Tartar and Mongolian invaders, native Russian dancing, enhanced with exuberance and joined to grace, took on a special look. Whether in their simplest folk dances or the most complicated stage forms of dance, Russian performers have long been acclaimed for dancing with the entire body, giving the impression that the dancer is full of music.

As early as 1250, versatile entertainers known as *skomorokhi* roamed the land providing street entertainment for the general population with juggling, joking, comic songs, and virtuoso acrobatic stunts. On occasion bands of dancers joined the *skomorokhi*, contributing to the show with their energetic folk dances called *pliaski*. The *skomorokhi*'s popular antics were curtailed in 1551 because their performances included satirical commentary on the hypocritical lifestyles of some of the Russian Orthodox Church leaders. A long period of persecution of the *skomorokhi* followed, causing them to migrate northward. Many settled on the immense estates of prominent nobility in the environs of Moscow. Here they were welcomed, perfecting their most dominant talents in a more sheltered setting. Those with superior musical ability concentrated on becoming masters of their instruments, while the dancers among the *skomorokhi* were able to expand their dancing techniques. Officially outlawed by the autocratic Orthodox Church, *skomorokhi* were actually cherished in the household of the czar as well as his noble boyars. Their performance in festive revels was considered to be of paramount importance.[1]

During the years when Louis XIV was embellishing his reign with splendid court ballets, word of these royal functions trickled into far-off Russia via returning diplomats and other travelers. Russian archives recorded sincere attempts to reproduce "French entertainments" for the Romanov court. Without the institutional superstructure and awesome talent commandeered by a Lully or a Beauchamp, these early productions were undoubtedly mere shadows of their French inspirations. In any event, Russian efforts at spectacle-making met with approval and encouragement from the ruling class. Around this time there was even a feeble undertaking afoot to train impoverished children in the skill of dancing so that Russia might develop its own expertise. However, a serious venture to introduce formal dance in Russia came only after the reign of a young and ambitious leader determined to break with centuries of isolation and tradition-bound ways.

## PETER THE GREAT: A WINDOW TO THE WEST

In 1697 the new Russian Czar, Peter the Great, made an incognito tour of Europe and became enamored with Western culture.[2] Wishing his own land to forsake its heavy cloak of medievalism in order to usher it into the European sphere, Peter began the habit of importing numerous artists, artisans, architects, engineers, and scientists to develop Russia. One of his earliest projects, and certainly the most arduous and labor intensive, was creating a new capital city, which he founded on the marshy shores of the Baltic Sea. Supported on a bed of millions of tree trunks forced upright into the mud, massive stones, gravel, and earth, St. Petersburg grew into one of the most beautifully planned cities ever built. Named for the czar's patron saint, the city soon shone with Italian-styled palaces elaborately decorated in the Austrian manner. Most obvious in its reflection in the rivers and canals, St. Petersburg represented a bridge from old to new, from the darkly Byzantine to the eighteenth century of Western Enlightenment.[3]

Implementing the transition from the past, Peter went about making radical changes based on German influences long felt at the Russian court. Virtually overnight, his boyars were commanded to cut their great beards, don wigs, and powder their faces. Off came their floor-length and fur-lined robes to be replaced by frock coats, satin breeches, silk stockings, and heeled and buckled shoes. Noblewomen, released from their seclusion in the *terem*, more willingly underwent external changes. Forsaking their *kokoschniki* or traditional head-dresses and *kaftans*, which were heavy and beltless court dresses, they readily adapted to teased and powdered coiffures, daring *décolletages*, and wide skirts extended by *paniers*. Within half a century, Western etiquette was imposed without mercy on a semi-barbaric nobility distantly separated from Western Europeans. Struggling with the refinements of eating with knives and forks, following the intricacies of court protocol based on continental standards, and above all, mastering French (the official court language during the reign of Peter's daughter Elizabeth), must have prematurely aged many a boyar and his boyarina.

Peter was intensely curious and impressed with all aspects of European culture during his grand tour of the Continent. On his travels he first saw theatrical dance when he attended the ballet *Cupidon* in Amsterdam. While a visitor in the French capital, he grew particularly fond of the lavish *ballets mascarades* so popular with Parisian society, and eventually instituted them at his own court. As a result, a fledgling theatrically touched ballroom dance form was introduced into Russian court life. Peter commanded his nobles, as part of their Westernization, to attend his "assemblies," wherein participation in European social dancing, taught by imported instructors, was obligatory.[4] Interestingly enough, it was during Peter's reforms that the word *tanets*, meaning dance as a formal body of steps, was introduced into the Russian language.[5] The event signaled a liberated attitude toward social dance as a legitimate part of the new culture. Prior to this time, the native folk dancing had been performed by skilled peasants for the entertainment of the ruling class. It would seem that the latter had been content to participate only as enthusiastic observers.

## ℒANDÉ AND THE *DANSE D'ÉCOLE* IN ST. PETERSBURG

Keeping with the precedent for importing Western culture, Peter's successor, the Czarina Anna, commissioned the French ballet master, Jean Baptiste Landé (died 1748), to teach court dances to cadets. All young nobles endured a period of compulsory military service in Russia, and part of the experience was dutiful attendance at official court balls. From the moment of his arrival at the St. Petersburg quayside in 1734, Landé was impressed with the energetic folk dancing that he witnessed while waiting to disembark from the ship. Delighted with the natural aptitude of his Russian pupils for ballroom dances, Landé soon won permission to instruct them further in the steps of the *danse d'école*. Several years later, he presented over 100 of these students as a *corps de ballet* in the finale of Francesco Araja's opera *La Forza dell'amore e dell'odio* (1736, The Force of Love and Hate), marking Russia's first professional ballet *divertissement*.[6]

With generous aid from the czarina and influential courtiers, Landé founded the St. Petersburg Ballet School in 1738. He chose for his three-year program twelve boys and twelve girls who were orphans of deceased palace servants. Daily classes were held in two rooms of the house where Landé and his wife lived before the school moved to the imperial palace. From ballet's inception in Russia, therefore, an educational institution filled with young aspirants was established to continuously supply performances with professional dancers.

Following the teaching tenure of Landé, Antonio Rinaldi, also known as Fossano (died c. 1760), took over the training of the Russian dance professionals.[7] The new ballet master was a prominent leader of a traveling troupe of *commedia dell'arte* players who had first come to Russia from the Meissen court of Augustin the Great around 1730. Highly praised by Noverre, Fossano was famous for both his comic and character dancing as well as his pantomimic skills. His virtuoso technique displayed acrobatic *tours de force* that, it was said, he tempered with good taste. Catering to his Russian students, Fossano introduced movements into their vocabulary that included complex steps of elevation and beaten steps called *batterie*. The Italian *commedia dell'arte* had become highly sophisticated with a technique of its own and it was probably the likes of Fossano who first coached the Russians in the *danse noble*, *demi-caractère*, and *grotesque* categories of ballet styles.

Formally introduced to the *danse d'école*, Russian dancers already versed in their national folk dances pronounced the new language in their own way,[8] creating a unique synthesis of Slavic ballet. While a small number of the dancing masters and a large *corps* of the dancers were Russian, the choreographers and soloists were obtained from France or Italy for their superior expertise and audience appeal as foreign artists. Thus, professional ballet was brought to Russia, an immense backward country that was totally untouched by the momentous changes in human life introduced during the West's great Renaissance period.

# IMPERIAL BALLET: FROM HILVERDING AND ANGIOLINI TO VALBERKH

Many events conspired to provide Russian theatrical dance with a healthy atmosphere for growth and refinement. Contributing largely to the quality of Russian ballet was the criterion for importing the very best talents from Europe. Upon the request of Anna's successor, the Czarina Elizabeth, fellow empress

Marie Thérèse of Austria sent her court ballet master, Franz Hilverding, to St. Petersburg to contribute to the embellishment of Russian court life. Based on his reputation as an innovative choreographer, he was asked to upgrade the general level of performances and to introduce the "new taste" in ballet to the Russian court.

Hilverding worked in St. Petersburg from 1758 to 1764, teaching and coaching Russian dancers and revising and creating ballets. Although he took a number of dancers with him, he was interested in training talented Russians, just as he had developed artists in his native Austria, and this he did with admirable success. Hilverding's work marked the beginnings of *ballet d'action* in Russia, as the plots of his wordless ballets were painstakingly supported by generous amounts of pantomime to advance their stories. Unlike European ballet, Russian ballet never had to struggle to remove itself from the service of opera. From the very beginning, theatrical dance was treated as a self-directing entity.

Hilverding introduced comic ballets incorporating local scenes, Slavic dances, and humorous situations taken from everyday life. It was recorded that he was the first teacher to introduce to the St. Petersburg students a *pirouette* after the four beats of an *entrechat quatre*.[9] One of his last tasks before leaving Russia was preparing a ballet for the coronation of Elizabeth's successor, an anacreontic work entitled *Amour et Psyché* (1762, Love and Psyche).[10]

So favored was the presence of ballet in Russia that the next czarina, Catherine the Great, founded in 1766 the Directorate of the Imperial Theaters. This institution gave enormous status and support to the development of all the performing arts, but especially to that of ballet.[11] While Peter had given Russia a window to the West, Catherine established the country as a European power. Organizing and profiting from Russia's immense natural wealth, Catherine acquired from France entire collections of paintings, sculpture, artifacts, and books, handsomely expanding her palaces to house the many thousands of objects. On a magnificent scale she acquired the best of Western culture for St. Petersburg. In all, four imperial theaters were designated to replace the *poteshnaia palata* that had been built around 1640 by the first Romanov ruler, Mikhail. These had served as select places for special amusements in the palace complex, but were hardly suitable for the production of Western-style ballet, opera, and drama. Therefore, in both St. Petersburg and Moscow, a large theater was ordered for ballet and opera productions and a smaller one for dramatic presentations.

The Directorate laid the foundations for what would be in time an enormous institutional apparatus for the training of personnel in the performing arts and in all the production aspects of dance, music, and drama. In 1773, Catherine called for the establishment of a theatrical school in Moscow. The ballet school that the Directorate set up was placed in the care of an obscure Italian ballet master, Filippo Beccaria, and his wife. The couple began the instruction of academic dance in an orphanage for children born to parents who had worked as bureaucrats in government offices or at court as gardeners, cooks, valets, etc. Thus, orphans of civil servants became the institution's first

185

dance, music, and drama students. Once finished with their ballet schooling, most dancers were engaged to entertain the Imperial Court in St. Petersburg. Completely autonomous and self-sufficient, the result of the Directorate's grand plan was so successful that it continues to function today.

As Russian theatrical dance developed, it was augmented by a unique Slavic phenomenon, the private serf theater. During Catherine's reign, wealthy landowners, emulating the imperial support of the ballet, instituted satellite ballet schools and built private theaters on their great estates. Among many, the Sheremetiev, Golovkin, Yussupov, and Apraxin families all employed foreign dancing masters to instruct their serfs in performing the strict *danse d'école*, in addition to refining their brilliant native folk dances. Serf dancers,[12] a class of performers unique to Russian culture, were wonderfully skilled artists whose lives centered on dancing classes, rehearsals, and working in the fields. Frequently they were bartered or sold to other estates, while others remained to dance in the service of their owners. One of the most widely recognized supporters of serf dancers was the director of the Imperial Theaters, Count Nicholas Sheremetiev. In his wooden palace at Ostankino, outside Moscow, he staffed his own theater with 166 serfs, twenty-six of who were dancers trained and coached by Noverre's favorite student, Charles Le Picq. Due to the expense of their training, the custom of retaining serf dancers ceased to exist in the early 1800s and the Imperial Theaters absorbed the remaining serf dancers and musicians for their expertise.

In 1783 Catherine decreed that St. Petersburg's Bolshoi would be the crown's premier imperial theater. It maintained the St. Petersburg Ballet School as its training center, which now also functioned under the Directorate. The theater itself was to be used exclusively by the aristocracy, for whom it showcased the best dance talent coming out of the institution prefigured by Landé. In time, the Imperial Ballet would move to Russia's first stone theater, the Bolshoi Kamenny, and when it burned down, to the Alexanderinsky Theater and later, the sumptuous blue and gold Maryinsky.

The Italian ballet master Gasparo Angiolini, Hilverding's former student, succeeded his teacher at Empress Catherine's Imperial Ballet in 1766. Angiolini stayed in Russia longer than any foreign ballet master up to that time. From the beginning he enjoyed great success with his heroic ballet, *Didon Abandonnée* (1766, Dido Abandoned), in which he substituted pantomime to relay the plot, omitting operatic arias.[13] Abhorring long-winded *livrets*, he took great pains to dramatize his works with concentrated action and gesture.[14] Over the next twenty years, during three extended visits to Russia, Angiolini mounted old and new productions, ever striving to balance the elements of dance, drama, and orchestral score. He emphasized the necessity for economy of stage business to clarify and strengthen the dramatic impact of his ballets, which included *Don Juan* (1761) and *Orpheus et Eurydice* (1762). An extremely musical choreographer for his era, he constantly endeavored to show the relationship between movement and music.

Angiolini was committed to drawing psychologically sensitive characterizations out of his Russian dancers. He believed ballet had the potential to deeply stir the emotions without the traditional use of spoken or sung words. When works were created to produce genuine emotional response from the audience, he reasoned that the art of dance showed its greatest beauty. Eventually he chose stories inspired by Russian history and folklore for his subject matter, not only writing the *libretti* but the music as well. Based on his musical qualifications, Angiolini eventually attempted to construct a system of dance notation.

Charles Le Picq replaced Angiolini when the latter finally left his post at the Imperial Ballet. While not especially creative in his own right, during his twelve-year stay, Le Picq met with great success staging the works of his old teacher Noverre. Due to the fact that Le Picq managed to have the definitive version of Noverre's *Lettres* published in Russia, the master's precepts of *ballet d'action* became available in 1803 to the French-reading theatrical circles.[15] Although Noverre himself never stepped foot on Russian soil, the Russian audiences developed a profound appreciation of his aesthetic philosophy as it manifested itself in the ballets set by Le Picq. Undoubtedly, the works also benefited from the lavish production budget of the Imperial Ballet. Noverre's emphasis on the importance of expressiveness in dancing found fertile ground in the passionate Russian personality. To be sure, his progressive balletic ideas put forth in the *Lettres* were seriously received by his Russian readers.

Ivan Valberkh (1766–1819), a pupil of Angiolini, was the first native Russian ballet teacher and choreographer of note.[16] Upon his graduation in 1786 he danced under the direction of Le Picq and was imbued with Noverre's precepts, which greatly augmented his dance education. Valberkh experienced first-hand Noverre's criticism of the rigid and decadent style of the Paris Opera and the revolutionary *fêtes* that he observed during a brief visit to France in 1792. His own ballets therefore reflected careful preparation, using the advanced ideas on mime and dance of Noverre and Angiolini. In his thirty-six ballets Valberkh frequently created characters drawn from historical and literary personalities. His most famous and successful ballet was based on Goethe's novel, *Die Leiden des jungen Werthers* (The Sorrows of Young Werther) from which he derived *The New Werther* (1799).[17] With his unique artistic perceptions, Valberkh inaugurated a move toward the sentimental in Russian ballet that resulted in rousing works on political themes. It is this emotional trend in his work that marked him as a genuine forerunner of the Romantic era in Russia as well as a choreographer of *ballet d'action*.

Valberkh was the first Russian to be appointed director and manager of the Imperial Ballet School in St. Petersburg in 1794. He was responsible for strengthening the curriculum and upgrading standards at the school. From the beginning of his tenure, he was a fierce advocate for Russian dancers who were often overlooked in the presence of imported performers from France and Italy. Throughout his career and until his death, Valberkh formed a number of excellent Russian artists who were, by many accounts, on a par with their European peers. One of the most notable was Eugenia Kolosova; it was said that her glances and gestures were more meaningful than speech. Kolosova's great personal beauty was underscored by the effectiveness of her dancing, making her the pride of her teacher.

# CHARLES-LOUIS DIDELOT: FATHER OF RUSSIAN BALLET

A decisive factor in the course of Russian ballet was the arrival of Charles-Louis Didelot (1767–1837). Count Sheremetev, a great lover of musical theater (he even married a serf dancer), had been instrumental in contracting the French ballet master. Although ballet had existed in Russia for sixty years prior to his arrival, it was Didelot who laid the foundations for the great artistic achievements to come. Working in St. Petersburg during two extended and highly productive periods, Didelot transmitted classical academic elegance to the fledgling Russian ballet. By numerous reliable accounts, his productions and his dancers were considered to be sheer magic.[18]

Didelot was the son of a Frenchman who had been first dancer and choreographer at the Royal Swedish Theatre. When the young Charles-Louis displayed a talent for the art, the Swedish king sent the boy to study in Paris. As a student of Dauberval, Noverre, and the Vestris family, Didelot had exceptional training in the tradition of the *danse d'école*. He danced in the finest ballets of the time, and for a few years he even performed in France's deplorable revolutionary ballets.[19] Didelot also gained extensive experience dancing in the theaters of Lyons and Bordeaux. As an outsider he suffered the same frustrations as Noverre had experienced in not being acceptable to the administration of the Paris Opera. Although his debut there as a dancer was a public success, professional envy and the usual petty intrigues associated with the history of the house kept him from any hopes of realizing his ambitions as a resident choreographer. Like Noverre before him, he sought a better working atmosphere and before long enjoyed profitable theatrical activity and critical acclaim in London.

During the next six years, Didelot danced in the creations of Noverre and Pierre Gardel. He also staged fourteen productions for English audiences, including pastorals and dances that were incidental to operas.[20] Didelot adapted the anacreontic format for *L'Amour Vengé* (1796, Love Avenged), in which the classical scenario was prettified to suit the tastes of the middle class. The story retold an ancient theme decoratively enhanced with fantasy and illusion, elements made possible by a myriad of mechanical devices. An arrangement of a dramatic ballet in three acts, *L'Heureux Naufrage* (1796, The Happy Shipwreck) was full of local color and real people, and relied on arresting stage effects. Giving enormous pleasure to the audience, Didelot's one act *Flore et Zéphire* (1796, Flora and Zephyr) deftly employed machines to enable dancers to fly.[21] That his artists seemed to take off into the air on a whim emphasized the ballet's ethereal thematic material.

188

Since the 1600s, stage machines had been used for lowering, lifting, or moving dancers in and out of the stage area to heighten the spectacular moments in a production. While often effective, the huge machines could be awkward, noisy, and to some extent visible to the audience. Didelot, however, developed a more advanced technology in the service of theatrical illusion during his London stay. As a child performer, he had observed the popular puppet shows on the sidewalks and in the boulevard theaters of Paris. On several occasions when puppets were exchanged for real children in the Théâtre Audinot where he was engaged,[22] the five-year-old Didelot probably experienced first hand a crude form of stage flying. It is thought that in the following years, when he so skillfully manipulated his own dancers harnessed to wires, that his knowledge was based on practical acquaintance stemming from this early training.

Didelot presented another novelty of even greater historical significance to British audiences, the ballerina occasionally rising on the tips of her slippers. Since Magri's first mention of the novelty in Pitrot's dancing, the use of the *pointe* was beginning to occur elsewhere in Europe.[23] Speculation has it this unusual feat resulted from the dancer momentarily holding her position as the flying machine took her weight in preparation for suspended flight. That the dancer herself was standing on the point of her foot was, of course, illusory, but Didelot may have seen the moment as a desirable effect, and that the logical progression from *demi-pointe* to full *pointe* could be developed into a gravity-defying reality.

In spite of Didelot's success as dancer and choreographer, London could not offer him and his wife, the elegant Rose Paul, the financial security that a permanently state-supported ballet company could. Many were his frustrations, which his zeal for ballet making could not tolerate. For example, in one theater where he worked, the stage was built outward so that the lowest tiers of boxes rested on the stage thrust itself. During this period the relaxed atmosphere of the English theater allowed members of the audience access to the stage during performance.[24] Not only were unruly young swains disconcerting to the dancers, but their close proximity interfered with the dramatic flow of the ballet, the dancing space, and scenery changes, all of which contributed to less-than-polished productions. Didelot and his wife chose not to remain in England. Instead they accepted a contract to go to St. Petersburg, Didelot as dancer and second ballet master, and Rose Paul as a leading female dancer.[25]

189

## RENOVATING RUSSIAN TRAINING

Shortly after their arrival, Didelot made his Russian debut as a choreographer[26] with *Apollo et Daphne* (1802) in the court's exquisite Hermitage Theater. In St. Petersburg Didelot discovered aids to his creative maturation that could be found nowhere else in such abundance. The new Russian culture, established on principles of French and Italian art, was experiencing a period of unprecedented growth that was largely attributed to the lavish imperial support of the theater. To have the opportunity to work in Russia was, therefore, a highly attractive prospect for an unsettled ballet artist. When Didelot arrived in the city, thanks to the groundwork of Angiolini, Le Picq, and his new colleague Ivan Valberkh, it was a highly sophisticated dance atmosphere that the Frenchman entered. The company of 114 dancers had a repertory of ballets, a school, and strong audience interest. Organization, discipline, and solid financial backing provided the imperial theatrical operation with a healthy permanence. To his delight, Didelot was pleased to find imperial Russian costume ateliers and scenic workshops that far surpassed any that he had access to before.[27]

Didelot's first stay in Russia (1801–1811) centered on the upgrading of dance training, although he also prepared several ballets including *Roland et Morgan* (1803, Roland and Morgan) and *Psyché et L'Amour* (1809, Psyche and Love). In the first months he and Rose were much acclaimed for their dancing talents and enjoyed unequivocal celebrity. When Didelot sustained a serious leg injury, he was kept from performing virtuoso parts and began to concentrate his energies on teaching. Before choreographing major ballets for the Russians, he set to work molding the company according to his ideas of excellence, and improving their level of technical achievement, which he knew would have to begin in the schooling.[28]

In revising the curriculum, the ballet master extended the period of study beyond the usual three-year program. Within a short time the enrollment grew to some sixty males and females.[29] He developed a technique for the dancer's execution of more refined *pirouettes*. He experimented with exercises to strengthen the female dancer's feet for the rudimentary demands of *pointe* work—seventy years before the blocked *pointe* shoe came into being. Didelot intensified the study of mime and gave special attention to music lessons in the curriculum. He faithfully adhered to the school's tradition of teaching students the social dances that had been brought by Landé in 1734, as well as teaching more recent ballroom forms. Referred to as the study of historical dancing, the class is still rigorously taught in the first three years and last two of the eight-year study program.[30] Most significantly, he introduced to his students the manner of executing simple lifts, supported *arabesques* and supported turns in *pas de deux* work.

Didelot's productive teaching expanded the Russian dancer's vocabulary of ballet steps beyond the meager twenty-five or so in the repertory.[31] His art had been greatly influenced while living through the changes wrought by the French Revolution. He now busied himself with extracting the rhythms, dynamics, passion, and freedom from dances of the common people, which expanded and embellished the classical lexicon of old. In applying folk elements to the precepts of the *danse d'école*, Didelot gave a new vitality to existing steps and poses and extended them with greater amplitude and range. For example, many versions of the *pas de basque* from northern Spain were further polished by changing spatial directions, by adding jumps, and by converting the outward flow of movement (*en dehors*) to inward (*en dedans*). In the same fashion the old French folk step *pas de bourrée* took on numerous refinements in the context of the *danse d'ecole* rules when manipulated with turning movement, the sharp or soft quality of execution, or forward and backward direction of movement.

Accounts of Didelot's tempestuous classroom demeanor were legendary[32] in their time and rank high among the most colorful stories to come down from thirteen generations of dancers. On becoming the school's director in 1804, Didelot introduced longer classes for the older students. A dynamo of energy and impatience, for up to five hours he would cajole, demand, slap, and rage at his youthful charges. He spared neither his foot nor his stick to elicit the proper execution of exercises and steps of the *danse d'école*. The more gifted the dancer, the harsher the blows. The students feared him and dreaded his classes. At the same time Didelot's ferocious artistic integrity inspired his pupils and they worshipped their terrifying teacher.[33]

When the Directorate decided to concentrate on the greater development of Russian artists and reduce the excessive expense of importing foreigners, theatrical schools were reorganized to educate children up to the age of thirteen in all the arts and in general subjects. Students were funnelled into small and select classes with a master teacher in the art for which they were thought most suitable. Every six months their work was assessed to determine progress. If, by the age of twenty, one had not achieved an appropriate level of artistry, the aspirant was dismissed.

## POETIC EXPRESSION AND FLYING MACHINES

Didelot espoused the cause of Russian dancers[34] who were often overlooked in favor of foreign artists. Over the years, he trained an impressive array of professionals. Among them, Maria Danilova was the first Russian to attempt *pointe* work when he coached her in *Zéphyr et Flore* (1804). By all accounts, Danilova was Didelot's masterpiece during her short life, combining great personal beauty with a soul of fire and grace of movement. Another student to become immortal in the story of Russian ballet was Anatasia Novitskaya whose dancing was said to have anticipated the qualities of Taglioni in the tenderness and perfection of her steps. Avdotia Istomina was acclaimed as a dark-eyed Russian beauty and a gifted mime. She demonstrated marvelous presentation and aplomb, dazzling elevation, and was one of the first females to command exceptional *pirouette* technique. So great was her fame and her following of balletomanes that Pushkin, who briefly courted her, immortalized her when he wrote:

> The house is crammed. A thousand lamps
> On pit, stalls, boxes, brightly blaze,
> Impatiently the gallery stamps,
> The curtain now they slowly raise.
> Obedient to the magic strings,
> Brilliant, ethereal, there springs
> Forth from the crowd of nymphs surrounding

*Charles-Louis Didelot*

Istomina the nimbly-bounding.
With one foot resting on its tip
Slow circling round its fellow swings
And now she skips and now she springs
Like down from Æolus's lip
Now her lithe form she arches o'er
And beats with rapid foot the floor.[35]
*Eugene Onegin*

By 1806 the school had graduated a genuine *premier danseur* in the person of Yakov Liustikh, who had been Didelot's *protégé* and who would, in time, become a teacher and ballet master. Nicolai Holtz was a splendid dramatic dancer in his prime. In middle age he matured to become a mime of extraordinary power and performed in the French Romantic ballets introduced in Russia in the 1850s. Adam Glushkovsky, beloved ward, disciple, and ardent chronicler of Didelot's Russian career, made many significant contributions to ballet, but one was of particular consequence. Several years after his graduation, when Napoleon's army was over-running Russia during the War of 1812, it was a heroic and far-sighted Glushkovsky who evacuated the Moscow Ballet School, saving its faculty and students for the time when peace and national security returned.[36]

Didelot's creative need to make ballets and his fruitful overhauling of the curriculum allowed him to resume the role of choreographer. His experiments with flying dancers to create illusory and artistic effects were unique for the audiences of St. Petersburg. The public had become bored with the obviousness of the little platforms called "glories" that were hung on heavy ropes that carried dancers up and down amid cardboard clouds. By means of virtually invisible wires, Didelot could raise and lower a ballerina to the floor in such a way that she seemed poised on the tips of her toes, greatly adding to the illusion of floating. Eventually, he even incorporated into his works an aerial *corps de ballet* operated by machinists who used counter-weighted wires to support dancers on their toes and fly them in all directions.

Onward from the 1808 production of *Zéphire et Flore*, Didelot was fortunate to have the participation of the French *demi-caractère* dancer Louis Duport, renowned for his *ballon* and *pirouettes* of astonishing variety. According to Didelot's biographer, Adam Glushkovsky, Duport always performed his *pirouettes* on *pointe* and finished them in an attractive pose. In addition to flying the dancer in the role of "god of the westerly winds," Didelot incorporated bounding leaps into Duport's more terrestrial solos, allowing the dancer to traverse the huge stage in a matter of seconds. Duport's dancing was reported to be truly ethereal in its use of expanded *grand allegro* steps enhanced with the flying-by-wire passages. His bravura technique created a sensation while his extraordinary virtuosity, which never showed a trace of fatigue,[37] opened up one more facet of the range of ballet's possibilities. Apparently, the conceited, haughty, and dazzling Duport was not a good actor, but it was said that Didelot deftly shaped the choreography so that it conveyed the meaning in and of itself.

192

The theater in which Didelot worked, the Bolshoi Kamenny, was the earliest permanent stone theater built in Russia. All previous performing sights had been palace ballrooms or the *teatralmaia khoromina*,[38] which were temporary wooden structures used only in summertime since they were not heated. Equipped with special machinery, the Bolshoi Kamenny's state-of-the-art technical facility fueled Didelot's imagination for creating aerial ballets. Unfortunately, this theater was razed by fire in 1811, consuming Didelot's wonderful sets and costumes for *Zéphire et Flore*.

## FROM LONDON TO BALLET MASTER AT THE PARIS OPERA

Early in 1811, Napoleon was on the doorstep of Russia, having already expelled Russian forces from Poland. Fearing Napoleon's advancing *Grand Armée* of a half million soldiers, the czar required all Frenchmen in his service to leave the country. With few regrets the choleric and proud Didelot vacated his position. He had been angered by an unfair cut in his salary, and needing a change of venue and renewed inspiration, he abruptly departed for England.[39] Relying on his previous London associations, he spent several successful years there creating over a dozen ballets and *divertissements* during the theater seasons, which lasted from February through June. The choreographer's work loudly proclaimed his artistic merit and maturity to the British audience.

His reputation preceding him, Didelot hastened to France in 1815 to accept yearly employment and the coveted position of director of the ballet at the Paris Opera. By this date Russian troops, which were mightily allied against Napoleon, occupied Paris. Through the presence and the political influence of Didelot's powerful Russian acquaintances, Grand Duke Constantine and Count Mikhail Miloradovich, he was able to break through Gardel's stronghold and assume the duties of ballet master. In character with its customary treatment of those whom it considered iconoclasts and outsiders, the Opera responded to Didelot's innovative ideas with hostility and sabotage. He had, however, the last word regarding his professional worth in the eyes of the public when he staged a new and spectacular production of *Zéphire et Flore* (1815), in which all the central characters were seen to fly in and out of the stage space.[40] In spite of the many intrigues during its production stage, the ballet had an enormous success. On opening night Louis XVIII invited Didelot to the royal box and praised the choreographer's accomplishment, a compliment not given to any of the Parisian ballet masters.[41]

During Didelot's brief engagement at the Paris Opera, audiences were not only fascinated with his penchant for flying dancers, but they also witnessed the introduction of a lesser innovation. Didelot was the first choreographer to require his dancers to wear flesh-colored tights. In *Zéphire et Flore* they gave the male dancer a more realistic appearance[42] and they clearly revealed the beauty of the female dancer's legs, especially when she was suspended in poses on the point of her foot. Designed by Monsieur Maillot, a costumer at the Opera, flesh-

193

colored tights became standard leg apparel for female dancers. In France, to this day, tights are called *maillots* in honor of their inventor.

The popular Parisian reception of *Zéphire et Flore* was followed by the conservative establishment's enthusiastic plans for Didelot's future. With a large box office success, the administration was only too pleased to bask in the choreographer's glory. Even so, it was but a short time before the improved atmosphere was tarnished with more back-stabbing and disillusionment. As a result of this trying situation, Didelot tendered his resignation.[43]

## *BALETOMANIA:* DIDELOT AND THE HEROIC BALLET IN RUSSIA

With Napoleon defeated and France no longer a threat to Russian life and limb, Didelot was able to negotiate a favorable return to St. Petersburg in 1816. The quality of his work had been sorely missed by the city's theatergoers during his absence. His many admirers, who included high-ranking members of the Russian aristocracy, helped pave the way for his much-welcomed reinstatement in the Imperial Ballet. Fortunately for the growth of the art, Didelot's decision was based on an understanding with the Directorate that he would be given undisputed authority and have a working situation conducive to all his creative needs.

The concept of *baletomania* (or balletomania in its anglicized form) emerged during Didelot's second period in St. Petersburg, when he raised the love of ballet to fever pitch. The term was originally coined to denote the feverish partisanship overtaking avid male ballet enthusiasts from the moment of their initial "infection" with the art to their acquisition of true connoisseurship.[44] While still at ballet school, young dancers were "discovered" as future stars and their careers were closely monitored. Not only were the personal preferences of balletomanes passionately aired in the press, but they were also a central topic for discussion at private men's clubs and several elegant cafes in the city. Partisan tastes were hotly demonstrated in the theaters during performances, as well. Favorite dancers supported by one set of balletomanes were lavished with flowers and applause while other artists found lacking were defamed, only to be redeemed by their own admirers.

The ballets Didelot created upon his return were prepared as vehicles for the growing body of excellent Russian performers. Equally significant at this point in his career was the consensus that his choreography demonstrated a new synthesis of artistic expressiveness. He took advantage of the Russian dancers' keen ability to identify with the characters they portrayed, passionately projecting ideas with force and clarity.[45] Because of their dramatic intensity, Didelot began to prefer working with the Russian artists he was training rather than their imported peers.[46] More often than not, he was engaged in opposing the Directorate's preference for foreign soloists. Important in the development of his choreography, Didelot's works from his second Russian period no longer relied on mythology, but drew on genuine Romantic characteristics. In his later ballets, which included *Raoul de Créqui* (1819) and *The Prisoner of the Caucasus* (1823), Didelot developed plots based on historical events and Slavic legends, with scenes that effectively mixed the comic and tragic styles of dancing.

Didelot produced a number of great pantomimic ballets that tied his work to the ballets of Noverre's Enlightenment classicism, while their emotionalism linked them to the forthcoming Romantic era. Whatever the melodramatic situation, the characters were related to the age of reason by their idealism, sense of duty, and noble spirit. For a benefit performance of a colleague, the dancer Auguste Poirot, Didelot created *Raoul de Créqui*.[47] The ballet told the complex tale of a virtuous crusader using lengthy stretches of pantomime. The incomparable mime of Didelot's favorite ballerina, Eugenia Kolosova, enthralled the audience in the central female role. The four-act ballet was hailed as a living tableaux, so skillfully were all the elements of theatrical presentation assembled. In crafting *Raoul*, Didelot surpassed himself in displaying a Romantic love of extravagant spectacle by including battles, shipwrecks, and violent acts of nature to underscore the drama.

The *Prisoner of the Caucasus* was Didelot's most important dramatic contribution to the Russian repertory. Inspired by Russia's greatest poet and Didelot's admiring friend, Alexander Pushkin, the choreographer adapted the introspective poem of the same name to the ballet medium. According to Glushkovsky, never before had ". . . one poet translated another into new forms as fully, closely, as eloquently as Didelot did, adapting the beautiful verses of our national poet into the poetical wordless prose of pantomime."[48] Highlighting the ballet's Russian characteristics, Didelot emphasized exotic locale and the Slavic culture in what became an immensely popular patriotic ballet. As in *Raoul de Créqui*, he used the formula of a high-minded hero who is imprisoned and then rescued by an equally noble friend. The success of *Prisoner of the Caucasus* was due to its nationalistic elements, but the fact that the ballet also used Didelot's highly competent Russian dancers was not lost on the audiences.

Didelot's second period in Russia was marked by his continued interest in all aspects of pedagogy. During his five-year absence, the school had fallen into disarray so that it was essential to oversee its return to excellence. Young dancers once again were firmly grounded in mime so that his works accomplished an elevated level of dramatic action. In addition to Didelot's modest use of *pointe* work, expressive *pas de deux*, and simple lifts, his perceptive understanding of the Slavic physical and artistic temperament shaped a Russianized *danse d'école* and established the beginning of Romantic ballet there.

# ROMANTICISM IN RUSSIA

Didelot's great legacy to the balletic body of knowledge was his development of danced mime and mimed dance, each of which was employed to enhance the dramatic flow of the story.[49] While dancing prevailed in the ballets of his first

Russian period, Didelot gave more attention to miming the story line in his later works. He merged the two facets of Noverre's dance so that the mimed part necessary to the drama took on the quality of dance movement and, at the same time, the dancing integrated meaningful gesture into its kinetic flow.

Didelot was obsessed with the notion that his ballets should be soulful expressions of ideas performed with faultless virtuosity.[50] Never sparing himself or the stick on his dancers to achieve his stunning artistic results, Didelot established a standard of excellence from which Russian ballet has rarely deviated. To this day the ultimate artistic goal of Russian dancers is to create deeply felt expression of ideas. It is this unique spiritual approach to the interpretation of roles that pervades their art, a concept initially worked out by Didelot and instilled into subsequent generations of Russian dancers.

On the technical side of his choreographic approach, Didelot augmented the impact of a danced story by furthering the development of the *pas de deux*. The male–female relationship in the *pas de deux* became more distinctly contrasted when he devised chest-high lifts to express the dominant role of the male while emphasizing the submissive and womanly qualities of the ballerina. Furthermore, he eliminated the man and woman's dual performance of the same steps and supplied in their place contrasting steps and body positions denoting dramatic interaction for each dancer. He thereby created a powerful and visually interesting conversation in movement pioneered a hundred years earlier in the artistry of Sallé and her partners.

Didelot's position was threatened in 1829 after one of many confrontations with the administration of the theater. Unlike the all-powerful artistic direction of twentieth-century Western ballet, the supreme power and ultimate artistic authority in nineteenth-century Russian ballet resided with the chief administrator of the Imperial Theaters. This office was traditionally held by a highly cultivated and aristocratic personage who, as often as not, was a retired military officer. Unfortunately, Didelot's current superior, the overbearing Prince Sergei Sergevich Gargarin, was not sympathetic in his dealings with the fiery old foreign ballet master. When Gargarin attempted to interfere with a production one evening, the situation became intolerable and Didelot's ensuing outburst against Gargarin landed the choreographer in prison for a short time. A war of nerves with the administration over money, benefits, and his pension followed for the next several years.[51] Finally, Didelot received a notice of his termination, which nevertheless acknowledged his ". . . outstanding talent, indefatigable zeal, and laudable conduct in the service of the Imperial Theaters."[52]

During Didelot's thirty-some years in Russia, he had helped educate audiences to appreciate a higher standard of ballet art. Press and public refused to forget him, decrying his absence on the St. Petersburg ballet scene. The Didelot years coincided with the notion of *baletomania* first entering the Russian psyche, so powerful was his impact on cultural life. With no copyright laws in existence, the choreographer's works were still performed even without his presence because of their great box office appeal. At the same time, no one filling the vacancy created by Didelot's departure could master his skill in presenting a poetical idea invested with mime and dance. Visiting French ballet masters valiantly tried to carry on, but they lacked Didelot's genius and the breadth of experience that his long years of work had given to the Russian stage. As a consequence, the return of superficial dance *divertissements* marked the end of this brilliant era, to the displeasure of knowledgeable journalists and informed audiences.

The quasi-talented French ballet master Antoine Titus succeeded Didelot in St. Petersburg.[53] Russian critics and historians dealt harshly with him for his treatment of Russian themes and blamed the failure of Mikhail Glinka's operas, *A Life for the Czar* (1836) and *Ruslan and Ludmilla* (1842), on his lack of ability. Later, Titus staged the first St. Petersburg production of Taglioni's *La Sylphide* in 1839 and *Giselle* in 1842, both said to be weak imitations. By one Russian account, an artillery officer, Alexis Scipion Blache, "who turned out to be worse than mediocre," was a French choreographer from Bordeaux who was also hired to fill Didelot's vacancy.[54] Even less appreciated in St. Petersburg than Titus, he still managed to stay employed and produced a number of original ballets for the Russian theater.

In Didelot's absence the press refused to drop their piercing criticism of productions that now appeared on the Imperial Ballet's stage and remarked, "As for our ballets, it is better not to speak of them. . . . They are feet without a head, language without speech, gestures without understanding. For them it suffices to have five thousand yards of silver lace, five hundred candles, fifty dressmakers, five scenic painters and their success will be brilliant and sure."[55] While some of this invective surely fell on the shoulders of Titus and Blache, it reflected to a certain degree the change in public taste (or lack of it) in the absence of a talent worthy to continue in Didelot's footsteps.

Charles-Louis Didelot, as a direct artistic descendant of Noverre, linked the pre-Romantic and Romantic styles of ballet by way of his innovative efforts in pedagogy as well as the production of genuinely artistic works. Didelot's voracious pursuit of knowledge was implicit in planning his productions. Throughout his career in Russia, he steeped himself in historical, geographical, and sociological studies to ensure the creation of interesting and informative ballets.[56] Because of his great scholarship, Didelot could convey to his audience an understanding of human psychology as it worked itself through the historical process.

From Didelot's studies evolved the important Russian concept of the ballet master being educator to his dancers in order to help them fulfill the choreographic intent. Essentially, he believed that the ballet master must have a complete grounding in music, without which there can be no true collaboration between the dance, the composer, and the conductor. In addition, Didelot thought the ballet master must be able to write competently in the preparation of his program notes. He also emphasized acquiring a working knowledge of drawing, design, and stage mechanics, which pertain to the total visual effect of a ballet.[57]

Didelot's contributions to the importance of training Russian dancers was enormous; the effect of his work was felt for years after his departure. When the

197

school finally moved into a refashioned five story building overlooking the city's sparkling canals in 1836, its quarters were greatly improved. Here all aspects of the students' lives were handsomely addressed. Numerous classrooms for dancing were designed to develop future artists in the best possible way. Academic subjects including studies in literature, music, drawing, and history were taught on the premises. Once students got through the probationary period, they occupied special living quarters that included large dormitories and dining halls. Transportation for students to and from the theater was provided by special carriages. The highlight of the year was the czar's annual visit to the school, when merit awards were dispensed to the most worthy. Nearby, the magnificent Alexandrinsky Theater had opened its doors in 1818, replacing the destroyed Bolshoi Kamenny. With the school's proximity to the theater, a new shrine to ballet was completed. Situated on Rossi Street, which commemorates the Italian architect of the school's perfect neoclassic proportions, it continues to strive for the very highest artistic and technical achievements of nineteenth- and twentieth-century ballet.

Didelot was committed to Noverre's maxim for furthering the development of the ballet as an expressive art rather than a decorative one. His chief intent was to create ballet that was the "soulful expression of an idea."[58] As a result of Didelot's efforts, ballet earned a prominent and enduring place in Russian art as an institutional superstructure. So all-encompassing was his great life work that when the feisty Frenchman finally left his post in 1834, he had accomplished enough to go down in history as the father of Russian ballet.

198

# $\mathcal{S}$UMMARY

The beginning of ballet in St. Petersburg was followed by exactly one hundred years of steady and careful progress. Dating from the time of Landé's arrival to teach military cadets ballroom dancing, a foreign art was transplanted and then transformed. One after another, a stream of Europeans worked, continuously refining the craft and the art of theatrical dance in its new home. A student of the visiting Angiolini, Ivan Valberkh and his superior talent were soon recognized in his native country. His contribution provided strong evidence that Russians had made ballet their own domain.

On the retirement of the greatest ballet master of his generation, Charles-Louis Didelot, Russian ballet had surpassed its French counterpart. Under Didelot the extent of ballet's popularity grew to such an extreme that it was seen as a mild form of madness, giving rise to the concept of balletomania. Ostensibly the art of dance enhanced the imperial majesty of the Romanov dynasty. More profoundly, ballet soon provided a unique means for the Russian soul to reveal itself as never before. While fresh ideas continued to be imported, generous imperial support and keenly appreciative audiences ensured ballet of its permanence in Russian culture.

# Chapter Notes

1. Natalia Roslavleva, *Era of the Russian Ballet: 1770–1965* (New York: E.P. Dutton & Son, 1966), p. 19.
2. Robert Massie, *Peter the Great* (New York: Ballantine Books, 1980), pp. 355–66. The author gives a particularly strong accounting of the numerous innovations that the czar brought to his land.
3. Ibid., pp. 355–66.
4. Roslavleva, p. 21.
5. Ibid., p. 17.
6. Ibid., p. 21.
7. Ibid., p. 22.
8. Ibid.
9. Winter, p. 98.
10. Ibid.
11. Roslavleva, p. 32.
12. Ibid., p. 30.
13. Winter, p. 136.
14. Ibid.
15. Ibid., p. 121.
16. Roslavleva, p. 34.
17. Ibid., 37.
18. Mary Grace Swift, *A Loftier Flight: The Life and Accomplishments of Charles-Louis Didelot, Balletmaster* (Middletown, CT: Wesleyan University Press, 1974), p. 166.
19. Ibid., pp. 45–53.
20. Ibid., p. 195.
21. Ibid., p. 63.
22. Ibid., p. 8.
23. Johannes Jelgerhuis, *Theoretische Lessen over de Gesticulatieen Mimiek* (Amsterdam, 1970). See illustration on p. 142 of this volume. Returning from a ballet performance by the Kobbler sisters in 1812, Johannes Jelgerhuis (1770–1836) said he drew his impressions of what he had just seen while they were still fresh in his mind. One of the dancers is unmistakably on the *pointe* of her foot. The sketch, which is judged to be reliable, is the earliest known drawing to document *pointe* work although Magri had written of witnessing it as early as 1779. The commentary in a reproduction of the rare 1827 edition owned by the Dutch *Theatermuseum* records that Jelgerhuis was a gifted actor who taught acting and mime. To help his students excel, he became practiced in drawing numerous sensitive pictures of arm and hand gestures, body positions, and facial expressions for his students to study. He must have found drawing the Kobbler sisters an irresistible task.
24. Swift, p. 79. From her personal collection of dance memorabilia, Marian Hannah Winter published an English cartoon, "Dr. Syntax at the Opera" in *The Pre-Romantic Ballet*, p. 231. The print illustrates the proximity of dancers and audience, a situation that would understandably upset a ballet master of Didelot's uncompromising idealism.
25. Ibid., p. 80.

26. Ibid., p. 95.
27. Ibid., p. 85.
28. Roslavleva, p. 43.
29. Swift, p. 101.
30. Victoria Schneider, conversations (1996).
31. Swift, p. 190.
32. Ibid., pp. 98–101.
33. Ibid., p. 100.
34. Ibid., pp. 101–2.
35. Beaumont, pp. 174–75.
36. Nikolai Ivanovich Tarasov, *Ballet Technique for the Male Dancer*, trans. Elizabeth Kraft (Garden City, NY: Doubleday & Co., 1985), Introduction.
37. Roland John Wiley, *A Century of Russian Ballet: Documents and Eyewitness Accounts, 1810–1910* (Oxford: Clarendon Press, 1990), p. 20.
38. Roslavleva, p. 21.
39. Swift, p. 113.
40. Ivor Guest, "Ballet Under Napoleon," *Proceedings*, Society of Dance History Scholars (University of California: Riverside, 1998), p. 238.
41. Wiley, p. 7.
42. Judith Chazin-Bennahum, "Women of Faint Heart and Steel Toes," *Rethinking the Sylph: New Perspectives on the Romantic Ballet*, p. 124. Dr. Chazin-Bennahum notes that Didelot himself had worn flesh-colored tights at the Paris Opera in 1791 and his innovation soon caught on.
43. Swift, pp. 132–35.
44. Koegler, p. 36. The hysteria of balletomania reached new heights following Taglioni's farewell performance in 1842, when certain balletomanes of St. Petersburg dined on soup made from her tattered dancing slippers. Not until 1934 was the term introduced into Western usage with the publication of Arnold Haskell's *Balletomania*.
45. Roslavleva, p. 45.
46. Ibid., p. 44.
47. Swift, pp. 152–55.
48. Wiley, p. 13.
49. Swift, p. 192.
50. Ibid., p. 169.
51. Ibid., pp. 183–84.
52. Ibid., p. 185.
53. Roslavleva, p. 57.
54. Swift, p. 176.
55. Ibid., p. 185.
56. Wiley, p. 17.
57. Ibid.
58. Swift, p. 191.

# 10

# $\mathcal{I}$mperial $\mathcal{R}$ussian $\mathcal{B}$allet

Peter the Great opened Russia's doors to Western Europe in founding the city of St. Petersburg on the banks of the Neva River in 1703, developing it into a major seaport, and establishing his residence there. Peter's successors continued his ambitious scheme and the city rapidly grew into one of Europe's most august cultural capitals. St. Petersburg was the home of Mikhail Lomonosov, the great humanitarian and education reformer whose universal genius made him first in philosophy, all the natural sciences, linguistics, and literature. Residing there, too, was the lyrical poet and balletomane, Gavrila Derzhavin whose magnificent imagery in solemn odes expressed the sensual side of the Russian appreciation of life. Alexander Pushkin spent his brief literary career as an inhabitant of the city, honoring with his work the birthplace of modern Russian literature.

In 1800 St. Petersburg reached a peak of particular splendor, boasting a culture resplendent with theater, opera, and ballet. It was then that the city acquired its classical stamp and the distinctive character it retains today as an international center of the arts and sciences, a marketplace for trade and commerce, and one of the world's great harbors. The arts played a central role in transforming Peter's city into the capital of an enormous empire. Once largely dominated by foreign artists, in time St. Petersburg witnessed the blossoming of native talent under foreign tutelage. The Slavic character and tradition combined with the inspiration of European expertise to form a harmonious expression of Russian experience.

In the nineteenth century an extraordinarily refined and cosmopolitan lifestyle took shape for the aristocracy and the newly affluent merchant class. Russia's boundless natural resources produced an almost unimaginable wealth for the powerful. At the same time an industrious middle class generated an economic apparatus for effectively utilizing what the land produced. Urbane society developed a prideful self-awareness of its very Russianness. As enlightened rulers, the Romanov dynasty established the concept in imperial Russia that all institutions would be designed to be the leading examples to the world. With the private purse of the czars at their disposal, the arts profited. Although not understood outside of Russia, theatrical dance, which held a position of enormous cultural importance, became the world's supreme model by century's end; hence its richly appropriate title: Imperial Russian Ballet.

Russian theatrical dance had received lavish protection and support since the days it first existed as court entertainment. In the early 1800s the talents of Valberkh and Didelot had steadily combined to generate Russia's own Romantic age that engendered intense dance activity and public interest. Although there were some excellent Russian dancers in St. Petersburg, particularly those formed by Didelot, foreign soloists were usually engaged as were foreign choreographers. During the Romantic era, various French and Italian ballet masters, choreographers, and dancers had traveled back and forth between the capitals of Europe to St. Petersburg and Moscow, spreading their skills and sharing in the popularity that a new age of dance brought to the theater. As a result, the ballet in Russia was enjoying a healthy existence at the very time it was beginning to recede in Western Europe's cultural life. The greatest names of the ballet stage were drawn like magnets to the far-off cities. The most celebrated of the Romantic ballerinas of the Paris Opera counted the adulation of Russian audiences in their lists of successes even though they appeared there past their artistic primes. Taglioni had performed in Russia after the peak of her career, but was still eulogized by the public as the "synonym of air." One by one, Elssler, Grisi, and Cerrito took their turn at enchanting the Russian audiences and setting new standards for Russian dancers.

## ℰERROT AND SAINT-LÉON IN ST. PETERSBURG

Visiting French ballet masters were highly valued for their choreographic talents, enriching the ballet in Russia with their most refined works. Shortly after its premiere, *Giselle* was staged in St. Petersburg by Anton Titus for Yelena Andreyanova, who became the country's first native Romantic ballerina.[1] In 1849 Jules Perrot was appointed ballet master for the Imperial Ballet at the Alexandrinsky Theater where his professionalism was fruitfully exploited over a ten-year period. Thriving in an artistic atmosphere that had been Didelot's legacy to Russian dance, Perrot recreated his earlier action ballets, in which the dance was an intrinsic part of the unfolding drama. Giving the *corps de ballet* more and more to do, he dramatically involved the well-disciplined dancers into the plot.[2] He perfected his use of integrated crowd scenes, animating the stage in ways that had not been seen before. Indeed, it was during his lengthy Russian sojourn that he took advantage of the opportunity to try out many of his original ideas, particularly in the presentation of *Giselle*. In his revision of the production for the Imperial Ballet, Perrot was able to establish himself as the legitimate joint-author of *Giselle*, a credit which had been denied him for its 1841 premiere at the Paris Opera.

Perrot's new versions of *Esmeralda* and *Catarina* in 1849 were resounding triumphs and secured his position as ballet master, dancer, and mime. He was promptly acclaimed a master choreographer capable of filling the deplorable gap left by Didelot's departure more than a decade earlier. One critic commented that since the days of Didelot, the excellent ballet company had lacked a choreographer of distinction, but Perrot's arrival filled the void.[3] While his dancing was praised, it was his usefulness as a choreographer that was most appreciated. Particularly noticed was Perrot's intelligence and care in handling scenes where masses of dancers needed to be effectively balanced and pleasingly grouped.[4] In blocking out his choreography, he was greatly influenced by the paintings of the early nineteenth-century French artist Léopold Robert, who had excelled in creating dramatic events on canvas. In Perrot's mature works, therefore, the choreography for the entire *corps de ballet* was always realistically designed as opposed to arranging dancers to resemble a military drill. Instead, each artist was carefully and attractively placed in a multitude of shifting images.

In her memoirs Ekaterina Vazem recalled Perrot's skillful integration of dances and mime, noting that ". . . Perrot, who always composed his own scenarios, was a great master of conceiving effective stage situations, which fascinated and at times even stunned the spectators." Vazem went on to say that in his early ballets in Russia, there were fewer dances, and in composing them Perrot took care to make the choreography supplement and develop the dramatic action.[5] In this sense, Perrot was actively engaged in carrying on the legacy of Noverre and Didelot who, in their own days, insisted on dance as a vehicle for conveying matters of the heart.

Every year Perrot oversaw at least two major productions marked by intense creativity. *The Naiad and the Fisherman* (1851), *Gazelda* (1853), *Armida* (1855), and *Eoline* (1858) were among his Russian works made with diligence and greatly pleased Russian balletomanes. Commenting on Perrot's dramatic works, the critic Rafail Zotov wrote in *Severnaya Pchela* (*Northern Bee*) that in recent years ballet consisted of ". . . no more than graceful poses, supple movements, lightness, speed, and strength: here we saw *acting* in the dances. Each movement spoke to mind and heart; every moment expressed some feeling; every look was in keeping with the action. It was a new, charming revelation in the sphere of choreography."[6]

Perrot re-introduced the trend toward realism in ballets that was ignored after Didelot's retirement.[7] He was truly admired in Russia as a poet of movement. His choreographic ideas were said to spring from his imagination fully and beautifully formed as a result of his inspiration and craftsmanship. One Russian commentator considered him to be a painter of living pictures that were full of naturalness and yet remained true to the choreographer's intent. Like a sculptor, Perrot endowed his dancers with the plastic charm of beautiful poses and flowing lines of movement. All were presented harmoniously through the measure of music.[8] Not since Didelot had Russian audiences witnessed such animated ballets where vitality of thought, passion, mime, and dancing invested human beings with images of the choreographer's fantasy.

Over time, however, Perrot felt his creativity was being increasingly frustrated by the theater's Directorate, under whom he functioned. Arguments and disagreements on both sides escalated, making the work setting unpleasant.[9] A final dispute erupted over a scene in *Esmeralda* where the townspeople were engaged in a revolt against the government of Paris. This inflammatory scene presented on a Russian stage was intolerable, viewed as an evocative threat to the autocratic rule of the imperial family.[10] The outcome of the *Esmeralda* incident ensured Perrot's dismissal. In addition, the ballet master's health problems, financial irritations, personality conflicts, and the changing public taste all conspired against his contract being renewed. With little regret he left his post in 1858, returned to Paris with his Russian wife, and began teaching in semi-retirement. On several occasions, Edgar Degas painted the choreographer giving class to the lackadaisical dancers of the Paris Opera Ballet's post-Romantic period.

Following the tenure of Perrot, Arthur Saint-Léon, who was more agreeable than his demanding predecessor, assumed the position of first ballet master and set a number of old and new ballets on the Imperial Ballet, including *La Perle de Seville* (1861, The Pearl of Seville), *Fiammetta* (1864), and *The Little Hump-Backed Horse* (1864).[11] Unfortunately, Saint-Léon's health was failing so that his ten years in Russia were not as productive as they might have been considering his reputation. Still, he significantly advanced the cause of native Russian soloists in place of foreign talent, promoting the careers of Ekaterina Vazem, Lubova Radina, and Marfa Muravieva.[12] Proving his esteem for Muravieva, he arranged an engagement at the Paris Opera where she debuted in her much acclaimed interpretation of *Giselle*.

Saint-Léon met with mixed success in Russia. He was often criticized for his ballets, which were said to concentrate on choreography for soloists,[13] de-emphasizing the logical development of the dramatic plot. It was also noted that Saint-Léon's ballets failed to make a skillful use of the *corps de ballet*, which, in the long run, rendered his works incomplete compositions. In *The Little Hump-Backed Horse*, Saint-Léon used a Russian fairy tale that had been translated for him. The inevitable reshaping of literary ideas occurred, as they must when adapting a story to dance, but this led several commentators to accuse the ballet of having a pseudo-Russian flavor. However, in the end, the Russian theme attracted audiences and delighted dancers even though its critical reception was bitter. The ballet's limited story line allowed a number of marvelous and inventive dancers—two in particular, Muravieva and Vassily Geltzer—to give the ballet more of a Russian spirit until it ended up as a truly Russian creation.[14] In 1868 Saint-Léon returned to his position at the Paris Opera and shortly thereafter created his masterpiece, *Coppélia*.

When Théophile Gautier visited Russia in 1866, he was duly impressed with the Imperial Ballet of St. Petersburg and was forced to admit that the development of Russian theatrical dance, cultivated by Perrot and Saint-Léon, surpassed that of France. After his brief stay, Gautier wrote that the Russian audiences were most discerning. He noted that balletomanes demanded ballets with several acts that involved dramatic plots handsomely conveyed by means of much dancing. Gautier also commented on the excellent quality of both the soloists and the Russian *corps de ballet*, remarking on their perfection of unity, speed, and line. He particularly admired the *corps de ballet*'s lack of coquettishness, giggling, and amorous glances so prevalent in the post-Romantic ballet in Paris.

# MARIUS PETIPA: FROM APPRENTICE TO ARTISTIC DIRECTOR

A new age of Russian ballet was on the horizon when yet another Frenchman, Marius Petipa (1818–1910), arrived in St. Petersburg. Just as had happened in the days of Didelot a half-century earlier, Russia again became the dominant center of world ballet. For the next fifty years the Imperial Ballet of St. Petersburg nurtured classical dance's most significant advances. During his lengthy career Petipa initiated a fresh thrust in the growth of ballet by building upon the foundations laid by the most significant artistic and technical achievements of the Russian and European Romantic eras. His remarkable synthesis manifested itself as one of the highest attainments of ballet, a perfect blend of superb physical skills with sumptuous spectacle.[15]

205

Born in Marseilles, Petipa had studied with his father, Jean Petipa, and later with Auguste Vestris in Paris. During his formative years, he received a strong music education at the conservatory in Brussels where his father had founded the ballet academy for the city. As a young dancer, he frequently partnered Carlotta Grisi and Fanny Elssler at the zenith of their careers. The Petipas went to New York City in 1839 for an engagement, but after some unfortunate financial dealings on the part of the theater's management, they returned to France to seek more fruitful employment. Marius succeeded his father as ballet master in Bordeaux and in the next four years choreographed his first works there in addition to performing leading roles. In 1845 he appeared in Madrid where he absorbed the colorful rhythms and steps of *escuela bolero*, the Spanish national dance that flavored much of the choreography of his mature works.

The opportunity to dance in St. Petersburg presented itself to Marius Petipa in 1847. Accompanied by his father, who took up a teaching post, the ambitious young Frenchman embarked on the path of his destiny. As *premier danseur*, he achieved critical success in the Russian productions of Perrot's greatest ballets. A mark of his dexterity, he excelled in character dancing and was a superb mime. In time Petipa became Perrot's assistant and was encouraged to teach in the school as well as choreograph *The Star of Granada* (1855). When Perrot was forced to leave his position after ongoing disagreements with the Russian management, followed by the *Esmeralda* scandal, it was Saint-Léon who filled the vacancy left by the choreographer. Continuing to grow in stature in the eyes of the Directorate, Petipa was appointed ballet master under Saint-Léon in 1862. The same year he choreographed his first important ballet, *La Fille du Pharaon* (The Daughter of the Pharaoh), the success of which clearly indicated the breadth of his capabilities.[16] When the exhausted and ailing Saint-Léon left Russia in 1868, the helm of St. Petersburg's ballet fell to Petipa. Over the years and in the course of events, he had painstakingly prepared himself for the task ahead, spearheading the authorship of a new ballet style.

With Petipa's leadership, the Imperial Ballet of St. Petersburg became the world's vital dance center,[17] while Western Europe forgot about the art that Noverre had ushered in a century earlier. Petipa had inherited the triumph of Romantic ballet in Russia and by imprinting it with his own genius, the dance arrived at a new level of development. It is noteworthy that the young Petipa had spent more than twenty years working in St. Petersburg prior to becoming principal ballet master. Observing firsthand the masterful approaches to the choreography of his mentors, Perrot and Saint-Léon, he distilled his impressions into a unique style. Petipa's apprenticeship was an invaluable preparation for the following thirty-five years that he worked in Russia.[18] His concepts of training, insights into the choreographic task, and comprehensive directives on production dominated the dance at the St. Petersburg Ballet School, the Alexandrinsky and Maryinsky Theaters, and to a certain extent the Bolshoi Theater in Moscow. Petipa's long tenure is attributed to his diverse talents as well as his prodigious choreographic output. His natural gifts for diplomacy, when interacting with the cultured and all-powerful administration, were combined with a charming skill for soothing the ruffled feelings and the fiery temperaments of his ballerinas.

Essential to Petipa's impact on dance history was his determination to please an audience without compromising his artistic vision. He created ballets that fit the general Russian theatrical taste of the times while he was able to meet the hearty approval of the keenest balletomanes. When Bournonville visited St. Petersburg in the spring of 1875, he expressed amazement with the stage effects, beautiful decors, and huge company of dancers. He found the "gymnastic powers" of the females remarkable, but commented that beauty and grace were sometimes lacking in the effort to emphasize virtuoso dancing. He pointed out to Petipa that some of his choreography lacked logical development and dramatic interest. Petipa concurred, but noted that since the public and the dancers wished such displays, he was forced to comply as best as he could while striving to maintain his artistic integrity.[19]

As a young man, Petipa acquired from Perrot the finer points of crafting brilliant combinations of steps for his bevy of ballerinas. During the nine years of their association, he learned that a powerful impression could be achieved with a carefully rehearsed and prominent *corps de ballet*.[20] When revising Perrot's works later on, Petipa held closely to the old master's intentions, reshaping with consummate taste passages for individuals only when deemed

206

necessary. From Saint-Léon, Petipa learned to exploit strong *pointe* work in the many variations he choreographed for his principal dancers. He acquired the skill from Saint-Léon to tailor a ballet to the unique gifts of the ballerina.[21] Petipa always took into account the different personalities and individual styles of the dancers he cast in central female roles. Ekaterina Vazem's powerful stage presence and virtuoso *pointe* work ensured the success of *La Bayadère* (1877, The Temple Dancer). In *The Sleeping Beauty* (1890) Carlotta Brianza's girlish charm and exceptional balance were perfectly suited to the classical French style of Petipa's greatest masterpiece. Pierina Legnani's dazzling feats in *Swan Lake* (1895) contrasted with her dramatic lyricism in the dual role of Odette-Odile.

## TECHNICAL INNOVATIONS

In the 1860s only soloists were required to work on *pointe*, but with his newly acquired position of power Petipa made the study of *pointe* work obligatory for all female dancers.[22] Up to this time the slippers in use limited the amount of *pointe* work to *relevés* on two feet and momentary balances in *arabesques* and *attitudes*. Petipa first put his entire *corps de ballet* on *pointe* in the "Entrance of the Shades" scene *La Bayadère*.[23] By then, slippers reinforced with leather and cork had been devised and they allowed for an expansion of what was possible on *pointe*.

Encouraged by the advice of August Bournonville, who had found Slavic folk dancing one of the most fascinating aspects of Russian culture,[24] Petipa decided to make more use of the national dances in his choreography. In subsequent ballets like *Le Corsaire* (1880, The Pirate), *Swan Lake,* and *Raymonda* (1898), the color and sparkle of reworked folk dances heightened the theatrical excitement on stage. Character dancing also lent a broad artistic contrast to a ballet when intermingled with the stricter form and style of *danse d'école*.

Incorporating folk dances into the curriculum, Petipa relied on the expertise of Felix Kschessinsky, a Polish artist at the Maryinsky who was renowned for his vibrant performances of a huge repertory of national dances.[25] Together they theatrically shaped the folk idiom by developing a character *barre* to prepare the dancer to deal with the unique dynamics and subtle differences of various traditional dances. They also created a body of refashioned steps and a repertory of glamorized dances for the curriculum. Petipa included a number of Spanish dances that he had studied during his time in Madrid. By and large, however, the largest contribution was made by Kschessinsky, who possessed an extensive knowledge of folk forms handed down for centuries by Slavic peoples. Dances ranged from those of the nobility to those of land-bound serfs. Beginning with the fourth year of training, the school required all students to study character dancing to the end of their student days, a practice still in service.[26]

Petipa's outward tact and courteous manner, as seen from the point of view of the Directorate, dignified his work. This was significant to the growth of the ballet because it gave the choreographer appreciable clout with the theater's administration. By the time he replaced Saint-Léon, Petipa was in a position to map out a long-term plan for the ballet to prosper in, and for him to produce an extensive repertory. Although Petipa's singular domination of the Imperial Ballet was eventually decried by the next generation, in his heyday of the 1880s and 1890s, his clear-sighted and iron-fisted control contributed much to his own volume of work and to the general healthy state of the dance.

In the early years Petipa had been responsible for overseeing the training of new pupils at the St. Petersburg Ballet School. The investment bore fruit in the development of native talents with principal stature such as Evgenia Sokolova, Ekaterina Vazem, Mathilda Kschessinska, Olga Preobrajenska, and Pavel Gerdt, the most famous male dancer of his generation.[27] Heavily subsidized by the personal fortune of the czar, the ballet school was the centerpiece of all the establishments for artistic education. Application for acceptance to the school on Theater Street was so rigorous that only a small number out of hundreds of children were taken in yearly. Exacting physical requirements and musicality were of primary concern in pupil selection. Even then, there was a long probationary period. If they qualified, students entered a world apart to complete eight years of training.

The school was surrounded by a protected atmosphere in which the best ballet masters handed down a revered and unbroken heritage to their pupils in a "legs to legs" manner.[28] After their preparation period, the most promising dancers officially entered the Imperial Theater to become part of a peerless temple of art. Following sixteen to twenty years' service, dancers were assured of a lifelong pension. Those wishing not to retire had the possibility of staying on as teachers, coaches, or assuming many of the other occupations necessary to the artistic function of the institution. In the case of the principal dancers, they could continue to perform in various other Russian theaters as guest artists and they could accept engagements abroad.[29]

As Petipa took on more and more choreographic responsibilities, he relied on the school's elite teaching staff to produce dancers for a company that consisted of almost two hundred members. One of the greatest and perhaps best known teacher was Christian Johansson (1817–1903), a Bournonville-trained Swede who had come to Russia in 1841 to dance leading roles and had taken up permanent roots.[30] In the course of his forty-year teaching career, Johansson blended the charm, poetic *port de bras* and the *ballon* of his Danish schooling with the prevailing French and Italian techniques taught in St. Petersburg. So remarkable were his results that he was in his own right a pedagogical force, becoming a major architect of the Russian system of training.[31]

## ITALIAN BALLERINAS IN THE IMPERIAL BALLET

Even though Russian dancers filled the company's ranks, Italian soloists engaged to dance in the Mikhailovsky Theater (where Italian opera was presented) found their way into the Imperial Ballet. Pierina Legnani, a visiting bal-

208

lerina from Milan's La Scala Opera, achieved immortality when Petipa utilized her special aptitude for thirty-two *fouettés en pointe* by inserting them into her variations in *Cinderella* (1893) and the third act of *Swan Lake* two years later. From visiting Italian dancers the Russians learned the technique of "spotting" to avoid dizziness in order to achieve multiple turns, although the foot strength to do so on *pointe* presented a major problem for them. Legnani, however, had brought with her the secret of her virtuosity, which was significant for the development of ballet everywhere. The Italian shoemaker, Nicolini,[32] custom-created all the ballerina's slippers. They had strong leather soles and box-like forms encasing the tips, which consisted of hardened layers of molded fabric. It was immediately apparent that Legnani's specially constructed dancing shoes were what assisted her natural strength in accomplishing her extraordinary feats on *pointe*.[33] From this time onward, the Imperial Ballet began to craft its own version of the slippers in its theatrical ateliers.

Legnani became the mistress of Grand Duke Mikhail Alexandrovitch. Accordingly, the duke requested his nephew, the czar, to grant Legnani membership in the Maryinsky so that she might have a benefit performance. Once per-

Pierina Legnani as the Fairy of the Golden Vine in Petipa's *Sleeping Beauty*. (Courtesy of the Victoria & Albert Museum, London.)

209

mission was granted to her, other foreign dancers were also allowed status beyond that of guest artist in the Imperial Ballet.[34] The loosening of the institution's ironclad rules regarding visiting soloists opened the way for principal dancers like Carlotta Brianza, who became the first Sleeping Beauty in Petipa's crowning achievement, to officially become members of the Imperial Ballet. At the request of Petipa, Enrico Cecchetti (1850–1928), who was esteemed for his staggering endurance and technique, was granted a permanent teaching position and stayed on in St. Petersburg for ten years. His own dance lineage, rooted in the pedagogy of Carlo Blasis, reinforced and enriched the classroom practice of countless Russian dancers.

The Milanese beauty, Virginia Zucchi, was one of the most admired foreign ballerinas to dance for Petipa.[35] Zucchi achieved so much success that she personally inspired a number of artists who, in the years to come, would be instrumental in reviving the popularity of ballet in Western Europe and in America. The Italian ballerina's virtuosity on steely Nicolini *pointes* never failed to cause a sensation and her glamour always insured audience interest. The last foreign ballerina to dance in St. Petersburg was Carlotta Zambelli, especially loved for her interpretations of Swanhilda in *Coppélia*.[36] The practice of allowing foreign artists to receive invitations or to have company memberships ended abruptly in 1901. Mathilda Kschessinska, powerful through her close relationship with the imperial family, rallied for the priority of Russian soloists and guest artists were seen no more.

## PETIPA'S CHOREOGRAPHIC METHOD

During the 56 years that Petipa devoted himself to Russian ballet, he brought the art of choreography to a new level. He prepared forty-six original ballets, many of which were full-length productions; further, he was responsible for reviving seventeen ballets, including those of Perrot. He re-choreographed parts of *Giselle* and *Le Corsaire*, put together five *divertissements*, and contributed thirty-five dance sequences to Maryinsky opera productions.

In establishing his choreographic method, Petipa orchestrated principal dancers, groups of soloists, and the *corps de ballet* of his ensemble much in the same way a composer disposes the various instruments in an orchestra. In his mature works the dance imagery matched the musical imagery. To accomplish these searches for the relationship of dance to music, Petipa analyzed the classical steps of the *danse d'école* and then categorized them according to quality and importance. He listed seven divisions, which comprised the classical vocabulary from which he created his ballets:

1. Auxiliary steps (such as *failli*, *tombé*, *glissade*, and *pas de bourrée*) serve to link one step or movement phrase with the next.
2. Large and small elevation steps (such as *pas de chat*, *ballonné*, and *grand jeté entrelacé*) contribute to the lightness and breadth of ballet movement.

3. *Batterie* or beaten steps (such as *entrechat quatre, brisé*, and *cabriole*) lend brilliance to the compositional structure.
4. *Port de bras* and *épaulement*, which are subtle arm movements and upper body positions, provide the completion of the dancer's body line as well as the design of the choreographic pattern.
5. *Pirouettes* (turning steps executed on one leg in a variety of body positions) add speed and excitement.
6. The classical poses (such as *arabesques* and *attitudes*) are effective in creating lyrical and elegant high points within a phrase of movement.
7. The tasteful use of *pointe* work is the finishing touch to the total compositional picture created by the first six categories.[37]

Among the characteristic elements in Petipa's choreography for the *corps de ballet* were dazzling successions of exquisite, kaleidoscopic patterns. His masterful juxtaposition of embellished *leitmotivs* and movement themes unfolded one after another. For principal dancers and soloists, he placed great emphasis on variations that afforded artists the opportunity to perform choreography designed to highlight their particular qualities. Regarding the intricately composed solos, duets, trios, and quadrilles of his ballets, Petipa arranged combinations of steps that were executed three times and then concluded with a variant step.[38] So extensive was the final result of Petipa's compositional approach that a new look appeared on the Maryinsky stage. The spectacular dancing and his dexterous use of extravagant decor, rich in special effects, completely overshadowed the delicate expressionism and heavily mimed human drama of the previous age.

Petipa's aspirations toward virtuosity marked an inevitable moment in the evolution of ballet, out of which grew a further enrichment in the language of dance. Not better than the best of Romantic ballet, Petipa's approach to making ballets was simply a natural progression of ideas. His aim was the evolvement of the major expressive device of ballet—the dancing itself—separated from pantomime. In this way, like symphonic music, ballet metaphorically revealed humanity's spiritual side in abstract terms rather than through storytelling. It was not by chance that Petipa's "greatest triumphs were achieved when dance found support in equivalent music, in the ballets of symphonic composers."[39] Under his aegis a new style—one charged with a greater vitality and expansiveness—the imperial Russian ballet style, emerged and matured for a new time and for an educated audience eager to welcome it.

## COLLABORATION WITH PETER ILYICH TCHAIKOVSKY

Petipa became a master at orchestrating movement. His earliest choreographic efforts at the Maryinsky, however, relied on banal scores from the Italian composer, Cesare Pugni. Of the three hundred pieces Pugni turned out over two decades, thirteen were tailored to fit the needs of Petipa. The Austrian composer, Alois Minkus, produced eleven tuneful compositions for him beginning with *Don Quixote* in 1869. Riccardo Drigo, the Maryinsky's visiting Italian choir master, composed two undistinguished ballet scores in the service of the choreographer. By contrast, for Petipa's later ballets, Alexander Glazunov provided three important symphonic compositions while the most stunning collaboration of Petipa's career was with Peter Ilyich Tchaikovsky (1840–1893).

Russian music, which had been dominated by Italian musicians at court during the reign of Catherine the Great, enjoyed a flowering under the surge of nationalism. Mikhail Glinka (1804–1857) had been the first major Russian composer to find his inspiration in the folk melodies of his homeland. His opera, *Ruslan and Ludmilla* (1828), was initially produced with Didelot's student, Adam Glushovsky, choreographing its dances. Glinka introduced principles of symphonic development into *Ruslan and Ludmilla* so that its dances grew out of an integral whole. The score remains an early example of first-rate ballet music.

By the 1860s two camps that reflected all artistic thinking in St. Petersburg and Moscow were in heated controversy. The "Slavophiles," believing that the Russian national heritage was sufficiently adequate to meet their aesthetic needs, championed art born of "Russian genius." The "Occidentalists," on the other hand, claimed that Russia was part of Europe according to the reforms begun in the time of Peter the Great and that Western elements were therefore both justifiable and crucial to the development of Russian culture.[40]

This philosophical dichotomy was present in nineteenth-century Russian musical compositions and was eventually bridged with the concertos, symphonies and opera compositions of Tchaikovsky. Russian music is greatly indebted to him for having brought the mainstream of Western sounds into the Slavic tradition. Trained as an academic musician, Tchaikovsky created genuine folk melodies, expressing their color and charm with treatments derived from the Western musical concepts. He was the only Russian composer of his generation who did not draw on orientalizing influences favored by the "Slavophiles." While Tchaikovsky preferred classical forms, he gave life to an abundance of sentiment that was at times profound, completely revealing himself and his intensely felt "Russianness" in music.[41]

Tchaikovsky had remarkably fine instincts with respect to ballet music. While his orchestration was richly textured, he avoided spectacular effects. His musical themes were ample and striking, and he used them as *leitmotivs* in successive waves of long crescendos. His three ballet scores, *Swan Lake*, *Sleeping Beauty*, and *The Nutcracker*, created between 1877 and 1892, are among the world's best and most performed. When Tchaikovsky was about to compose his first ballet, *Swan Lake*, he completed an exhaustive analysis of Adam's score for *Giselle*. In so doing he discovered the subtle emotional interactions between musical sound, dramatic idea, danced steps, and broad choreographic design that had made *Giselle* the masterwork that it was. Tchaikovsky built on what he had learned from his research and composed ballet scores of such beauty that beyond their presence in ballet companies they are recorded for listening pleasure by orchestras worldwide. Since Tchaikovsky's lifetime, numerous choreographers have also used his eminently danceable concertos, symphonic poems, and opera scores with enormous success, as exemplified by George Balanchine's *Serenade* (1934) and *Ballet Imperial* (1941) and John Cranko's *Eugene Onegin* (1965).

## THE SLEEPING BEAUTY

Among Petipa's masterpieces that continue to be performed, the most popular are *Don Quixote* created for Moscow's Bolshoi in 1870, *La Bayadère*, *Swan Lake* (Acts I and III), *The Sleeping Beauty*, and *Raymonda*. The last three ballets are especially meritorious in that they have outstanding musical scores solidly based on symphonic laws employed by their composers.[42] For *Sleeping Beauty* the revered Tchaikovsky provided Petipa with a collaboration that would endure over the years. Petipa, who wrote his own ballet scenarios, enjoined the composer to coordinate precisely designated musical measures and counts with the moment-by-moment choreographic action. On occasion Petipa even specified the orchestral instruments for a given passage of music. As an indication of Tchaikovsky's respect for Petipa's inspiration, the composer obligingly complied with the choreographer's 101 detailed instructions, which resulted in a perfect harmony of dance and music. In one of his last efforts, Petipa created *Raymonda* (1898) to music composed by Alexander Glazunov. The score was filled with splendid musical imagery, melodic beauty, lush orchestration, and sweeping symphonic breadth that the choreography duly matched.

213

Petipa's penchant for composing *divertissements* for his ballerinas was essentially a return to the classical form of the French court's decorative *ballet à entrée*. Petipa knew first-hand Perrot's experimentation with the genre of *divertissement* ballet in which dancing prevailed over a thin thematic line. *Pas de quatre*, *Les Eléments*, and *Les Quatre Saisons* had reawakened a taste for dance movement unencumbered by overly complex narrative. The gradual development of the female dancer's bravura technique and other advancements during the height of the Romantic era made dancing, without the trappings of heavy mime scenes, pleasurable to watch in and of itself. It was from this point of departure that Petipa shaped his numerous ballets.

Major emphasis on magnificent dancing culminated in the *divertissements* and the grand spatial patterns devised for the *corps de ballet* in *The Sleeping Beauty*. The ballet's choreographic structure employed a minimum of plot that served to string together, in the late seventeenth-century manner, intricate solos and *pas de deux* work. In a strictly historical context *Sleeping Beauty* was in every sense a court ballet rendering, in the greatest possible manner, homage to the Romanov lineage. The opulent production was reminiscent of Louis XIV's Court at Versailles, a flattering allusion not lost on the urbane upperclass of St. Petersburg. Thus it was that an elite body of citizens delighted in knowing that their imperial Russian family, their capital city, and its ballet outdid precedents set by the much-admired French culture. While the technical vocabulary had made enormous strides since the time of Lully, Beauchamp, and their *ballets à entrées*, great elegance and dignity remained as hallmarks of Petipa's work, just as they had set the tone in the ballets produced for the Sun King.

Petipa's longevity allowed him to contribute a wealth of ballets to the profession and his best efforts remain a significant part of the dancer's heritage. Petipa was over sixty years old when he began his most creative period and he magnanimously accredited the noble and cultured Director of the Imperial Theaters, Ivan Vsevolojsky, with good management policy that allowed him seventeen years of unbroken success. The choreographer later recalled that during this period he had led the entire company of dancers, musicians, and designers in over thirty successful collaborations. The high point of this period was *The Sleeping Beauty*, created at the suggestion of Vsevolojsky who himself designed the costumes.

It was in this late period that Petipa found his ideal ballerina. He possessed the ultimate exponent of his classicism in Mathilda Kschessinska (1872–1971), who was trained by Johansson and Vazem. The first Russian to execute thirty-two *fouettés* on *pointe*, her unshakable aplomb, strong dramatic gifts, and an exceptional bravura technique complimented Petipa's interest in choreographic shape. Kschessinska's artistry, as well as her intimate ties to the imperial family,[43] earned her wealth and enormous influence in the theater. Her achievements were crowned with the imperial entitlement of *prima ballerina assoluta*, an accolade that she shared with only one other ballerina, Pierina Legnani.

Hand in hand with Petipa's new choreographic style came a fresh look in woman's costuming. The long bell-shaped skirt, thickly gathered at the waist, which was first introduced by Marie Taglioni in *La Sylphide*, lingered as a theatrical convention. When the female's technique began to expand under Petipa's increasingly complex choreography, the voluminous skirts minimized the effect of the dancer's steps and often constricted her freedom of movement. Costume designers, in noting the necessity for the abbreviated shape of the skirts worn by Italian acrobats and circus girls riding bareback, adapted the shorter, knee-length style to the ballet during the 1860s.

Toward the end of the century, a further development in the costume occurred at the request of Kschessinska. A yoke was added to the bodice, extending and slimming the line of the torso, to create a more streamlined look for the ballerina. Numerous layers of tarlatan, a stiffened open-weave muslin of Indian origin, were attached to the yoke. They were cut so that the topmost skirt was the widest, giving the effect of a flower in full bloom.[44] At some point the newly styled costume acquired the name tutu. It is generally thought that the French word *cul*, meaning end or one's posterior, was reduced to *cucu* and then mispronounced in an infantile rendering to become tutu. Henceforth, the little skirt that encircled the dancer's hips was so named and the term was absorbed into the ballet lexicon.

# ᴄᴢᴀʀɪꜱᴛ ʙᴀʟʟᴇᴛ ᴄᴜʟᴛᴜʀᴇ

In Russia, only aristocratic families, the higher government officials, and the upper echelon of the military had access to the two imperial theaters in St. Petersburg. For this educated and cultured stratum of society, entrance to ballet performances was by annual subscription. Boxes or a select section of seats were rented for the entire season; hence there was no need for the function of a box office. Access was guaranteed for as many or as few evenings as one wished to attend. Seats in distant areas of the house with limited stage visibility were made available to music students of the imperial conservatory and to a small number of people who had family members employed in the theater.

Attending the Maryinsky was always a special event. The theater itself was named for Grand Duchess Marina, the crippled daughter of Czar Nicholas I. The beautiful house, with its pale blue silk and gilt interior, had been converted from an indoor circus in the 1860s and became the main venue for ballet in Russia. It was mandatory to dress formally for the occasion, which was always graced by the presence of some members of the imperial family. It was also a tradition to dress appropriately as a mark of honoring the artists of the ballet. The boxes and best seats were ever filled with fashionable and bejeweled women accompanied by escorts in elegant attire, befitting the nobility and highest-ranking military officers. With his political acumen and theatrical wisdom, Petipa saw to it that the Romanov court and the audience were, in turn, flattered by their superb mirror images on stage. Unfailingly, the glamour of the Imperial Ballet reinforced the autocratic self-image just as it reflected the glittering lifestyle of the capital city.

Under Petipa's guidance the Imperial Ballet grew to such a level of popularity that it was only a matter of time when theatrical dance would become available to all inhabitants of St. Petersburg. In 1901 Czar Nicholas II built the Narodny Dom, the so-called National Palace, which was a theater of three thousand seats offering low-priced tickets to the general public. Here a broader form of musical theater provided high-quality vaudeville entertainment, operettas, circus acts, and modified ballet performances for the less sophisticated populace. To meet the growing demands of the public for genuine ballet and opera, the Narodny Dom was enlarged by incorporating an additional stage and seating capacity within its perimeters.

Petipa was the major force in accomplishing an about-face to the melodramatic narrative of the Romantic style of dance. While his ballets contained all the earmarks of Romanticism (i.e., the exotic, the demonic, passionate emotionality, and escapism), he significantly renewed the seventeenth-century emphasis on choreographic form. Hand in hand with his output of some fifty works, he and his ballet masters and teachers built on all the pedagogical advancements engineered by the techniques of the Romantic ballerina to evolve an academic dance just as complex as that of the previous age, but different.

215

By the turn of the century, Petipa's choreographic formula and its inherent idolization of the ballerina within his unrelenting pyramidal scheme had exhausted itself.[45] Change was once again in the air. Too close to his own life's work to view it as it would be understood in historical perspective, Petipa died deposed and embittered by a new administration at the Maryinsky. How pleased he would have been to see a number of his ballets still beloved while his choreographic concepts enjoyed expansion in the works of George Balanchine, and, in due course, the myriad choreographers he has influenced.

## ℒEV IVANOV: PIONEER OF SYMPHONIC BALLET

Lev Ivanov (1834–1901) is remembered as one of the most musical choreographers in the history of theatrical dance, becoming the earliest pioneer of symphonic ballet. Even if Petipa's position at the Maryinsky had not been so omnipotent, Ivanov would not have achieved more opportunities, recognition, and personal fulfillment in his work. While Petipa avoided creating a rival for himself, Ivanov's weak character and indecisiveness were against him, despite his talent.[46] Moreover, in the latter half of the nineteenth century, the theater administration still considered French ballet masters superior and judged no native Russian capable of directing the St. Petersburg company. As it was, the work Ivanov accomplished was often circumstantial, as exemplified by the time when Petipa had become ill and Ivanov assumed choreographic responsibilities for *The Nutcracker*.[47] Petipa had previously shaped a libretto from the E.T.A. Hoffman story for which he formulated choreographic plans. He and Tchaikovsky had also mapped out in great detail the musical requirements relative to the story line. Ivanov's lack of close collaboration with Petipa and the composer impaired his having a free artistic hand in the creation of the ballet since others had already laid the groundwork for the production.

Aside from professional and psychological difficulties, Ivanov crafted a small body of extremely refined choreography during his career. His method was to interpret the aural essence of the music and then transmit the idea into movement. Often cited as a perfect example of this creative process, Ivanov's arrangement of steps in the "Dance of the Sugar Plum Fairy" from *The Nutcracker* was said to illustrate the sound so perfectly that the dance seemed to blossom forth from the music.[48] Ivanov's choreography underscored the Romantic elements in Act I which portrayed Hoffmanesque storytelling at its best. The sinister Drosselmeyer, a nutcracker that turns into a prince, toy soldiers who fight rodents, and a girl who "flies" to the land of sweets, perfectly fit the Romantic criteria in vogue sixty years earlier. In Act II of the ballet, Ivanov closely followed Petipa's format, which emphasized dancing by choreographing classical and ethnic-styled variations within a grand *divertissement* setting.

During its first eight years, *The Nutcracker* did not play well and received much criticism. The "Battle Scene" was declared a complete failure, having been staged in semi-darkness with inexperienced children from a military school. As

"Rats," they bustled about blocking and muddling the direction of the "Soldiers," who were the stage-wise children of Theatre Street. By the same token, Ivanov's choreography and Mikhail Bocharov's decor triumphed with the "Waltz of the Snowflakes." The symmetrical but fleeting entrance of trios, one after another, mimicked a winter breeze, linking the choreography to its topic in the scenario. Throughout the waltz, the choreographic imagery was a metaphor for a real snowstorm. The *corps de ballet* in knee-length white tutus adorned with puffs of snow, carried ". . . snowy boughs which they gently shook, and with snowy rays about their heads; when they sat down and lay down they formed, beckoning, a pleasant and even warming mound of snow."[49]

## *SWAN LAKE:* FROM REISINGER TO IVANOV

The most poetic sample of Ivanov's work is thought to be preserved in his choreography for *Swan Lake*. Laboring under a heavy demand on his time, Petipa was frequently so involved in creating dances for the ballerina that he relegated large *corps de ballet* sections, character dances, and male variations to his assistants. The prime example of Petipa's delegation of a choreographic assignment to a subordinate was *Swan Lake*, for which Ivanov prepared Acts II and IV.[50] The work firmly established his ability to weld inventive movement to musical phrases. Whereas Petipa's rigid compositional approach sometimes made working with Tchaikovsky's symphonic music a challenging task, symphonic continuity was the precise musical element that inspired Ivanov. He used the device of movement *leitmotiv*, inspired by musical imagery to heighten the emotional impact of his choreographic design. While he did not duplicate Perrot's simpler formula of using signature steps as in *Giselle*, he managed to contrive expressive poses and a kinetic flow in the upper body and the carriage of the arms to suggest swans in flight, in fear, alighting onto water, soothing feathers, and so on.

217

   *Swan Lake*'s first production had been choreographed in 1877 by the Austrian, Wenzel Reisinger (1828–1892), for the Bolshoi Theatre. Before becoming ballet master in Moscow in 1871, Reisinger had enjoyed a long and distinguished career as a character dancer and choreographer throughout Middle Europe. In the eyes of Russian (and Soviet) writers assessing his production of *Swan Lake*, it was a failure. According to other accounts, the bad press generated at the time of its premiere was probably politically motivated, due to the fact that the choreographer was a foreigner. Furthermore, audiences of 1877, including the critics, were not used to seeing ballets with symphonic scores. The magnitude of *Swan Lake*'s sweeping sound was overwhelming to balletgoers accustomed to melodic pleasantries. The composer and choreographer were breaking new ground for which the public was as yet unprepared to accept.

   In Reisinger's version of the ballet, which showed much originality, all the swans from ballerina to *corps de ballet* danced on *pointe* only a few months after

218    A modern staging of the Petipa-Ivanov *Swan Lake,* Act III with Rudolph Nureyev, Cynthia Gregory, and Lucia Chase. American Ballet Theatre. (Photo Courtesy of Jack Vartoogian.)

this had been achieved in Petipa's *Bayadère.* The familiar swan motifs were all originally developed by Reisinger. The Russian sixth *port de bras* came into the technical body of knowledge at this time.[51] In an effort to show the swans peering at their reflections while leaning over the lake's edge, a deep lunge position was used in the choreography. Once this pose had been cast into exercise form in the classroom, it was effortlessly achieved by the dancers on stage and added to the curriculum as the sixth *port de bras.* In addition, Reisinger's deep knowledge of character dancing allowed him to theatrically develop the national dances for Acts I and III beyond their previous level of intricacy in ballets by earlier choreographers.

As to the controversy surrounding the artistic quality of the 1877 version of *Swan Lake,* comment in other quarters strongly defends Reisinger's talent as a choreographer.[52] During the 11 years following its Moscow premiere, Reisinger's *Swan Lake* was given seventy performances, a respectable achievement by any account. Its renowned composer Tchaikovsky would never have collaborated with a ballet master of less than exceptional ability. They had worked closely and even traveled together to Germany where they visited the remote Schloss Hohenschwangau and its mysterious mountain lake of swans. The beautiful site and the castle's ballroom became the actual inspiration for the ballet's realistic and the ephemeral decors, which were faithfully reproduced for the ballet's production. The German story had been adapted to Russian tastes by Vassily Geltzer, a dancer and extraordinary mime of German extraction who was a much admired and respected forty year veteran of the Bolshoi Ballet. In any case, various aspects of the first *Swan Lake* were still in living memory when Petipa assigned Ivanov to revive Act II for an 1894 memorial matinee commemorating the composer. Unquestionably, Reisinger's "swan movements" acted as a springboard for Ivanov's poetic imagination and wonderful musicality.[53] Shortly after the presentation of Act II, Ivanov prepared Act IV and Petipa choreographed Acts I and III for the Maryinsky's magnificent and eminently successful production.

In the "white acts" of *Swan Lake*, Ivanov significantly improved upon the music-movement breakthrough that was first manifested in the musical *leitmotivs* of *Giselle*. Adam's music was composed in sections to accommodate the story as it unfolded through Perrot's integrated dances and mime scenes. Their associated melodies in turn were reflected in the movement motifs of the characters in the ballet. Tchaikovsky's unbroken streams of sound were, however, of a musically superior nature and Ivanov's expert handling of this music vastly enlarged the expressive scope of the *danse d'école*. He was responsible for a closer unification of music and movement than had been known up to that time.

While often a silent victim of Petipa's personal domination, Ivanov's skill in joining music to exquisitely shaped *port de bras* and classical body positions has influenced a veritable flood of choreographic advances down to the present time. He absorbed the latest forays of technique from the visiting Italian ballerinas and quickly turned them from tricks into art. For this Ivanov must be credited along with Petipa for reconciling the Italian and French schools and assisting in forging a characteristic Russian school. [54]

219

# ALEXANDER GORSKY AND THE BOLSHOI BALLET

At the turn of the century, Alexander Gorsky (1871–1924) was the first Russian to introduce reforms that led to the present style of Moscow's Bolshoi Ballet. His influence on Russian dance was important, due to his ability to organize and implement his ideas. Gorsky trained in St. Petersburg and as a student he obtained a thorough knowledge and love of character dancing as well as the classical dance of the old French school. Conversant with Vladimir Stepanov's system for notating choreography, he was able to have it adapted into the curriculum of the ballet school in St. Petersburg and later in Moscow. He was interested in choreographic experimentation and he particularly admired the independent artistic values of Isadora Duncan, who was performing in Russia at the time.[55] Influenced also by the views and choreography of Lev Ivanov, he favored the softer approach to classical dance as it was utilized by the Romantic choreographers, thus instituting reforms of his own. He strove to give movement the greatest expressiveness by increasing its relationship to music.

Gorsky traveled to Moscow in 1898 to set Petipa's *Sleeping Beauty* for the Bolshoi Ballet, using the Stepanov notation from the original Maryinsky production. His painstaking approach to the work did not go unnoticed and he was invited to stay on as ballet master. What Gorsky inherited when he assumed his post at the Bolshoi was a company that traced its existence back to 1776. For some years a large segment of the personnel had been serf dancers. In addition to a healthy tendency toward Slavic folk dancing inherent in its style, the Bolshoi had the European influences of Saint-Léon forty years earlier when he staged choreography using Western ballerinas.

Prior to Gorsky's arrival at the Bolshoi Ballet, the company had experienced a decline owing to a wholesale lack of artistic leadership. Never a match for the Maryinsky, various descriptions of the Bolshoi during this period suggest a style of ballet reminiscent of the music hall variety. Although gifted dancers waited to have their talents tapped, machines, masks, and motley-colored costumes dominated the productions and invariably distracted the viewer from questioning the lack of competent choreography. In spite of the mediocre situation he came to, Gorsky embraced the opportunity. He was fortunate in that Moscow was far removed from the strict tastes of the court and governmental bureaucracy overshadowing the Imperial Theaters of the capital. The Bolshoi Ballet was more egalitarian in its administration than was the Maryinsky. It permitted artistic innovation and even broad comedy unlike the tradition-bound Maryinsky. In restaging much of the St. Petersburg repertory for Moscow, Gorsky took the liberty of breaking up Petipa's ensemble patterns, which he thought were too rigid. The ballets were therefore no longer authentic Petipa creations, although some critics pointed out that they were not different enough to be totally original works. While never losing sight of his revered classical legacy, Gorsky shaped the Bolshoi Ballet into a mature artistic ensemble based on sound innovations.[56]

During Gorsky's time in Moscow, he was caught up in the excitement of a regional movement to develop Russian drama, opera, painting, and literature. He knew and admired the work of artists like Konstantin Stanislavsky in theater, Nicolai Rimsky-Korsakov in music, Ilya Repin and Valentin Serov in painting, and Maxim Gorky and Anton Chekov in literature. Their interests called for the preservation of the crafts and lore of Russian peasants, which were in danger of being lost as times changed. The general trend of the Russian art movement was away from artifice and toward realism. Gorsky was perfectly in tune with the movement by bringing his own ideas to bear on overhauling the dance in Moscow; his desire to create realism in ballet underscored his approach to all choreographic assignments. When Gorsky began re-staging Petipa's works (*Swan Lake* and Petipa's revision of *Giselle* and *Le Corsaire*) or creating his own ballets, *The Magic Mirror* (1905) and *Stenka Razin* (1918), he used the coaching techniques of Stanislavsky so that his dancers would "live" their parts as did the actors of the extraordinary Moscow Art Theatre. The

220

choreography, accordingly, gave each dancer individualized movement sequences so that crowd scenes established a realistic atmosphere.[57]

Gorsky always subordinated his choreography and his ego to the creation of the whole. To his credit, he felt the dance, drama, design, musical score, as well as their respective creators, should serve each other toward the common aim of an artful production. In keeping with the development of Russian art, he strove to make the final outcome more distinctly Russian by employing a great deal of character dancing and by using only Russian composers and designers to collaborate on ballet productions of Russian stories and fairy tales. Gorsky's experimentation eventually led him to construct symphonic ballets that were, in essence, the forerunners of abstract ballets. In this genre the ballets created in the twentieth century would be made without any narrative content whatsoever; their sole purpose was the kinetic interpretation of musical dynamics.

Gorsky's efforts toward achieving a more national spirit in Russian ballet were possible because he worked in Moscow at the right point in time and in an atmosphere conducive to his vision. Whereas St. Petersburg had been influenced by all styles and vogues of Western Europe, it was constricted by theatrical conventions and the elegant but restricted tastes of the court. Moscow, in its comparative geographic isolation, was the scene of the awakening Russian artistic consciousness. In time this nationalistic identity manifested itself in all the arts. In the ballet it produced works brimming with exotic folklore that were interpreted by vivid imagination and performed with Tartar energies. These essentially Russian characteristics were noticeably present in the ballets engineered by the Diaghilev-Fokine team for Paris audiences some years later. So overwhelming was the effect of Russian ballet on the French public in the early twentieth century that a lustrous new age in Western ballet dawned. The characteristically unique Russian elements of colorful and vigorously performed folklore are still visible in current Bolshoi productions. The first appearance of the Bolshoi in the United States in 1959 initiated an intense and ongoing interest in Russian ballet for American dance enthusiasts.

# ANNA PAVLOVA

Complementing the choreographic forces that encouraged the growth of ballet at the beginning of the twentieth century, Anna Pavlova (1881–1931) greatly influenced the art as a dancer. While a student at the Maryinsky, her talent was evident long before graduation. Frail and slim with exquisitely formed legs and feet, Pavlova embodied the antithesis of the muscularly powerful, turn-of-the-century Russian and Italian ballerinas. Her teachers, principally Gerdt, Johansson, and Cecchetti, recognized her unusual gifts and they were jointly instrumental in developing her artistry. Instead of allowing her to compete with the athletic feats of her contemporaries, they encouraged her to develop her delicacy, lightness, and natural grace. Pavlova's highly personal style marked a

ANNA PAVLOWA

Anna Pavlova in "the Swan" cre-
ated for her by Fokine in 1907.
The solo was later named "The
Dying Swan" for audiences out-
side Russia. (Courtesy of Jerome
Robbins Dance Division, The New
York Public Library for the Per-
forming Arts, Astor, Lenox and
Tilden Foundations.)

222

revival of the appreciation of the ethereal qualities made so famous by Marie
Taglioni, whose artistic heir she came to be.

From an early age, Pavlova aspired to travel following the example of the
Romantic ballerinas, and so she never lost an opportunity to venture on foreign
tours during her vacation periods at the Maryinsky. She was the first twentieth-
century Russian ballerina to dance outside of Czarist Russia when she guested
in Stockholm, Prague, and Vienna in 1908 as an established star from St.
Petersburg. Pavlova's ambition soon led her to determine her artistic autonomy
by forming her own company in England. In 1913 she purchased Golder's
Green, a permanent residence on a beautiful estate near London from which she
planned and embarked on her arduous tours.

By most accounts Pavlova's troupe lacked genuine artistic direction. Rather,
it served to provide the ballerina with a showcase for her own marvelous danc-

ing, enhanced by such superb partners as Adolf Bolm, Mikhail Mordkin, Pierre Vladimirov, Alexander Volonine, and Laurent Novikov. Eyewitnesses agree that so great was her genius, the undistinguished choreography and choices of music that she selected were completely transformed into beauty when she interpreted them.

Pavlova's company was her personal vehicle for realizing what she felt to be a sacred mission, to take her art to the ends of the earth. Due to improved transportation throughout the world, touring conditions afforded many thousands of people the opportunity to witness Pavlova's performances. Indefatigable, the ballerina visited every country to which travel was feasible. For the rest of her life she performed constantly, journeying nearly half a million miles, an incredible feat in those days of slow boats and trains. Tirelessly giving of herself, she danced before loincloth-covered natives in the Orient and on makeshift stages in Egypt. While in New York, she appeared at the Hippodrome on the same bill with magicians and elephants. Pavlova's effect on audiences was prodigious, owing to an almost hypnotic power she exerted in each of her roles. Some said her bow-taking was an art in itself and that the applause grew rather than diminished as her artful acknowledgements enraptured the audience.

# Summary

223

Marius Petipa's domination of the ballet in Russia was immensely significant in the history of dance. On assuming artistic direction in the wake of Perrot and Saint-Léon, Petipa and his staff set about the advancement of Russian ballet. His vision, handsomely supported by the Romanov crown's great wealth and patronage, evolved a resplendent style of ballet that reflected the imperial aura of St. Petersburg and its aristocracy. Not only did Petipa and his colleagues refine the art from a technical and compositional point of view, but his unswerving devotion to traditional principles also preserved the Imperial Ballet's connection back beyond its Romantic heritage to the *danse d'école* of Le Picq and Vestris. While the link to the past was broken and forgotten in France during the Romantic decline in Western Europe, it continued vibrantly alive in far-off Russia.

Petipa founded his choreographic style and his pedagogic theories on principles reinforced by years of working side by side with his great French mentors, Perrot and Saint-Léon. He thereby generated around him remarkable dancers and teachers sympathetic to the realization of their leader's artistic intent. Up to this period in time, Russian ballet was created almost entirely by Frenchmen. Soon the circle completed itself and Russians such as Lev Ivanov and Alexander Gorsky, while adhering to the very same ancient rules passed onto them by Petipa's generation, brought fresh interpretation to the balletic life line.

Although the next step forward in the development of ballet was master-minded by Russians, it did not take place on Russian soil. Indeed, the dance of the brilliant Imperial Ballet, shaped by Frenchmen on Russian bodies, was eons away from the extraordinary artistic event that would rocket the Paris of 1909 into a veritable dance renaissance.

## Chapter Notes

1. Roslavleva, p. 60.
2. Wiley, *A Century of Russian Ballet*, p. 176.
3. Guest, *Jules Perrot*, p. 232.
4. Ibid., p. 233.
5. Wiley, p. 176.
6. Ibid.
7. Guest, *Jules Perrot*, p. 247.
8. Ibid., p. 244.
9. Ibid., p. 318.
10. Erkki Tann, conversations (1996).
11. Roslavleva, pp. 68–69.
12. Wiley, p. 279.
13. Ibid., p. 262.
14. Roslavleva, pp. 71–75.
15. Humphrey Searle, *Ballet Music* (New York: Dover Publications, 1973), p. 67.
16. Roslavleva, p. 89.
17. Ibid., p. 85.
18. Lawson, p. 74.
19. Bournonville, pp. 581–82.
20. Roslavleva, pp. 86–89.
21. Ibid.
22. Erkki Tann, conversations (1996).
23. Ibid.
24. Terry, p. 110.
25. Erkki Tann, conversations (1996).
26. Ibid.
27. Elvira Roné, *Olga Preobrazhenskaya: A Portrait*, trans. Fernau Hall (New York: Marcel Dekker), p. 29.
28. Erkki Tann, conversations (1996).
29. Konstantin Russu, conversation (1995).
30. Bournonville, p. 303.
31. Roslavleva, pp. 110–11.
32. Janice Barringer and Sarah Schlesinger, *The Pointe Book: Shoes, Training and Technique* (Princeton, NJ: Princeton Book Company, 1990), p. 4.
33. Ibid.
34. Erkki Tann, conversations (1996).

35. Guest, *The Divine Virginia: A Biography* (London: Marcel Dekker, 1977), pp. 78–79.
36. Guest, "Zambelli," *Dance Magazine: Part II* (March 1974), pp. 44–58.
37. Carol Lee, *An Introduction to Classical Ballet* (Hillsdale, NJ: Erlbaum & Associates, 1983), pp. 122–23.
38. Roslavleva, p. 98.
39. Elizabeth Souritz, *Soviet Ballet in the 1920s*, trans. Lynn Visson and edited with additional translation by Sally Banes (London: Dance Books, 1990), p. 22.
40. Hindley, pp. 348–50.
41. Solomon Volkov, *Balanchine's Tchaikovsky* (New York: Simon & Schuster, 1985), p. 126.
42. Marius Petipa, *The Memoirs of Marius Petipa: Russian Ballet Master*, ed. Lillian Moore (London: Dance Books, 1958) p. 60.
43. Richard Buckle, *Diaghilev* (New York: Atheneum, 1979), p. 13.
44. Alexandra Danilova, *Choura: The Memoirs of Alexandra Danilova* (International Publishing Corporation, l988), p. 175.
45. Lynn Garafola, *Diaghilev's Ballets Russes* (New York: Oxford University Press, 1989), p. 22.
46. Roland John Wiley, *The Life and Ballets of Lev Ivanov: Choreographer of The Nutcracker and Swan Lake* (Oxford: Clarendon Press, 1997), p. 50.
47. Ibid., p. 132.
48. Lawson, p. 84.
49. Wiley, *The Life and Ballets of Lev Ivanov*, pp. 142–43. Quote from *Novoe vremya*, 7 Dec. 1892, p. 3.
50. Ibid., p. 174.
51. Erkki Tann, conversations (1996).
52. Konstantin Russo and Mikhail Lavrovsky, conversations (1995).
53. Konstantin Russo, conversation (1995).
54. Wiley, *Lev Ivanov*, pp. 211–12.
55. Roslavleva, p. 166.
56. Souritz, pp. 30–31.
57. Roslavleva, p. 159.

# 11

# Sergei Diaghilev and the New Dance

In May of 1909, the last vestige of the great Romantic ballerinas, ninety-two-year-old Fanny Cerrito, was all but forgotten as she lay dying in her Paris home. At the same time in another part of the city, feverish activity consumed a troupe of Russian artists who prepared to open a ballet season at the Châtelet Theatre. The account of this sensational event, which began with the *Saison Russe* of 1909, makes a fascinating story. But more extraordinary for us, the event and the twenty years of dancing that followed it are still close enough to our own times that we can recognize ourselves among the multitude of forces that continue to round out this unprecedented period in the evolution of classical ballet.

The Ballets Russes, as this company of artists would eventually be known, resulted from a complex process in which a variety of creative urges manifested themselves through the ballet medium known as "the new dance." Master minding this amazing effort was Sergei Pavlovich Diaghilev (1872–1929) whose veritable genius for organizing, educating, talent scouting, and accomplishing the impossible earned him immortality in the chronicles of Western theater art. The Ballets Russes was inseparably bound up with his dynamic personality, while his leadership accomplished a reawakening of ballet in Europe and Great Britain.

Under the aegis of Diaghilev, ballet in the West reclaimed its former status won in the golden years of Romantic ballet. In various ways the seminal ideas of centuries of dance-making were revived and surpassed in the highest fashion by the Ballets Russes. In the European public's eye, ballet was viewed once more as a full-fledged art form, equal to music, drama, and painting. After Diaghilev's death, his dancers turned to teaching and his choreographers created the foundation for the development of American ballet.

Diaghilev's conception, brilliantly actualized through his artists, proposed that classical ballet should represent a more timely, natural, and unified style of movement, plot, music, and painting reflective of the twentieth century. Three hundred years earlier, the Italian Renaissance searched for the perfection of combined elements in its attempt to rediscover the power of antique mime and spectacle. Equipped with technical information developed since the founding of Louis XIV's professional academy of ballet, Jean Georges Noverre, child of the Enlightenment, sought the expressive powers of dance to convey the narrative completely, without depending on a sung libretto. While the master of Romantic ballet, Jules Perrot, emphasized the story telling side of dance, Marius Petipa masterfully brought forth broader spatial and musical dimensions of choreography. As direct heirs of this vast accumulation of knowledge, it was Diaghilev's choreographers who drew from diverse elements of their heritage to serve up a new form of theatrical dance commonly referred to as modern ballet.

Diaghilev's unique position allowed him to preside over the extraction of the Russian technical advancements in dance and its production and apply them as he saw fit. Hence, the latest in theatrical innovation was enjoined to the fresh ideas of the gifted young Russian choreographers he personally selected to create for him. Diaghilev also discovered and promoted a number of composers and designers who became the artistic giants of the age. The ballets that his chosen artists composed shaped an entirely new dance theater. Masterworks of relatively short duration, their scenario, music, decor, and the dancing itself were enmeshed in a made-to-order format, admirably in tune with the advent of "modern times" of the early twentieth century.

# Catalyst of Genius

Born into a family of minor nobility, Diaghilev grew up in Perm in a provincial but genteel atmosphere that encouraged a love of the arts, especially music and painting. His early years were marked by the tender care of his stepmother who ruled over a household devoted to art and artists. At eighteen he journeyed to St. Petersburg to enter the university as a student of law, which was considered to be a proper line of study for a gentleman. Diaghilev stayed in the city with his cousin, Dimitri Filosofov, and through him was introduced into a circle of artists and intellectuals, all of whom shared intense ambitions in the arts. At first the group viewed Diaghilev as a "country boy," coming from the provinces as he did. In a short while, however, life in the culture capital of Russia polished his manner and sufficiently strengthened his well-founded artistic opinions so that he became readily accepted among his peers. In a letter to his stepmother in 1895, he prophetically described how history would assess him when he exuberantly reported:

> I am firstly a great charlatan, though *con brio*; secondly, a great *charmeur*; thirdly, I have any amount of cheek; fourthly, I am a man with a great quantity of logic, but with very few principles; fifthly, I think I have no real gifts. All the same, I think I have just found my true vocation—being a Maecenas. I have all that is necessary save the money—*mais ça viendra*.[1]

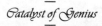

The circle of friends' unofficial leader was Alexandre Benois (1870–1960), a deeply cultured young painter and art historian who counted water colorists, sculptors, and architects in the embellishment of St. Petersburg among his distinguished ancestors. Figuring equally important in the life work of Diaghilev was the talented designer Leon Bakst (1866–1924), whose sensational costumes strongly influenced the style of the day. Other members of the group were Evgeny Lanceray, Constantin Somov, and an intellectually inclined musician, Walter Nuvel, who would eventually assist in the administration of the Ballets Russes. The group of friends met regularly and their ardent conversations stimulated discussions on a variety of art-related topics.

In time Diaghilev received his law degree but began thinking seriously that he would pursue a career in music. His teachers prepared him with courses in singing and musical theory. When he eventually asked Rimsky-Korsakov for an opinion of a composition he had written, the great composer discouraged him, bluntly pointing out his lack of musical talent. Undaunted, Diaghilev turned his attention to pictorial art, becoming a rabid connoisseur of painting; he also began collecting pictures with a small inheritance from his family.

During these formative years, several trips to Western Europe served to broaden Diaghilev's tastes in painting as well as hone his native instinct for recognizing creative potential in others. Keen to improve his social standing, he began to show a flair for attracting prominent personages, enlisting their interest in his projects. By means of his aesthetic convictions, which were reinforced by his ingratiating personal charm, Diaghilev began making his way as a controversial figure in the art circles of St. Petersburg. Contrary to the Slavophile thinking of the establishment, Diaghilev and his friends believed that there was no morality in art. What completely justified the existence of art was its beauty. Passionately holding to this "art for the sake of art" idea, he and his friends were labeled Decadents for their subversive notions.[2] While his brightness and energy were favorably recognized, having even come to the notice of the imperial family, his unconventional opinions were gathering him severe critics. Diaghilev also managed to call attention to himself in another and more unacceptable way. He had settled down to a homosexual style of life, regarded as scandalous at the turn of the century. Be that as it may, in 1897 Diaghilev had sufficient connections and authority to organize a successful exhibition of English and German watercolors in St. Petersburg. He also began contributing art criticism to a daily newspaper.

## THE WORLD OF ART

The following year Diaghilev persuaded two wealthy art lovers who sponsored thriving art colonies, Princess Tenichev and Savva Mamontov, to back the publication of a new magazine to be prepared by the circle of friends that he now led.[3] With Diaghilev as editor, *Mir Iskusstva* (World of Art) was a beautiful and extravagantly designed review of painting, drama, and music devoted to encouraging modern art. The magazine was intended to be a means of revealing to Russian readers their precious aesthetic heritage. Of course, the group used *Mir Iskusstva* as a platform for its own passionate views, allowing it to be outspoken in its criticism of the St. Petersburg art establishment. Diaghilev prepared sixteen sponsored *Mir Iskusstva* exhibitions that traveled from St. Petersburg to Moscow, various German cities, and Venice, and attracted considerable publicity for the magazine. With the first issue the review became the most advanced and vital force in Russian art, significantly promoting the careers of its staff until it ceased publication in 1904.

By 1900 Diaghilev was a respected, if often disputed, authority on artistic subjects. Joining the administration of the Imperial Theatre as special assistant to the director, he found a setting equal to his ambitions. Although occupying a very minor post, he worked to make the most of whatever possibilities came his way. Shortly thereafter, Diaghilev was appointed editor-in-chief of what was considered to be a dull but necessary document, the *Annual Report of the Imperial Theaters*. To the astonishment of all concerned, so competent and complete was his work in assembling a marvelously printed and illustrated yearbook that even his enemies bowed to his accomplishment. Up to this point, Diaghilev's life in the capital had been fruitful but by no means free of professional aggravation. He had enjoyed praise for his work from the czar and was beginning to move in certain court circles. This unfortunately led him to have undue confidence in his situation. In a heated altercation over a tentative production of *Sylvia* at the Maryinsky, his dictatorial attitude caused him to overstep his bounds. Ignoring the theater's hierarchical functioning, he rashly insisted on being given full artistic control of the undertaking. In the course of hours, he was outmaneuvered and banned from further association with the Imperial Theaters.[4]

Turning his attention to writing monographs for *Mir Iskusstva*, Diaghilev edited an album of lithographs by various Russian artists. In 1904 the Academy of Sciences awarded him the Uvarov Grand Prize for his published study on the Russian painter Dmitri Levitsky. Undeterred by the eventual demise of *Mir Iskusstva* for lack of funds, he engaged himself in the preparation of an exhibition of 2,500 historical portraits, which he gleaned from all over Russia. These pictures dated from the time of Peter the Great when the czar had sent Russians to Europe to study painting. Upon their return the artists' task was to paint the likenesses of distinguished Russians in order to decorate the walls of the great many palaces being built in St. Petersburg and environs. Diaghilev's exhibit was held in the Tauride Palace and his organization and stylish mounting of the display caused a sensation in the way he presented the amazing pageant of Slavic history to the public.

So successful was the venture that the Imperial government agreed to back Diaghilev and his associates in underwriting an exhibition of Russian art in Paris. This exportation, ranging from icons to contemporary painting, came at a politically favorable time in 1906. The Franco-Russian alliance had just been signed and the visit served as a gracious Russian gesture toward public relations with France.[5] The exhibition proved to be fascinating for the cultured French elite, and as a direct result it was decided that the next year the highly motivated Diaghilev would bring Russian music to Paris. The music concerts of 1907 generated great excitement when Diaghilev was able to boast to the press the personal participation of composers Alexander Glazunov, Nicholai Rimsky-Korsakov, Alexander Scriabin, and Serge Rachmaninoff. Like the success of the art exhibition held earlier, their music was enthusiastically received by the Parisians, adding enormously to Russian prestige abroad.[6]

With the financial backing of his close circle of Russian friends and important new French ones, Diaghilev and his associates undertook preparation for a presentation of Russian opera in the French capital in 1908. No expense was spared to achieve an artistic success for a production of Modest Mussorgsky's *Boris Godunov*. The opera turned out to be a triumph for the magnificent basso, Feodor Chaliapine, as well as the chorus and orchestra of the Imperial Theater of Moscow. Neither a composer nor designer himself, Diaghilev involved himself in all facets of creation and operation of the production and during rehearsals he offered advice on numerous artistic matters. His urge to create and his keen aesthetic judgment were matched only by his business skill in managing the financial end of the operation. Living at peak excitement over the impact of *Boris*, another Paris opera season was inevitable. In working out the details, the die was cast for ballet to be added to the program. Ultimately, theatrical dance reappeared in the West in all its glory.

230

# BALLET RETURNS TO THE WEST

For decades the Imperial Ballet of St. Petersburg, vitalized by French ballet masters and primed with czarist subsidies, had produced sumptuous three- and four-act ballets that presented brilliant dancing in every facet of spectacle. The grand manner of the Petipa choreographic style served to reflect the glittering life of the Russian aristocracy in the same way that the baroque ballets of Lully and Beauchamp mirrored the elegant artifice that was the way of life at Versailles. It was this form of ballet that Diaghilev had grown to admire in his student days when Benois' abiding love and knowledge of the art were most influential in his aesthetic development. Surely, had fate decreed otherwise, it would have been some dimension of the Petipa repertory that Diaghilev would have wished to show Paris. Yet in 1901 he had been abruptly dismissed from the Maryinsky in the fray over *Sylvia* and his access to the theater had ceased permanently. From the outset it was never within his power to transport the Imperial Ballet to Western Europe; in any case, such an ambition would have been managerial and artistic folly.[7]

The ballet that would be seen in the Paris of 1909 was in an entirely new and modern form. To accomplish his plans, Diaghilev encouraged a collaborative method of working whereby the various artists associated with a project jointly shaped the production at hand. Diaghilev was familiar with this democratic approach to art-making that had proven its effectiveness in several Russian art colonies established on large estates by wealthy patrons. In these settings enthusiastic amateurs practiced uniquely Russian peasant arts and crafts. Workshops were set up for artists and craftsmen to produce folkloric artifacts which were then sold in the cities. In addition, large collections of antique folk objects were catalogued and preserved on the site in museum fashion by curators.

# $\mathscr{T}$HE COLLABORATIVE METHOD

In the art colony at Abramtsevo, which was supported by the railway magnate, Savva Mamontov, amateur theatricals featuring native music eventually turned into lyrical productions that presented nineteenth century works of Russian opera. Large design studios hummed with the activities of producing sets and costumes for numerous performances. Using folk art as a springboard, artists primed their imaginations with ideas from the West and devised new techniques for building and painting sets and scenery. The artists and intellectuals who gathered in these centers were free to study, explore, experiment, and expand their talents. They were also free to interact with each other in developing original work. The collective exchange of ideas spawned a hotbed of creative activity, a state prerequisite to the creation of art.[8]

Diaghilev appreciated the refreshingly productive teamwork of the art colonies, which was in sharp contrast to his own experience of the hierarchical management of the Imperial Theaters. In his position at the Maryinsky, he had observed that tradition and bureaucracy often obliterated talent, while change and innovation of any kind were categorically disdained. Consequently, as Diaghilev commenced his efforts to bring Russian ballet to Paris, he gathered around him many artists who had been associated with the collaborative method.[9] Creative cooperation was to be the foundation of his enterprise over the course of the next twenty years.

In his biography Alexandre Benois credits himself as the one who suggested to Diaghilev and the others that they should include ballet in the opera season of 1909.[10] In his youth, Benois had been overwhelmed by the dancing of Virginia Zucchi in *The Daughter of the Pharaoh* when the famous Italian virtuoso guested in St. Petersburg. So profound had been the ballerina's effect on the young painter that he became a devoted balletomane, never missing performances of *Giselle* or *Sleeping Beauty*, and attending the Russian premiere of *Coppélia*. Currently, Benois was part of Princess Tenichev's art colony, acting as curator for her collection of paintings and drawings. In this setting he was cognizant of the newest and most exciting advancements in Russian art. From frequent visits and extended stays, Benois knew that ballet in Paris in its present trivial form was all but forgotten, so he reasoned that the showing of a sample of the magnificent Russian ballet, in addition to opera, would be a welcome change for the novelty-loving French.

Recently, Benois had worked on the Maryinsky production of *Le Pavillon d'Armide* (1909, The Pavilion of Armide), which was based on Gautier's story, *Omphale*. Mikhail Fokine (1889–1942) was the ballet's promising young choreographer and his unconventional ideas about dance greatly impressed Benois. He urged Diaghilev to invite Fokine into the project and that *Pavillon d'Armide* be taken to Paris with several additional pieces by the choreographer. A number of exceptional dancers who had been classmates of Fokine were willing to join him in the venture during their summer vacation time. And so, ideas turned into action, plans were laid out and they materialized with fanatic energy.

Over the months and with a labyrinthian turn of events, the Russian court's financial support, which had secured the previous Paris seasons, was withdrawn upon the death of the sympathetic and influential Grand Duke Vladimir. Diaghilev was forced to rely on his newly cultivated French associates to supply funds for the undertaking, which at this point, became entirely the product of the European financial leaders. As a Russian he was treading on new ground. By establishing the 1909 season on the foundation of Western merchant capitalism, Diaghilev made ballet a business.[11]

While his earlier projects had received imperial subsidy and monetary gifts from generous aristocrats, Diaghilev's ballet enterprise depended on the dictates of the marketplace. In outlining the programs for the Paris opening, he economized by presenting only one full opera in its entirety, *Ivan the Terrible*. On alternate nights he combined acts from various other Russian operas in addition to the ballets that were slated for every program. The major shift toward Western financing necessitated that certain adjustments be made to Fokine's existing ballets.

In planning new works to fit the needs of the ballet evenings, novel ideas abounded among the collaborators. Instead of the spectacular full-evening Petipa-styled ballets so familiar to Diaghilev, a program of four one-act ballets was devised by Fokine and Benois wherein each piece differed stylistically from the other. Thus, the program format of the new dance, which became one of many of the Ballets Russes' unique contributions to the twentieth century, was almost accidentally created. That the magnificent Russian opera was a part of the 1909 Russian season in Paris is now but a footnote in the history of the ballet's return to the West.

232

Diaghilev's company took on its original formation in 1909 to provide a temporary organization for presenting Russian ballet abroad. In view of the personal, social, and political obstacles that he had created for himself over the years, Diaghilev understood that he would have to make his mark outside Russia and this fact, no doubt, weighed heavily when he created a permanent dance company in 1911. In the face of both success and hardship, he kept his enterprise in almost continuous operation until his death in 1929. These twenty years are commonly viewed in two distinct phases during which the Ballets Russes echoed its maker's ever-changing tastes, his unerring judgment in assembling the right combination of artists to bring about the creation of new ballets, and his showmanship instincts that attracted, stimulated, and educated the public.

## *THE* BALLETS RUSSES (1909–1914)

The first phase of Diaghilev's Russian ballet began in Paris and lasted until the outbreak of World War I, which interrupted travel and engagements. In many ways these early years made up the most extraordinary period of the company. Diaghilev's aesthetic conceptions were well formed after an intensive period of zealous study and observation. Therefore, it only remained for him to take the reins in guiding his collaborators toward the broad artistic ends he foresaw. Russian dancing, drama, music, and decor were newly presented in what was seen as a perfectly blended product, developed according to the joint dictum of duo-leadership. Benois took responsibility for the general artistic direction while Diaghilev shouldered the awesome burden of organization and management. With few exceptions all the dancers had come from the Imperial Theater in the first years, but the ballets they danced in no way resembled those at the Maryinsky. The ballets choreographed by the innovative Fokine for the company were brief, compact, dramatic, and chic.

With the contribution of Fokine, whose choreography was the foundation of the entire project, the work began on a firm footing. A common thread of understanding ran among the choreographer, Bakst, and Benois. Like Bakst, Fokine reveled in the unleashing of the senses, and like Benois, he sought the beauty of the idealized past. Fokine had under his authority some of the finest young principal dancers and soloists the Imperial Ballet had yet produced. Eager to be part of Diaghilev's maverick successes and to have the opportunity to work with Fokine, Anna Pavlova readily accepted the budding impresario's invitation. Fokine had previously created *Le Cygne* (1907, The Swan) for her, an exquisite solo that will forever be synonymous with her name, her life, and her style of dancing. During the first Paris season, Pavlova danced with the young Nijinsky in *Pavillion d'Armide* and the premieres of *Les Sylphides* (1909, The Sylphs), and *Cléopâtre* (1909).

233

When Pavlova, already an established ballerina in St. Petersburg, agreed to join the Paris venture, so did the luminous, doe-eyed Tamara Karsavina (1885–1978). Both women, while differing in style, were dancers of exceptional beauty and command of the stage. Vaslav Nijinsky (1889–1950), whose stupendous technique had already canonized him as a dance deity in his school days, led the male contingent of powerful performers. Diaghilev went to Moscow to engage the Bolshoi artists Vera Karalli and Theodore Kosloff and his wife, the Maryinsky trained Alexandra Baldina. Other dancers, including the *corps de ballet*, were all of soloist rank so that the quality of dancing was remarkably high. Diaghilev was closely advised by Benois and Bakst who created the sets and costumes for Fokine's ballets, while continuously exerting their long-standing knowledge of ballet. Diaghilev was fortunate to have the good will and worldly sophistication of Gabriel Astruc who managed the Parisian theater where the ballet would appear.

Being displeased with the run-down state of Astruc's building, the Châtelet, Diaghilev insisted on improvements. As part of his grand plan for the 1909 opening, workmen set about replacing tattered red velvet hangings, re-upholstering worn seats, and re-carpeting the faded theater, all to enhance the beauty of what was presented on stage. To make room for the large orchestra, Diaghilev had the first nine rows of seats removed. In a frenzy of effort, carpenters laid a new stage floor, finishing only at the hour of dress rehearsal. Up-to-date stage machinery and lighting equipment were installed in the old house to render the best possible production of the new ballets. For the premier performance the carefully selected audience was picked by Diaghilev and Astruc to ensure the strongest impression. The most suitable aristocrats, socialites, politicians, writers, composers, theater directors and glamorous actresses eagerly lent their presence to the event. Making a shrewd although absurd promotional decision, in the very visible front row of the rose-bedecked first balcony, they seated the lovely actresses, alternating brunettes with blonds and redheads.

## THE CHOREOGRAPHIC CONTRIBUTION OF MIKHAIL FOKINE

The ballets shown the first season were those of Fokine except for *Le Festin* (The Feast), which was made up of various *divertissements* that were the personal vehicles of the artists performing them. Fokine's new style of choreography took shape in *ballets d'époques*,[12] period pieces that evoked times and places gone by. Their compact format found an appropriate showcase in the Russian season offered to Paris. Four complete one-act ballets were prepared, all of which Diaghilev and his collaborators had modified to suit the event.

Choreographed in 1907 for a graduation performance at the Maryinsky, *Pavillon d'Armide* opened the program. The dancing of Vera Karalli, Mikhail Mordkin, and Nijinsky created a storm of excitement while the exquisitely detailed French rococo scenery was duly appreciated by the Paris *cognoscenti*.

As a period piece in miniature format, *Pavillon* was unique in the Fokine repertory. The choreographer followed a traditional approach, reminiscent of Petipa's classical steps and style, in which he had been trained during his school days. Benois, who designed the ballet's sets and costumes, had previously lived in the town of Versailles, spending countless hours researching the historical period, the art, and the architecture of its great palace and gardens. This experience had provided him with a scholarly authority as well as inspiration in his collaboration with the choreographer.

Chopiniana had been another of Fokine's school projects in 1907. It now made its appearance under the title of *Les Sylphides*, with Chopin's piano pieces orchestrated by Glazunov. The work had undergone several choreographic revisions, but received its final and much-edited form in 1909. The new name was purposely devised by Fokine and Diaghilev to recall for the Parisians the legendary figure of Marie Taglioni, the renowned sylph from a past era who had fascinated the French public during the 1830s. Indeed, the choreographer even supplied the reincarnation of Taglioni by casting the mesmerizing Pavlova in the ballet. Fokine's invocation of Romantic ballet style enchanted the audience, and time has proven it to be his hardiest masterpiece.

The season's greatest successes were *Cléopâtre* and *Prince Igor*, both presenting exotic themes. These colorful productions, full of eroticism and violence, caught the public's imagination. Diaghilev's theatrical flair for presenting the unexpected showed itself when he introduced the beautiful actress mime, Ida Rubinstein (1885–1960), in the leading, non-dancing role of *Cléopâtre*. Fokine staged her entrance so that Rubinstein was carried onto the scene wrapped in twelve differently colored scarves that her bearers then unfurled, one by one, to display the exotic queen of the Nile. Supported by a cast of outstanding classical technicians, Rubinstein was a sensation without herself dancing a step.

235

The soaring leaps and barbaric energy in Fokine's choreography for the male dancers led by Adolph Bolm (1884–1951) in *Prince Igor* stunned the refined French audience. Since Gautier's caustic writings had all but banished men from the stage during the Romantic age, masculine participation in dance performances outside Russia and Denmark had been negligible. By 1909 no one in the audience of the Châtelet Theatre had ever seen the likes of the aerial grace of the androgynous Nijinsky or the virile bounding of the manly Bolm. By presenting Fokine's abridged form of Russian ballet (i.e., ballet that omitted lengthy spectacles that included long pantomime scenes and a decorous *corps de ballet*), Diaghilev succeeded in establishing a modernized form of theatrical dance.

In Fokine's anti-academic ballets, the grand ballerina lost her place of pride as the centerpiece around which all revolved.[13] Gone was the Petipa-styled *pas de deux* crafted to show her off along with her resplendent solo variations followed by a rousing coda. The appearances of Nijinsky outweighed even the impressions created by the ballerinas, although Fokine's craftsmanship still endowed Karsavina and others with outstanding roles. Diaghilev was insistent on making the most of Nijinsky's genius for his personal satisfaction, but also for the dancer's effect on box office receipts. Diaghilev's liaison with the younger man inspired him to devise ballets with Fokine in which Nijinsky danced the central role.

Virtuosity remained in Fokine's ballets, but he used it sparingly and only to the extent that it elucidated the emotionality of the characters. Fokine wrought beautiful visual images of the human form that replaced technical tricks guaranteed to bring forth applause. The dancers' classically trained bodies were cast into a modified form, a special *plastique* that reflected the particular ethnology of the ballet. Torso, head, arm, and hand positions aimed to heighten the expressiveness of the dancer. Fokine manipulated the upper body and invented steps to suggest the historical setting of the works and provide nuances that gave each ballet its particular flavor. The choreographer's skill, developed through the comprehensive training he received at the St. Petersburg Ballet School, was indispensable to the wildly successful outcome of the first phase of the Ballets Russes. For his part, Diaghilev was quick to access Fokine's originality, which paralleled his own conceptions of what kind of dance the Russian troupe presented in Paris.

# $\mathcal{T}$HE INFLUENCE OF ISADORA DUNCAN

Fokine and Diaghilev appreciated the ideas of Isadora Duncan (1877–1927), whom they had met when she performed in St. Petersburg. Duncan, who was technically unschooled in dance, created her own style of movement *plastique* by which she radiated the meaning and the emotional content of music through the force of her personality. Her art was a very intimate form of expression and this individualism interested the choreographer. During four visits between 1904 and 1909, Duncan had given concerts in St. Petersburg that turned out to be major cultural events attended by the artistic and social elite of the city.[14] Her lilting, uncorseted, and lightly draped torso, her bare feet and legs, the abandon she displayed in head and arm movement in the service of the natural and expressive, captivated Fokine. Duncan's performances coincided with his first efforts at dance-making and her impact on him clearly marked the ballets he would prepare for the Ballets Russes.

It was Duncan's iconoclastic use of concert hall music for dance that affected Fokine most profoundly.[15] Her all-Chopin concert in 1904 signaled the choreographer to forsake the specialist composers like Pugni, Drigo, and Minkus, who had prepared countless scores of tuneful waltzes and polkas for the Imperial Ballet. The wonderful musicality evident in Duncan's emotional performing had made it clear to Fokine that there was a wide field of musical choices suitable for ballet. He was, accordingly, inspired to create new forms of movement to correspond to the characteristics of each of his musical selections so that the dance was organically linked to the music. With the exception of *Les*

236

*Sylphides*, all the music used for the 1909 season was Russian and eminently suited to Fokine's choreography.

## BALLET FOR MODERN TIMES

While still a student, Fokine had fervently believed in the need to reform the ballet. Although Petipa had raised the art to new heights, his style of ballet had spent itself in the eyes of the next generation. Changing times called for a new approach to theatrical dance, and it was the visionary Fokine who was among those to lead the way. By dispensing with the grandiose choreographic format of Petipa conventions and by adjusting the classical steps and poses for his purposes, Fokine shaped original and exuberant movement that was tailored to the story line of each work.

Fokine's most significant and lasting accomplishment was to create ballets founded on realism and naturalism that underscored the element of human expression. He insisted that the purpose of ballet was to extol beauty through the portrayal of the individual and his feelings. The major aesthetic of the Moscow Art Theatre had strongly bolstered Fokine's choreographic style. He coached his artists to develop their roles with "arabesques of their own personalities"[16] so that the dancing became conversations in movement, filled with emotional subtleties. Influenced by the symbolist art movement prevailing at the time,[17] Fokine believed that man's innermost self could only be truly revealed by the use of symbol, myth, and mood. Therefore the characters in his ballets were universals. His poets, puppets, spirits, slaves, and seductresses shared their joyful, tragic, victimized, and futile experiences with Everyman and Everywoman. In this context Fokine managed to achieve the desire for consummate expressiveness begun by Sallé and continued down through the years by Angiolini, Noverre, Dauberval, Didelot, and Perrot. For him, the dancer needed to be an expressive instrument from head to foot—an idea overlooked in the technical fireworks of most of the Italian and some of the Russian ballerinas of the previous generation.

Diaghilev's company provided the platform for Fokine's outpouring of an array of choreographic works that showed a new kind of dance genre, one that disclosed the social tensions of a new century. In various guises Fokine revealed the individual's need for spiritual freedom set against a desire for a vision of community. By aligning himself with the first Paris season, Fokine was able to actualize his burning ambition to enforce change in the ballet. Fortunately, he inhabited a milieu where prominent artists and musicians joined him in the creation of his choreographic projects, which were performed by excellent dancers.

Eventually, Fokine formulated a five-point choreographic aesthetic that elaborated the following maxims:

237

1. Each ballet should have a style of movement created especially for it according to the demands of the subject matter and the musical scores. The classical steps should be modified or restyled according to the dictates of the thematic material.
2. The dance movement itself should convey the unfolding of the dramatic action, thus eliminating the inclusion of mime.
3. The formalized pantomimic gesture of the previous ages should be replaced by an expressiveness created from total body movement, which would, in turn, meaningfully communicate ideas and feelings.
4. All dancers in a work, including the *corps de ballet*, should be an intricate part of the whole and not serve to decorate the stage at various interludes.
5. All aspects of the ballet should be on an equal footing. Namely, the dancing, the music, sets, and costumes should reflect the collaborative effort toward a cohesive creative product.[18]

In reviewing Fokine's principles, one is struck with the notion that his comprehensive thought seemed so innovative at the time. Indeed, his fifth point was the very basis for what had made the *Ballet Comique de la Reine* the extraordinary event it was in 1581. It is even more astonishing when one considers that much of what Fokine advocated had been seminal in Noverre's practical theorizing on the *ballet d'action*. Now the aesthetics from earlier times were once again addressed in the making of twentieth-century ballets, this time in the person of a Russian choreographer.

The Russian painters' contributions to Fokine's productions made the strongest possible artistic statements in their marriage of vibrant color to choreography. Benois and Bakst were highly skilled, first-rate easel artists who also happened to be creating stage designs at a period when the work of theatrical hacks was commonplace in Paris. Benois' decor for *Pavillon*, with its real water-jetting fountains, was exquisitely conceived with regard to the sheer beauty of its coloration. The moonlight and woodland scenery for *Les Sylphides* received a delicate treatment reminiscent of the Romantic epoch, perfectly suited to Fokine's harmonious choreographic configurations. Bakst's sensuous rendering of sets and costumes for *Cléopâtre* suggested a strikingly exotic atmosphere that enthralled the French theatergoers. The Russian painter Nicholas Roerich was engaged to design a huge curved backdrop for *Prince Igor* and the stunning result effectively evoked the vastness of the Russian plains. A new horizon in theatrical history, not since Boucher and Fragonard created sets in the eighteenth century had painting of superb quality been magnified and transferred to the huge parameters marked out by the proscenium arch.

The extraordinary dancing of the Russian artists proved also to be of intense interest for press and public. Regarding the French critics' impression of the 1909 season, however, ballet was such a forgotten medium of expression that the writers failed to appreciate the specific contribution of Fokine as choreographer in their extensive previews and reviews. Instead, in their comments they ineptly lumped his choreographic contribution together with the dancers' performances.

At the close of the first season, Benois enthusiastically wrote that everyone connected with the project felt that they were bringing to the artistic capital of the West all that was best in Russian art. The designer rightly prophesied that the event would begin a new European theatrical art. While it certainly did achieve a renaissance for the European ballet and theater arts in general, the presence of the Russian ballet in Paris eventually stimulated radical changes in fashion styles, jewelry design, interior decoration, and commercial art all over the Continent. Benois summed up the visit by generously concluding that the greatest triumph did not belong to anyone in particular, but to Russian culture itself with its uniquely Slavic characteristics that overshadowed decadent Western sophistication. Evident in the ballets presented to the public that first season were the Russian culture's great sense of conviction, its freshness and spontaneity, its wild force, and its concurrent tenderness and deep spirituality.

# $\mathcal{S}$ECOND PARIS SEASON

So celebrated was the Russian ballet in Paris that a return engagement for 1910 was inevitable. Up to this time Diaghilev and his collaborators did not think ballet evenings alone would be acceptable to French audiences. However, the Russians had demonstrated in their dance productions that the ballet was indeed capable of being an autonomous and timely art. Due to the company's prominence, the lofty Paris Opera was offered as a proper setting for the forth-coming season. Returning to Russia, Diaghilev set plans in motion to prepare for the next Paris season, knowing he would have to match the success of 1909.

As it turned out, the second visit of the Ballets Russes to Paris surpassed the first. Five ballets were added to the original repertory. Four of them were works by Fokine, while Benois persuaded Diaghilev to produce a revival of *Giselle*. A staple of the Maryinsky repertory since 1842, the cherished old Perrot-Corelli-Gautier ballet had been lovingly preserved and last revised by Petipa in 1884. However, as Diaghilev had predicted, the time was not yet right for the French public to accept its reappearance. Next to the flamboyant and sensuous Fokine ballets, *Giselle*'s story, pantomime scenes, and musical score appeared out-of-date, despite an exquisite interpretation given by Nijinsky and Karsavina.[19] Fokine's new works for 1910 were another matter. In creating *L'Oiseau de feu* (Firebird), *Schéhérazade*, *Carnaval*, and *Les Orientales*, the chore-ographer wrought four distinct ballets that were added to his previous material in the repertory.

*Firebird* was by far the most significant artistic offering of the season. Both Diaghilev and Fokine had wanted to do something based on genuine Russian folklore and seized upon the Slavic *zhar-ptitsa* theme, which they contrived from several old fairy tales. Diaghilev had heard a composition by Igor Stravinsky (1882–1971), a rising young Russian composer, and determined that he could provide a fitting score for *Firebird*. During its preparation in St.

Petersburg, the composer and the choreographer worked closely, and the final result was a musical event of the first order. Stravinsky's ultra-modern tonalities and complex rhythmic structure altered and advanced the quality of ballet music. The score also provided an unexpected challenge for the performers, who were used to highly danceable, four square melodies. Stravinsky's novel sounds and rhythms stimulated the musically trained Fokine to create exciting and original choreographic movements. For the final touch Diaghilev engaged the established Russian painter Alexander Golovin to create the decor for the enchanted atmosphere. On hearing the composition Pavlova, who was to dance the part of the Firebird, disliked the contemporaneous music.[20] By bowing out of the project, Pavlova opened the way for Karsavina to replace her and thus create the role in which the younger dancer proved to be incomparable.

*Schéhérazade* was the second ballet readied for the Paris season. The plot was conceived by Benois, who had been inspired after researching the stories depicted in Persian miniature paintings. Overtly presenting eroticism and brutality, *Schéhérazade* turned out to be one of the most stunning theatrical successes of the entire Diaghilev era. Fokine was at the height of his inventiveness during its creation. After the difficulty of acclimating the dancers to the complex rhythms of Stravinsky's *Firebird*, the melodic Rimsky-Korsakov score was a relief for the artists, so work progressed swiftly. In his chronicle of the troupe, Serge Grigoriev (1883–1968), the company's *regisseur*, recalled the dancers' perplexity when Fokine started rehearsals with the *corps de ballet* and soloists sitting on the floor, sensuously moving arms, head, and upper torso. It was necessary to assure them that they would eventually be allowed to rise and dance in a more conventional manner.[21]

A number of elements contributed to *Schéhérazade*'s overall effect, but the art of the colorist is what is most remembered. Bakst's riot of paint and fabric lent a startlingly exotic texture to the production. A harem atmosphere was achieved with the daring juxtaposition of peacock green and blue contrasted with coral red and rose pink, painted on billowing silken tent hangings. Glittering pendant lamps of pierced silver added an authentic touch to the scene as did luxurious oriental carpets. The visual effect of Bakst's decor was stupendous, bringing a new importance to stage dressing in theatrical dance. Years later, however, it would often be said that Diaghilev's designers killed the central role of dance in the making of ballets for his company.

The *corps de ballet* of *Schéhérazade* were elaborately costumed as voluptuous odalisques to aid in creating atmosphere. The non-dancing, leading female part was designed for Rubinstein while Nijinsky interpreted the golden slave whom she seduces in the course of the story. At the ballet's end Nijinsky's acrobatic death spasms electrified the audience. According to numerous accounts and passionate memories of the opening night, the public's reception of the shockingly brutal ballet was overwhelming.[22] Indeed, *Schéhérazade*'s premiere proved to be such a triumph that the public's reaction caused the management some effort in restoring order in the theater before the next ballet could be presented. With the production of *Schéhérazade*, according to Grigoriev,

240

Diaghilev achieved an aim once dreamt of by Noverre when the old master wistfully complained that if only a painter, composer, and choreographer could work harmoniously, what wonders they could show the public.[23]

The third ballet slated for the season was *Carnaval,* a revival of a delightful work Fokine had recently done for a charity benefit in St. Petersburg. Based on the Italian *commedia dell'arte* characters of Harlequin, Colombina, and Pierrot, with costumes by Bakst and music by the nineteenth-century German composer Robert Schumann,[24] *Carnaval* provided the repertory with another aspect of dance's capabilities, a humorous satire. Paris got its first look at the newly graduated Lydia Lopokova (1891–1981) in the role of Colombina. A born comedienne, Lopokova was eminently suited to the role as was her Harlequin partner, the idolized Nijinsky. *Les Orientales* was a *divertissement* consisting of old and new Fokine dances, and made up the fourth original presentation of the season.

In reviewing the Ballets Russes' second Paris season, the company's developing problem of personnel change was threatening its artistic integrity. While Diaghilev achieved a great coup in discovering Stravinsky, he lost Pavlova. The great ballerina not only disapproved of Diaghilev's modern tendencies, but was offended when he spoke of her as secondary to Nijinsky. To some extent she also resented the public's acclaim of Nijinsky and Karsavina for their success in Fokine's modernist ballets. Shortly thereafter, Pavlova formed her own troupe, which was to be essentially a showcase for her unique artistry for the rest of her career. By season's close, Benois had also left the company over an uproar concerning the authorship of *Schéhérazade.* Although Benois had provided the ballet's scenario, Diaghilev arbitrarily gave Bakst the program credit.[25] Diaghilev reasoned that Benois already had *Pavillon* on his list of accomplishments while Bakst needed the authorship as well as the design credit for a ballet. Diaghilev's monomania and paranoia caused him to be dismissive at times and controlling at others, which contributed to slighting one artist in favor of another. Unfortunately, the instability of personnel was a mere preview of what lay ahead for the Ballets Russes with respect to its artistic staffing.

The successful repetition of the Ballets Russes' season in Paris secured the company's position as a major event in the artistic life of the city. The principal dancers, namely, Karsavina, Lopokova, Nijinsky, Bolm, and Fokine were treated as heroes, even though Fokine's choreography had deprived the ballerinas of their exclusive importance established during the Romantic era and reinforced in all of Petipa's ballets. The almost superhuman quality of the Russian male dancing remained a great joy for Paris. The ensemble dancing was a revelation to the public. With Fokine's skillful manipulation, even a curtailed *corps de ballet* was an expressive instrument.

Significantly, the second appearance of the Russians affirmed that ballet seasons could be financially as well as artistically viable. Due to production cost overruns, the first season had incurred a debt of 86,000 French francs and this was not allowed to repeat itself the following year. More knowledgeable planning for 1910 had discontinued the magnificent but costly presentations of Russian operas. Furthermore, management improvements had dictated that a

241

Russian orchestra would not accompany the troupe to the West because competent musicians could be found in Paris.

# THE PERMANENT ESTABLISHMENT OF THE BALLETS RUSSES

Diaghilev received enough requests for performance engagements after the 1910 success to officially establish a permanent troupe.[26] Prior to the next season in Paris, the company was contracted to appear in Monte Carlo, Rome, and London. Again Diaghilev rallied round himself an array of devoted artists eager to participate in the now famous Diaghilev organization. With the company on a firm footing, Fokine was hired as choreographic director to continue his innovative work. This was an opportunity for him to create ballets without constraints of any kind, which was not possible within the tradition-laden Imperial Ballet.

Karsavina was engaged as the company's prima ballerina since she was senior enough at the Maryinsky that she was only bound there for a certain number of months during the year. Other luminaries to join included Adolph Bolm, who was particularly distinguished as a character dancer. The celebrated Maryinsky prima ballerina Olga Preobrajenska agreed to commit herself to Diaghilev during her free periods in St. Petersburg. The company's acquisition of Nijinsky was finally made, but only after considerable scandal.

In preparing Nijinsky for *Giselle* in St. Petersburg, Nicholas Legat had choreographed a male variation for Act II that replaced the pantomime originally set by Perrot according to Romantic tastes. The variation was, of course, meant to focus greater attention on male dancing and the role of Albrecht. The traditional costume for the role called for mandatory trunks worn over tights, which were particularly unattractive on the muscular Nijinsky. For some time balletomanes, including the staff of the defunct *Mir Iskusstva*, had voiced their opinions regarding costume conventions that they deemed outmoded and irrelevant. Strongly influenced by those around him, Nijinsky omitted the bulky trunks of his costume on a particular occasion when the dowager czarina and several grand duchesses attended a performance of *Giselle*. The former sovereign was reportedly shocked at the revealing costume, calling the administration's attention to the incident. Nijinsky had failed to meet the Imperial Theater's regulations, and as a result of this insubordination to authority he was expelled from the Maryinsky,[27] while Diaghilev was only too pleased to engage him on a full-time basis.

Recruiting minor soloists and an adequate *corps de ballet* for the company was Diaghilev's most pressing problem. *Corps* dancers had to be acquired outside of Russia since lower-ranking dancers of the Maryinsky were not permitted foreign engagements. At the same time there were very few sufficiently capable dancers in Europe who could meet the challenge of performing alongside the

242

Russians. After considerable search and intensive company training, the new dancers were found and cast. In many cases they were English, since there were a few teachers giving instruction in classical dance in London. The quest for qualified performers continued to be a major concern for the duration of Diaghilev's enterprise.

Once the troupe was permanently established, acquiring a company teacher for the dancers was imperative. Diaghilev was fortunate to secure the services of Enrico Cecchetti, who had recently left his post at the Maryinsky. The maestro's formidable classroom methods were rooted in the pedagogy of Carlo Blasis and broadened to include firsthand influences of Johannson and Petipa with whom he had worked in St. Petersburg. As coach and pedagogue, Cecchetti not only pulled the technically uneven group of *corps* dancers together, but was able to homogenize their efforts into a single style.[28] The soloists were overjoyed to have the opportunity to benefit from separate classes with him. Consequently, morale as well as technique remained on a high level.

To the amazement of the French, Cecchetti's classes were conducted with a pianist. In Russia the *violin de poche*, which had provided the musical beat for dance practice since the eighteenth century, was set aside in 1883 when one of Petipa's assistants, Alexei Bogdanov, was transferred to Moscow to head the Bolshoi Ballet. In an effort to upgrade the troupe, Bogdanov introduced a number of reforms, one of which was that all classes should have piano music just as all rehearsals were conducted to the accompaniment of the piano.[29] The practice was subsequently adopted for classroom work in the imperial companies and, somewhat later, in the schools. It was therefore standard Russian practice for piano music to accompany Cecchetti's classes in Diaghilev's company.

Four new Fokine ballets were added to the repertory in 1911. The pieces were, for the most part, planned before the company assembled for rehearsals and their opening in Monte Carlo. Fokine and Stravinsky repeated their exceptional collaboration in realizing *Petrushka* (1911),[30] named for a character in Slavic folklore and a theme that Diaghilev had fervently wished to see materialize into a ballet. After lengthy negotiations carried on before the enmeshing Diaghilev charm, Benois returned to the company to create the ballet's sets and costumes. His inspiration was fueled by vivid childhood memories of *balagan*, the lively street fair in St. Petersburg. Benois' particular love had been the colorful and raucous stunts of the street players, who drew the presence of the entire city, as well as the *balagani*, little booths that sold sweets and housed puppet shows. *Balagan* would now become the dramatic setting for his set and costume design.

*Petrushka* is generally considered the pinnacle of all the masterworks produced under the aegis of the Diaghilev collaborators because of the particularly harmonious balance of its components of libretto, choreography, music, and decor. A ballet within a ballet, *Petrushka* takes place in the pre-Lenten Butter Week *balagan* prior to the Russian Easter. The chief characters are puppets who act out a poignant love triangle in their rooms behind the stage of their little theater. Each puppet is loosely based on a composite of personalities from

243

Russian legend and *commedia dell'arte* figures. Extraordinary interpretations of the leading roles were rendered by Nijinsky as Petrushka, a straw-stuffed puppet with the soul of a human being. Karsavina danced the role of the flighty ballerina whom he loves, and Alexander Orlov portrayed the handsome but empty-headed Moor whom the ballerina prefers. Fokine's handling of the joyfully milling crowd scenes gave each dancer an individual characterization that added vitality and flavor to the festive setting. Diaghilev's theatrical instincts for assembling the particular talents that created *Petrushka* confirmed once again his cataclysmic impact on twentieth-century dance.

The second great achievement of the 1911 season was *Le Spectre de la Rose* (The Spirit of the Rose), with libretto by Jean-Louis Vaudoyer, after a poem by Théophile Gautier and set to the nineteenth-century music of Carl Maria von Weber. Bakst provided a delicate decor and exceptional costumes for the two characters danced by Karsavina and Nijinsky. The haunting theme depicts a young girl returning home after her first ball. In a dream she is visited by the spirit of the rose given to her at the party. In a genuinely romantic manner they dance, recreating the pleasures of the waltz. At the end of the duet, the spirit disappears as fleetingly as it came, leaving the girl alone in her room to dream on, as the rose falls from her hand.

*Spectre*'s exquisite *pas de deux* met with immense success for both dancers. Nijinsky outdid himself in a solo in which Fokine exploited the dancer's unmatched elevation, academic beats, and *pirouettes* to the fullest. Fokine choreographed the spirit of the rose leaving by one of the large windows in Bakst's set. Because of Nijinsky's extraordinary command of the air, the dancer was able to accomplish a leap so amazing, an illusion was created that the spirit soared beyond the window clearing and into the night sky. Nijinsky timed his *grand jeté* so that the audience only saw him leap upward, his descent being off stage and out of view.[31] Just as in his soul-wrenching interpretation of Petrushka, Nijinsky as the spirit of the rose transformed himself into the role, at the same time androgynous, enigmatic, and utterly beautiful.

The full extent of the audience's reaction to *Spectre* became clear in the days ahead. When Bakst's carefully tinted silk petals on Nijinsky's costume began mysteriously disappearing, it was discovered that the dancer's valet, Vassily Zuikov, was the culprit. In an effort to benefit from the frenzied souvenir-seeking society matrons, he nightly clipped off and sold the damp petals to enraptured fans.[32] The other Fokine ballets, *Narcisse* (1911), created for Nijinsky, and *Sadko* (1911), an undersea ballet from an opera, completed the bill, but they met with minor success in comparison to *Spectre*.

When the third Paris season was received by an ecstatic public, the company felt confident to venture to London for performances in the autumn of 1911. While French tastes had preferred the exotic works in the repertory, the English favored the romantic ones. British theatergoers, accustomed to post-Romantic style dance of the musical-hall variety, responded passionately to the Russian ballet, becoming faithful and informed devotees of the art; they continue to be so to this day. The *prima ballerina assoluta* of the Maryinsky, Mathilde

244

Tamara Karsavina and Vaslav
Nijinsky in *Le Spectre de la Rose*.
(Courtesy of Jerome Robbins Dance
Division, The New York Public
Library for the Performing
Arts, Astor, Lenox and Tilden
Foundations.)

Kschessinska, joined the troupe in London, agreeing to dance a modified version of *Swan Lake*. The year was to end with a special season in St. Petersburg
where Diaghilev dearly hoped to present his new company, but fate intervened.
Naraodny Dom, the national theater where they were to perform, burned to the
ground, dashing Diaghilev's hopes for a triumphant homecoming. The unofficial
reason for cancelling the engagement, however, was that Diaghilev's abrupt dismissal from the Imperial Theater was still an issue with his old enemies in the
powerful Maryinsky Directorate.

## $\mathcal{C}$HOREOGRAPHIC DEBUT OF VASLAV NIJINSKY

Notable changes occurred in the Ballets Russes in 1912 that influenced the
future direction and artistic policies of the company. Fokine was already preparing *Thamar*, *Daphnis et Chloé* (Daphnis and Chloe), and *Le Dieu Bleu* (The Blue

God). Having French librettists and composers, these ballets signaled the end of the company's pure "Russian" ballet identity. By engaging French collaborators, wags of the moment claimed Diaghilev was ingratiating himself with Parisian salon society to gain its financial support for his projects.

The most dramatic upheaval the company had yet experienced arose when it became apparent to Fokine that Diaghilev was grooming Nijinsky to create ballets. Despite Fokine's proven excellence in bringing forth a number of exquisite works (made possible by his superior education and musicianship), Diaghilev and Bakst thought that Nijinsky could be molded into a choreographer. Nijinsky was open to the idea of exploring a new medium of self-expression and began to discuss possible topics and ideas for his choreographic debut. From the onset of their homosexual relationship, Diaghilev had immersed himself in directing and broadening the artistic education of the young dancer and his efforts were now to bear fruit. Whether Diaghilev's intentions were purely in Nijinksy's best interest, or whether he was in some sense encouraging Nijinsky to be the medium of his own artistic urges as a creator of talent, is a moot point.[33] In any case, by introducing him to famous artists as well as the cream of Parisian society, by squiring him to concerts, museums, and exhibitions, Diaghilev was convinced that he was preparing a choreographer. For hours at a time both Bakst and Diaghilev worked with the dancer behind locked doors, influencing him in ways that can never be known. Thus was an intolerable professional situation created, leading to Fokine's resignation.

When Nijinsky's experimental work finally appeared, it vaulted dance into the future by overthrowing traditional concepts of beauty on the ballet stage. Stimulated by early Egyptian and Greek art he had seen at the Louvre, Nijinsky found the inspiration for his first choreographic essay, *L'Après-midi d'un Faune* (1912, Afternoon of a Faun). The ballet, according to Stravinsky,[34] was conceptually devised by Diaghilev, while the choreography was strongly influenced by Bakst. Based on Stéphane Mallarmé's poetic monologue of sexual discovery, a faun first pursues and then loses nymphs in a forest. In a mood of erotic languor perfectly set by Claude Debussy's score, the faun relives their memory and expresses his thwarted desire.

Nijinsky's initial experiments for his ballet were in search of a new style of movement that included ways for suggesting the two-dimensional archaic figures on Greek vases. His neoprimitive approach dissected human movement and restructured it in geometric forms. Washing away the sentimental and romantic, Nijinsky introduced sexual ambiguity and raw emotion to the ballet stage. He abandoned all virtuosity[35] and the academic technique in developing the choreography, and used non-dance movement to link the angular bas-relief poses of the faun and the nymphs. In a complete departure from classical ballet, the dancers were directed to move without turnout and to show their bodies in profile to the audience. Diaghilev allowed 120 rehearsals to be called in the birthing of the nine-minute piece, and through Nijinsky, he achieved his aim to present something that he deemed disturbingly new to the public who was accustomed to hearty Fokine fare.[36]

246

Unexpectedly, *L'Après-midi d'un Faune* evoked a riot in the theater and a scandal in the press. Nijinsky, who danced the part of the faun, chose to end the ballet with movements designed to imitate the sexual climax. Chaos broke out in the theater between those who were morally outraged and those who responded to the beauty of Debussy's score and Bakst's intoxicating effects of decor and costumes. The press joined the uproar the next day by censuring Diaghilev for allowing the offending final moment of the ballet. In the long run, however, *Faune* weathered the storm and actually achieved a certain success due to its beguiling originality. Today it is still performed, enjoyed for its hypnotizing marriage of aural and visual beauty. The publicity created by the initial reaction to the ballet served nicely to increase box office receipts, all of which fired Diaghilev's tendency for risk-taking. With its ground-breaking newness, the piece encouraged Diaghilev's growing predilection for avant-garde trends in which he was the first to involve ballet.

IN THE DANCELESS BALLET OF HIS DEVISING, WHICH WAS PRESENTED TWICE ON ITS FIRST PRODUCTION IN LONDON : M. NIJINSKY AS THE FAUN IN "L'APRÈS-MIDI D'UN FAUNE."

*L'Après midi d'un Faune.* Nijinsky surrounded by some of the choreographic motifs that he created for the nymphs. (Courtesy of the Victoria & Albert Museum, London.)

247

*Choreographic Debut of Vaslav Nijinsky*

Fokine was deeply hurt that his professional competence, highly respected in Russia and now in Europe, had been publicly devalued in deference to Nijinsky's novice attempts at dance-making. Still, and with little regret, Diaghilev allowed the disgruntled Fokine to leave when his contract expired even though his creative capacity was far from exhausted. Fokine's departure left the Ballets Russes without a proven choreographer, but Diaghilev evidently felt Nijinsky would provide the company with important works given the opportunity. Until that time arrived, however, Fokine's ballets would necessarily remain the largest part of the repertory.

The company continued its successful tours to major European cities during the 1913 season, and Nijinsky served as the leading male artist and sole choreographer. The dancer began a new ballet set to Stravinsky's *Le Sacre du Printemps* (1913, The Rite of Spring). As a work-in-progress it had no clear plot and began with a collection of dances performed by a large ensemble. The ballet suggested primitive rites that climaxed with the sacrificial death of a tribal maiden. Going beyond the parallel leg positions in *Faune*, Nijinsky's experiments now demanded turned-in legs, clenched fists, non-classical steps and positions, and body-straining movements for which the dancers were untrained.

Due to the complexities of the music, Nijinsky's inexperience, uncommanding off-stage personality, and the dancers' unwillingness to cooperate with their choreographer, it soon became clear to everyone involved that the projected ballet would not be finished. The dancers openly disliked the unmelodious music and resented the violent stomping patterns they were made to perform. In desperation Diaghilev sought the advice of the music theoretician, Emile Jaques-Dalcroze, who recommended that he engage his Polish assistant, Marie Rambert. Her assignment was to disentangle the rhythmic intricacies of Stravinsky's score for Nijinsky and the dancers so that the choreographer could proceed with the work.[37] When Diaghilev heard of the unpopularity of *Sacre du Printemps* (1959, Rite of Spring) with the cast, he noted that their irritation augured well because it confirmed the originality of Nijinsky's composition. Grigoriev wrote years later that he resorted to calling occasional rehearsals of the eminently danceable Fokine ballets simply to restore the dancers' morale.

When *Sacre* was finally presented in the middle of the 1913 season, it was intentionally included amidst the beloved Fokine ballets. Even then, at the premiere, the hostile indignation in a section of the audience was so pronounced that it became all but impossible for the orchestra and the dancers to continue. The boldness of Stravinsky's music shocked to such an extent that fighting broke out in the theater. No sooner were the offenders ejected by police and the lights turned back down then the commotion again erupted and continued to the end of the ballet. Stravinsky later recalled how his life was endangered later that night when his carriage was mobbed by members of the irate audience. The unnerving experience deterred Stravinsky from composing another ballet score for some years.

The aftermath of the public's outcry over *Sacre* was proof that Diaghilev had succeeded again in the production of new and provoking artistic creations.

248

Nijinsky was hurt by his ballet's lack of acceptance and its brief life of nine performances, while many of the dancers grew to recognize that they had participated in a history-making event. After overcoming the trials of so many difficult
rehearsals, they began to appreciate this compelling ballet, born as a precursor
of its time. Indeed, years later, when Stravinsky was asked what he thought
about the many choreographed interpretations of *Sacre*, he replied that, in retrospect, Nijinsky's was the best.[38] *Sacre du Printemps* had awakened an awareness
in the public of the need for daring self-expression and originality. With
Nijinsky's choreographic revelation of the unknown in art, the traditional
notions of grace and beauty in ballet were dethroned. He had made a radical
dance statement in the conception and realization of *Sacre* and with this production, the Ballets Russes irrevocably changed the course of theatrical dance.[39]

The 1913 Paris season of the Ballets Russes had coincided with the occasion of the opening of the Théâtre de Champs Élysées. A third ballet by
Nijinsky entitled *Jeux* (1913, Games) preceded the premiere of *Sacre* and was on
the opening night program. It was the first time a ballet costumed in sport
clothes was seen on stage.[40] Set to commissioned music by Debussy, its theme
evolved around a tennis game, which provided the enigmatic basis for the
movement of its trio cast of Karsavina, Nijinsky, and Ludmilla Schollar. The ballet's strangeness as a stage work puzzled the uncomprehending audience and it
was not a success. However, the standard Ballets Russes fare primarily created
by Fokine, as well as a new work by company member Boris Romanov, *La
Tragédie de Salomé* (1913, The Tragedy of Salomé), the scandalous *Sacre du
Printemps*, and a segments of Russian operas provided the company with a successful showing in the new theater.

# $\mathcal{T}$HE BALLETS RUSSES VISITS THE NEW WORLD

The company sailed for engagements in South America toward the end of the
summer of 1913. Diaghilev, both a hypochondriac and superstitious (a fortuneteller once told him he would die on the water), stayed behind. The most sensational occurrence of the South American tour was that Nijinsky married Romola
de Pulszky, a pretty Hungarian socialite who had attached herself to the
troupe.[41] She had recently become a ballet student, working intensely under
Cecchetti's tutelage. Diaghilev tolerated her presence with the company because
he invariably made a practice of courting rich and influential people, which her
actress–mother was. Little did Diaghilev suspect Romula's girlish infatuation
with the introverted dancer and her determination to marry him. In a fit of rage
and jealously, Diaghilev responded to Nijinsky's marriage as a personal betrayal.
Although he was allowed to keep his position as premier dancer, he lost his
place as choreographer to the "hated" Fokine.[42]

Under the influence of his new wife, Nijinsky refused to dance one night,
the reasons being difficult to discern. Diaghilev used this incident to claim the

249

dancer had officially broken his contract and summarily fired him. Unfortunately, as happened all too often in the course of twenty years, Diaghilev's personal involvement with his artists threatened to jeopardize the functioning of the company. His strong need to control and direct the work of his artists tended to restrict their creative freedom, causing frequent emotional ruptures and untimely departures from the Ballets Russes.

Diaghilev began plans for the 1914 season by coaxing Fokine back to the Ballets Russes, not only to resume his choreographic responsibilities, but also to substitute for Nijinsky as the leading male dancer. The replacement of Nijinsky did not seem to affect the usual successes of the company, now firmly established as part of European culture. Besides, Fokine enjoyed the distinction of having fifteen of his ballets in the repertory that were still popular with the public. The same year Diaghilev added Léonide Massine (1895–1979) to the roster. Sensing in the young man rich possibilities as a choreographer, Diaghilev took charge of educating Massine and of cultivating the dancer's sensibilities.[43] He was exposed to the elements of composition, he was taken to galleries and concerts, he was given pictures, and he was introduced to the leading artists and performers of the day. Massine, who had trained as both an actor and dancer at the Bolshoi in Moscow, was put to intensive study with Maestro Cecchetti. Clearly, Diaghilev was grooming him to artistically and personally fill the absence left by Nijinsky's dismissal.

Of four ballets produced that year, only Fokine's *Le Coq d'Or* (1913, The Golden Cock) was an unqualified success. This ballet was set to Rimsky-Korsakov's opera and incorporated both singers and dancers on stage. Natalia Goncharova's vibrant decor produced an effect of glowing color and Slavic fantasy that admirably enhanced the impression made by Karsavina, who danced the role of the golden cock. The orchestra and the magnificent Russian singers and chorus were under the baton of Pierre Monteux. *Le Coq d'Or* was an experiment in the best Ballets Russes tradition. With its success Fokine once again took his rightful place as master choreographer while Diaghilev was exonerated by the public for the more sensational or weaker creations of the previous two years.

In addition to the impact that the Ballets Russes had on the European culture scene in the early phase of its existence, a growing awareness and interest in dance were also being fed by other pockets of activity. Since the 1908 appearances of Anna Pavlova in Scandinavia and Germany, there had been small and sporadic showings of individual Russian dancers, and even temporarily organized groups of established artists, contracting themselves out to theater managers in some European capitals. At one point all the major music halls of London boasted a Russian ballerina on their programs. In 1911 Ida Rubinstein supported a rival company to Diaghilev's in Paris, and with her substantial fortune, periodically commissioned works by Fokine and Diaghilev's later choreographers. She engaged composers, artists, and dancers to fulfill numerous engagements for more than twenty years. In 1913 Anna Pavlova formed her

250

own troupe and from her London home she continuously toured the world, her interpretive art becoming a legend in the dancer's own time.

The infant modern dance movement was making itself felt on European soil and contributed to the growing interest in theatrical dance because of its experimental tendencies and its concern with social and political issues. Loie Fuller, the American pioneer, was admired on the Continent for her lighting experiments in the creation of theatrical illusion. The iconoclastic Isadora Duncan was an outspoken, veteran celebrity in Paris and St. Petersburg some years before the Ballets Russes permanently existed. When Mary Wigman made her debut in 1914, German modern dance took its first important steps as a serious new art form. Thus, in the period prior to World War I, was a reawakened interest in dance art demonstrated by audiences who welcomed the creative work of young and vibrant artists wherever they appeared.

# Summary

Diaghilev's enterprise had the farthest-reaching impact on renewed public interest in theatrical dance in the early decades of the twentieth century. The Ballets Russes' superlative artistic merits, particularly as exhibited in its first six years, distinguished it as an incomparable apparatus devoted to the presentation of new forms of visual and aural beauty. Under the aegis of the maverick Diaghilev and his chief collaborators—Benois, Bakst, Fokine, and Stravinsky—a brilliant new dance, one designed for modern times, took shape and ravished a public hungry for an exotic, dramatic, and sensuous performing art. When Nijinsky moved to the domain of choreography, by testing even newer waters, he tore asunder the standard concepts of beauty. The grace and elegance that ballet had traditionally expressed were replaced with dissected and reconstructed geometric shapes, infused with overt sexuality and primitive emotion.

In an extraordinary unfolding, the Ballets Russes of Sergei Diaghilev had returned ballet to the West in a new and often shocking guise after an absence of seventy years. If any one person can be credited for shepherding the growth of twentieth-century ballet, it was Diaghilev, who lifted it from the rarified realm of the aristocracy and offered it to the man on the street.

251

## Chapter Notes

1. Arnold Haskell, *Ballets Russes: The Age of Diaghilev* (London: Weidenfeld & Nicolson Gollancz, 1968), p. 32. Translation for *mais ça viendra*: "but that will come."
2. Richard Buckle, *Diaghilev* (New York: Atheneum, 1979), p. 31.
3. Ibid., p. 38.

4. Ibid., p. 63.

5. Ibid., pp. 84–85.

6. Ibid., pp. 95–99.

7. Surviving on a piece of stationery in the Astruc papers at Lincoln Center is a proposed repertory for 1909 that indicates that *Sylvia, Giselle,* and *Pavillon d'Armide* were being considered for the season. The notes are in the handwriting of Gabriel Astruc, who was the French theatrical entrepreneur dealing with Diaghilev's Russian projects in Paris.

8. Buckle, p. 38–40.

9. Lynn Garafola, *Diaghilev's Ballets Russes* (New York: Oxford University Press, 1989), p. 15. Garafola gives a detailed account of Diaghilev's activities and points out that the musical and artistic blueprint for his first ballet season grew out of the collaboratively produced operas at the Abramtsevo art colony during the 1880s.

10. Buckle, p. 120. Astruc claimed it was he who originally gave Diaghilev the idea of bringing Russian ballet to Paris. In a verbatim account of a conversation over dinner during 1908, Buckle records that Astruc expressed his admiration for the dances in *Boris Godunov* to Diaghilev. The latter countered with a diatribe on the splendid merits of czarist ballet, whereupon Astruc told him that he must bring Russian dance to Paris in the forthcoming season.

11. Garafola, p. 177.

12. Ibid., p. 19. Fokine viewed the concept of style in his period pieces as the "creation of historical illusion based on direct observation of reality combined with historical reconstruction."

13. Ibid., p. 21–22.

14. Ilya Schneider, *Isadora Duncan: The Russian Years*, trans. David Magarshack (New York: Harcourt, Brace & World, 1968), p. 33.

15. Garafola, p. 41.

16. Ibid., p. 87.

17. Ibid., p. 28.

18. Carol Lee, *An Introduction to Classical Ballet* (Hillsdale, NJ, & London: Erlbaum Associates, 1983), pp. 137–38.

19. Buckle, p. 174.

20. Haskell, p. 69.

21. S. L. Grigoriev, *The Diaghilev Ballet, 1909–1929*, trans. and ed. by Vera Bowen (Harmondsworth, Middlesex: Penguin Books, 1960), p. 43.

22. Garafola, p. 22.

23. Grigoriev, p. 46.

24. In choosing Schumann's music for *Carnaval*, Fokine and his colleagues marked the Ballets Russes' first step toward using non-Russian composers. While *Les Sylphides'* score was comprised of music composed in France, Chopin was a citizen of Russian-dominated Poland; the Russian court composer, Glazunov had orchestrated the ballet for Diaghilev.

25. Buckle, pp. 172–73.

26. Ibid., pp. 182–83.

27. Vera Krasovskaya, *Nijinsky*, trans. John W. Bowlt (New York: Schirmer Books, 1979), p. 154.

28. Buckle, *Nijinsky* (New York: Equinox, 1975), p. 172.

252

29. Erkki Tann, conversation (1996).

30. The name Petrushka is the diminutive of the Russian *Petuhh*, meaning "little rooster," which inspired Benois' cockscomb design in Nijinsky's costume.

31. Alexander Schouvaloff, *The Art of Ballets Russes: The Serve Lifar Collection of Theater Designs, Costumes, and Paintings at the Wadsworth Atheneum* (New Haven, CT, & London: Yale University Press, 1997), pp. 67–70, ff. 6. The British critic and historian, John Percival, stated a less dramatic description of Nijinsky leaving the stage in *Spectre*. He recalled that the dancer stepped onto the window ledge and then "floated down."

32. Krasovskaya, p. 165.

33. Haskell, p. 82.

34. Charles Spencer, *Leon Bakst* (London: Academy Editions, 1973), p. 98. Madame Nijinsky's account in the biography of her husband was at odds with that of Stravinsky. She insisted that the dancer came up with the idea for the Grecian ballet himself and that he was as dissatisfied with Bakst's decor as he was with Debussy's music, complaining that neither suited his choreography.

35. Buckle, *Diaghilev*, p. 247.

36. Haskell, p. 79. In defending his artistic policies, Diaghilev once said: "I am accused of treating classicism with neglect and contempt. Rubbish. Classicism like everything else evolves. We must first make up our minds as to what is classicism. There were outcries, at first, about the music of Igor Stravinsky—now it is classic. . . . classicism is the university of the modern choreographer, but to develop theatrical creation we cannot remain academic. We have all learned algebra and Greek but not in order to solve problems nor to speak Greek. The dancer and ballet master of today must matriculate, just as Picasso must know anatomy and Stravinsky his scales."

37. Buckle, *Nijinsky*, pp. 267–68.

38. Bronislava Nijinska, *Early Memoirs* (New York: Holt, Rinehart and Winston, 1981), trans. and ed. by Irina Nijinska and Jean Rawlinson, p. 471.

39. Garafola, p. 74.

40. Buckle, *Diaghilev*, p. 249.

41. Krasovskaya, pp. 277–80.

42. Buckle, *Diaghilev*, p. 263.

43. Ibid., pp. 284–85.

253

# 12

# The Ballets Russes from the Pursuit of the Avant-Garde to Neoclassicism

Diaghilev's Ballets Russes had established itself as a major force in the life of European culture within its first few seasons. Not since the Renaissance had the Continent witnessed and welcomed such an intense artistic interchange as that stimulated by Diaghilev and his roster of collaborators. The company's triumphs reflected a bourgeois public's need to see itself as part of a growing, modern, mechanized, and worldly society. Whatever the Ballets Russes presented, Paris eagerly embraced, at least for the moment, and the rest of Europe followed her lead. Once the company's dance style established itself as an art form comprised of elegant, compact, and astonishing ballets, Diaghilev's ongoing task was the motivation of the creative process with whomever it was to be found. As time passed and fame and demand grew, the need to replenish the repertory and sustain his assembly of dancers became an unending quest.

## THE WAR YEARS (1914–1918)

The outbreak of World War I interrupted the workings of the Ballets Russes and marked a turning point in the development of the company. When engagements in Germany and England were cancelled due to the growing hostilities, Diaghilev spent the time in preparation for a tour of the United States. A new generation of leading dancers was engaged to replace the absence of Karsavina, who was in Russia with her English diplomat husband and about to give birth. Fokine, for the second time, parted ways with Diaghilev, leaving the troupe bereft of a principal dancer and choreographer. Nijinsky, under house arrest in Budapest, was unavailable even if Diaghilev had decided to forgive him for marrying Romola de Pulszky.

Leading the list of new principals was the brilliant soubrette, Lydia Lopokova. She had joined the company in 1910 following her graduation from the Imperial Ballet School of St. Petersburg. After five years under Diaghilev's discriminating eye, he deemed her ready to inherit a number of Karsavina's *demi-caractère* roles. Endowed with enormous charm on and off stage, Lopokova was widely acclaimed and enjoyed particular favor with the growing number of London balletomanes. Aside from several short tours, Lopokova danced exclusively for Diaghilev to the end of his organization. From the Imperial Ballet School, Lubov Tchernicheva entered the Ballets Russes ranks, eventually distinguishing herself in many important character roles that Massine would create for her over the years. Sixteen-year-old Vera Nemchinova, from the Moscow school, joined the company and would also excel in the soon-to-be-seen Massine repertory. Lydia Sokolova, born Hilda Munnings, was the first of Diaghilev's several English soloists. She had studied with Pavlova, Mordkin, and Cecchetti during times when they were in London. Sokolova was appreciated for her dramatic flair and her Slavic-like exuberant dancing in character roles. Stanislas Idzikovsky and Leon Woidzikovsky, two Polish dancers who had trained at the National Ballet School in Warsaw, were a welcome addition to the rank of male soloists for their versatility and virtuosity.

The end of the year marked Léonide Massine's debut as a budding choreographer with the premiere of *Le Soleil de Nuit* (1915, Midnight Sun). In Massine, Diaghilev felt he had discovered someone who could respond to and interpret the fruits of his own highly active imagination. As an administrator, Diaghilev played an unprecedented role. Although a well-known lover of all the arts and a sophisticated dilettante, Diaghilev was not professionally trained in any medium. Yet he used young, fledgling talents to actualize his own ideas of appropriate artistic subject matter, musical style, and scenic and lighting design. Just as he had done with Nijinsky, his efforts to educate Massine bore abundant fruit in a very short time.

# *C*HE BALLETS RUSSES IN AMERICA

The Ballets Russes opened its North American season with fifty dancers, giving two weeks of performances at the Century Theater in New York in January 1916. Aroused by a barrage of advanced press notices initiated by Diaghilev and the American management, the public showed great interest in what was a novel form of theatrical entertainment in the United States. Following the opening performance, the press issued exceedingly favorable reviews, despite the fact that Nijinsky and Karsavina had not yet arrived because of travel complications in Europe. New York was seeing a smaller company compared to that shown in the initial Paris and London seasons. Although the number of dancers was reduced, the choreography represented the full glory of the repertory. Twelve of the fourteen ballets were by Fokine, with one each representing the choreography of Nijinsky and Massine. While *Petrushka* was appreciated for the intrinsic merit of its perfectly matched components, *Faune* again succeeded in shocking, this time the puritanical American audience. Lopokova became the great favorite of the New York season, enhancing her popularity by enchanting the press with innumerable interviews in quaint English.

Departing New York for an arduous eight-week tour of the United States— with dancers, large orchestra, and stage technicians—was an immense and complex undertaking for train travel. The entourage occupied numerous coaches in addition to box cars needed for scenery and equipment. The company's schedule included many one-night stands as far west as Kansas City and provided the troupe with an amazing array of American experiences. Upon finishing the tour, the Ballets Russes returned to New York to dance another four weeks at the Metropolitan Opera House.

In April, Nijinsky had been released from his incarceration in Hungary through the intercession of the Metropolitan Opera and various European powers, including the King of Spain and Pope Benedict XV. Nijinsky finally arrived to fulfill a contractual stipulation that he dance with the company when he was freed. In need of the great dancer's box office appeal, Diaghilev tolerated his return, and there was a short-lived effort to reconcile their differences. However, tensions created by Nijinsky's wife over money matters, the dancer's growing paranoia, and his aloofness from company members caused matters to go from bad to worse. On several occasions he refused to perform, and more than once he walked out of rehearsals. It has been frequently noted that the first signs of the dancer's madness began to surface at this time in his antagonistic and unfriendly behavior toward the company.

At season's end the Ballets Russes sailed from New York to Spain for performances and to plan new works for the coming year. In the fall of 1916, the company returned to the Metropolitan Opera, this time without Diaghilev. Otto Kahn, the socially ambitious New York impresario and great admirer of the Ballets Russes, insisted on Nijinsky's presence, asking him to direct the second North American tour. From the beginning it was apparent that Nijinsky was incapable, by nature or training, to handle the managerial responsibilities that go with running a ballet company.[1] Finding the famous troupe a threat to its tradition-bound opera productions that were studded with a mediocre level of classical ballet, the administration of the Metropolitan Opera proceeded to interfere with the company's touring arrangements and a number of bookings were lost. Consequently, under Nijinsky's direction the Ballets Russes ended the American season by incurring heavy debts and damaging the company's artistic reputation.

Trouble had been brewing since the earliest negotiations between the Metropolitan and the Ballets Russes. The opera's general manager, Guilo Gatti-Casazza overtly disliked Diaghilev and had been against the New York visit to the point of wishing to sabotage it. Leading the Met's opera *corps de ballet* was

Rosina Galli, an accomplished technician trained at La Scala, who was also Gatti-Casazza's mistress. The couple viewed the appearances of the sensational Russians as a threat to Galli's hold on the New York audience. From behind the scenes, they were only too pleased to add to the many problems occurring under Nijinsky's lack of leadership.[2]

Early in the New York season, Nijinsky premiered *Tyl Eulenspiegel* (1916), his fourth and last ballet. A centuries-old German tale of a roguish prankster served as the dramatic basis that was set to Richard Strauss' tone poem by the same title. The ballet's stylish and ultra-theatrical costumes and decor were created by the American designer, Robert Edmund Jones. The work's choreographic conception represented more of Nijinsky's unorthodox approaches to dance making. Ineffectual in communicating his intentions to a cast who failed to appreciate his innovations, the ballet was unfinished on opening night, leaving the dancers to improvise as best they could during sections of incomplete choreography.[3] Nevertheless, it was considered a success by audience and press who awarded it fifteen curtain calls. Although the ballet was given twenty-two times in America, it did not survive its premiere season. *Tyl Eulenspiegel* was the only ballet produced by the Ballets Russes that Diaghilev never saw in rehearsal or performance. It was also the only ballet of the company's large repertory to have an American as one of its major collaborators.

It has often been said that under different circumstances Nijinsky would have been a more fulfilled and productive choreographer. What we can glean from his own words, his sister Bronislava's commentary,[4] critical interpretations of his choreographic aesthetic, old photographs, and first-hand memories, confirm that the dancer was a genuine harbinger of the radically unconventional in ballet. Indeed, his few works shared common elements with the experimental efforts fostered by the great American trailblazers of modern dance some years later. Unfortunately, Nijinsky lacked the ability to win support for his ideas from those who could have helped him the most, his dancers.

Cut off more and more from his prewar sources of Russian artists, Diaghilev was forced to seek inspiration elsewhere for new works that the public had grown to expect each season. For some time, futurist art theory had interested Diaghilev. Futurism extended the limits of traditional art by bending, reshaping, and combining conventional ideas while also absorbing new material. Aided by an abundant use of modern technology, the new genre distracted, entertained, and astonished; and, to varying degrees, it played a part in determining the direction of the Ballets Russes. Diaghilev took his first public steps into Futurism by producing a stage work for Stravinsky's score *Feu d'Artifice* (1916, Fireworks).[5] Giacomo Balla's concept for presenting the music was a complex light show that played on a stage setting of geometrical solids. It is thought that Diaghilev himself designed and executed the complex illumination. The musical and visual effect harmonized to display the essential futurist characteristics of abstraction, brevity, and dynamism.

257

# $\mathcal{T}$HE BALLETS RUSSES (1917–1929)

## MASSINE: FUTURISM AND CUBISM IN BALLET

By 1917 Léonide Massine had developed into an experienced choreographer with the productions of the Spanish-inspired *Las Meninas* (1916, The Maids of Honor), *Kikimora* (1916), which later became part of *Contes Russes* (1917, Russian Tales), and *Les Femmes de Bonne Humeur* (1917, The Good Humored Ladies), the first modern comedy of manners in ballet. An intellectual as opposed to instinctual approach to choreography came into dance-making with Massine. Unlike most novice choreographers who form their work by imitating or rebelling against the previous generation, Massine learned the basics of choreographic grouping and designing poses from the painter's static images. By studying canvases of the masters, Diaghilev encouraged Massine to imitate gestures and movements in pictures that they most admired. The young man proved to be a serious, eager student and quickly grasped the style of different periods as well as the unique expressiveness revealed in every good painting. Under the influence of the neoprimitive designer, Mikhail Larionov, Massine replaced ballet's soft, beautiful lines and harmonious flow with angular, mechanical, and short movements. Massine's *ballets d'atmosphère* tied their action together by evoking the quality of a particular mood that cloaked the idea with which he was immediately concerned. Filled with character dances, his ballets during this period were of the present; they were concerned with the commonplace and were presented in a vanguard format.

Diaghilev leaned upon Massine's creativity to provide the company with a new work called *Parade*. The ballet embodied the futurist elements of an alogical format, concrete sounds, mechanistic movements, and structured costumes. It was a startling collaborative effort that included Jean Cocteau's scenario involving various characters at a parade. Cocteau led a group of six young French composers called *Les Six* whom he encouraged to find inspiration from the witty, worldly art of the circus and music halls.[6] The musicians were hostile to the emotionalism in French music that had been introduced by the German composer Richard Wagner. As a result, Erik Satie, who was a staunch member of *Les Six*, produced a score for *Parade* that was at times less music than a collage of twentieth-century sounds including whistles, machinery, and the clatter of the typewriter.

Diaghilev commissioned Picasso to design a drop curtain that filled the proscenium arch with a vast, glowing canvas.[7] It imposed itself upon the vision of the viewer, giving no hint of the *mise en scène* that would follow the overture for the iconoclastic production. Picasso's cubist experiments with sets proceeded in the same manner. No longer bound by the logic of ordinary perspective, the artist provided the Ballets Russes with traditional backdrops bearing extremely untraditional images. He analyzed three-dimensional space and then disassembled and reassembled it according to new principles.

258

Vera Nemchinova and
Tadeo Slavinsky in
Massine's *Les Femmes de
Bonne Humeur.* (Courtesy
of the Victoria & Albert
Museum, London.)

*Parade*'s plot gave little to the ballet, but the visual impact of Picasso's
cubist impulse was at its strongest in this jarring work. In ways distinctively his
own, Picasso allowed his costume designs to share in the freedom already
attained by avant-garde painting and sculpture that influenced his decor. His
concepts signaled a new point of departure for the company. Two of the
dancers, portraying "managers" of the parade, were encased in nine-foot tall
box-like structures, creating an extraordinary impression with very little mobil-
ity. The astonished audience noisily reacted to the fragments of tap dancing,
everyday movement, and peculiar behavior of the dancers that replaced the
familiar Ballets Russes brand of choreography. Yet *Parade* was rewarded with
much applause according to eyewitnesses. The condescending press, however,
deemed the ballet an interesting failure. By abjuring classicism and its roots in
the *danse d'école*, Massine's research into the avant-garde lost for ballet its very
language and rationale for existing, resembling, as *Parade* did, any number of
other theatrical experiments going on in Paris at the time.

The Ballets Russes returned to South America without Diaghilev and
Massine following a brief season in Spain, a country less affected by the ongoing

war. It was in Buenos Aires, the locale of his marriage and now the place of his professional turning point, where Nijinsky performed for the last time. The dancer's meteoric career ended as his schizophrenic behavior erupted in a series of eccentric incidents, making the continuation of his dancing impossible. Nijinsky's illness progressively worsened over the next months while radical attempts to cure him failed, and he receded into thirty-five years of twilight existence.

The Ballets Russes ended its tenth year with a season in postwar London. Due to a lack of continental engagements, the company was fortunate to share a music hall bill with other entertainers at the Coliseum, performing one of several ballets twelve times a week. Later, an additional season at the Alhambra Theater allowed the troupe to resume offering full-length ballet performances for the faithful, enthusiastic British public in a more appropriate setting. Two new Massine ballets, which would win immortality for the choreographer, were added to the repertory. The premiere of *La Boutique Fantasque* (1919, The Fantastic Toy Shop) marked the company's most durable and popular success since 1914. With its charming 1830s story of a bourgeois family and animated toys, the ballet revealed Massine's great gift for characterization and provided Lopokova with her signature role as the can-can doll. Massine's toyshop theme for *Boutique* was not new but reconfirmed itself as an ideal plot for the ballet medium and a timeless favorite of audiences. Saint-Léon's *Coppélia* survived as a masterpiece of the empire ballet style in France, and Joseph Hassreiter's *Die Puppenfee* (The Fairy Doll) used the toyshop theme in an enormously popular Viennese production choreographed in 1888.[8] Although *Coppélia* and *Puppenfee* were still being performed in 1919, Massine's *Boutique* was up-to-date in the eyes of the modern audience. Its design by André Derain undercut the sentimental nostalgia inherent in the plot of the earlier ballets with a clever play on the past and present. Gioacchino Rossini's music, orchestrated by Ottorino Respighi, provided an air of clarity and freshness to the piece.

An even finer ballet by Massine, *Le Tricorne* (1919, The Three Cornered Hat) was the first of several Spanish-styled works that displayed his choreographic versatility. His superb flair for the flamenco and *escuela bolero* techniques had been acquired on frequent visits to Spain. Studying in Barcelona and high up in the caves of Granada's Sacramonte under the gypsy Félix Fernández García, Massine had mastered dances that imbued his ballet with atmosphere and authenticity. Three Spanish artists were his collaborators under Diaghilev's watchful eye. Martínez Sierra adapted the libretto from a nineteenth-century novella based on a popular folk tale, and the dynamic, colorful score produced by Manuel de Falla invoked the Iberian passion for life. Highlighting the comic tale of love and jealousy, Picasso created evocative sets and costumes that combined the complexities of cubism with reminiscences of traditional Spanish architecture and dress. Massine danced the character role of the miller, and, with Karsavina as the wife, the two artists became the toasts of London.

An important effort of the Ballets Russes was a revival of the *Sacre du Printemps* in 1920, totally rechoreographed by Massine. The strenuous role of the virgin was danced by the English girl whom Diaghilev had renamed Lydia Sokolova.[9] This time the cacophonous music, not heard for eight years, was accepted by the British audience in contrast to the French pandemonium that had greeted Nijinsky's 1913 premiere. The production was underwritten by the generosity of the fashion designer Coco Chanel who was to remain a close friend and supporter of the company to its last. Compared to Massine's much beloved *Le Tricorne*, his version of *Sacre* was only a relative success despite its extraordinary score and not seen again for several years.

At the halfway mark of the Ballets Russes's twenty years of existence, not only had the various European cities become accustomed and educated to its fresh style of theatrical dance, but to some extent so had cities in North and South America. By the end of the decade, the Ballets Russes had accomplished a revolution in Western stage design. Dating from the early contributions of Benois and Bakst, artists had abandoned the traditional *tromp l'oeil* style with its false perspective that had created the baroque theater. Instead, the painter's brush swept flat surfaces of contrasting colors onto the stage.[10] The costumes themselves formed integral parts of the set. Bakst noted that the dancers became moving elements in a painting. Although they were in perpetual motion, dancers played the part of the easel painter's accents. To enhance the effect of the shimmering movement of colors, costumes were composed of richly patterned surfaces. Painting on textiles, designers were just as important as the seamstresses in garment construction. Those who remembered the costumes in action noted that they made an even more powerful impression on the stage.[11] The radical new costuming presented by the Ballets Russes reinforced the possibilities for entirely new choreographic ideas introduced by those who provided the dance material in Diaghilev's epoch-making productions.[12] After a decade of touring, wherever the Ballets Russes appeared, its inimitable style was applauded and appreciated by an ever-eager public.

While the art of dance in the West was resurging as a product of capitalism under the guidance of Diaghilev, internal affairs within the company often produced a less than ideal situation for its members and the health of the ongoing venture. The Massine era of the Ballets Russes ended with the creation of two marginal works that were only in the repertory briefly. *Le Chant du Rossignol* (1920, Song of the Nightingale) in collaboration with Stravinsky and Henri Matisse, was a one act interpretation of the Hans Christian Andersen fairy tale. While Stravinsky's score and Henri Matisse's decor and costumes were important contributions, in a misdirected effort to be creative, Massine formulated a rhythm on the dance steps that was unrelated to the musical beat. The choreographic result gave the impression that the dancers had no ear for music and were poorly rehearsed.[13] Audience and critics alike made known their disapproval at the ballet's premiere.

The second work was *Pulcinella* (1920), based on the adventures of a *commedia dell'arte* hero. The old Italian theme led Picasso to revive a cast of *commedia* figures from his "blue and rose" periods, contriving some of his most energetic and appealing theatrical creations. Stravinsky reworked themes of

261

Giovanni Pergolesi in which the crisp sounds of seventeenth-century music sat well with those of the composer's modernist strains. The completed work, however, received a lukewarm reception at its Paris premiere while the Barcelona public was actually insulted by the avant-garde humor that Massine imposed on the characterization of Pulcinella.[14] The ballet is primarily remembered today for its lively and very important score that spearheaded the neoclassic movement in music.

The postwar phase of the Ballets Russes was marked by an ever-increasing taste for novelty on the part of Diaghilev. With the scandalous productions of *Faune* and *Sacre*, Diaghilev embraced the idea that instead of courting public opinion, art must shock its audience by defying established concepts of beauty and traditions. He became convinced that the spirit of rebellion was indispensable in the act of artistic creation,[15] which was made so clear in the compositions of Stravinsky and the canvases of Picasso. The great entrepreneur's oft-quoted command to Cocteau, *"étonne-moi, Jean"* ("astonish me, Jean"), summed up his constantly changing aesthetic in regard to new productions. As years passed, genuine artistic quest was often overshadowed in an effort to invoke audience shock with the use of gimmickry for its own sake. Productions progressively appeared to justify themselves as matters more of chic than of art.

One of the strangest ballets of this period was a Russian legend about peasant buffoons, entitled *Chout* (1921) and set to a score by Sergei Prokofiev. Planning with Massine and the designer Larionov, Diaghilev's intent in producing *Chout* was to present new ideas in Russian art to the West.[16] Although Massine had already made preliminary choreographic plans, he suddenly left the company in a temperamental outburst. Because Larionov was familiar with Massine's plans, Diaghilev asked him to be an advisor to the dancer, Tadeo Slavinsky, whom he had assigned the chore of setting the futurist ballet in the absence of Massine. Slavinsky was not only an untrained choreographer, but was also without creative ability. Lacking an experienced choreographer, *Chout* was doomed from the outset and the unprecedented result was more like a pantomime. Furthermore, the critics and audiences decried the lack of harmony between Prokofiev's cool music and Larionov's strong geometric folk motifs. Heavy and over-designed costumes encumbered the dancers' bodies while odd half-masks, absurd makeup, and top-heavy headdresses hid the dancers' expressions. The collaboration that created *Chout* marked one more jolting example of experiment in ballet with its elements of dehumanization and anti-naturalism. Indicative of the company's direction, it was at this juncture that design totally superseded dance and music as the foundation of a Diaghilev production.[17]

When Massine left the Ballets Russes and formed his own group in Latin America, the company was again imperiled by lacking the primary creative force of a genuine choreographer. Unable to secure a replacement for Massine, Diaghilev imported a company of six flamenco artists from Spain led by María Dalbaicín and successfully produced their Andalusian singing and sensationally erotic dances under the title *Cuadro Flamenco* (1921, Gypsy Portrait). Picasso designed the sets for this prefabricated ballet, giving it a stamp of the company's contemporary look.[18] Without a choreographer at work developing collaborative ideas into new pieces, Diaghilev realized that the Ballets Russes would soon be at a loss for fresh material to present to its public. As a result of this dangerous state of affairs, he became involved in the planning of a production that recalled the ballets remembered from his former life in Russia.

## THE SLEEPING PRINCESS

In the wake of Massine's productive experiments, Diaghilev took an unexpected turn by retreating into the nineteenth-century ballet style that he had done so much to make obsolete. Along with many postwar artists and intellectuals, Diaghilev rediscovered the beauties of the classical past. Anti-German sentiment was rampant in Europe after the war and became the driving force that encouraged the exploitation of seventeenth- and eighteenth-century French themes and old and new French music. In conjunction with English theatrical producers and in a bow to traditional artistic endeavor, Diaghilev selected the glorious old Perrault–Petipa–Tchaikovsky masterpiece, *The Sleeping Beauty*.[19] By doing so he departed from the Ballets Russes' signature programming of three or four one-act ballets that had become progressively more experimental in nature. He decided to attempt the full-length classic for the London season of 1921, which he expected would run for six months, coinciding with the 100th anniversary of Petipa's birth. Diaghilev hoped the production would be the vehicle for providing the means to stabilize the troupe during a long and lucrative run. Ultimately, he planned that the projected box office receipts would also underwrite the cost of his continued experiments in the forefront of theater art. Seed money for the new project was eagerly provided by Sir Arthur Stoll, the entrepreneur of the Alhambra Theater where the Petipa ballet would be presented. Capitalizing on the Ballets Russes' popularity with the British public, Stoll stood to reap a handsome profit from what seemed to be a solid business venture.

Nicholas Sergeyev, a former dancer and *regisseur* at the Maryinsky, was engaged to stage the ballet in an effort to show London audiences a genuine sample of the imperial Russian ballet style. At the time of the Revolution, Sergeyev had left Russia with twenty-one ballets all or partially preserved in the Stepanov notation system, and among them was a fairly complete record of *The Sleeping Beauty*. Consequently the notated choreography, if not the original choreographer, was at hand, and it remained only for Sergeyev to mount the work on Ballets Russes artists.[20] A stellar array of additional Russian dancers was engaged to perform the leading roles. Recently emigrated from Russia were the ballerinas Vera Trefilova, Lubov Egorova, Olga Spessitseva, and the agile virtuoso, Anatole Vilzak. Pierre Vladimirov danced the role of Prince Florian while the role of Aurora was shared by the new ballerinas as well as Lopokova and Nemchinova. Carlotta Brianza, the Italian virtuoso who had danced the role of Aurora in the premiere in 1890, was coaxed out of retirement by Diaghilev to interpret the evil Carabosse.

263

Bakst was recalled and outdid himself in what was to be his final work for the company, creating the most ruinously lavish costumes and decor that the Ballets Russes had ever presented. His inspiration derived from the work of the Bibiena family, renowned Italian artists who were active in creating early eighteenth-century musical productions and *opéra ballet* on a magnificent scale. Although some of Bakst's 300 sketches had been drawn earlier for Pavlova's company when she produced an abridged version of *Sleeping Beauty* in 1916, his task was gigantic and became the artist's last great labor of love. The sheer luxury of the fabric and decoration that Bakst indicated on the designs announced a theatrical embarrassment of riches, while the labor-intensive beading and embroidery kept English and French seamstresses occupied for months.

Exercising his self-appointed prerogatives, Diaghilev made suggestions for rearranging the Tchaikovsky score. He also renamed the ballet *The Sleeping Princess* to avoid confusion with a traditional Christmas pantomime production playing during the season. Diaghilev encouraged Bronislava Nijinska (1891–1972), who had left the company when her brother departed, to return to the Ballets Russes fold as rehearsal mistress. He also asked her to arrange some additional choreography where he felt certain changes needed to be made in the Petipa classic.[21] Nijinska had been involved for the past six years with her own choreographic experiments in Soviet Russia. She was reticent about working on a Petipa ballet, but in the face of Diaghilev's persuasiveness, she finally agreed to do so. For Act II she contributed the "Hunting Dances" and a new variation for Aurora while she created additional choreography for Act III, including "The Three Ivans." Diaghilev was impressed with her work, sensing a new choreographer at his disposal.[22]

Western dance historians have generally considered the revival of *The Sleeping Princess* a grand artistic success, delighting the London public as it did. Unfortunately, it proved to be a financial fiasco. After 115 consecutive performances it was forced to close two months early, its magnificent costumes and sets impounded for outstanding debts. Enchanted though Londoners were with the Petipa fantasy and their firsthand look at a revamped imperial Russian ballet, there was simply not a large enough British dance-following to support a half-year run of one ballet.

It has often been noted that the financial turmoil surrounding *The Sleeping Princess* coincided with the beginning of Diaghilev's illness. The strain of the production in general, the exorbitant costs for its lavish beauty, countered by the glaring mechanical failures on opening night,[23] took their toll on the impresario. Numerous problems, unmitigated even by the dancing of a bevy of brilliant ballerinas, beset Diaghilev. Although deeply disappointed, in the end he managed to salvage some of the huge undertaking by presenting excerpts from *The Sleeping Princess* in Paris after renaming the new one-act ballet *Le Mariage de la Belle au Bois dormant* (1922, *Aurora's Wedding*). Sets from *Pavillon d'Armide* substituted for the original ones while Goncharova provided new costumes.

264

With Diaghilev's production of *The Sleeping Princess*, the West was introduced to the grandeur of imperial Russian ballet. Granted, the virtuoso technique and beauty of its ballerinas had been on Western display with the periodic appearances of Kschessinska, Preobrajenska, Pavlova, and others, but the large cast productions and fabulous *mise en scène* of czarist ballet culture was undreamt of even by elite theatergoers. English audiences before 1922 had grown enamored of the Ballets Russes' modern evocations of romanticism, ethnic-flavored drama, and savage, erotic glamour. Vanguard experiment on the ballet stage was also accepted or at least tolerated as a part of the times. Long after its premature closing, however, the strong impression of Diaghilev's *Sleeping Princess* lingered. The ballet's memory was to materialize in the reappearance of Petipa's masterwork in the repertory of the emerging English ballet during the 1940s. The 1921 performance had clearly introduced Russian balletomania to London but also had a seminal effect on the future of classical dancing throughout Western Europe. Its abbreviated form, *Aurora's Wedding*, encapsulated *danse d'école* classicism for its Paris audience in 1922 and was performed throughout Europe for the following seven years. Its presence in the Ballets Russes repertory was, in the long run, enormously influential because classical ballet as it had been expanded in Russia took root in the Western mind of the twentieth century.

## BRONISLAVA NIJINSKA: A RENEWABLE LEGACY

The spring season of 1922 began in Monte Carlo, followed by performances at the Paris Opera, and marked Nijinska's first complete work for the Ballets Russes. Her burlesque conception of the fable *Le Renard* (1922, The Fox) earned her the title of choreographer in Diaghilev's eyes. Similar to Fokine's *Le Coq d'Or*, the sixteen-minute duration of Stravinsky's score included singers whose words were interpreted by a cast of four dancers costumed by Larionov. Toward the end of the season, an all-Stravinsky program was presented that combined *Le Coq d'Or* with a revival of *Petrushka* and Massine's 1920 version of *Sacre du Printemps*. The program at the Opera was so successful that it was extended to continue at the Mogador Theater and was further enhanced with the return of Karsavina.

The year ended with the Ballets Russes' finding a permanent home in Monte Carlo's Garnier Theatre in the principality of Monaco.[24] Diaghilev, along with his collaborators and dancers, was delighted with the prospect of settling in for half a year at a time on the French Riviera after so many touring seasons. The inviting atmosphere of the locale's supreme elegance and international flavor was an additional pleasure added to the comforting note of permanence. For six months out of every year, Diaghilev contracted for the renamed Ballets Russes de Monte Carlo to have its own season, which involved creating, rehearsing, and dancing, on the premises of the beautiful little *belle époque* theater housed in the town's famous casino. The company also agreed to perform the ballets in operas during the opera season in its glamorous new home.

The only premiere slated for the 1923 season was *Les Noces* (The Wedding). For years Diaghilev and his colleagues had been wanting to bring into being a ballet centered around the arranged nuptials of a young Russian peasant couple in the presence of their families. Diaghilev believed it was one of the most beautiful and purely Russian themes he had ever considered for production. When Stravinsky completed the score in 1917, so appealing was the idea of realizing *Les Noces* that Nijinsky and Massine had quarreled violently over who would choreograph the work. The uncertainties of wartime had caused Diaghilev to put the project aside, but now he decided the time was ripe for Nijinska to give it life. In an all-Russian collaboration with Stravinsky and Goncharova, Nijinska's ballet turned out to be a poetic celebration of traditional Russian culture distilled by a modern generation. The choreographer gave full rein to her distinctly personal style, producing what in time would prove to be one of several masterworks.

While composing the music for *Les Noces*, Stravinsky had imagined various possibilities for the instrumentation of his score. He finally settled on solo voices backed by chorus, four pianos, and a strong percussion section. Initially Goncharova produced richly colored Russo–Boyar costume and set designs that reflected her interest in neoprimitivism, but these were flatly rejected by Nijinska. Bowing to the choreographer's demand that costumes and set be subordinated to choreography, she redesigned. Plain dark brown and white uniforms suitable for peasants working the earth provided an appropriately somber air. Goncharova also produced a backdrop of the utmost simplicity to mark the solemn occasion of a deeply felt religious ceremony.[25] The finished work was hailed as an intensely moving and austerely beautiful ballet. It gained immediate success in eight Paris performances led by Felia Doubrovska and Leon Woizikovsky as the bride and groom.

Like her brother, Nijinska was exceedingly inventive, but she also admitted his influence on her work. Unlike her brother, she remained closer to the bonds of classicism, regarding her heritage as a renewable legacy. While Vaslav Nijinsky had thrown away the very grounds of his early experience, as had Massine, Nijinska integrated the fundamentals of classical dance with the comings and goings, the human relationships, and commonplaces of contemporary life. By synthesizing her nineteenth-century heritage and her contemporary experimental efforts in dance-making, she formulated a neoclassic style for the Ballets Russes repertory. Nijinska succeeded in showing that choreography's way forward lay in classicism newly thought out, and not in departing from the mainstream vocabulary of the *danse d'école*.[26]

In the care of Nijinska's inspiration, classicism was extended, varied, and even distorted in *Les Noces* without altering the basic language of classical ballet. Feet still pointed, *plié* remained a fundamental of movement, and turnout was still present although Nijinska also incorporated the parallel sixth position of the legs introduced to the West by her brother in *Faune*. In Nijinska's neo-

266

classicism the traditional ballet steps and poses took on a new look with stylized arm and head positions that reflected meaning and music. Nijinska made use of *pointe* work to elongate the women's figures, which recalled the saints in Byzantine mosaics and which became a metaphor for female pain experienced in a world of male power.[27] She not only dispensed with partnering in the traditional sense, but gave men and women the same steps to perform. The premiere of *Les Noces* firmly established Nijinska as a creative talent of the first order, and it remains one of her greatest contributions to the choreographic evolution of ballet. She personally revived the work a number of times to the very end of her long career.

The next season introduced three Nijinska ballets in Monte Carlo that continued the company's trend toward producing French period pieces. *Les Tentations de la Bergère* (1924, The Temptations of the Shepherdess) exploited genuine classical French music, theme, and form, but Juan Gris's geometric costume designs overlaid on period silhouettes gave a bold, contemporary flavor. Diaghilev had also commissioned works from two young French composers, Francis Poulenc and George Auric, both members of the vanguard musical circle, *Les Six*. With new scores at hand, Nijinska began composing *Les Biches* (1924, *The House Party*) and *Les Fâcheux* (1924, The Bores). *Les Biches*, its thin plot conceived by Cocteau, consisted of a number of charming dances performed to Poulenc's light-hearted music. Marie Laurencin provided decor and costumes of fashionable street wear that were rendered from a predominantly pastel palette. On the surface the ballet concerned itself with frivolous behavior at an upper-class social gathering, but in Nijinska's ingenious handling, it turned into a piquant critique of sexual mores. A mixture of innocence and decadence, *Les Biches* dealt frankly with themes never or rarely seen on the ballet stage, namely, narcissism, voyeurism, female sexual power, and sapphism. Nijinska also redefined gender boundaries by endowing some of her female characters with male characteristics and vice versa, revealing her unease with traditional ideas of femininity.[28]

After two hundred years, the Molière–Beauchamp collaboration, *Les Fâcheux*, was again modeled as a ballet, although Beauchamp's choreography and music for the 1661 production had long disappeared as a historical reference. Diaghilev envisioned the period piece styled for modern tastes while Auric's rococo-touched score suggested the past. Nijinska carefully researched the poses and mannerisms of the Louis XIV period to recall the air of refined artificiality. To reinforce her idea, she created a *pointe* solo for the Irish dancer, Anton Dolin, and his fastidious interpretation effectively underscored the work's slightly decadent atmosphere.[29] Contemporary in every sense of the word, its original scenario was adapted by Diaghilev's secretary, the librettist, Boris Kochno. The cubist artist Georges Braque supplied stylized scenery and elaborate costumes for the updated French classic.

Nijinska created a third ballet toward the season's end entitled *Le Train Bleu* (1924, The Blue Train). This work utilized a scenario by Jean Cocteau that centered around beach activities on the French Riviera. The music was by another

French composer of *Les Six*, Darius Milhaud. The costumes by Coco Chanel consisted of bathing suits and sport clothes, while Picasso provided an act curtain with two luminous giant figures sprinting across the sand. The classically trained Dolin had a rare success in the ballet, displaying splendid acrobatic feats that Nijinska incorporated into her stylized movement.[30] When the dancer eventually left the company, *Le Train Bleu* was dropped from the repertory because no one could match Dolin's gymnastic skills.

It was during this period that an Irish girl, Ninette de Valois, and the child prodigy, Alicia Markova, joined the troupe. From 1911 onwards when Diaghilev's associates left the Ballets Russes, they often set themselves up as private ballet teachers in London. In addition to Pavlova and Maestro Cecchetti, who taught off and on for years in London, there were Serafina Astafieva, Nicholas Legat, and Nicholas Sergeyev who were particularly adept at developing British dance artists. Dolin, de Valois, and Markova emerged from the classes of these teachers, and during their lengthy careers all three would take a central role in the establishment of British ballet.

Diaghilev had a falling out with Nijinska when he refused to produce her abstract symphonic work, *Holy Etudes*, on the basis that it was storyless.[31] In later years Nijinska wrote that Diaghilev was never able to totally give up the idea of the literary element in a ballet in spite of his advanced aesthetic preferences. Perhaps Diaghilev's greatest failing was his tendency to discover and then discard artists when they disagreed with his ideas. Although Nijinska, like

268

Autographed photo of Enrico Cecchetti and his wife teaching company class for the Ballets Russes de Monte Carlo in 1925. From left to right, Mme Cecchetti, Doubrovska, Markova, Majerska, N. Nikitina, Geva, Klemetska, Komarova, Sokolova, Unger, Troussevich, Chamié, Lapitsky, Lifar, Tcherkas, A. Nikitina, Dolin, Danilova, Zalevska, Savina, and Maestro Cecchetti. (Courtesy of Jerome Robbins Dance Division, The New York Public Library for the Performing Arts, Astor, Lenox and Tilden Foundations.)

Fokine and Massine before her, had hardly exhausted her creative energies with seven ballets for the Ballets Russes, she was deprived of the most likely setting for her work by leaving the organization. She eventually produced *Holy Etudes* (1925) along with other ballets for her short-lived company, Théâtre Chorégraphique.

Ever searching for new choreographic talent, Diaghilev began to develop the potential of Serge Lifar, one of Nijinska's students in Moscow who had recently joined the Ballets Russes. Diaghilev proceeded to take charge of the still raw but eager dancer in the same manner he had educated Nijinsky and Massine. Making him gifts of a number of drawings and paintings, Diaghilev unknowingly precipitated the beginnings of Lifar's exceptional collection of Ballets Russes memorabilia, of which some of the most valuable portraits, costumes, and set and costume designs for thirty-seven ballets are now maintained by the Wadsworth Atheneum Museum. While Lifar never achieved worldwide renown as a choreographer, he would in time establish a renewed flourish of dance at the Paris Opera. Massine briefly rejoined the company in 1925 to create the comic *Les Matelots* (The Sailors), and a contemporary version of the mythological *Zéphyr et Flore* in which Lifar danced his first major role.

# SURREALIST AND CONSTRUCTIVIST EXPERIMENTS IN BALLET

Nijinska was persuaded to return to the Ballets Russes to prepare *Romeo and Juliet*[32] (1926), which only mildly touched on Shakespeare's play. An experiment in surrealism, which was of particular interest to Diaghilev at the time, the ballet was staged as a rehearsal of the story and was danced in practice clothes. Instead of dying together as a conventional Romeo and Juliet, the two principals, who were lovers in the rehearsal scene as well as in the context of their play, elope in an airplane. This feat was cleverly suggested by aviator costumes and the way Lifar spirited Karsavina offstage in a horizontal position on his shoulders.

The scenario of *Romeo and Juliet* reflected the aims of the surrealist Manifesto (1924) by uniting the fantasy of the subconscious to the everyday rational world to create an "absolute reality, a surreality."[33] The performances of Karsavina and Lifar were admired as was the music by the young Englishman, Constant Lambert. Nijinska's choreography pleased less because it was heavy with pantomime necessary to convey her ideas. To the delight of Diaghilev, the Paris opening of *Romeo and Juliet* proved to be a public scandal followed by the usual box office sell-out. During its first performance the ballet's designers, Joan Miró and Max Ernst, were attacked by the surrealist movement's spokesman, André Breton. The outraged poet caused hundreds of leaflets to be thrown from the balconies, denouncing the pair for associating their art with a capitalist venture such as the Ballets Russes. Forewarned of Breton's intention to create a riot, Miró and Ernst stayed away from the premiere.

---

Diaghilev never stopped being interested in the aesthetic trends of his native land. Constructivism, the experimental work in Soviet design that he had heard of indirectly, excited his curiosity. At one point the impresario had even planned a visit to Russia to witness this artistic activity firsthand, although the trip never came about. For the 1927 season Massine took on the task of preparing *Pas d'Acier* in accordance with the constructivist trend in avant-garde art. Attempting to portray Soviet life dominated by the heavy industry of factories, the ballet used stylized movement for dancers who were deprived of a deep, unhampered stage floor by the complex set. When the ballet finally came about, however, its decor was precisely what held the greatest interest for Diaghilev.[34] Georgi Yakulov's powerful constructivist set was the embodiment of the age of mechanics. Theater artists in Russia had been conducting vigorous research into new ways to articulate stage space by splitting the stage floor into platforms joined by ramps and ladders. Yakulov's construction for *Pas d'Acier* confirmed the clash between the new Russian art movement and the Soviet regime that eventually suppressed it in favor of Socialist Realism.[35] Although the choreography met with only modest success, the ballet was kept in the repertory because its novelty pleased and it afforded audiences the only opportunity to hear the Prokofiev score.

*Ode* (1928) was one of the most controversial works ever launched by the Ballets Russes. Intended as a Russian period piece, the spectacle in three acts was inspired by the eighteenth-century court poet, Mikhail Lomonosov, eulogist of the Empress Elizabeth. The ballet's modern score by Nicolas Nabokov sung to Lomonosov's poetic words, surrealist designs by Pavel Tchelitchev, and complex experimental lighting effects by Pierre Charbonnier both confused and pleased. Diaghilev initially intended the *mise en scène* to be based on eighteenth-century allegorical drawings and authentic engravings of the imperial court. Tchelitchev, however, wished to express himself through the use of modern technical devices, and *Ode* ended up with elements that were incompatible with Diaghilev's desire for a historically accurate reconstruction.[36] The ballet was, however, truly revolutionary in its use of phosphorescent costumes, film projections against screens, and neon lighting that was immediately forbidden as a fire hazard. The most recollected images of those who witnessed the production were the great bursts of light flooding the stage that imperceptibly changed color. *Ode* was as much an artistic experimentation in electric illumination as it was an entity consisting of choreography, music, and decor.

# GEORGE BALANCHINE AND NEOCLASSICISM

Of the trickle of Soviet dancers coming out of Russia and joining the company, George Balanchine (1904–1983) was the most promising from a creative point of view. As a student, Balanchine's endeavors at the ballet school in postrevolu-

270

tionary St. Petersburg had competed with his interest and formal study of music at the city's conservatory. Nearing graduation he had become interested in choreographic experimentation to the considerable displeasure of the school authorities. He was interested in the acrobatic style of Kasian Goleizovsky whose approach to dance-making explored movement outside the established ballet vocabulary.[37] One favored movement theme that Goleizovsky often used was hand-linked lines of dancers that he tied into knots, leading them in and out of serpentine patterns.[38] Balanchine would employ this choreographic chaining device countless times in his prodigious body of work.

Balanchine was also influenced during his fledgling years as a choreographer by Fyodor Lopoukhov, the brother of Diaghilev's adored Lydia. While less iconoclastic than Goleizovsky, Lopoukhov was beginning to shape his theories on symphonic dance. He reasoned that the musical curve should coincide with the dance curve. He also suggested that major key phrases in music should correspond to *en dehors* movements while the minor key should be reflected in *en dedans* movement.[39] As principal choreographer in the former Maryinsky Theater, Lopoukhov by example encouraged the youthful Balanchine to experiment in keeping with the revolutionary spirit of Russian times. Trained in the timeless tenets of classical ballet, Goleizovsky, Lopoukhov, and Balanchine contributed strongly to a reformulation of classical, kinetic expression that emerged as neoclassicism.[40] Fired by the efforts of his two mentors, Balanchine put together his own little group, which he called the Young Ballet. After the revolution, when Bolshevik and Menshevik power struggles made Russian life extremely arduous and dangerous, he worked with a group of sympathetic dancers on irregular and artistically uneven concerts.

On the pretext of a cultural exchange tour to Berlin in 1924, Balanchine, his wife, Tamara Geva, and ballet school classmates, Alexandra Danilova and Nicholas Efimoff managed by Vladimir Dmitriev, secretly planned to stay in the West following the German performances. After a brief engagement in London, the group traveled to Paris in an effort to find work. At this point they came into contact with the Ballets Russes. After a brief meeting and an even shorter audition, Diaghilev hired the newcomers. He had been cognizant of choreographic experimentation being carried on in Soviet Russia and hoped to locate a ballet master who could create startling new ballets for Western audiences. By the time he gave a creative assignment to Balanchine, the impresario was desperate for a choreographer who could quickly turn out dances for the upcoming ballet and opera season in Monte Carlo. Diaghilev did not use Balanchine as a personal medium of creation in the manner he had developed Nijinsky and Massine. The choreographer's work stood on its own merits, and his versions of *Le Chant du Rossingnol* (1925, Song of the Nightingale) and *Barabau* (1925, Bluebeard) proved to be effective ballets. In the last four years of the company's existence, Balanchine choreographed nine additional ballets for Diaghilev including *The Triumph of Neptune* (1926), *La Chatte* (1927, The Cat), *Apollon Musagète* (1928, Apollo), *The Gods Go A'Begging* (1928), *Le Bal* (1929, The Dance), and *Le Fils prodigue* (1929, The Prodigal Son)

Balanchine and Stravinsky launched one of the most important collaborations in the history of ballet with their creation of *Apollon Musagète*. A masterpiece in its own right, the string orchestral score with echoes of Bach and Tchaikovsky created a new, highly personal and twentieth-century sound for which Balanchine had to discover a fitting dance idiom. The work was a collection of ten dances with variations for Apollo and his three muses, a sublime adagio, coda and a stately apotheosis. The choreographer was free to give full reign to his inventiveness, and in so doing, he extended the language of dance in an unprecedented way to fit the extraordinary music. The ballet was well received along with its handsome support from Danilova, Doubrovska, Tchernicheva, and Lifar, but few in the audience realized the momentous dance event they had just witnessed.

Balanchine's neoclassicism, as realized in *Apollon Musagète*, was a veritable seedbed for all of his future ballets. He shaped his fresh ideas in *Apollon* by building variants and modifications onto the traditional vocabulary of ballet movement. He freely borrowed Goleizovsky's "sixth position" in which parallel feet touch heel to heel and toe to toe, suggesting archaic Greek sculpture. He also introduced syncopated movements and developed entire passages without traditional steps. Each dancer was given a unique symbolic gesture to illuminate the slight narrative. In the course of rehearsals Balanchine found new ways to manipulate *pointe* work, to present arabesques as symbols, and to use the intricacies of partnering for unusual sculptural effects.[41] The ultimate impression of *Apollo*, as it is now known, is a perfect distillation of what might also have been a ballet on a much larger scale.

Balanchine's last work for the Ballets Russes' final season was *Le Fils prodigue* (*The Prodigal Son*), a complete contrast to the cool classicism of *Apollo*. The element of powerful dramatization, absent since the Fokine years, reappeared in the frame of an updated academic dance.[42] The intensely emotional biblical parable was deftly reduced by Kochno to show the Prodigal's corruption to utter destitution by the Siren and her sordid companions. The son's repentant return and welcome into his father's arms achieved one of the most touching moments in all of ballet repertory. The sets repeated Georges Rouault's profoundly religious, jewel-like style of painting. The artist's costuming, especially that for the Siren, was a bona fide *coup de théâtre* with its double function of seductively alluring attire and ingenious prop. Prokofiev had already completed the score when Balanchine took on the project. Although tied to the plot, this factor in no way hindered the choreographer's inventiveness in the manner in which he gave layers of significance to the personalities of his characters. Rich with symbolic meaning, the resourceful use of set pieces by the dancers greatly extended the ballet's impression. Lifar triumphed in the title role as did the bewitching and statuesque Doubrovska who portrayed the Siren.[43]

Balanchine's originality and economy of means had a tremendous impact on Ballets Russes audiences of 1929. The exposition of debauchery on the ballet stage had astounded the public almost two decades earlier with *Schéhérazade*'s voluptuous caresses and overt sexuality. These elements in *Prodigal Son* were

272

portrayed even more effectively by the emotionally contained, acrobatic symbolism emerging from Balanchine's neoclassic style. A mark of their enduring quality, both *Apollo* and *Prodigal Son* survive in the active repertory of the New York City Ballet.

At the twenty-year mark of Diaghilev's organization, only his advisor and old friend, Walter Nuvel, and his régisseur, Serge Grigoriev, remained from the early days of the company. Long cut off from the rich progeny of the Maryinsky as a result of the 1917 Revolution and the passing of time, Diaghilev was constantly searching for adequate performers. The artists who danced in the ballets of this period were now a mixture of émigré Russians, one American, English, Polish, Belgian, and French dancers. The quality and style of dancing, however, fared more steady.

When Diaghilev hired Cecchetti as teacher for the 1911 season, the Maestro stayed with the Ballets Russes for fifteen years, imposing his rich Italian heritage on the company in addition to what he had drawn in mid-life from the Gerdt–Johansson–Petipa triumvirate at the Maryinsky. After Cecchetti's retirement and subsequent appointment to the academy of Milan's La Scala Opera House, Nicholas Legat was engaged to assume the company's teaching position. Trained at the Maryinsky, Legat followed earlier teaching methods in force at the time of Petipa. This older, highly disciplined and rigid approach, as effective as it might have been, met with severe criticism from the nomadic Diaghilev dancers, most of whom had never been trained in Russia. As a result, Legat was replaced by Lubov Tchernicheva. Not only was she one of the company's leading soloists, but she had developed into an accommodating teacher, having absorbed much of her knowledge from Cecchetti, which she then integrated into her Maryinsky schooling.

273

Toward the end of the 1929 season, Diaghilev was showing signs of exhaustion and ill health. He bade the dancers farewell for the summer and departed for a rest before the company gave its final performance. After a leisurely journey south, during which he attended opera performances in Munich and Salzburg, a weary Diaghilev arrived at a favorite summer retreat. The Hotel des Bains on the sandy island of Venice's Lido had frequently served as a vacation home where the impresario and his collaborators planned entire seasons. Almost immediately upon Diaghilev's settling in, the diabetes which he had all but ignored, despite grave warnings from his physician, progressed to its last stages. Within days Diaghilev succumbed.

Just as the fortuneteller had prophesied, Diaghilev died on the water, the sun-dappled sea of the Adriatic. European newspapers announced his death in broad headlines. His passing left the members of his company, who were dispersed and on holidays, in shock and without future prospects. The impresario was buried on the nearby cemetery island of San Michele and lies there beside his great musical discovery, Igor Stravinsky, who joined him some four decades later. Thus came the abrupt end of the saga of Sergei Diaghilev's fabulous Ballets Russes. Rightly so, he was "the last of the great Baroque princes . . . who knit together the arts of painting, music, literature, acting and choreography into a brilliant pattern. . . ."[44]

# Summary

Diaghilev's legacy to ballet in our time is inestimable. His activities inaugurated a major cultural interchange between East and West with artists from many countries lending their ideas to a common cause. In the years from 1909 to 1929, Paris again resumed its position as the world's most important cultural center, only briefly relinquishing it due to the effects of World War I. Never before had an artistic event like the Ballets Russes continuously intrigued the capitals of Europe for such a lengthy period of time.

Diaghilev founded an enterprise that was instrumental in creating a repertory of seventy-one ballets that raised dance art to new heights and diffused it over Europe and the Americas. The works he produced represented a modern approach in dance-making. Relatively short and dramatically compact, the Ballets Russes' best productions boasted an exquisite integration of choreography, music, painting, and plot. By producing *The Sleeping Princess* in London, Diaghilev opened up the eyes of the West toward the East. With the vision of Peter the Great transposed, Diaghilev recreated the glory of Russian classicism as it had evolved under the grand patronage of the czars.[45] During two decades Diaghilev employed the distinctively varied, world-class talents of five major choreographers. They shepherded ballet from the threshold of modernism to that of the avant-garde with experiments in joining dance to futurism, cubism, surrealism, and constructivism, and finally coming full circle in a return to the *danse d'école* of neoclassicism. Under Diaghilev's guidance, numerous contemporary composers and first-rate painters bestowed their genius on the foundations of all that is important in the development of twentieth-century ballet. A lasting contribution to the dance world, Diaghilev commandeered a staggering list of extraordinary dancers who graced Western theaters with their beauty before endowing the next generation with the secrets of their skill.

Upon his death, the company scattered across the face of Europe with some artists returning to Russia while a score of the finest ventured to the New World. It was precisely the disruption of the Ballets Russes that jettisoned a number of talents onto soil already made fertile by touring. Tragic on the surface that the company died with its director, in the long run it was a turning point. In seeking a livelihood as teachers and choreographers, Diaghilev's dancers were major forces in causing the ballet to begin its worldwide growth. Before this migration of artists, the ballet was known only to relatively small and elite cosmopolitan groups, but within three generations their knowledge, dedication, and energy touched the lives of millions.

# Chapter Notes

1. Nesta Macdonald, *Diaghilev Observed by Critics in England and the United States, 1911–1929* (New York: Dance Horizons & London: Dance Books, 1975), p. 183.
2. Ibid., p. 129.
3. Ibid., p. 192.
4. Nijinska, pp. 453–70.
5. Garafola, p. 81.
6. Hindley, p. 400.
7. Garafola, pp. 76–77.
8. George Jackson, et al, *Die Puppenfee* (Wien: Osterreichischer Bundestheaterverband, 1983). The ballet has been in the active Viennese repertory since its creation in 1888 and to date has received nearly 1000 performances.
9. Lydia Sokolova, *Dancing for Diaghilev: The Memoirs of Lydia Sokolova* (San Francisco: Mercury House, 1960), pp. 159.
10. Erik Näslund, *The Art of Extravagance: Larionov, Bakst and Matisse* (Stockholm: Dansmuseet, 1996), p. 26.
11. Ibid., p. 26.
12. Ibid., p. 27.
13. Boris Kochno, *Diaghilev and the Ballets Russes* (New York: Harper & Row, 1970), p. 138.
14. Ibid., p. 148.
15. Modris Eksteins, *Rites of Spring: The Great War and the Birth of the Modern Age* (New York: Anchor Books, 1989), pp. 33–39.
16. Kochno, pp. 156–60.
17. Garafola, pp. 84–85.
18. Buckle, *Diaghilev*, p. 383.
19. Ibid., p. 386.
20. Ibid., p. 387.
21. Ibid., p. 390.
22. Grigoriev, p. 178.
23. Buckle, *Diaghilev*, p. 392.
24. Sokolova, pp. 201–03.
25. Nancy Van Norman Baer, *Bronislava Nijinska, A Dancer's Legacy* (San Francisco: The Fine Arts Museum of San Francisco, 1986), p. 32.
26. Garafola, p. 127.
27. Ibid., pp. 128–31.
28. Ibid., p. 130.
29. Baer, p. 40.
30. Kochno, pp. 214–19.
31. Baer, p. 70.
32. Kochno, pp. 234–36.
33. Ibid., p. 237.
34. Garafola, pp. 248–49.
35. An unnamed Russian painter who was a victim of socialist realism once commented

that impressionism was painting what one saw, expressionism was painting what one felt, but socialist realism was painting what one was forced to hear.

36. Kochno, p. 148.
37. Souritz, p. 169.
38. Ibid., p. 85. Souritz gives a detailed account of Goleizovsky's choreography that culminated in *Joseph the Beautiful* (1925). See illustrations of his "chaining device," numbers 43 and 44.
39. Roslavleva, p. 204.
40. Garafola, p. 122. Nijinska was also part of this group of early neoclassicists based on her experimental work in Moscow and her conceptions regarding the preparations for *Les Noces* and *Les Biches*.
41. Richard Buckle, *George Balanchine, Ballet Master: In Collaboration with John Taras* (New York: Random House, 1988), pp. 44–47.
42. Ibid., p. 49.
43. Ibid., pp. 49–52.
44. A. Everett Austin, Jr. Austin was quoted by Serge Lifar in the "Foreword" of *Twenty-Five Years of Russian Ballet from the Collection of Serge Lifar*. Catalogue: Julien Levy Gallery, p. 2.
45. Eksteins, p. 22.

276

# 13

# Ballet in the Twentieth Century

## THE EXPANSION OF WESTERN EUROPEAN BALLET

During the first decades of the twentieth century the groundwork was laid for the establishment of ballet throughout the Western world. Despite ballet's decline in Europe following the Romantic era, at the turn of the century a number of Russian artists making guest appearances in major cities revived interest in the art. A sophisticated public was also stimulated by the advent of the modern dance that proclaimed itself an alternative to the classical form. From 1909 onward Diaghilev's efforts to produce brilliant dance art throughout the Continent had a huge impact on the future directions of ballet, and they were largely determined at the impresario's death. He had been the driving force for the creation of a number of the most perfect ballets ever conceived, thereby creating a new audience for dance.

In keeping with the spirit of his times, Diaghilev facilitated the injection of modernist attitudes into the tradition-bound classical ballet, thus freeing choreographers to seek ways to open the doors for a full-blown dance theater relevant to the twentieth century. Shortly after Diaghilev's death, a long-term effort to keep his work ongoing was made by the reorganization of remnants of his troupe into a new ballet company. The Ballet Russe of René Blum and Colonel de Basil was based in Monte Carlo, employed a number of Diaghilev's choreographers and dancers, and extensively toured the Continent, England, and the Americas until the outbreak of the Second World War.

Especially significant was the fact that Diaghilev's enterprise provided fertile ground for a handful of artists whose energies would nurture the new dance evolving from their mentor's vision. Two determined women, Marie Rambert and Ninette de Valois, founded a national ballet movement in England that would be the pride of this most civilized of countries. Lifar reestablished the ballet in Paris while the inventive Balanchine, along with Mordkin, Bolm,

Fokine, Massine, and Nijinska, would all contribute to the development of ballet in America.

## GREAT BRITAIN AND THE COMMONWEALTH

Ballet is more popular in Western countries than at any time in the art form's history. Modern ballet outside of Russia is a direct descendant of Diaghilev's great life work.[1]

In 1920 Marie Rambert (1888–1982) opened a ballet school in London after an unorthodox career in the dance world. As a Polish émigré in Germany, she had been influenced by the ideas of Isadora Duncan and later, as a pupil, by Emile-Jaques Dalcroze, whose unique studies in movement provided her with invaluable insight as a dance educator in England. Through Dalcroze, Rambert had been employed by Diaghilev to assist Nijinsky in his choreographic efforts. She continued on with the company as a dancer where she was able to observe firsthand the making of dance theater, partake in the joys and pitfalls of choreographic experimentation, and benefit from the company's strict technique classes.

Upon the advice of Nijinsky, Rambert left the Ballets Russes in 1918 and returned to England since that was where the great dancer suggested her artistic future lay. Armed with nothing but her experience and driving ambition, she began training students with an eye to presenting them in performances. Within the decade it was evident to her dancers and the small number of ballet lovers who supported their performing efforts that here was the making of the first twentieth-century English ballet company. Rambert proceeded to form the Ballet Club, later to become Ballet Rambert. Often the group was led by famous guest artists who were former colleagues including Kschessinska, Lopokova, Markova, and Dolin. The company offered regular performances in the humble Mercury Theater where several of her dancers made their first attempts at choreography. Throughout her career Rambert fought relentlessly to incorporate twentieth-century ballet into the cultural fabric of Great Britain by insisting on the development of British choreographers. Among her first protégés were Frederick Ashton and Antony Tudor whose distinctive works gave important dimensions to contemporary English ballet.

Frederick Ashton (1906–1988) created ballets remarkable for their variety of style, subject matter, and danceability. Emerging from Rambert's classical tutelage, all Ashton's works were rooted in the technique of the *danse d'école*, which he skillfully adapted to the specific requirements of each ballet. His choreographic output exerted the greatest influence in creating what might be called the English style of ballet, stately and elegant, yet witty, colorful, and well-bred. Ashton is credited with introducing back into European theaters the popularity of the full-evening spectacle ballet with his faultless taste and a cultivated understanding of historical nuance. Among these works were his choreography for *Cinderella* (1948), *Sylvia* (1952), *Romeo and Juliet* (1955), *Ondine* (1958), and *La Fille mal gardée* (1960) for the Royal Ballet. Numerous shorter ballets such as *Façade* (1931), *Les Patineurs* (1937, The Skaters), *Illuminations* (1950), *Monotones* (1965–66), *Enigma Variations* (1968), and *A Month in the Country* (1976) have been revived for the company's repertory for decades.

One of Ashton's most stunning accomplishments was developing the career of Margot Fonteyn in an extraordinary collaboration between choreographer and the woman who became England's first great twentieth-century ballerina. Ashton's immense influence on all facets of English ballet was confirmed by the British critic Perry Brinson's comment:

> To write about Sir Frederick Ashton is to write about the history of the Royal Ballet; in Ashton's ballets lie a portrait of the company; their range reflects the range of its dancers, their demands have enriched and ennobled its dancers' style and abilities. As Ashton's genius has developed, so has the Royal Ballet; the mutual stimulus existing between a choreographer and his company, between creator and instrument—and notably with Ashton, between him and Margot Fonteyn (their association having lasted longer and more fruitfully than any other in the history of ballet) has made for great ballets and a great company.[2]

Antony Tudor (1908–1987) spent his early career under the encouraging mantle of Rambert. After his studying a short three years, she produced his first ballet, *Cross-Garter'd* (1931). Within a few seasons a number of other ballets, including the psychologically sensitive masterpieces *Lilac Garden* (1936) and *Dark Elegies* (1937), were premiered. In 1940 Tudor left London for New York to join in a history-making project, the birthing of the American Ballet Theatre.[3]

In 1966 Rambert's company dropped its classical identity in preference of a more up-to-date look. During the codirectorship of Norman Morrice, English choreographers such as John Chesworth and Christopher Bruce emerged while the American, Glen Tetley, contributed a series of masterful modern ballets to the repertory in the 1970s. After Rambert's death a period of stylistic austerity followed under the guidance of Richard Alston and Robert North at which time the Ballet Rambert was renamed the Rambert Dance Company. In 1994 Rambert's last protégé, the dancer and resident choreographer Christopher Bruce, assumed artistic directorship. Staffed with artists equally at home in the classical and modern idioms, the company currently reflects a broader range of the latest in choreographic styles that educate and please a growing contemporary ballet audience in England.

Ninette de Valois (1898) has the unique distinction in British dance history of single-handedly founding a national ballet school and company for England. Such a feat is remarkable when one considers that similar accomplishments have traditionally taken the resources of a monarch and an incubation period of a century or two. While still in her teens, the Irish born de Valois had participated in pantomimes and musical reviews that were presented in London musical halls. Her early performing centered around working in frail productions of the postromantic style that were popularized at the Empire and Alhambra Theaters. Genuine ballet training was not available to her until Cecchetti opened a studio in London when he arrived during the war years with

279

Diaghilev's Ballets Russes. It was during this time that she received a thorough grounding in technical study. Shortly thereafter she was invited to join a short-lived Massine–Lopokova venture in 1922 and then Diaghilev's Ballets Russes. Several highly charged and colorful years with the renowned Russians proved invaluable to the destiny that awaited her.

In 1926 de Valois left Diaghilev to found her private London school, the Academy of Choreographic Art, which was the feeding source for a native English ballet. In five years she established the Sadler's Wells Ballet School, fortified with pedagogic knowledge derived from intensive company classes with Maestro Cecchetti, as well as with Nicholas Legat and Edouard Espinosa. Gifted with administrative and organizational talents that had been sharpened by close association with the Ballets Russes, de Valois set about founding the Sadler's Wells Ballet Company at the request of the theater's director, Lillian Baylis. As choreographer, de Valois was most productive between 1930 and 1940 when she created ballets for Sadler's Wells as well as the Carmargo Society and Ballet Rambert. Her works included *Job* (1931), *The Haunted Ballroom* (1934), *The Rake's Progress* (1935), *Checkmate* (1937), and *The Prospect Before Us* (1940).

During World War II the British armed forces asked the Sadler's Wells Ballet to tour the Continent with the intention of restoring morale amidst the enlisted troops and allied countries. Withstanding the enormous difficulties of wartime touring inadvertently seasoned the company sufficiently to attract the help of the British government once peace returned. In due course the dancers moved from their inadequate quarters to Covent Garden Opera House, and a new period of growth began with a production of *Sleeping Beauty* (1946) that brought a huge international reputation. The company continued to develop under distinguished guest choreographers when Massine and Balanchine set some of their finest works on it. Ashton greatly enriched the growing repertory, and his presence encouraged up-and-coming choreographic talents, namely Kenneth MacMillan and John Cranko.[4]

Kenneth MacMillan (1929–1994), a charter member of Sadler's Wells Theater Ballet, was Britain's most prolific dancemaker, employing a broad range of dramatic subject matter that he deftly expressed through the classical idiom. To a great extent MacMillan explored the Freudian perimeters of the psychological ballet first introduced by Antony Tudor in which passions, desires, loneliness, and frustrations of society are masked in hypocrisy and self-delusion.[5] In addition to his productions of the standard Russian classics for the Royal Ballet, *Sleeping Beauty* (1967) and *Swan Lake* (1969), MacMillan choreographed numerous memorable works that included *Danses concertantes* (1955), *Anastasia* (1971), *Elite Syncopations* (1974), *Mayerling* (1978), *Gloria* (1980), and *Isadora* (1980). When Ninette de Valois retired in 1963, MacMillan became Royal Ballet's second director followed by Norman Morrice in 1977. The Royal Ballet's former leading male artist, Anthony Dowell, is its most recent director.

Between his student days at Sadler's Wells and his departure for Germany to lead the Stuttgart Ballet in 1960, John Cranko (1927–1973) produced a large number of ballets for various groups in London and abroad. His skill and versa-

280

tility gained him an international reputation, marking him as one of the most important choreographers of the mid-twentieth century. Cranko's important ballets for English audiences included *Beauty and the Beast* (1949), *Pineapple Poll* (1951), *The Lady and the Fool* (1954), and *The Prince of the Pagodas* (1957). For the Paris Opera Ballet Cranko created *La Belle Hélène* (1955) and fashioned his first *Romeo and Juliet* for La Scala Ballet in 1959.

The solid foundation of de Valois's company accrued from the fact that the entire operation was always rooted in the systematic training of students.[6] From the time of the school's establishment, its pedagogy was dominated by the founders of the Royal Academy of Dancing (RAD), namely Adeline Genée, Tamara Karsavina, Phyllis Bedells, and Edouard Espinosa, whose purpose was continually to improve teaching standards throughout England and the Commonwealth. They devised a comprehensive teacher's training course, a

Jennifer Penney and Wayne Eagling in MacMillan's *Gloria*. The ballet was created for the Royal Ballet to commemorate those lost in World War I. (Photo courtesy of Jack Vartoogian.)

281

graded syllabus, and held yearly examinations for both teachers and students. To preserve the daily classes that Cecchetti recorded in his notebooks, the Cecchetti Society was formed in 1922 and incorporated in the Imperial Society of Teachers of Dancing in 1924. Elements of Cecchetti's methodology and his early influences on de Valois figured strongly in the first years of the school. From 1943 to 1950 Vera Volkova, who was the leading Western authority on the pedagogy of the twentieth-century Russian teacher Agrippina Vaganova, taught at the school as well as for the company. To Volkova went the credit of having been the dominant figure in the formation of a generation of excellent postwar British dancers. In the 1980s the Russian school of ballet further influenced the curriculum when the former Bolshoi ballerina, Sulamith Messerer, joined the teaching staff.

Having steadily grown despite the war and its ensuing draft of male dancers, Sadler's Wells began its great international tours. The company's appearance in New York dazzled the public with a lavish version of *Sleeping Beauty* in 1949. A bevy of superb dancers, led by Fonteyn, helped inaugurate the American ballet boom of the 1950s. By 1956 the company had become sufficiently distinguished to be honored by the Crown with a new charter and its present name, the Royal Ballet. When the first of the Russian dance defectors, Rudolf Nureyev, accepted an invitation to become Fonteyn's partner in 1962, an incomparable ballet team emerged to ignite the public with a newfound passion for ballet. The partnership of Nureyev and Fonteyn became the most celebrated in ballet history as they proceeded to touch the hearts of audiences all over the world.

282

Other companies have emerged in England, producing their own ballets and schooling dancers. A second touring company related to the Royal Ballet, called the Sadler's Wells Royal Ballet, provided additional repertory to feed the growing appetite for dance. Festival Ballet, later renamed the English National Ballet, was founded in 1950 by the former Diaghilev principals Markova and Dolin. Initially the company provided a special dimension to England's dance scene when foreign as well as English artists were invited to perform with the troupe.

The Manchester-based Northern Ballet Theatre emerged in 1973 from a small touring group, which presented original works of Laverne Meyer and others. In 1976 Robert de Warren took over the organization, doubled its number of dancers, and created a classically based repertory that featured full-length ballets, including his own versions of *Cinderella* (1979) and *A Midsummer's Night Dream* (1981). When the number of classical companies in London grew to four, the major industrial city of Birmingham won the presence of Sadler's Wells Royal Ballet in 1990. The troupe was renamed the Birmingham Royal Ballet and was directed for five years by a veteran of the Royal ballet, Peter Wright. In 1995 David Bintly, a former Royal Ballet dancer and choreographer, succeeded Wright as director. Bintly, who is considered the spiritual heir of Frederick Ashton, preserves Ashton's English classicism, and the repertory is strictly rooted in the energy, beauty, and variety of the classical vocabulary.

# CANADA

Extending to the commonwealth, the British ballet establishment has had a profound influence on the organization of world class ballet schools and touring companies in Canada. Toronto's National Ballet of Canada was founded in 1951 by the English dancer Celia Franca. After briefly touring with Diaghilev, Franca studied at the Royal Academy of Dance with Idzikowsky and Rambert before her move to Ontario. Under her guidance the company steadily developed, and Franca created major productions of *Nutcracker* (1964) and *Cinderella* (1968). Added to the classical repertory, the National Ballet has produced contemporary works by its resident choreographers, Brian Macdonald and Constantin Patsalas, and its most recent artistic director, James Kudelka, as well as a host of international dance makers. So successful is the National Ballet's school that since its development in the 1960s by the British teacher and ballet mistress, Betty Oliphant, its overflow of artists can be found in companies throughout the world.

Ludmilla Chiriaeff emigrated from Latvia to Canada after World War II and in 1957 oversaw the founding of Les Grands Ballets Canadiens of Montreal and its affiliated school. With Fernand Nault as co-director and Anton Dolin as artistic advisor, the company produced their stagings of *Giselle*, *Pas de quatre*, *Nutcracker*, and *La Fille mal gardée*. In 1970 Nault created *Tommy*, the first Canadian rock ballet. Its huge success unveiled a new dimension of Canadian dance. Since Lawrence Rhodes took over the directorship of the troupe of handsome young dancers, the standard classical repertory has been complemented with many twentieth-century ballets by Canadian, European, and American choreographers.

Canada's oldest organization is the Royal Winnipeg Ballet, founded in 1938 by the British dancer and teacher, Gweneth Lloyd. The group was semi-professional until Arnold Spohr, a Canadian who had studied under Volkova in London and Alexander Pushkin in St. Petersburg, assumed responsibilities in 1958. The pioneer company of twenty-five dancers and its repertory were sufficiently built up by Spohr to commence a heavy touring schedule.[7] In addition to contemporary works by guest choreographers, Canadians also contributed. Macdonald's *Rose Latulippe* (1966) was the first full-length work on a Canadian theme, and his later experiments with rock music underlined the company's taste for innovation. Norbert Vesak's *Ecstasy of Rita Joe* (1971), commissioned by the Manitoba Indian Brotherhood, framed regional folklore in balletic context.

# AUSTRALIA

Since the Melbourne opera production of *The Fair Maid of Perth* (1835), which featured a local chorus of dancers, Australia had been strongly impacted by theatrical dance imported from Europe and America. When Colonel de Basil began bringing his Ballet Russe to the Australian continent in 1936, the glamour and excitement generated by the ballets of Fokine, Massine, and Balanchine inspired

283

a passionate mandate for the country to develop a national company. Edouard Borovansky, a Czech dancer who had toured with Pavlova before joining Colonel de Basil's Ballet Russe, decided to settle in Melbourne in 1940. He opened a classical ballet school, formed a ballet club, and by 1944 established the Borovansky Ballet, which endured for fifteen years.[8]

Shortly after Borovansky's death, the dancers from his troupe were absorbed by the newly founded Australian Ballet in 1962, which made its debut with a four-act *Swan Lake*. Under the leadership of senior British artist Peggy van Praagh, the company flourished and became widely recognized as one of significant stature. Its school, founded and run by Margaret Scott who was a former Rambert and Sadler's Wells dancer, grew steadily from its inception. In 1965 the dancer and choreographer Robert Helpmann returned to his birthplace after an international career that peaked at England's Royal Ballet. Under Helpmann's directorship the Australian Ballet continued to encompass the classical tradition but scored its greatest success with *The Merry Widow* (1975), which Helpmann choreographed in collaboration with Ronald Hynd.

The Australian Ballet has a reputation for demanding of its dancers the ability to be at home in the divergent styles of Petipa, Fokine, Ashton, Balanchine, Tudor, and Jiri Kylian as well as various modern dance choreographers. Australian audiences, however, still favor full-evening-length ballets with powerful literary subjects. In addition to the nineteenth-century standard classics, Garth Welch's *Othello* (1971) was a strong box office draw in its day just as *Madame Butterfly* (1995) by his son, Stanton Welch, now is. The success of the Australian Ballet has been instrumental in inspiring support for other companies in the country and encouraging ballet training in the major cities of Sydney, Brisbane, Perth, and Adelaide.

New Zealand has developed its national ballet, which supports a repertory dominated by the classics. The group was founded in Wellington by Russell Kerr in 1961 with partial funding from the New Zealand Arts Council. The National School of Ballet was added in 1967. Over the years a number of dancers born in New Zealand have returned from careers in London to teach and direct, while the company in its early seasons invited principals from the Royal Ballet to augment its roster of native dancers. In 1973 the American, Una Kai, took over the running of the company, and with her skill of masterfully setting Balanchine's works, she extended the group's image. The New Zealand Ballet regularly tours the country's major population areas, cities in the Pacific rim, North America, and Europe. Like Canada and Australia, New Zealand regulates the standards of ballet teaching by following the guidelines and yearly examinations called for in Britain's Royal Academy of Dance method.

## FRANCE

The excitement generated by Diaghilev's first seasons in Paris affected the ballet at the Paris Opera, suggesting new approaches to an art that had been steadily in decline since the waning of the Romantic ballet some fifty years earlier. During the Opera's off-seasons the Ballets Russes had occasion to perform in the theater, which linked the company's modern flair and its elegant chic to the tradition-bound institution. Stellar guest artists such as Pavlova, Spessivtzeva, and Nijinska with her own company, did much to stir the French public's interest in ballet performances as well as increase awareness of the Opera's Italian-trained ballerina, Carlotta Zambelli.

Hoping to achieve acclaim similar to Diaghilev's Ballets Russes, several interesting dance companies were founded in France and enjoyed varying degrees of success and longevity. One of the most notable was organized by Ida Rubinstein shortly after World War I, and it continued sporadically until 1935. Staffing her company with many former Ballets Russes dancers including Nijinska, Massine, and Schollar, Rubinstein also gave choreographic opportunities to the promising Kurt Jooss, David Lichine, and the British dancers Dolin and Ashton. In modeling her repertory on the style of ballets introduced by Diaghilev, Rubinstein presented works in collaboration with first-rate composers and scenarists. The company gave performances in Paris and subsequently around the world.

Ballet Suedois was another company that enjoyed success when it appeared in Paris in 1920. Originated by Rolf de Maré, it sought an avant-garde repertory and functioned as a platform for Scandinavian dancers, painters, and composers when it toured Europe and the United States. Jean Börlin became the company's leading dancer and prolific choreographer, collaborating with some of the most interesting composers and artists of the day including Honegger, Poulenc, Picabia, and de Chirico. In 1924 Etienne de Beaumont organized a single season called Les Soirées de Paris that toured Massine's collection of dances and dancers. Balanchine served as the sole choreographer for Les Ballets 1933, which performed in Paris and London and also lasted only one season. One of the most attractive pieces produced was the first dance interpretation of Bertholt Brecht's *Les Sept Péchés capitaux* (*The Seven Deadly Sins*). Balanchine created the "ballet with songs" in collaboration with Kurt Weill, Lotte Lenya, and Tilly Losch whose husband financed the troupe.

Following Diaghilev's death, Serge Lifar, the impresario's last dance protégé, replaced the ailing Balanchine who had been invited to prepare an original version of *Prometheus* at the Paris Opera. Lifar's timely presence led to his appointment as director, and for the next quarter of a century he reorganized and stabilized the company, which then flourished as a result. From the beginning Lifar was the Paris Opera Ballet's principal dancer and choreographer. Two of his most notable roles were Albrecht in *Giselle* and the spirit in *Spectre de la Rose*. Lifar took on the duties of choreographer during these years, creating over sixty works of which *Icare* (1935, Icarus), *Le Chevalier et la Damoiselle* (1941, The Cavalier and the Young Lady), and *Suite en Blanc* (1943, Suite in White) are most often cited.

To Lifar goes the honor of being the architect of modern French ballet, but he liked to think of himself as a spiritual father of an entire generation of dancers. His long tenure with the Paris Opera Ballet provided the link for young artists to the traditional past that had been lost in Paris at the close of the Romantic age. His own training with Nijinska, Vladimirov, Legat, and Cecchetti echoed the Imperial School of old Russia and influenced the way in which he overhauled the Paris Opera's ballet school, which immediately began to thrive. Lifar's Ballets Russes years had provided him with a firsthand understanding for establishing new directions for theatrical dance at the Paris Opera and in the development of classical and neoclassical repertory. Although World War II interfered greatly with the workings of the house, a number of superb French dancers emerged. Under his direction the fabled Yvette Chauviré crowned a list of French artists including Ludmilla Tcherina, Lycette Darsonval, Claude Bessy, Serge Peretti, and Michel Renault.

By the 1970s the ballet at the Paris Opera was enjoying a revival with the addition of repertory by Balanchine, Jerome Robbins, and the modern master Merce Cunningham, danced by a large company of brilliant performers. In 1977 the French born Balanchine ballerina Violette Verdy directed the company for three years, and she was followed by the American dancer Rosella Hightower who had been a leading ballerina in Europe. Rudolf Nureyev assumed the directorship in 1983, giving life to new productions of his revered classics as well as presenting his own choreography. Although Nureyev left the post after six years, his inspiration, knowledge, and artistic integrity in all the various departments that comprise the Paris Opera Ballet have continued to fuel the company's renaissance throughout the 1990s.

**French Ballet beyond the Paris Opera.**  Lifar's influence extended to Roland Petit (1924) who displayed a genuine flair for making ballets that were uniquely French, due in part to his close collaboration with fashionable librettists and designers. Shortly after leaving the Paris Opera Ballet School, Petit choreographed for Les Ballets des Champs-Élysées and then his own company, Ballet de Paris. In 1972 he became director and choreographer for the Ballet National de Marseilles. From the premieres of his first works, he was an acclaimed master at combining the elements of chic, sex, and high theatricality in numerous ballets including *Le jeune homme et la mort* (1946, The Young Man and Death), *Carmen* (1949), *Cyrano de Bergerac* (1959), *La Croqueuse de diamants* (1960, The Diamond Eater), *La Dame de pique* (1977, The Queen of Spades), and *La Chauve souris* (1980, The Bat Mouse).[9] He also choreographed extensively for musical reviews, films, and the French television industry, frequently appearing with his wife, Renée Jeanmaire.

After World War II a number of large and small companies appeared in France, and other French choreographers of Petit's generation emerged. Greatly contributing to French ballet, Jean Babilée was a leading dancer of the Paris Opera who organized Les Ballets de la Jeunesse to showcase his ballets. For many years the privately trained Janine Charrat danced and choreographed works for her own touring company as well as numerous European venues. Before Maurice Béjart began his long association with the Ballet of the Twentieth

Monique Loudières and
Manuel Legris in the Paris
Opera Ballet's production of
*La Bayadère*. (Photo courtesy
of Jack Vartoogian.)

Century in Belgium, he performed widely as a leading soloist in various French
companies. In 1953 Béjart founded Les Ballets de l'Etoile, which grew into the
Ballet Theatre de Paris. Lifar's favorite protégé, Ludmilla Tcherina, established
her own International Ballet in 1958 and toured the Continent, featuring
Romantic ballets and contemporary dramatic works in which the ballerina
excelled.

The best known large French company, the Grand Ballet de Marquis de
Cuevas, was an international touring body that prospered from 1947 to 1962.
Lavishly supported with funds from the Marquis's wife, who had inherited a
Rockefeller fortune, the troupe was initially staffed with a partial contingent of
fledgling American dancers, most notably the Oklahoma born Rosella Hightower
and Marjorie Tallchief. The de Cuevas organization thrived under its ballet mistress, Bronislava Nijinska, presenting works by her and the American choreographers Edward Caton and William Dollar. Through the years the company
relied on the box office appeal of famous dancers including Markova, Massine,
and Nureyev, who found his first Western home in the Marquis's company.

The town of Monte Carlo in the Principality of Monaco hosts a ballet school and company that have been favored projects of the ruling Grimaldi family. In 1952 a highly structured institution, presently known as the *Académie de Danse Classique Princesse Grace*, was founded by Marika Besobrasova who had been a student of the former czarist ballerinas Lubov Egorova and Julia Sedova. A master teacher, Besobrasova prepared some of the finest dancers currently performing. The Ballets de Monte Carlo was formed in 1985 and is housed in the jewel-like Casino Theater in the same building with the famous gaming establishment. The troupe began under the leadership of Paris Opera graduate Pierre Lacotte and his wife, the ballerina Ghislaine Thesmar. Recognized as a leading authority on reviving historic ballets, Lacotte gave to the present century acclaimed productions of Taglioni's *La Sylphide* (1972) and *Nathalie* (1980) and Saint-Léon's *Coppélia* (1973), which were incorporated into the Monte Carlo repertory. In 1993 the company adopted a more updated look when the ballets of the succeeding director, Jean-Christophe Maillot, replaced the former repertory. The company's sleek neoclassic look, as demonstrated in pieces such as Maillot's *Vers un Pays Sage* (1996, Toward a Wise Land), strongly suggests influences of Balanchine at work in its use of the classical idiom in a contemporary approach. The works of Kylian, Nacho Duato, and William Forsythe have also entered the Monte Carlo repertory.


## SCANDINAVIA

Denmark holds a unique position in twentieth-century ballet. The pedagogic system of August Bournonville had been handed down in unbroken succession at the Royal Danish Ballet School in Copenhagen. Unaffected by the general disintegration of the ballet toward the end of the Romantic period, Danish ballet kept intact all the precise aspects of training that gave it the unprecedented ballet style originally shaped by Bournonville. The Danes continued to perform the master's ballets as they were intended, without revision or restaging, so that one can presently observe Danish ballet as it appeared over 150 years ago.

Early in this century Edel Pederson was the leading expert on the Bournonville pedagogy in Copenhagen, having been trained by Hans Beck, one of the master's most trusted students. Directly passed down to her were the six codified ballet classes and three ballet barres that comprise the Bournonville syllabus composed by his disciples after his death. While the syllabus as such is not currently taught, the classes at the school are based on the Bournonville principles of *épaulement*, *port de bras*, and musicality. Technical innovations and creative trends occurring elsewhere, such as those introduced by Diaghilev's choreographers, never fully penetrated the Danish Ballet, leaving its lively art uniquely archaic. Fokine worked briefly with the Danish Ballet in 1925, setting a number of his works for the Royal Theatre. Balanchine likewise spent a brief time in Copenhagen, but neither his presence nor Fokine's seemed to have had a lasting effect on the established Danish traditions.

From 1932 to 1951 the Danish ballet master Harald Lander oversaw a period of extraordinary creativity. Closely advised by Beck in an unbroken line of tradition, Lander supported the beginning of a Bournonville renaissance.[10] He choreographed thirty works for the company, most notably, *The Little Mermaid* (1936), *Qarrtsiluni* (1942), and *Études* (1948). By balancing his own works with fresh productions of Bournonville's ballets, the company flourished and gained international recognition on its first foreign tour in 1948.

Vera Volkova was invited to Denmark in 1959 to reorganize and update the Royal Danish Ballet School, just as she had done for London's Sadler's Wells Ballet School. Adding to the peerless Bournonville training, she incorporated the Vaganova pedagogic method, and in the course of her tenure Volkova succeeded in eliciting a greater technical range from the dancers. As a result, the Danes have since that time been remarkably equipped to perform the contemporary works of twentieth-century choreographers from all over the globe while maintaining the skill to recreate their precious heritage. Today the Royal Danish Ballet is recognized throughout the dance world for the training given at its school, the women noted for their femininity, *ballon*, and *batterie* and the men for their elegance and prodigious elevation. With the broadening of the Danish dancers' technique, Flemming Flindt, who began his directorship in 1966, was able to build a repertory that balanced the Bournonville inheritance with standard classic, neoclassic, and modern ballets including his own works, *The Lesson* (1963), *The Three Musketeers* (1966), and *The Miraculous Mandarin* (1967).

Other Scandinavian countries have absorbed ballet into their cultural life. Sweden was the earliest of the northern lands to adapt the artistic trappings of seventeenth-century France. The first court ballet was produced there in 1638 by the French ballet master Antoine de Beaulieu. Some years before he made his epic journey to Russia, Jean-Baptiste Landé was actively creating an excellent foundation for ballet training in Stockholm between 1721 and 1727. Stockholm's Royal Opera housed the country's major ballet company, which dates from 1773. The senior Charles Didelot, Antoine and August Bournonville, and Filippo Taglioni all worked there in succession for a number of years after which a long decline set in.[11] Starting in 1913 Fokine made several visits to the Royal Swedish Ballet, staging his work and generating enthusiasm among the dancers, but there was no continuity, and only very limited ballet activity persisted.[12] Early in this century public interest in theatrical dance was renewed when the appearances of Isadora Duncan, Mary Wigman, and Kurt Jooss introduced modern dance to the capital. So successful were the moderns that young Swedes such as Ivo Cramér, Birgit Akesson, and Birgit Cullberg were inspired to form a synthesis of the classical and modern idioms that brought about the current stylistic basis of Swedish repertories.

Interest in traditional ballet was rekindled in 1950 when Antony Tudor was installed as director and choreographer. He was followed by Mary Skeaping, and during nine years she concentrated on cultivating the classics for the company while she also enlarged the repertory with works by Massine and Balanchine. Skeaping took an avid interest in eighteenth- and early nineteenth-century ballets and revived them for the Drottningholm Palace court theater where they are still shown during the summer months.

For decades the widely recognized Swedish dance maker, Brigit Cullberg, sustained the Cullberg Ballet, staffed with both classically trained and modern dancers. Among her most acclaimed works were *Miss Julie* (1950) and *The Moon Reindeer* (1957). Her sons, Niklas and Mats Ek, have continued the company's artistic policies to produce dramatic ballets that have strong philosophical and psychological underpinnings. Mats Ek's *House of Bernarda Alba* (1978), his unsettling *Giselle* (1982), *Swan Lake* (1987), and *Sleeping Beauty* (1996) are representative of the company's originality.

Norway has made valiant efforts to establish a permanent company in Oslo. Known today as the Norwegian National Ballet, the Norske Ballet was founded in 1953 by Gerd Kjolass and Louise Browne who functioned as its leading dancers and sole choreographers. Directed by the Bulgarian ballerina Sonia Arova, the company was put on a firm footing and quickly expanded to some forty dancers. In the early 1970s Nureyev's spectacular guest performance focused huge attention on the male dancer, which improved the climate for a budding national art, and the company began touring outside the country. In 1990 Dinna Bjorn, who is an expert in Bournonville pedagogy, staging, research, and reconstruction, took on the leadership and role of resident choreographer for the Norwegian National Ballet.

The National Ballet of Finland has its roots in the origins of the Finnish State Opera. When the theater opened its doors in 1879, a *corps de ballet* was formed to serve opera and operetta productions. When occasional ballet evenings were offered, the soloists were imported from nearby St. Petersburg. At the beginning of his fourteen years in Helsinki, the Russian ballet master George Gé formed the first independent company in 1921 and set a version of *Swan Lake* on the Finnish dancers. After World War II Finland's ballet widened its horizons, taking on an international look with the works of a long list of guest choreographers. While all the great classics were staged, Finnish dance makers began to emerge when the country's first native choreographer, Irja Koskinen, created *Scaramouche* (1955). The National Ballet of Finland has been greatly influenced in its training methods by the proximity of its Russian neighbor and has produced excellent dancers who exhibit the thorough technical schooling of the Vaganova method.

## THE LOW COUNTRIES

The Théâtre Royal de la Monnaie in Belgium's capital supplied the necessary *corps de ballet* for its opera seasons in the nineteenth century. Since the Romantic era there had been a tradition of visiting French and Italian dancers coming to Brussels on a regular basis. This was of particular significance when Jean Petipa founded the national ballet school in 1843. Antwerp, the country's second city, hosted a ballet troupe made up entirely of Russian émigrés led by

Sonia Korty in the 1930s. For years Jeanne Brabants (1920) studied with the German modern dancer Kurt Jooss, but later diverted to classical dance at the Royal Ballet School in London. She danced, taught, and choreographed for her own group in her native city of Antwerp. In 1951 she became director of Antwerp's Institute for Ballet, a tuition free public school controlled by the city's education department. Brabant's sisters, Jos and Annie, greatly assisted her efforts as ballet teachers at the Institute. Due to Jeanne's lifelong dedication to ballet and her additional work as a dance publicist, professional dance activity expanded beyond Antwerp. The Ballet de Wallonie based in Charleroi was formed in 1966. Antwerp's Ballet de Flandres came into being in 1970 with Jeanne Brabants as director while Jos took over the Institute. Annie dedicated herself solely to teaching and became particularly adept at training boys, a number of whom developed into leading dancers.

The French dancer Maurice Béjart (1927) dominated the dance scene in Brussels from 1960 to 1980 as director of the Ballet of the Twentieth Century. The company was the result of a sensational Stravinsky evening produced through the participation of a specially formed group made up of dancers from Ballet de la Monnaie, Ballet Janine Charrat, Ballet de Milorad Miskovitch, and Western Theater Ballet. The performance was highlighted with Béjart's choreographic rendering of *Sacre du Printemps* (1959), which caused scandal. In handling the score, the choreographer removed the familiar theme of tribal sacrifice within a primitive setting, which had been used by choreographers since Nijinsky's premiere in 1913. Instead, Béjart created a highly contemporary looking, brutal confrontation of the sexes not seen before on the ballet stage.

Béjart became one of Europe's most avant-garde choreographers, specializing in an eclectic exploration of dance. He created or staged a huge body of unconventional works that ranged from total spectacle in *The Merry Widow* (1963) to his highly personal brand of ballet mysticism suggestive of Far Eastern influences that pervade *Bakhti* (1968) and *Nijinsky, Clown of God* (1971). In a brief time Béjart shaped Ballet of the Twentieth Century into one of the world's leading companies, which continuously toured the globe when not performing in Brussels. He captivated large and young new audiences for ballet, although he remains a controversial figure in the eyes of the most discriminating balletomanes because of his untraditional treatment of subject matter.

Ballet in the Netherlands was not part of its national tradition due to its nation's political and religious history. From the beginning of their great power in the 1650s the Dutch Parliament curtailed the extension of absolute monarchy, thus removing the need for their king to elevate his prestige through royal patronage of the arts.[13] Therefore, the traditional purpose for the development of a national ballet in Holland never existed. While the early seventeenth-century Dutch court did indeed enjoy social dancing and ballets as part of their aristocratic entertainments, these were acquired secondhand from France by Dutch ballet masters or arranged by Frenchmen of minor reputation.

Beyond the rarified life at court, there had been a long history of thriving commercial activity among Dutch dancers and managers at Amsterdam's first and foremost public theater, the popular Stadsschouwburg. Ballets were performed shortly after the house opened in 1638, but their primary attraction as French-inspired allegorical works was decorative rather than choreographic. Although imitative of French models, eighteenth-century baroque and rococo ballets in Amsterdam began to feature healthy doses of Dutch-flavored comedy, acrobatic slapstick, and ice skating in their productions, which were enormously successful with the middle class audiences.

Throughout the nineteenth century well-known French ballet masters supervised ballet at the Stadsschouwburg. Eventually the genre of *ballet d'action* caught on and flourished, beginning with the presence of Jean Rochefort who had escaped to Holland from revolutionary France. He was followed by Jean Aumer, François Albert, and Arthur Saint-Léon, all of whom introduced Romantic influences into choreography seen at the theater. The Dutch ballet master Andries Voitus van Hamme (1828–1868) came to the fore as one of the period's most prolific directors and choreographers of classical ballet and comic pantomime reminiscent of the *commedia dell'arte* style. For his company of sixty dancers, the prodigiously hard working Dutchman created 115 full-length ballets. Van Hamme also introduced to Amsterdam the most important ballets of Taglioni and Coralli. As the Romantic era waned, the city's attraction to ballet declined as it did elsewhere. Interest in ballet revived in the 1920s, especially due to the frequent appearances of Pavlova and her touring company. The ballerina's memory remains enshrined in the heart of the Hague. On one of her tours in the winter of 1931, the ballerina died of pneumonia at the elegant Hôtel des Indes where a permanent and gracious memorial is on view.

A broad public awareness of dance in Holland stems from the post-World War II years. When the country was engaged in its massive reconstruction program, all the arts enjoyed new life, and the nation's great collective courage seems to have been reflected in the birth of a truly vibrant interest in dance. Since that time, two major government-supported companies have dominated the presence of many partially subsidized dance groups on the cultural scene: the Dutch National Ballet resides in Amsterdam and Nederlands Dans Theater is housed in the Hague in studios and a theater complex marvelously designed to meet its needs.

One of the Netherlands' most important dance pioneers was the Lithuanian born Sonia Gaskell (1904–1974) who had toured briefly with Diaghilev during the last seasons of the Ballets Russes. After teaching for some years in Paris, Gaskell emigrated to Holland where she opened a school and began to choreograph for her group, Ballet Recital. Exercising her exceptional gifts for organization, Gaskell established a ballet academy in the Hague in 1954. Next she formed the Dutch National Ballet in 1961, which resulted from a merger with Mascha Ter Weeme's postwar Amsterdam Ballet. Under Gaskell's direction, the Dutch National Ballet boasted an unusually extensive repertory and a large company of dancers who were as at home performing the classics as they were at dancing contemporary ballets.

In the vanguard of the Dutch creators at the National Ballet has been Rudi van Dantzig (1933) whose choreography contributed greatly to the distinct profile the company has today. His many works for the troupe, including *Monument for a Dead Boy* (1965), *Epitaph* (1969), *The Ropes of Time* (1970), *Ramifications* (1973), and *Four Last Songs* (1977), showed his interest in themes based on personal feelings and experience, while even his more abstract ballets were equally filled with emotional implications. Social and environmental themes have also been used in his work as seen in *Painted Birds* (1971), which focused on the dangers of pollution.

Hans van Manen (1932) is the most productive Dutch choreographer to date, having complemented van Dantzig's work at the National Ballet. He has also produced over forty outstanding works for Nederlands Dans Theater where he is house choreographer. His ballets have ranged widely from the experimental *Mutations* (1970) and *Situations* (1970) to the neoclassic lyricism of *Four Schumann Pieces* (1975), which he prepared for England's Royal Ballet. *Grosse Fuge* (1987, Great Fugue), *Black Cake* (1989), and *Déjà Vu* (1995, Previously Seen) are among his most popular ballets. His choreography emphasizes form, but his use of structure does not prevent a sense of the drama inherent in the relationships of dancers on stage. Because he is a superb photographer in his own right, it has often been noted that van Manen's choreography is more influenced by modern art and films than by other ballets.

Elke Schepers and Johan Inger in Kylian's *Petite Mort* for Nederlands Dans Theater I. (Photo courtesy of Hans Gerritsen.)

Nederlands Dans Theater was formed in 1959 by a breakaway group from the National Ballet, which included Willy de la Bye, Jaap Flier, and Aart Verstegen. It remains dedicated to producing ballets only by living choreographers. The dancers are thoroughly trained in the technique of the classical dance, but they also possess a practical knowledge of the technical system of Martha Graham and other modern dance exponents. At the beginning, Nederlands Dans Theater profited from numerous efforts of van Dantzig, van Manen, and several Americans, namely, Glen Tetley, John Butler, Charles Czarny, and Benjamin Harkarvy, who was also one of the company's founders. Possessing remarkable gifts as a teacher and artistic coach, Harkarvy contributed greatly to the development of young Dutch dancers and to the groundbreaking direction of the company during its first ten years.[14]

Jiri Kylian, who had come under the influence of the nurturing atmosphere of Cranko's Stuttgart Ballet, became the artistic director of Nederlands Dans Theater in 1975. He created a repertory of startlingly moving ballets that includes *Verklärte Nacht* (1975, Transformed Night), *Sinfonietta* (1978, Little Symphony), *Psalmensymfonie* (1978, Psalm Symphony), and *Soldatenmis* (1980, Soldier's Mass). In this early phase his choreography was uniquely characterized by a subtle pervasion of deeply felt patriotism for his Czech homeland, giving his ballets a particularly poignant tone. Over the years Kylian's creative output has ranged from the spectacular *L'Histoire de Soldat* (1986, A Soldier's Tale) and *Kaguyahime* (1988, She Who Shines Through the Night) to the tantalizing *Sechs Tänze* (1986, Six Dances), *Falling Angels* (1989), *Petite Mort* (1991, Little Death), *Bella Figura* (1995, Beautiful Figure), and *Wings of Wax* (1997). His work continues to draw praise for its sheer craft and exquisite musicality. In addition to Kylian's body of extraordinary work, the ballets of Mats Ek, William Forsythe, Nacho Duato, Ohad Naharin, and Paul Lightfoot complement the ever-changing repertory.

As in the case of many professional companies, Nederlands Dans Theater has developed a smaller troupe, NDT II, which is currently led by Gerald Tibbs but remains under the artistic direction of Kylian. While first and foremost a performing group, it serves as a stylistic training ground for young dancers who are chosen with the intention that some will enter the major company after two years. NDT II performs works prepared for the troupe by various international choreographers, although two of the most important creations remain Kylian's *Un Ballo* (1991, A Dance) and Duato's *Jardí Tancet* (1983, Secret Garden).

Unique in the world is the enormously successful NDT III led by former NDT dancer Arlette van Boven under the artistic direction of Kylian. It is staffed with veteran artists of Nederlands Dans Theater and occasionally by dancers from other companies who range between forty and sixty years of age. Resident and guest choreographers create works that are precisely tailored to the dancers' vast stage experience and physical maturity. NDT III's repertory consistently displays powerful artistic and theatrical statements. The repertory consists of works by Kylian, *Double You* (1994); van Manen, *Old Man and Me* (1996); Naharin, *Two Short Stories* (1997); and Johan Ingar, *Couple of Moments* (1997).

Ballet has had a home in Germany since the eighteenth century. The considerable trafficking of foreign dancers and choreographers across the continent brought the latest talent and trends coming out of France's Royal Academy to the upper class. The wealthy nobility of Germany's various city-states vied with one another in subsidizing theatrical entertainments at their magnificent baroque palaces from Mannheim to Potsdam. Not only were estate theaters built to house these activities, but entire retinues of dancers, actors, musicians, and singers were maintained for participation in performances arranged for the inhabitants and their unending flow of guests. We have seen, for example, that Noverre, patronized by the Duke of Württemberg, created many of his greatest ballets on the era's finest artists for the Duke's theater in Stuttgart and at his summer home, the nearby Schloss Ludwigsburg.

Because the German states were not unified into a republic until 1871, the concept of a central national ballet never emerged. The number of ballet schools was minimal compared to other European countries, and, as a consequence, did not produce many native dancers or choreographers. In the eighteenth century, interest in ballet shifted from city to city, depending on the taste and purse of the particular court and the capabilities of the artists it engaged. In the early nineteenth century, members of the Taglioni family worked in Stuttgart and Berlin, and the ballet flourished.[15] Around 1860 interest expanded in the city of Hamburg for the light and colorful ballets directed by Kitti Lanner. Just so, it grew in Munich during the six years that Lucile Grahn worked as ballet mistress at the Munich Court Opera.

At the beginning of the twentieth century, the concerts of Isadora Duncan and Ruth St. Denis began a rage for modern dance in Germany that put a shadow over the appreciation of ballet. The modern movement culminated in the 1932 production of *The Green Table* by Kurt Jooss shortly before the choreographer left Germany for political reasons. During the 1920s occasional tours of Diaghilev and Pavlova provided seasonal ballet performances in Berlin while several schools continued to function in the capital. However, due to the ideology and growing power of the Nazi Party, professional dance activity receded sharply prior to and during World War II.

When Germany was divided after 1945, the eastern section came heavily under the influence of Soviet Russia. Although the theaters were destroyed, ballet was shown in makeshift houses in East Berlin, Dresden, and Leipzig. Tatjana Gsovsky culminated a six-year tenure with Germany's first production of Prokofiev's *Romeo and Juliet* (1948) in Berlin. She was succeeded by Lilo Gruber who was able to build a balanced repertory of the classics in East Berlin. In Dresden the Soviet choreographer Vasily Vainonen introduced his ballets, which strongly reflected socialist realism.[16] By 1958 ballet began to overtake the predominance of modern dance in Leipzig with Emmy Köhler-Richter's highly idiosyncratic productions of the classics. Tom Schilling was one of the most productive East German choreographers in Berlin and Dresden with numerous ballets to his credit in Germany and elsewhere.

By contrast the western part of Germany, rebuilt with the encouragement of the Western powers after World War II, was marked by a rich diversity of classical ballet that existed side by side with numerous forms of modern dance and a growing interest in jazz and tap dancing. Currently, all cities in what was once West Germany have opera houses with attached ballet companies that have been heavily influenced by American and British dance styles.

Following the reconstruction of Germany, the growing economy produced enormous wealth, which encouraged the enhancement of the quality of life through the promulgation of the arts. New theaters replaced the war-wasted ones in the larger cities while the smaller cities acquired state of the art facilities. Resort towns, famous for their mineral waters, polished up their theaters which are often baroque or rustic architectural jewels. At the close of the twentieth century Germany has been swept with a veritable dance craze for cutting edge, experimental work represented by countless groups of varying quality. Due to the cost of reunification of the country since 1991, however, financial strains have called for budget cuts that closed down various dance programs and temporarily limited the growth of the art.

In the 1960s the city of Stuttgart began reliving the brilliant years of ballet brought to it by Noverre two centuries earlier. A part of a large cultural complex called the Württemberg State Theater, the Stuttgart Ballet came under the guiding hand of Nicholas Beriozoff who began laying the groundwork in 1957.[17] He was followed by the Royal Ballet-trained, South African John Cranko (1927–1973) who developed a company that grew to be praised at home and in the world's dance centers as "the Stuttgart ballet miracle." Although Cranko worked in many styles, his major ballets were full-length dramatic pieces exemplified by *Romeo and Juliet* (1962), *Onegin* (1965), *Taming of the Shrew* (1969), and *Carmen* (1971). From the beginning the company was made up of many foreign dancers, and Marcia Haydée, its Brazilian ballerina who became Cranko's muse, was recognized as being in the highest echelon. A number of native German dancers began to develop, and the honor of being the first German ballerina of the twentieth century went to Birgit Keil.[18]

In common with other major companies like those in Frankfurt, Hamburg, Berlin, Düsseldorf, and Munich, the Stuttgart Ballet shares the policy of hiring dancers and choreographers from around the world. Especially noteworthy is the presence of the American choreographers John Neumeier, who has directed the ballet in Hamburg since 1973, and William Forsythe, whose work has created an enthusiastic audience for ballet in Frankfurt. While he was still a dancer in Cranko's Stuttgart company, Neumeier's choreographic talent began to show itself. He was readily encouraged by Cranko to create ballets for the Noverre Society's matinees, the city's famous showcases for aspiring choreographers. Like Neumeier, Forsythe had the good fortune to cut his choreographic teeth at Stuttgart. He has built the Frankfurt company into one known for iconoclastic ballet, and his works are in demand internationally.

The munificent Viennese court supported a ballet company that was one of the most active and handsomely funded in eighteenth-century Europe. Since the

296

days of Hilverding and Angiolini, the Kärntnertor Theater, which in time became the Vienna State Opera, maintained accomplished ballet masters and a thriving company and school. As ballet began to enter the public theaters of Vienna, France's most celebrated choreographers were drawn to the city and produced their old and new works at the Volkoper, the Theater an der Wien, and the Kärntnertor with leading dancers from Italy and France. During the Romantic era ballet remained important to Viennese cultural life, and it was continuously graced with the finest artists who appeared in all the important works of the period. By the end of the nineteenth century, Austrian ballet masters and directors once again assumed major responsibilities. One of the most important was Joseph Hassreiter who choreographed *Puppenfee* (1888, The Fairy Doll). The production enjoyed such popularity that it remained in the repertory and has had over 1000 performances to date.

After the dissolution of the Hapsburg Empire in 1919, the overthrow of its 900-year-old monarchy, and the establishment of a democratic government, the ballet at the Vienna State Opera experienced internal troubles. Frequent turnover of personnel from 1920 to 1942 persisted until Erika Hanka became ballet mistress and later director. She stabilized the organization by choreographing a strong repertory of dramatic works. Following Hanka's death in 1958 a new period of unrest beset Austrian ballet although the Nureyev production of *Swan Lake* (1964) and Grigorovich's *Nutcracker* (1973) were outstanding dance events. Rigorous concentration on the quality of choreography occurred under the directorship of Gerhard Brunner who was succeeded briefly by Elena Tschernichova and Anne Wooliams. In 1994 the 100-member ballet company of the Vienna State Opera came under the direction of Renato Zanella, a neoclassicist from La Scala who has created his own versions of Stravinsky's ballet scores.

In Switzerland the modern dance movement stemming from Rudolf von Laban's school had a strong following in the early twentieth century. Ballet was entirely in the service of operatic productions in the major cities. In 1934 Pia and Pino Mlakar, two classical dancers who had studied with von Laban, assumed the directorship of the Zürich Ballet and briefly proceeded to call serious attention to professional dance with *The Devil in the Village* (1935) and *The Ballad of Medieval Love* (1936). A number of successive ballet masters in the postwar years contributed works created to contemporary scores, but it was not until Nicholas Beriozoff's presence dating from 1964 to 1971 that a solid repertory was put on a firm footing, featuring the classics and his own works. Nureyev's 1972 production of *Raymonda* brought international attention to the Zürich Ballet, but the unstable direction that followed seriously threatened the company's artistic growth. In 1978 the American ballerina Patricia Neary took over and based the largest part of a new repertory for the Zürich Ballet on Balanchine revivals, which gave the company a unique status during her tenure.

The Festival of Lausanne had long hosted seasonal visits from leading foreign ballet companies. In 1973 wealthy community-minded industrialists established the Prix de Lausanne, which is awarded to promising young dancers who

Marcie Haydée and Richard Cragun rehearsing Tetley's *Voluntaries* for the Stuttgart Ballet. (Photo courtesy of Jack Vartoogian.)

come from all over to compete internationally. In view of these activities, the city was committed to sponsoring a ballet company and in 1992 won the presence of the highly visible avant-garde choreographer, Maurice Béjart, and his dancers. Firmly established in Lausanne with his new company, Ballet Béjart, the choreographer's much disputed theatrical work continues to attract a diverse and youthful audience.

298

## ITALY

Since the seventeenth century onward, many Italian ballet masters from Lully to Galeotti, Angiolini, and Taglioni did their best work outside the country. The contributions of Italian choreographers and ballerinas in the nineteenth and twentieth centuries played an integral part in the development of the Romantic ballet and the present form of the classical technique. The country itself, however, has not maintained the reputation it enjoyed as the dance center during the Renaissance. While the systemization of the daily class by Carlo Blasis in the 1830s produced distinguished teachers for Milan's conservatory, *La Regia Accademia di Ballo*, generations of stellar dancers found their fame in foreign theaters. Italy has upheld its reputation as the mecca of musical theater, with ballet in the secondary position of dutiful servant to sung drama. Grand opera further increased in importance toward the end of the nineteenth century when the waves of nationalism overtook the Italian peninsula. The zeitgeist coincided with the creation of Giuseppe Verdi's politically rousing and melodious masterworks. Thus on a national scale the opera has continued to dominate the performing arts, and a broad interest in ballet has failed to develop in modern times.

La Scala Ballet is Italy's only major classical company. A sharp decline was evident after World War II when conditions insupportable with the needs of art destabilized the ballet establishment. Overwhelming governmental bureaucracy, which oversees the workings of all theatrical activity in Italy, counteracted the nurturing of ballet. There have been relatively few recognized Italian choreographers at La Scala with the exception of Ugo dell Ara who trained in the school of the Rome Opera and became a principal dancer there and later at La Scala. He produced a revival of the Romantic era's famous "Ballet of Nuns" from Meyerbeer's opera, *Robert le Diable* (1966) and a restaging of Manzotti's *Excelsior* (1967). Coming out of the same tradition, Mario Pistoni created ballets that aroused considerable interest, notably, *La Strada* (1966, The Road) and *The Miraculous Mandarin* (1981). Since then the company has had various foreign directors and guest principal dancers to augment its staff and to stage ambitious full-length productions. From 1987 to 1994 Robert de Warren upgraded the quality of ballet and shaped a fuller repertory for the company. De Warren's efforts are currently continued by Elisabetta Terabust. The former ballerina is bringing in outside choreographers in an attempt to invigorate the company's intermittent dormant creative spirit and elevate La Scala to the level of major European troupes.

## THE IBERIAN PENINSULA

Spain was the last European country to develop professional ballet. Although a plentiful store of dances performed at the royal court since the 1700s and folk dances of the countryside had been a joyous aspect of Spanish culture for generations, professional ballet had no tradition and was only seen when foreign companies visited.[19] Centuries of prejudice had condemned street entertainers and Spanish theater people as immoral. This attitude rendered theater work socially unacceptable and served to discourage native talent and ambitions. In Spain the profession of dance had always been associated with poverty. People danced in order to live. Only peasants and the country's most derided social group, the Gypsies who performed their distinctive flamenco sets, danced for money.[20]

In an effort to get in step with other countries, in 1979 Spain's Ministry of Education and Culture commissioned Victor Ullate to form a national classical group, which he struggled to lead for four years on a limited budget. An uncertain period followed when Ullate left the troupe and established a ballet school in Madrid. With his students he was able to renew his choreographic pursuits, debuting his own Ballet Ullate in 1988. The Spanish government then engaged the Soviet ballerina Maya Plisetskaya for the purpose of developing a large-scale classical company, but results were not forthcoming. Aside from the absence of a long tradition of gradually evolved ballet culture in Spain, the lack of the obligatory, large number of uniformly trained *corps de ballet* dancers derailed the project from the start.

In a continued effort to establish a dance company equal to those of other European capitals, the Ministry invited Nacho Duato back to his homeland to develop a national company in 1990. Armed with training and experience in the forefront of modern European and American ballet, Duato set about shaping Compañía Nacional de Danza with its own identity, a place where, without forgetting the classic precepts, it would be possible to move toward a more contemporary style. After only four years, the dance critic of the British newspaper *The Observer* noted that Duato had done more for Spanish dance than anyone had done in the last half century. Recognized during the ten years that he danced under Kylian at Nederlands Dans Theater, Duato fashioned a contemporary ballet company that is a showcase for his choreography as well as works by Kylian, van Manen, Forsythe, and Naharin. Since his award-winning first piece, *Jardí Tancat* (1985) for NDT II, Duato has created a number of ballets that have been in his company's repertory including *Synaphai* (1986), *Arenal* (1988), *Raptus* (Rapture 1988), *Rassemblement* (1991, The Assembling), *Por Vos Muero* (1995, I Die for Thee), and *Romeo y Julieta* (1998, Romeo and Juliet). Later the same year, the Spanish choreographer was commissioned by American Ballet Theatre to create *Remansos*, a *pas de trois* for three males inspired by poems of Federico Garcia Lorca and set to Spanish folk melodies.

Like its Spanish neighbor, Portugal lacked the presence of ballet in its heritage. There was never an effort to create a font of Portuguese dancers and ballet masters. Classical dance was only seen during the rare visits of foreign artists. The Romantic ballet fared poorly since the virile Portuguese considered themselves too serious for melodrama spun out by frivolous beings like sylphs and

300    Members of Compañía Nacional de Danza in Duato's *Mediterrania*. (Photo courtesy of Carlos Cortés.)

mermaids. Only Saint-Léon was appreciated for work he did in Lisbon early in his career. By 1870 ballet was only seen as an accessory to operas. Diaghilev's Ballets Russes passed through in 1916, but audiences seemed to like the sets and costumes of Benois and Bakst better than the dancing. In the 1940s there was an effort to resuscitate an interest in dance when Francis Graça formed Verde Gaio. Without a long tradition and no established school, however, the group remained essentially a folkloric company.

In 1965 the Gulbenkian Foundation, using its exceptional financial means, founded a Portuguese dance company under the direction of the Scottish chore-ographer Walter Gore.[21] Housed in splendid quarters centrally located in Lisbon, the group established itself as a modern ballet company, showing the works of the period's most energetic and productive choreographers including Butler, Van Manen, and Lar Lubovitch. Milko Sparemblek took over the group in 1970 and brought forty-four works to the repertory including twelve of his own ballets and a production of *Nutcracker*. Sparemblek began the tradition of workshops for the purpose of developing Portuguese choreographers, and they began to contribute to the repertory.[22] He also began touring the company inter-nationally. For a brief period after Sparemblek's departure, the Gulbenkian Ballet was run by an artistic committee elected by the dancers. The repertory was cur-tailed, and becoming more hybrid, programs consisted of conflicting styles.

Jose Salavisa, a Portuguese dancer working in London, was drafted to return and lead the company in 1977. Salavisa not only eliminated traditional choreography, but eventually all of the earlier modern works disappeared including those of the Portuguese dance makers. In the 1980s he returned clas-sical ballet to the repertory to augment the Gulbenkian's newer repertory of modern ballets. An international repertory comprised of works of well-known Europeans including Kylian, van Manen, Ek, Bruce, and Duato was chosen, and to it were added the creations of Salavisa's compatriots Vasco Wellankamp, Vera Montra, and Olga Roriz.[23] When Salavisa retired in 1997, he was succeeded by the Brazilian Iracity Cardosa.

# BALLET IN SOVIET RUSSIA

## POST-REVOLUTIONARY RUSSIA

Before the Communist Revolution, Russian ballet, which had achieved the fullest aesthetic and technical development the art had yet attained, was con-centrated in the Imperial Ballet of St. Petersburg and to a lesser extent in the ancient capital of Moscow. Because of the radical changes in thinking and living that the hurricanes of history brought on in 1917, ballet aesthetic, pedagogy, and production underwent drastic reforms like all other facets of life. During the 1920s there were deliberations on whether ballet should survive at all and whether it was necessary to the vast Soviet audiences. Most politicians considered ballet a worn-out manifestation of bourgeois culture, while the artists themselves passionately defended their profession.[24]

Once the authorities understood that art could be useful as a tool of propaganda, the Soviet struggle to stabilize and extend the services of government encouraged the reorganization of the ballet. Heated discussions on the future direction of ballet continued among dancers, choreographers, and teachers, and their ongoing debate was over the lexicon of dance. Should it hold to the strict academic rules of the past or should it be renewed by assimilating elements of nonclassical dance, using novel themes, and adopting experimental techniques of production?[25] Little by little, the road to a Russian ballet of the future solidified. In 1930 the Moscow Lunacharsky State Institute for Theater Art (GITIS) added a faculty for training ballet historians and critics. At the end of World War II greater focus was placed on the dance training and production at the Bolshoi. In 1946 the Institute developed a faculty for training choreographers, and in 1958 a division was added to prepare teachers of ballet. The full program is extraordinarily comprehensive, requiring five years of study, and awards a degree equivalent to a Doctor of Philosophy.

During World War II the Imperial Ballet of St. Petersburg, renamed the Kirov Ballet Company of Leningrad, was evacuated to the distant city of Perm. Its performances there over several years started a wide public enthusiasm for ballet that ultimately helped to strengthen Perm's own company. In 1958 ballet productions and training in Perm progressed enormously under the direction of the GITIS graduate Murat Gaziev. Today Perm is the third major dance center in Russia and is recognized for the large number of stellar dancers it develops.[26]

More than any country, Russia has embraced Noverre's ideas to the fullest possible extent in the systematic preparation of dancers, teachers, and choreographers. From the outset Soviet dancers, just as those in czarist times, received comprehensive training for careers in ballet. Their education dealt with the complete physical, emotional, and spiritual aspects of the work. Under communism an official mental attitude was also dictated for the preparation of artists. As future dancers, students were taught that they were individually responsible to the state and, therefore, to all people in the USSR to achieve maximum goals for themselves. As the next generation of artists, they had a predetermined place in the scheme of Soviet life and a duty to fulfill it. This politically derived philosophy influenced the total development of Russian dancers making them, on the whole, the best-prepared, best-equipped, most capable, and secure in the world. On the other hand, periodic defections of a long list of dancers from all the former iron curtain countries focused worldwide attention on the festering demand for uncensored artistic experimentation, a central element of creativity that is contrary to the values of any totalitarian government.

We have seen in Chapter 11 that prior to the Revolution there had been considerable advanced thinking in the art circles of Moscow. In ballet it was clear that the long years of Petipa's influence had run their course. While fate and youthful impatience allowed Pavlova, Karsavina, and Fokine to realize their destinies in Western Europe, for those who stayed in Russia, reforms did not occur until after the Revolution had succeeded in annihilating the old order. By 1920 the ballet masters Alexander Gorsky, Fyodor Lopoukhov, and Kasian Goleizovsky were not only questioning choreographic tradition, but were breaking with it while antagonizing colleagues and bureaucrats.[27]

Under the auspices of the Soviet government the very purpose of dance art acquired political goals. By 1932 the aim of socialist realism was officially declared to be the sole criterion of art. No longer was ballet for the enjoyment of the privileged few. In line with new objectives, art was now meant to ennoble the feelings of Soviet audiences committed to recreating a Russian nation built on Marxist ideas. Ballet was to project meaning, having human emotions at the center of choreographic works. Due to the nature of dance, according to Party thinking, the thematic material of socialist realism was required to reflect the positive aspects of life, which meant the glorification of the Communist Party and the proletariat working force.[28] Tragic, sordid, or grotesque subject matter had to be minimal to blend with the essentially joyful nature of dance. Soviet ballet prided itself in having retained selected aspects of its 200-year-old national treasure that stood the test of time. Artists living under a drastically altered system harmonized the past with novel theatrical ideas and new technical discoveries worked out in the classroom. Fresh artistic concepts in choreography were sought to promote and blend with the sociopolitical needs of the Communist regime.

**Twentieth-Century Russian Choreographers.**   Soviet choreography went its own direction, having been cut off from Western trends until the historic visit of American Ballet Theatre in 1960. *The Red Poppy* (1927) by Lev Lashchilin and Vassili Tikhomirov was one of the most enduring of the early Soviet ballets and the first to introduce a heroic theme in which its political format staunchly praised the new order. During this period Lopoukhov was recognized as the custodian of the classic heritage; he firmly believed that it was the springboard of all choreographic invention.[29] Yet his rejection of classical technique in his avant-garde ballets including *The Ice Maiden* (1927), *Taras Bulba* (1940), and *Pictures from an Exhibition* (1963), caused controversy regarding their break from tradition. Similarly, the experimental ballets of Goleizovsky, *Joseph the Beautiful* (1925) and *The Red Whirlwind* (1927), in which Goleizovsky used no classical steps, led to his temporary resignations, periods during which he choreographed for music hall productions. Bureaucratic interference with the work of artists was due to the overriding Marxist political thought that all activity should be subservient to the needs of the state. Artistic work was subsequently guided by dictates of the government to provide a kind of ballet for inexperienced proletarian audiences, one that was easily understood and appreciated. As a result, the compositional output of Soviet ballet was uneven.

Vasily Vainonen (1901–1964) was considered by Russian critics to be one of the guiding lights of the new Soviet choreography seen at the Kirov Theater. His first work, *The Golden Age* (1930), was disputed on account of its incorporation of daring acrobatics. Soviet authorities felt that the production minimized the conflicts of class war and ideological destruction and it was soon dropped from the repertory. Vainonen is best remembered for *The Flames of Paris* (1932), which showed that historical subject matter could be strongly effective when used in ballet. His widely hailed version of *Nutcracker* (1934), *Partisan Days* (1937), and *Sleeping Beauty* (1952) made him one of the most important chore-ographers of his day. The 1930s produced some of the best Soviet ballets for the Kirov repertory including Rostislav Zakharov's *Fountain of Bakhchisaray* (1934) and Leonid Lavrovsky's *Prisoner of the Caucasus* (1938) and *Romeo and Juliet* (1940), which inspired countless versions in the West after a film of it was exported.

Although primarily a ballet master and teacher, Asaf Messerer (1903–1992) contributed occasional choreography during his long career. In 1962 he created *Ballet School* for the Bolshoi, and his 1949 concert pieces, *Spring Water* and *Melody*, have been danced by virtuoso performers the world over. One of the most prolific Soviet dance makers was Vladimir Bourmeister whose *Straussiana* (1941), *Coast of Happiness* (1956), and *The Lonely White Sail* (1970) were his best-known works. His production of *Swan Lake* (1958) used the Tchaikovsky score in its original sequence and was later set on the Paris Opera Ballet. He was the first Soviet choreographer to work in the West when he created a new ver-sion of *The Snow Maiden* for London Festival Ballet in 1961. Equally productive was Leonid Jacobson (1904–1975) whose collaboration on *The Golden Age* (1930) won him early recognition. Many of his ballets incorporated unusual movements and patterns and caused controversy at every performance. Jacobson was particularly adept at choreographing concert pieces, some of which were inspired by the paintings and sculptures of Marc Chagall and

Nadezhda Pavlova and Vyacheslav Gordeyev in the Bolshoi Ballet's *Spartacus*. (Photo courtesy of Jack Vartoogian.)

Auguste Rodin. Toward the end of his life, he formed his own company that he named Choreographic Miniatures.

Konstantine Sergeyev (1910–1992) became one of Soviet ballet's most elegant principal dancers, partnering Galina Ulanova and his wife, Natalia Dudinskaya. Between 1951 and 1979 he directed the Kirov Ballet on two separate occasions, during which he was plagued with political difficulties. He created new productions of *Raymonda* (1948), *Swan Lake* (1950), and *Sleeping Beauty* (1952). The demi-character dancer Yuri Grigorovich (1927) was one of the most successful choreographers and producers to emerge after the war. His first full-scale ballet *The Stone Flower* (1957) was followed by his sweeping spectacle, the equally praised *Legend of Love* (1961). Under his directorship of the Bolshoi Ballet, the company rose to enormous distinction. Grigorovich created the definitive version of *Spartacus* (1968) and new versions of *Swan Lake* (1969), *The Sleeping Beauty* (1973), and *Romeo and Juliet* (1979).[30]

At the breakup of the Soviet Union, the Bolshoi's repertory had become a virtual museum under Grigorovich's thirty-year rule. It consisted of the same classics, Grigorovich's ballets, and only a few works by Balanchine and Bournonville. The company experienced a perilous crisis, ravaged by artistic, economic, and spiritual depression. In a calculated effort to save the bleak situation, the government abruptly dismissed Grigorovich in 1995 and replaced him with his former protégé Vladimir Vasiliev who had been an exceptional Bolshoi virtuoso. In attending the transition from old guard to new, the genial Vasiliev's task is to move the large artistic enterprise of dancers into the next century without losing the Bolshoi's essential past.

Oleg Vinogradov (1937) directed both the Kirov company and the smaller Maly troupe, during which time he prepared very unorthodox stagings of *Cinderella* (1964) and *Romeo and Juliet* (1965). His later works included a version of *La Fille mal gardée* for the Maly Ballet in 1970 and *Yaroslavna* in 1974. In 1995, Vinogradov was removed as director of the St. Petersburg company and replaced by Makhar Vaziyev. The highly respected Igor Belski, who is committed to a contemporary classical style, heads the Vaganova school.

**Agrippina Vaganova.** Agrippina Vaganova (1879–1951) was most responsible for the intensive and swift reforms in ballet schooling during Soviet times. As a pupil of Gerdt, Vazem, and Legat, her early training had represented the highest attainments of the St. Petersburg Ballet School, and over time she also absorbed the strong influences of Cecchetti and Fokine. Acknowledged for her outstanding *batterie* and *ballon*, Vaganova was known as the "Queen of Variations" during her dancing career. Today her contribution to Russian dance reaches far beyond the accomplishments of her performing years. Achieving a revered place in the archives of ballet history, Vaganova was personally responsible for renovating the pedagogic system that produced Russian dancers. Her methods reorganized and, in some instances, expanded the entire body of technical knowledge in such a comprehensive manner that it continues to be the hub of all ballet training in the country. A new period in dance pedagogy began with the

305

publication of her *Basic Principles of Classical Ballet* (1934) in which generations of experience were distilled in a clear, concise approach to teaching the complete classical vocabulary. Resulting from the exacting demands of the graded syllabus worked out in Vaganova's methodology, ballet teaching in Russia became completely professional in the sense that no longer could retired dancers claim the right to teach. Before passing the art on to the next generation, dancers undertook a two-year training course that reinforced and refined their own classroom education and stage experience in terms of its breadth and balance.

After the Revolution, which to some extent precipitated Vaganova's premature retirement from the stage, she was invited to teach at the St. Petersburg Ballet School, renamed the Leningrad Choreographic Technikum. While the Western dance world was unaware of the intense ballet activity behind the Iron Curtain, Vaganova proceeded to add new significance and historical importance to dance training. At once she began to blend the knowledge of personal experience with her ideas on ballet instruction. As the Technikum's leading teacher, Vaganova soon turned out a bevy of ballerinas, unique in their ability to conquer space. Never before had *pirouettes* and *grand jetés* been so dazzling and yet pure in their classical line as when performed by her students, according to firsthand observer, historian Natalia Roslavleva. The expressive capacities of the elegantly poised head, back, and arms had never reached such degrees of subtlety. For sheer amplitude Soviet ballerinas out-soared the leaps of any dancer in living memory. Leading the list of Vaganova's renowned pupils were Marina Semenova, Natalia Dudkinskaya, Olga Lepeshinskaya, and Galina Ulanova, the latter being the only one seen by Western audiences when she appeared in Europe and in the United States toward the end of her career.

Vaganova's teaching methods were implemented in the entire training system throughout the Soviet Union. Her concepts further expanded the technical horizons of male dancing, which had been, in any case, well developed in St. Petersburg since the days of Didelot. Carefully following the choreographic trends of her times, Vaganova was able to break down numerous daring innovations in partnering that were being attempted in the contemporary choreography of her colleagues. Once these novel movement ideas were systematically analyzed, they were absorbed into the syllabus, thus extending the male's technical expectations in *pas de deux* work. Often acrobatic, the complex and demanding lifts achieved by the Russian male dancer went through considerable artistic refinement in the hands of Vaganova to become genuine amplifications of the *danse d'école*. Roslavleva best sums up the impact of Vaganova-trained dancers in words that still apply to the Russian artists who are trained in her method.

> Everything was subordinated to the main goal of bringing the human body into a state of complete and harmonious co-ordination of all parts. However, the "Vaganova back" was the first thing that struck the eye in Vaganova trained dancers. This was due to the exceptional placing of the [torso] that, according

to the professor's maxim, should be the "master of the body." She taught the pupil to "dance out of the body," so that the muscles of the [torso] governed the movement of the limbs. This could be reached only after a prolonged education of muscular sensations on the part of the dancer, learning how to bring into action any part of her body and any muscles without applying unnecessary energy to its other parts. Vaganova pupils were famed for their *équilibre*. At the same time, while being firmly placed on the ground, the strength of their backs enabled them to "take off" at any given moment and soar in the air, continuing to move and to maneuver their body *during* the flight.[31]

The teaching methods of Nikolai Tarasov (1902–1975) did for the Russian male dancer what Vaganova did for the Russian ballerina. One of the most important methodologists of Russian classical ballet, Tarasov taught without interruption at the Moscow Choreographic School between 1923 and 1960. Like Vaganova, he firmly believed in the classical school as the foundation of ballet art. Yet Tarasov understood the inevitability of change in art, of new

Larissa Lezhnina and Alexander Grulyaev in the 1992 St. Petersburg production of *Romeo and Juliet*. (Photo courtesy of Jack Vartoogian.)

307

Altynai Asylmuratova and Konstantin Zaklinsky in the Kirov production of Balanchine's *Theme and Variations*. (Photo courtesy of Jack Vartoogian.)

styles, and contemporary themes. He also understood the limits of the genre and taught that disregarding them would lead to artistic failure. During the disastrous years of World War II, Tarasov saved the ballet in Moscow from certain destruction by evacuating the faculty and students to Vasilsursk. There he found living quarters and a studio to continue the Moscow School's teaching activities. Tarasov devoted his career to masculine dance, and shortly before his death he published the prize-winning *Ballet Technique for the Male Dancer*. His students have staffed the state schools of Russia and all the countries of Eastern Europe.[32]

The West was able to observe Soviet dancers on a number of occasions since 1956 when the Kirov and the Bolshoi began visiting the capitals of Europe and North America. Both companies had tremendous impact on their audiences from the standpoint of their individual styles and the superlative qualities of their dancers. While the Kirov astonished the Western public with the exquisite lyricism of its artists, the Bolshoi won the day for the sheer exuberance of its dramatic performers. These central characteristics in each company are traceable back many decades and were present prior to the artistic reforms instituted by the Soviets.

Since the dissolution of the Soviet Union in 1991, ballet has suffered financial instability and uncertainty regarding its future in all of Russia's theaters. Internal power shifts in the renamed Maryinsky and the Bolshoi companies, however, have not interfered with the performing schedules, high quality of dancing or with the continuing development of young dancers in the three major ballet schools. Worldwide company tours and smaller touring groups made up of company dancers have, in fact, increased as a means of acquiring foreign currency, which replaces the lost government subsidies of recent years. While tours are generally successful, it is too early to say how the Russian choreographic style will be affected by outside influences. At the same time, the unleashing of an ever-increasing number of Russian teachers and dancers eager to learn Western repertory is adding a new dimension to dance technique and performance everywhere.

# Summary

The touring companies of Pavlova and Diaghilev were the primary instruments that initiated a renewed Western European interest in an art form that had been absent since the waning of Romantic ballet over a half century earlier. Subsequently, the 1930s were witness to the widespread revival of ballet across the Continent. The seasons and series of concerts provided by Rubinstein, Fokine, Nijinska, Massine, and Balanchine kept modern ballet in the imagination of society. The effort to reestablish the work of Diaghilev by René Blum and Colonel de Basil produced Ballet Russe organizations that handsomely served Europe and sparked ballet's firm establishment in North and South America. European opera houses began renewing their ballet troupes and schools or instituting them for the first time as a consequence of general interest in theatrical dance.

The pioneering efforts of Rambert and de Valois were heroic, marking their contributions to British society with a significance that goes beyond their place in dance history. Lifar managed to give a wake-up call to the Paris Opera that once again came to revere the art it had birthed. When peace and prosperity returned after World War II, ballet spread and flourished as never before. Companies staffed with fresh young dancers could be found almost everywhere in Western Europe. Only Spain, long embroiled in civil war and fascism, failed to join the trend until the 1980s.

By 1950 European ballet clearly fell into two geographical camps. Western European ballet, in a free world setting, covered the broadest possible spectrum of choreographic styles from the storehouse of the classics to contemporary forms touched by the modern, jazz, and ethnic idioms. Quality of training, too, was reflected in a wide range from conservatory schooling to commercially driven private studios. Eastern European ballet, by contrast, had a linear development based on its control by Soviet Russia as a foreign propaganda tool and as an appealing opiate for its long-suffering citizens. While Russia's elitist, systematic training produced superlative artists for the state, the merit of its chore-

309

ographic output was uneven, encumbered with bureaucratic interference and its disdain for artistic individuality and creative freedom.

Vaganova's reorganization of methodology, her pedagogy, professionalism, and lack of compromise regarding the rules of *danse d'école* systematically produced a new brand of ballerina. In the same fashion, Tarasov's forty years of teaching in Moscow formed unmatched male dancers. Europe and America got its first look at what had been happening in Russian ballet in the late 1950s, and the Western dance world was swept off its feet by the technical level of Russian artists and the superb mounting of its spectacles.

Even before the overthrow of communist governments, Western ideas began seeping into the Russian dance establishment and its former satellites, but now they are open to explore wherever the muse points. A wealth of Western choreographic styles is imposing itself on Eastern European dancers and choreographers, which was not possible before 1989. Expert teaching of the Vaganova syllabus is more widely available in Europe and North America because Russian teachers, dancers, and directors are moving Westward in droves. They mingle in the free marketplace where they can share their unique heritage in theaters and classrooms.

# Chapter Notes

310

1. Haskell, p. 116.
2. Peter Brinson and Clement Crisp, *Ballet for All: A Guide to One Hundred Ballets* (London: Pan Books, 1970), p. 114.
3. John Percival, *Modern Ballet* (London: Herbert Press, 1980), p. 8.
4. Alexander Bland, *The Royal Ballet: The First Fifty Years* (Garden City, NY: Doubleday, 1981), pp. 77–112.
5. Ibid., pp. 175–76.
6. Ibid., pp. 249–54.
7. Koegler, p. 357.
8. Ibid., p. 26.
9. Ibid., p. 324.
10. Percival, *Modern Ballet*, p. 49.
11. Gustaf Hilleström, *Theatre and Ballet in Sweden*, trans. Anne Bibby (Stockholm: The Swedish Institute, 1953), p. 75.
12. Ibid., p. 84.
13. Simon Schama, *The Embarrassment of Riches: An Interpretation of Dutch Culture in the Golden Age* (Berkeley: University of California Press, 1988), pp. 221–28.
14. Coos Versteeg, *Nederlands Dans Theater: Een revolutionaire geschiedenis* (Amsterdam: Uitgeverij Balans, 1987), pp. 13–21.
15. Hartmut Regitz, *Tanz in Deutschland: Ballet seit 1984, Eine Situationsbeschreibung* (Berlin: Quadriga Verlag, 1984), p. 7.
16. Koegler, p. 56.

17. Regitz, p. 33.
18. Ibid., p. 36.
19. Luis Bonilla, *La Danza en el mito y en la Historia* (Madrid: Biblioteca Neuva, l964), p. 316.
20. Ian Woodward, *Ballet* (London: Hodder and Stoughton, 1978), p. 255.
21. José Sasportes and António Pinto Ribeiro, *History of Dance*, trans. Joan Ennes (Portugal: Casa Da Moeda, 1991), pp. 60–72.
22. Ibid., pp. 63–67.
23. Ibid., p. 68.
24. Nikolai Ivanovich Tarasov, *Ballet Technique for the Male Dancer*, trans. Elizabeth Kraft (Garden City, NY: Doubleday, 1985), p. xiv.
25. Ibid., p. xv.
26. Roslavleva, p. 270.
27. Souritz, pp. 86–87.
28. Roslavleva, pp. 190–91.
29. Souritz, p. 256.
30. Alexander Demidov, *The Russian Ballet, Past & Present*, trans. Guy Daniels (Garden City, NY: Doubleday, 1977), p. 132.
31. Roslavleva, p. 200.
32. Tarasov, pp. xiv–xix.

# 14

# $\mathscr{T}$he $\mathscr{D}$evelopment of $\mathscr{B}$allet in the $\mathscr{U}$nited $\mathscr{S}$tates

When ballet arrived in the New World, it took a different shape from that of its extravagantly gilded European counterpart. While there had been a modicum of theatrical dance activity in the states from 1700 onwards, various reasons manifested themselves for its less-than-steady growth, and several factors shed light on this aspect of United States history. First, the art form of dance, which was a centuries-old tradition in European court life, had no breeding ground in the United States. No tradition existed to establish its presence as meaningful in the cultural life of the country. In the 1600s the settlers exerted all their energies merely to sustain life in a rough new land. Starvation, disease, Indian attacks and harsh weather were only a few of the perils that the early Americans faced daily.

312

Religious reforms present in the thought of John Calvin (1509–1564) provided the second set of circumstances antagonistic to the development of American theatrical dance. The Puritans in Rhode Island and Connecticut represented the largest of the religious sects affected by Calvinist thinking. So far-reaching was the French theologian's influence in dictating moral conduct that public merrymaking and entertainment on any scale were considered degenerate and not tolerated as a part of the proscribed pattern for Christian living. The Puritans chose to profess a severe faith rooted in a firm adherence to sobriety and simplicity, values intrinsic to the Reformation. The Protestant work ethic bred by the Reformation prevailed, meaning that each person was required to fulfill one's "calling." Any activity beyond life-sustaining daily labor was frowned upon and, as a consequence, theatrical amusements were customarily banned. While predominantly Catholic Maryland and other Southern colonies were not against dancing, there were simply no theaters providing theatrical dance a venue in community life.

Dance as a performing art is a byproduct of leisure in the noblest sense of the word; not until the new society could meet the basic needs of life was it able to revel in public artistic expression. By the early 1700s colonial cities were growing, and their internal security and prosperity helped to raise people's expectations of life and their standards of living. When the effort to survive became less arduous and the American colonists gained time to turn their efforts toward aesthetic development, they had long been cut off from their European cultural roots. Even if it were available to them, the American merchant and farmer could not be expected to adopt a vigorous interest in ballet, an expression of ideas and sentiments derived from foreign court entertainment. When an enthusiasm for theatrical dance did emerge around 1790, it began with performances that included a variety of movement idioms ranging from acrobatics, pantomimes, and questionable fragments of imported ballet technique.

# ℱROM MINUETS TO MORAL LECTURES

In the eighteenth century, ballroom dancing was considered an appropriate part of education, a notion remembered from ancestral ties to the English way of life. A number of immigrant dancing masters imparted their knowledge of *gigues*, *gavottes*, and *menuets* to the more prosperous colonists. It was not unusual that Thomas Jefferson kept Kellom Tomlinson's *The Art of Dancing* in his library at Monticello. A certain Captain George Bush, who served in the Pennsylvania Line of the Continental Army, was a well-traveled gentleman who began recording in his pocket notebook musical directions and a number of minuets and country dance figures that he himself probably enjoyed dancing. Judging from this little collection of observations and remarks preserved by his descendants, he dined with officers and hosted parties for friends where immigrant French, English, and Italian dancing masters arranged the social dancing. The notes give a lively and personal glimpse into the Army's leisure moments during the American Revolution.[1]

313

As life improved, religious bans against public entertainment were relaxed. On occasion, amateur groups organized by ambitious dancing masters presented balls where recreational dancing was featured as a form of spectator entertainment. A number of theatrical troupes from abroad also appeared, mediocre though they were, with repertories of tightrope dancing, mime, hornpipes, tumbling, prestidigitation, and other specialty acts. These shows were often advertised as "moral lectures" to elude the persistently staunch ethical standards of religious zealots. The lack of quality in these productions was due in part to the fact that there was little money to be earned by artists as theatrical presentations and performers were still looked down upon. Since no real theaters existed, the better singers, dancers, and actors remained in Europe and only third-raters plied their trade on American shores.

During the years that the foremost European ballet masters were perfecting the *ballet d'action* as an ennobling and lofty medium of expression, the value of stage dance went unnoticed on this side of the Atlantic because almost nothing of worth was to be seen. Consequently, a third fact transpired to deter the establishment of the art of dance. At the framing of the Constitution in 1789, its authors were not pressured by the States that they represented to provide for the performing arts. No stipulation calling for a Secretary of the Arts was designated in the Constitution. It is important to understand that at the time the document was written, the country was straddling the fence of inexperienced nationhood on the one hand, and possible renewed oppression from England on the other should ratification not occur. The task of the authors of the Constitution was to achieve a working instrument whereby the new country could operate in an effective manner. Practically speaking, the document needed to be as succinct as possible, and as open to interpretation as it could be for the future. The performing arts, particularly ballet and opera, were traditionally associated with royalty, and being indicative of a distant aristocratic culture they were not perceived as a welcome or natural part of the new country in 1789. Therefore, the most dignified forms of dance and music were not reckoned with in the creation of United States government, because they had no previous existence in the States and because they were considered to be offspring of a heinous political heritage.

Despite the lack of conditions for the development of a dance art, there were foreign touring companies and individuals mentioned in eighteenth-century newspapers and pamphlets that confirm the periodic presence of genuine dance performances. In 1738 an Englishman by the name of Henry Holt gave the first ballet performance in Charleston[2] when he danced in a production inspired by a *commedia dell'arte* theme, *The Adventures of Harlequin and Scaramouche*. In mid-century, Lewis Hallam introduced his English troupe of entertainers on a tour of various colonial cities, giving a variety of incidental dances. The Williamsburg *Virginia Gazette* mentions a Monsieur Denoier, member of a well-known French family of dancers, performing a "grand tragic dance" in the town's New Theatre in the autumn of 1751.[3] After New York's John Street Theater opened in New York in 1767, week-long performances of ballet spectacles were frequently presented by visiting companies from Europe. Pietro Sodi, a much experienced Italian dancer and choreographer arrived in Charleston in 1774.[4] During his long career in Europe he had been a promoter of *ballet d'action* along with his close colleague De Hesse. He made his way in America by offering his services as a dancing master to the public. Sodi's highly praised gift for composing and performing pantomime dances no doubt led to some theatrical activity even though he was at the end of his career by this date. While theatrical events ceased during the American Revolution because of various bans and prohibitions, they returned in 1781 when a new Baltimore theater began hosting various dance attractions. Theatrical entertainment disappeared again with an antitheater law that was passed by Congress in 1787. When it was repealed two years later, European artists returned on a regular basis.

# ℬALLET IN COLONIAL AMERICAN CITIES

In 1791, Alexancer Placide and a number of his French compatriots immigrated to the United States in flight from the holocaust of the French Revolution. Trained in classical ballet, Placide had held the title of tightrope walker to the French king and he was equally proficient as an acrobat, actor, and theater manager.[5] The following year, under the management of Lewis Hallam and John Henry, New York opened its first extended ballet season that gave twenty-seven performances and lasted over three months. It featured Placide and his group in a list of works including *The Bird Catchers*, *The Two Philosophers*, and a pantomime entitled, *Harlequin Protected by Cupid, or, The Enchanted Nosegay*. In addition to operettas, patriotic spectacles, and pantomimes, the Placide repertory included many ballets derived from the works of Noverre, Dauberval, and the Gardels that were eventually shown in cities as far north as Hartford and as far south as New Orleans. When Placide ventured to South Carolina, however, he was forced to resort to tightrope dancing and other forms of outdoor entertainment since there were no theaters.

A young Philadelphian, John Durang, debuted with Placide's company and was destined to be remembered as the first American professional dancer. Durang's association with these well-schooled stage veterans allowed him to profit greatly from their instruction and example. By 1795 Durang had learned enough to partner the elegant Anna Gardie, a ballerina in Placide's company. Both dancers enjoyed considerable acclaim, according to the Boston press, in what could be regarded as the first full-fledged ballet in the United States, *La Forêt Noire* (1794, The Black Forest). It featured a complex plot employing all sorts of daring-do and was well received in a number of performances. The beautiful and mysterious Gardie also starred in popular pantomimes before she was murdered by a jealous husband in 1798.[6] A British choreographer, James Byrne, introduced ballet spectacles to Philadelphia in 1796, but it was the Placide company and its 1792 New York season that represented the avantgarde of America's first golden age of ballet.[7] In 1796 Placide's wife, Suzanne Vaillande, left him after he wounded her lover in a duel. She then moved to Louisiana with her recovering new husband and in New Orleans she became the leading dancer and America's first female choreographer for the next nineteen years.[8]

After the American Revolution, theaters were constructed as business ventures by entrepreneurs at an increasing rate. In conjunction with the necessity of housing the visiting opera, mime, and ballet troupes from abroad, theaters proved to be highly profitable for the new capitalists. Moreover, the presence of the theaters served to whet the public's appetite for more entertainments and enterprising theater managements did this by engaging the most popular, amusing, or amazing acts that could be found.

315

Most of the foreign performers were French and had often been schooled at the Paris Opera. As theaters appeared, better artists were attracted so that the form and content of dance improved until classical ballet became a recognized elitist entertainment among the *cognoscenti* of the seaboard cities. To some degree ballet's popularity was due to the exotic note lent by its very Frenchness. Even before the American Revolution, all things French, thanks to the dynamic flowering of French Renaissance civilization, had been considered the ultimate in taste and fashion. And now, there were Americans informed enough to appreciate and, indeed, demand them.

By the mid-1800s, when the United States had achieved its national identity through the energy and wealth generated by the Industrial Revolution, American society's attitudes and lifestyles were altered. Public entertainment was clamored for. The healthy curiosity of Americans, fed by a booming economy, required the excitement and luxury of amusements that only theatrical productions could provide. Boston, New York, Philadelphia, Richmond, Charleston, and New Orleans were the foremost theatrical cities, and they continuously extended lucrative invitations to European troupes and individual artists to visit.

A number of dancers displaced and unsettled by reoccurring political strife in Europe found their way to American shores and began, on a small scale, to teach their craft. As a result, at the dawn of the Romantic ballet, some talented Americans emerged on this side of the Atlantic. Paul Hazard, a French dancer, trained Mary Ann Lee at one of the country's first ballet schools at 96 Fifth Street in Philadelphia. Hazard and his wife had gained their experience at several European opera houses and were reputed to be excellent teachers, forming a number of aspiring American dancers. Lee danced *La Sylphide* and a parody of *The Maid of Cashmere*, entitled *Buy It, Dear, 'Tis Made of Cashmere*.[9] She also learned Fanny Elssler's most famous roles during the Austrian's American tour. Lee traveled to Europe, and after a year of private study with Jules Perrot and others in Paris, she returned to produce from memory a version of *Giselle* for a theater in Boston. She was America's first Giselle as well as its first ballerina to gain international recognition. Julia Turnbull, who also trained with Hazard and danced with Elssler's touring group, was Lee's strongest rival. Turnbull performed solos on programs that resembled variety shows, and occasionally danced in copies of popular European ballets such as *La Sylphide* and *Nathalie*.[10]

According to the French critic Gautier, one American was a match for the greatest of the Romantic ballerinas. She was the remarkable Augusta Maywood (1825–1876) who had received her early training at Hazard's school. Following only two years of classes, twelve-year-old Augusta made sensational appearances as a child prodigy, which led her to try her wings abroad; she enjoyed so much success that she never returned home. When the Paris Opera engaged her after she had studied there with Joseph Mazilier and Jean Coralli, the critics marveled at the unique flexibility and graceful buoyancy in the dancing style of the ballerina from the "land of savages."[11] When Maywood eloped and disappeared with her partner, Charles Mabille, the two were dismissed from the Opera, but continued to have engagements all over Europe. She danced in Italy at the height of her career for twelve years. Not willing to put up with the loss of lucrative engagements brought about by the frequent incompetence of the businessmen who managed her bookings, Maywood, in true Yankee spirit, established her own company independent of any theater. Hence, the American ballerina became the first female dancer in history to lead a traveling company that included a ballet master, her various leading male partners, *corps de ballet*, costumes, and props.

The long career of America's first *premier danseur*, George Washington Smith, faired better as the lot of homegrown dancers went. He was one of several Americans who had joined Elssler's troupe in America and learned immeasurably from the experience.[12] Smith was able to study with Elssler's Irish partner, James Sylvain, from whom he learned the role of Albrecht. By 1859 Smith was the principal dancer with the Ronzani Ballet, the first Italian troupe to visit the country. Among the dancers listed on the Ronzani roster were little Enrico Cecchetti and his parents. Smith's own son took up the occupation, and in the early twentieth century performed and arranged vaudeville dances.

Well-known foreign dancers were beginning to appear in the United States. Francisque Hutin introduced the "new French style of dancing" that emphasized greater virtuosity than had been seen before, including the first *pointe* work performed in America. The Ravel family toured the country for over thirty years with a broad repertory of original ballets, pantomimes, tumbling, and tightrope acts. After going down the Atlantic coast, the Ravels traveled the waterways to the Gulf of Mexico, performing in New Orleans at the same time as Léon Espinosa, the famous Portuguese Jew who founded one of the last great dance dynasties. Jules Perrot danced in New York briefly as did Paul Taglioni, Jean Petipa, and Petipa's son Marius; the Romantic ballet style evolved from the *danse d'école* was first introduced to America by all of them. Prior to the appearance of these four contributors to Romantic ballet, few of the growing audiences had seen anything beyond Irish reels and African-American minstrel clogs.

## A ROMANTIC BALLERINA VISITS

When Fanny Elssler arrived in 1840, a large number of Americans were ready for her glamour, even if they were unschooled in her art. The general quality of the ballets in which she appeared was far from the Paris Opera productions that had been the stunning settings supporting her fame, but Elssler's stage genius could not fail to penetrate the sensitivities of even basically unsophisticated ballet audiences. When she appeared in Washington, D.C., one of her most ardent fans was the son of President Martin Van Buren, who attended all her performances. Elssler returned to Europe following two years of American engagements, which included a tour up the Mississippi River and a voyage to Cuba that greatly enriched her pocketbook. While many Americans treasured the sweet memories of Elssler's visit, her presence had been essentially the personal success of a famous and exciting foreigner. Elssler's American tours did not generate a strong enough desire for the development of ballet, one that was sufficient to overcome a situation where there were almost no ballet schools and no companies. Lack of opportunity kept the profession of dance a precarious and impoverished one for young Americans. Although ballet had received its most significant airing in the United States with Elssler's appearances, it would not begin to develop as a flourishing American art until the times provided the right circumstances.

More Italians danced in America when Maria Bonfanti and Rita Sangalli starred in *The Black Crook* (1866). They were followed by such beautiful and colorful women as Carlotta Brianza, Malvina Cavallazzi, and Josefina Morlacchi. After her dancing career, Cavallazzi established the ballet school at the Metropolitan Opera. Morlacchi met and married Texas Jack and then danced for many years on the circuit of Buffalo Bill's Wild West Show. Elizabetta Menzeli was also an important Italian ballerina who toured all over the United States, and when she eventually settled in New York taught ballet at the Knickerbocker Academy in Greenwich Village. Kitti Lanner came from Vienna in 1870 and was praised for her performances in *Giselle*, which was also the last time the ballet was seen in New York until Pavlova danced it in 1910. The Danish ballerina Adeline Genée culminated her five visits and a coast-to-coast tour in partnership with Alexander Volinine at the Metropolitan Opera House in 1912.

318

## PAVLOVA'S CROSS-COUNTRY TOURS

The indefatigable Anna Pavlova was extremely influential in the United States, calling attention to the art by taking her company to communities where ballet was previously unknown. Trained to perform before Russian aristocracy, Pavlova delighted in dancing for the common laborer in cities and towns across the country. Far from an audience of cultural elitists, Pavlova danced in front of crowds of Americans from various backgrounds. They came out of curiosity to high school auditoriums, convention halls, and movie houses, and her beauty, talent, and devotion to her art sent them away deeply touched. A person might not have read Shakespeare but could easily have seen Pavlova dance. Not since the advent of Fanny Elssler to these shores had people been so excited by a dance artist. Pavlova succeeded in being the personal inspiration for an entire generation of dancers. She aroused a desire to dance in the hearts of countless young women long before there was a supply of properly trained teachers. Pavlova was, indeed, a dance pioneer to the world, but her contribution has a very special meaning in America.

The appearance of Diaghilev's Ballets Russes, bolstered by enthusiastic press releases in 1915, left indelible impressions with its New York performances and its lengthy tour westward. The successful impact of Diaghilev's enterprise on

America was the result of an appealing repertory, fitting musical scores, superb decor, and star-studded choreography. Even before Diaghilev's death and the end of his company, a devoted fleet of his artists began to arrive and help institute the teaching force that founded American ballet. After World War I, Theodore Kosloff and his wife Alexandra Baldina settled in California, turning out dancers the calibre of Nana Gollner and Paul Petroff in their ballet school, coaching Hollywood stars, and choreographing spectacular scenes in Cecil B. De Mille films. In 1919 there had been performances in Chicago staged by the Ballets Russes principal, Adolph Bolm. A number of productions prepared by Bolm's compatriot, Mikhail Mordkin and his Russian Ballet Company, were given in New York. Between 1928 and 1931 Léonide Massine staged *Schéhérazade* at the Roxy Theater, giving four presentations daily. Later, he recreated *Rite of Spring* for performances in Philadelphia and at the Metropolitan Opera House.

That the arts were not specifically provided for in 1789 was not necessarily the misfortune that it was once made out to be. Let it suffice to say that things happen in their own time as is witnessed by the immense popularity of American professional, regional, and campus ballet.

The growth of ballet in the United States has been unparalleled in the entire history of the art. From its modest beginnings during the early years of the twentieth century, participation and interest in classical dance has steadily expanded to a point where the United States stands alongside England and Russia. Based on numbers alone, the incalculable list of ballet students in the United States by the century's end, the staggering amount of performances ranging from professional to amateur, the wealth of creative talent, technological know-how, and enthusiastic audiences all combine to outshine any other country, past or present.

319

# BALLET RUSSE DE MONTE CARLO

The dissolution of Diaghilev's enterprise unleashed an entire company of dancers in Europe, many of whom were unwilling to retire, teach, or go abroad in search of work. When René Blum and Colonel Vassili de Basil established the Ballet Russe de Monte Carlo in 1932, a number of these artists were brought back into close association. Léonide Massine created for the company his first abstract choreographic interpretations of symphonic music including *Les Présages* (1934, The Omens), *Choreartium* (1934), and *Symphonie Fantastique* (1936, Fantastic Symphony). Balanchine contributed to the Ballet Russe repertory also, setting *La Concurrence* (1932) and *Cotillon* (1933). In 1933 Sol Hurok, a New York impresario, negotiated with Colonel de Basil to bring his touring company Ballet Russe de Monte Carlo to the United States. The arrival of the troupe at this time is usually cited as the long term major event that permanently established an American interest in dance that accelerated uninterruptedly to the present.

For the historic visit of the Ballet Russe, the heavily dominated Massine–Balanchine repertory that evolved from an extension of Diaghilev's artistic policies was led by the veteran Russian ballerina Alexandra Danilova. The three "baby ballerinas," Irina Baronova, Tamara Toumanova, and Tatiana Riabouchinska, discovered in the Paris classrooms of Preobrajenska and Kschessinska, proved to be a great theatrical draw, catching the American imagination for the novelty of their youth as well as virtuoso talents. The character dancer Leon Woizokowski headed the male contingent including David Lichine, André Eglevsky, Roman Jasinsky, and Paul Petroff. Before long, however, a number of American dancers were swelling the ranks of the Russian-dominated company, demonstrating that nationality had no special claim on sheer dance ability.

Paradoxically, the Ballet Russe's 1933–1934 season was a time of incredible glamour for the ballet even though there was virtually no educated ballet audience in America. The press made the most of the exotic and temperamental stars, and intrigued Americans flocked to theaters in the cities where the Ballet Russe appeared. Hurok's business acumen helped the Ballet Russe gross over a

Alexandra Danilova as the Firebird in *L'Oiseau de feu*. Col. de Basil's Ballet Russe de Monte Carlo. (Photo courtesy of the Victoria & Albert Museum, London.)

320

million dollars in the first year, proving that an extravagant form of entertainment could be a financial success in a capitalistic setting. As a result of the company's continuous touring, ballet was fast becoming ingrained in American cultural life.

The annals of the Ballet Russe between 1933 and 1940 are fraught with administrative entanglements and a number of name changes for the organization. They record Blum's and de Basil's efforts to set up rival companies, which Hurok attempted to merge. In 1936 Massine, who wanted to be artistic director, broke with de Basil. Since Blum had the title to the Ballet Russe de Monte Carlo, Massine joined him and that became the official company. Colonel de Basil formed another company bearing his own name, which he later renamed the Original Ballets Russes. It toured the world, presenting much of Massine's creative output. The company's extended visits to South America were particularly important to the establishment and growth of classical ballet in Argentina and Chile. Upon de Basil's departure, Blum revitalized the Ballet Russe de Monte Carlo under his own name, with Serge Denham as business manager. He secured the services of Mikhail Fokine, who staged old and new ballets for Alicia Markova, Igor Youskevich, Frederic Franklin, and the indomitable Danilova. A man of impeccable taste and culture, it was largely due to René Blum that so much of Diaghilev's legacy survived.[13]

Massine continued to be enormously productive, and in 1938 he created *Gâité Parisienne* (Parisian Gaiety), *Seventh Symphony*, and *Capriccio espagnol* (Spanish caprice), among many new ballets. On the administrative side the situation was filled with turmoil when dancers shifted their allegiances from one company to the other. Most devastating, perhaps, was Massine's legal battle over his choreographic rights arising from the fact that the rival companies were both claiming his earlier ballets as their exclusive property. While artistic deterioration took its toll, for over three decades the magic name of Ballet Russe managed to retain its fascination for the American public.

After World War II, the Ballet Russe severed its connections with Monte Carlo and became an American troupe although it retained its famous name. The Ballet Russe de Monte Carlo's historical significance is that the company bridged the period between the demise of the Pavlova and Diaghilev organizations and the establishment of the first national companies in the United States. It provided the public with the opportunity to develop an appreciation for genuine professional ballet. Nationwide, audiences in cities saw a substantial amount of classical dancing during years of cross-country tours. Perhaps the most charismatic and versatile ballerina of her time, Alexandra Danilova, and her partner, Frederic Franklin, thrilled the public with their irresistible stage charm and elegance. The popular triple bill of *Swan Lake* Act II, *Schéhérazade*, and *Nutcracker* always ensured a good house. It became known within the troupe as the "ham 'n' eggs"[14] program for its lucrative box office appeal and the relative ease in hanging and striking the scenery of these ballets for one-night stands. The Ballet Russe was the gateway for countless dancers who eventually set up ballet schools all over the nation, created climates for performing wherever they settled, and contributed hugely to the evolution of the classical dance in America. The Ballet Russe rang down its final curtain in 1962, done in by an overwhelming array of legal and economic problems.

The burgeoning interest in ballet generated by the Ballet Russe de Monte Carlo brought about the successful inauguration of the first two national American companies, the New York City Ballet and the American Ballet Theatre. While the inspiration for and establishment of these organizations were independent of the Ballet Russe itself, much of their initial strength derived from the individual dancers and choreographers who, at one time or another, had affiliation with the original Diaghilev organization. Thus, the honored traditions of the dancer's heritage passed naturally from an old-world reservoir into the mainstream of American ballet.

# $\mathscr{N}$EW YORK CITY BALLET

In the late summer of 1929, an exhausted and ailing Diaghilev had come to the end of his productive life. A few days later a daring and inspired Harvard graduate strolled through the narrow Venetian streets, gazing at the city's blue-green canals and dreaming of the possibility of American ballet. In a curious turn of fate, circumstances were finally right for ballet to journey from Europe to a permanent home in the New World. The young man, Lincoln Kirstein (1907–1996), was destined to be one of Diaghilev's heirs in the United States. Perhaps a momentous sign of something to come, during his stroll Kirstein quite unknowingly had observed the funeral cortège of the great impresario as the black gondola wound its way from the church toward the cemetery island of San Michele.[15] While Diaghilev's journey was ended, Kirstein was at the threshold of his professional life. Throughout his long career Kirstein remained a major figure in the development of American ballet.

Both scholar and patron of the arts, Kirstein was the visionary behind the lengthy and arduous fostering of one of the country's brightest cultural assets, the New York City Ballet. As a result of his extensive dance research during his university years, Kirstein and his Harvard classmate Edward Warburg formulated the core of a long-range plan that established the timeless *danse d'école* on American soil to train and prepare American dancers for American audiences. Like Diaghilev, Kirstein did not possess any specific artistic talents to be used in the ballet companies he founded. Yet, his immense erudition, his sense of history, and his unerring aesthetic judgment enabled him to be the creative spirit behind a lifetime of forming artistic organizations. In emphasizing the importance of developing a new classicism, Kirstein believed that not only must those who create ballets understand their ancient language, but in a more profound sense, choreographers must comprehend the emotional and moral spirit of their own times. In other words, the richer a choreographer's contemporary experi-

322

ence, the greater impact his or her art can have on the quality of a society's cultural life.

Kirstein reasoned that the chief directorial position of the enterprise must project an artistic and productive potential extensive enough to move into the future. He found such a man in Diaghilev's last choreographer, George Balanchine, whom he saw as an exponent of the purest contemporary rendering of classical theatrical dance.[16] After lengthy negotiations and considerable persuasion on Kirstein's part, the choreographer came to the United States. The first major undertaking in Balanchine's grand design was the foundation of the School of American Ballet in 1934. Dancers from the Littlefield School of Ballet in Philadelphia were taken to New York to audition; ten were chosen, becoming charter members of the Kirstein/Balanchine project. First established at the Wadsworth Atheneum Museum in Hartford, the group moved a year later to the Manhattan studios that had once served Isadora Duncan. At the helm of the school, Balanchine was the central figure steeped in ballet's great tradition, while at the same time, open-minded to contemporary trends. Dedicated to the preservation and growth of the classical dance, the school aimed to train the finest dancers to provide the essential human material for a new national art. Begotten as a means toward an end, the school polished its dancers for performing, and in a little over a year the newly designated American Ballet gave a New York season. Although Balanchine's choreography and the technical competence and vitality of the young Americans were lauded, some critics lamented that the style of the company did not exhibit a true American genre. The short season, however, clearly indicated that the systematic approach to training young people for the ranks of the company was on solid ground.

In November 1935, the Metropolitan Opera engaged the American Ballet to create the ballet segments for opera and to further develop its own repertory.[17] While this affiliation with the prestigious Metropolitan was a great boon for the recently formed company, it was short-lived. Balanchine set a substantial amount of choreography for operas, but it became clear that the Met's administration was not serious about the development of the ballet as an autonomous art within its precincts. In 1938 the troupe's relationship with the Met was dissolved, the American Ballet disbanded, and Balanchine turned to choreographing Broadway musicals and Hollywood films to support himself.

Determined not to forsake his vision, Kirstein formed a new group in 1937, which was called Ballet Caravan. The dancers were former members of the American Ballet and additional recruits from the school. This time Kirstein, in an effort to underscore the presence of homegrown talent, engaged only American choreographers, namely Lew Christensen (1909–1984), Eugene Loring (1914–1982), and William Dollar (1907–1986). A number of ballets with indigenous themes were created in a short time. *Filling Station* (1938) and *City Portrait* (1939) were conceived by Kirstein himself and choreographed by Christensen and Loring. These works, along with a number of others in the growing repertory, employed colloquial gesture in conjunction with the classical technique to achieve an atmosphere of Americana.

323

Loring's prototype for the western saga *Billy the Kid* (1938) passed the test of time with flying colors and became an American classic. Dollar began his substantial choreographic output for Ballet Caravan by creating two works in the classical vein, *Promenade* (1936) and *Air and Variation* (1938). Ballet Caravan reorganized in 1941 for a Latin American tour. Balanchine joined the company and added his early masterpieces, *Apollon musagète* to *Serenade* (1934), *Ballet Imperial* (1941), and *Concerto Barocco* (1941, Baroque Concerto). In these ballets, but in particular *Concerto Barocco*, he created a new classicism for a new time. Balanchine's modern works were essentially amplifications of the centuries-old *danse d'école*, a theatrical instrument capable of infinite manipulation and variation.

When Kirstein's enlistment in the war interrupted his activities, Ballet Caravan ceased to exist, although the operation of the School of American Ballet continued. At war's end, Kirstein announced plans for a new company to be called Ballet Society.[18] The troupe presented original works prepared in the Diaghilev manner, employing first-rate collaboration among progressive choreographers, composers, and designers. The self-conscious American idiom, which Kirstein favored earlier, was no longer emphasized. Instead, a broader, more encompassing artistic vision emerged. Avoiding the pitfall of Diaghilev's wandering Ballets Russes, Kirstein was able to maintain his organization on sounder footing provided by the school because a continuous flow of proficient dancers was always available to staff the company. The formation of Ballet Society made provisions for scholarships to talented students and young choreographers, while the publication of books, periodicals, records, and films served to promote public interest in ballet. In 1948 Ballet Society became affiliated with the New York City Center of Music and Drama and was renamed the New York City Ballet. From that time onward the company, under the artistic leadership of Balanchine, achieved international recognition taking its unique place among the world's major companies.

324

## GEORGE BALANCHINE IN AMERICA

George Balanchine, more than any other dance personality, has had the greatest impact on the development of American ballet. The choreographer left Russia during the transition years marked by the end of the imperial era and the firm establishment of the new Soviet style of ballet. After a highly productive period with Diaghilev, which lasted from 1925 until the impresario's death in 1929, he engaged himself in several choreographic assignments that led to his own company in Paris, *Les Ballets 1933*. It was at this point that Kirstein invited Balanchine to America with the intention of implanting the heritage of classical ballet in relatively virgin soil.

During his lengthy career Balanchine created a vast body of work, so varied and extensive that adequate discussion of it is far beyond the scope of this

Merrill Ashley and Peter Martins in Balanchine's *Stars and Stripes*. New York
City Ballet. (Photo courtesy of Linda Vartoogian.)

chapter. The majority of his ballets were unchallenged for their intimate relationship with the musical score and the sheer beauty of their choreographic
invention. In his development of neoclassicism, Balanchine emphasized the
dominance of the choreography over the component dancers so that they function like the instruments of an orchestra. He required his dancers to submerge
their individuality for the sake of the greater whole, absorbing themselves in the
classical purity of the academic technique. Thus Balanchine was able to employ
the *danse d'école* through his living instruments to create works that bespoke
the essence of "nowness." The movement his dancers generated was brilliant,
infused with speed and clarity, reflecting the kinetic spirit of a free and open
society in the modern world. In precisely this way Balanchine amplified the
classical style of Petipa to renew the aesthetic validity of "dance for the sake of
dance." When the New York City Ballet first visited the Soviet Union 1962, the
public and critics found it unimaginable that their ballets were without plots, so
differently had Russian dance evolved under Communism. A much-relished
remark was made by Balanchine during the welcoming ceremonies when the
Russians greeted him with, "You have come to the home of classical ballet."
Balanchine countered with, "No, we are bringing classical ballet to you."

In addition to ballets like *The Four Temperaments* (1946), *Symphony in C*
(1947), and *Scotch Symphony* (1952), Balanchine initiated a revival of *The
Nutcracker* in 1954 that became a worldwide event. For years the Ballet Russe
had been touring an abridged version of the work, much loved for its colorful
variations in Act II. Balanchine's spectacular production for the New York City
Ballet, however, established a perennial Christmas tradition, and its overwhelm-

ing success ensured that annual *Nutcracker* performances would take hold virtually everywhere ballet exists.

One of the most influential choreographers to have worked in the New York City Ballet was Jerome Robbins (1918–1998). He began his dance training with modern dancers Gluck Sandor and Felicia Sorel. Unusually well prepared in music and drama for a theatrical career, Robbins choreographed and directed for Broadway and the cinema and created dance for his own jazz company. The musical comedies that he choreographed have become classics and are known throughout the world; they include *The King and I* (1951), *West Side Story* (1957), *Funny Girl* (1964), and *Fiddler on the Roof* (1964). From 1949 to 1959 Robbins was associate artistic director of the New York City Ballet,[19] while continuing his exceptionally productive collaboration with the composer Leonard Bernstein with whom he created *The Age of Anxiety* (1950). In *Afternoon of a Faun* (1953), a particularly interesting work, Robbins created a reflection of Vaslav Nijinsky's ballet when he transformed the faun and one of the muses into two dancers rehearsing in a ballet studio. Robbin's choreography manifested a highly individual *demi-caractère* idiom that effortlessly absorbed nuances from academic, modern, jazz, and social dance forms. The range of Robbins's ballets for the company has been lyrical, comical, and controversial, and has included diverse works such as *The Cage* (1951), *Fanfare* (1953), *Dances at a Gathering* (1969), *Goldberg Variations* (1971), and *Dumbarton Oaks* (1972). *The Cage* caused a scandal at its premiere because it suggested a parallel between the sexual rites of insects and certain aspects of human behavior.

The New York City Ballet has hosted the careers of an enormous list of dancers, including Maria Tallchief whom the press dubbed the first American prima ballerina although the company gave no such aristocratic rank. The lengthy contributions of principal dancers Melissa Hayden, Patricia Wilde, Diana Adams, Allegra Kent, Nicholas Magallanes, Francisco Moncion, and Jacques d'Amboise helped stabilize the early years. The diversity of foreign personalities also enriched the company's style. Violette Verdy, Peter Martins, Mikhail Baryshnikov, Valentina and Leonid Koslov, who were products of the French, Danish, and Russian technical systems, explored another dimension of their talent under the cloak of Balanchine's neoclassicism. The more recent careers of Suzanne Farrell, Merril Ashley, Kyra Nichols, and Darci Kistler have continued the company's emphasis on female dancing. Since Balanchine's death, Peter Martins has run the company that continues to be a major cultural attraction in New York City. His choreographic contributions, along with those of upcoming choreographers, grace programs that continue to present the works of Balanchine.

# AMERICAN BALLET THEATRE

In 1938 the distinguished Bolshoi artist and Diaghilev soloist Mikhail Mordkin revived the Mordkin Ballet formed in 1926 to provide the students of his New York school with dancing experience. With this effort Mordkin became one of the most important pioneers in establishing American ballet. Taking the leading roles in his group's limited traditional repertory was the New England heiress Lucia Chase, Dimitri Romanoff, and Leon Varkas. After several brief but encouraging seasons, it was decided by general manager Richard Pleasant to expand the company into a major effort. Hence, Ballet Theatre came into being in 1939. Pleasant believed, and rightly so, that there was an enormous audience in the United States waiting to be molded and shaped into ardent lovers of the lively art of ballet.[20]

The magnanimous patronage of Lucia Chase (1907–1987) made the project feasible on a continuing basis. She became codirector with Oliver Smith (1918–1994), a designer who would contribute decor for the company's most signature pieces. Their ambitious vision led to an idealistic plan of action. The emerging organization intended to harbor vital tradition while preserving choreographic masterpieces of every style and period. It also desired that modern trends in dance be encouraged and that a healthy artistic enterprise, by its very nature, should offer provocative works created by contemporary artists.

When Ballet Theatre debuted in 1940, it boasted the largest collaboration in dance history, comprising eleven choreographers, eighteen ballets, fifty-six classical dancers of whom fifteen were soloists, nineteen Spanish dancers, fourteen African American dancers, eleven designers, and three conductors preparing the music of numerous composers. The company's opening was an extraordinary success, offering a varied program comprised of ballets by Fokine and Mordkin. An adoring New York audience, already initiated by the mercurial Ballet Russe de Monte Carlo seasons, was ready to follow the proverbial piper. While the choreographers represented in the company were heavily Russian and European, the Americans, Agnes de Mille and Eugene Loring, choreographed their fresh inspirations that in time would become American classics. Anthony Tudor's revival of *Lilac Garden*, Dolin's production of *Giselle*, and the dancing of Patricia Bowman, Karen Conrad, and Nana Gollner confirmed the company's world-class status. While Ballet Theatre was not made of strictly native-born artists, it was a representative American company for American audiences, and has ever since maintained that honor.

Tudor's influence on contemporary American ballet was central in the establishment of Ballet Theatre as a major company. As a former student of Rambert, he was well prepared to make dances, as were a number of his British counterparts. Before Tudor arrived in America as staff choreographer for Ballet Theatre, he had created highly original ballets in England. Just as Noverre, Didelot, and Fokine opended up frontiers in the conceptualization of theatrical dance, Tudor brought a new and electrifying form of expressiveness to his incomparable works, often referred to as psychological ballets. In mounting his choreography, Tudor infused the classical technique with sublime sensitivity in a wealth of gestural nuances and economy of movement, giving insight into the human struggle. His collaboration with the dancers Nora Kaye and Hugh Laing produced some of the most dramatic ballet seen since the era of Diaghilev. *Lilac Garden* (1936), *Dark Elegies* (1937), *Pillar of Fire* (1942), *Dim Lustre* (1943), *Romeo and*

327

*Juliet* (1943), and *Undertow* (1945) are representative of his ballets that contributed heavily to the the company's diverse style.[21]

In 1941 Sol Hurok assumed responsibility for booking Ballet Theatre on international tours, which presented the company throughout the world. For a State Department-sponsored tour in 1957, the company added "American" to its title and the designation has remained. The troupe showed itself to be a virtual melting pot of ballet with the works of Michael Kidd, de Mille, Tudor, Ashton, Robbins, and Balanchine. Of its many leading dancers, only a few of the brightest are cited here, including Marie-Jeanne, Alicia Markova, Alicia Alonso, Nora Kaye, Lupe Serrano, Igor Youskevitch, Eric Bruhn, Royes Fernandez and the Russian defectors Natalia Makarova and Mikhail Baryshnikov, the latter of whom succeeded Chase as director in 1980. During Baryshnikov's tenure the company enjoyed a particularly brilliant period with productions of *Giselle*, *La Bayadère*, and *Raymonda*. Coached by Markarova and company ballet master Jurgen Schneider, the *corps de ballet* rivaled the world's finest. Under the directorship of former principal dancer Kevin McKensie, the American Ballet Theatre continues to absorb into its repertory such diverse choreography as that of Jiri Kylian, Nacho Duato, Clark Tippet, Mark Morris, and Lar Lubovitch to stand alongside the nineteenth- and twentieth-century classics.

Natalia Makarova and Mikhail Baryshnikov in *Giselle*, Act II.
**328**    American Ballet Theatre. (Photo courtesy of Linda Vartoogian.)

The achievements of Agnes de Mille rank among the company's most important contribution to the evolution of ballet. She was most successful in creating ballets that used American themes, such as *Rodeo* (1942), originally done for Ballet Russe de Monte Carlo, and the harrowing *Fall River Legend* (1948), which established her as a major American dance maker. Her choreography for the dance segments of the Broadway musical comedies *Oklahoma* (1943), *Carousel* (1945), and *Gentlemen Prefer Blondes* (1949) took the indigenous American art form of musical theater to new heights. By stylizing classical ballet movement to fit the characters, de Mille helped dramatize the American heartland atmosphere and added a dimension of dance art to popular theater.

De Mille's interest in folk dance was the basis for founding Heritage Dance Theatre in 1973. She passionately understood the importance of preserving all forms of American folk dances in the same manner other cultures cherish their dance traditions, but the venture failed to receive sufficient public support and funding. A born communicator, de Mille was widely acclaimed for her witty and informative lecture-demonstrations. Her outstanding writings on dance place her with the most engaging dance authors the dance world has ever known.

# ℘ROFESSIONAL BALLET ACROSS THE UNITED STATES

During the years that the Mordkin and Kirstein groups were shaping themselves into major organizations, other forces and dreams outside of New York City were at work. Inspired by the infrequent and scattered dance events available to them, a number of young Americans pioneered the permanent establishment of ballet in their home states. Born in Pennsylvania, Catherine Littlefield's (1905–1951) gift to the American ballet scene as a choreographer, teacher, and artistic director of her own company is inestimable. She had received training from their mother and from Luigi Albertieri in New York. Later she studied in Paris with Staats and the former czarist ballerina Egorova. In 1934 Catherine formed the Littlefield Ballet, supported by the virtuoso dancing of her younger sister, Dorothé. In 1936 the group became the Philadelphia Ballet. While it was not considered a national organization, Littlefield's company was a major effort touring the United States; it also played successfully in Paris, London, and Brussels from 1937 to the country's entry into World War II. Littlefield was exceptional for presenting the male dancer as athlete. Deftly synthesizing her eclectic training, she produced a number of ballets and strong American dancers. Of her American theme ballets, she is most remembered for *Barn Dance* (1937).

Genuine ballet in Chicago was first initiated in 1910 with the establishment of the Chicago Opera Ballet. Before that the primary dance activities centered on schools teaching ballroom dance and preparing vaudeville performers. A member of the Pavlova troupe, Serge Okrainsky, and Andreas Pavley became ballet masters for the Chicago Opera Ballet and also formed a school in Chicago in 1917. This gave rise to a successful company that generated much interest in the Midwest and wherever they toured. Remaining in America after World War I, the former Maryinsky and Diaghilev dancer Adolph Bolm devoted himself to several seasons at the Chicago Grand Opera. One of the most important artists pioneering ballet across America, Bolm's successful Chicago ballet school and his lifelong activism have been too little recognized despite the fact that he choreographed major ballets on both coasts and in the Midwest. He also prepared an entire generation of well-known dancers and teachers including Edna McRae.

A strong-minded woman, Ruth Page (1905–1991) was central to the growth of ballet outside of New York City.[22] A student of Bolm, Cecchetti, and Ivan Clustine, Page's earliest professional experience reached back to touring South America with Pavlova when she was only thirteen years old. In 1919 she danced in Bolm's first Chicago assignment, *Birthday of the Infanta*, and then became the leading dancer in his Allied Arts Ballet and Ballet Intime. Page spent 1925 dancing for Diaghilev in Europe. She returned home in 1928 and created the role of Terpsichore in Bolm's Washington, D.C., production of *Apollo musagète*.

Marrying a prominent Chicagoan, she decided to anchor her career in the Midwest although she continued extensive touring and concertizing. In 1933 Page choreographed *Hear Ye! Hear Ye!* to a score by Aaron Copland for an all-ballet program presented by the Chicago Civic Opera. Together with one of her leading dancers, Bentley Stone, she was named director of the dance section of the government-sponsored Federal Theater of the Works-Progress Administration (WPA). Page blossomed as a choreographer, producing ballets with Stone that exhibited their special brand of American ballet style. Among a number of works, the sordid tale of *Frankie and Johnny* (1938) was perhaps their most inventive, and was later danced by the Ballet Russe de Monte Carlo. When Congress closed the Federal Theater, Page and Stone formed a company to tour the repertory they had developed. From 1941 onwards, Stone and colleague, Walter Camryn conducted the city's foremost ballet school, which survived forty years.

In 1955 Page was named ballet director of the Chicago Opera, which represented the only major ballet force in the Midwest. She began demonstrating a penchant for converting operatic scenarios into ballets. Page turned musical masterpieces into unique dance works, earning substantial box office success that attracted a primarily music-oriented audience to the ballet seasons. Included in a number of her ballets was *Vilia*, based on Lehar's operetta *The Merry Widow* (1953); *Suzanna and the Barber* (1955) converted from Rossini's opera, *The Barber of Seville*; *Camille*, based on Verdi's *La Traviata* (1957); and *Mephistophela* (1966), adapted from Gounod's *Faust*. Page was responsible for bringing a cluster of international personalities to the Chicago stage including Henning Kronstam, Marjorie Tallchief, George Skibine, Alicia Markova, and Rudolph Nureyev.[23] After Page's retirement, Maria Tallchief assumed the directorship of the company for eleven years. Currently, Daniel Duell is at the helm.

The development of ballet on the West Coast has been ongoing since 1933 when Adolph Bolm founded the San Francisco Ballet as an affiliate of the Opera. The company holds the distinction of being the oldest troupe in the United

330

States. The brothers Lew, Willam, and Harold Christensen were among those largely responsible for the current expanse of ballet in the western part of the country. After World War II, Lew followed Willam as the director of the San Francisco Ballet while Harold (1904–1989) ran the company's school. Willam (b. 1902) subsequently distinguished himself by forming the ballet department at the University of Utah, and establishing a civic company for Salt Lake that grew into Ballet West in 1963.

Lew Christensen (1909–1984) was among the budding American choreographers encouraged by Lincoln Kirstein in the earlier days of the American Ballet. Not only did he compose exciting pieces, but he enjoyed innumerable successes as a dancer, being especially applauded for his creation of "Pat Garrett" in Loring's *Billy the Kid*. Lew Christensen crafted almost one hundred ballets, most of them being in the San Francisco Ballet's repertory at one time or another. His works demonstrated a style of dancing suited to the American temperament and physical characteristics. Lew Christensen's lengthy career inspired several generations so that many remarkable dancers continued to emerge from the school and into the ranks of the company. Due to his leadership, the enthusiasm stirred by the troupe's national and international tours sparked municipal pride and support for the organization.[24]

Since the 1950s professional ballet companies have continued to appear, enhancing the status of classical ballet. In 1954 Robert Joffrey (1930–1988), an ambitious young artist from Seattle who had danced in Petit's Ballet de Paris, formed a tiny touring company with six dancers, and proceeded to concertize in hundreds of school auditoriums and movie houses across the country. Following the tried-and-true formula, Joffrey and his associate, Gerald Arpino, established a school in New York City in 1957 to produce a steady flow of dancers for a major enterprise that became the Joffrey Ballet. In addition to being an inspired teacher and artistic director, he choreographed a number of works ranging from the rock *Astarte* (1967) to the romantic *Remembrances* (1973). One of Joffrey's most splendid and historically significant contributions to ballet was overseeing the task of researching, reconstructing, or reviving "lost ballets,"[25] notably Saint-Léon's *La Vivandière*; Nijinsky's *Sacre du Printemps*; Massine's *Parade*, *Le Tricorne*, and *Beau Danube*; and Jooss's *The Green Table*.

An impressive array of adjunct choreographers set their works on the Joffrey Ballet, but Gerald Arpino (b. 1928) remained the predominant creative personality, showing himself to be both prolific and a competent craftsman with *Viva Vivaldi* (1965), *Trinity* (1971), and *Kettentanz* (1971). Standard works by Bournonville, Fokine, Tudor, and Ashton have also graced the repertory. After the New York City Ballet vacated its home for quarters in the Lincoln Center complex in 1966, the company filled the space and was renamed the Joffrey City Center Ballet. In the 1980s the company developed a relationship with the West Coast, dividing its home base between New York and Los Angeles. After Joffrey's untimely death from AIDS, the struggle over leadership and severe financial ruptures led to the company's temporary closure in 1995, followed by its reorganization in Chicago. The Joffrey Ballet of Chicago, along with New

331

York City Ballet and American Ballet Theatre, are trustees of the world's great repertories.

Rebekah Harkness was a benefactress of the Joffrey Ballet in the early 1960s. When she wanted to change the company name to her own, Joffrey receded, regrouped, and flourished on his own. Harkness, who had contracted a number of the dancers and ballets in Joffrey's troupe, used them as the basis for her own company. Formed in 1964 and largely subsidized by its patroness, Harkness Ballet added another dimension to the country's growing dance awareness. During the eleven years it existed, the Harkness Ballet gained wide acclaim here and abroad for compelling productions of contemporary choreographers, composers, and designers that were danced by an international ensemble of gifted performers.

Unique in the United States is Dance Theatre of Harlem. Founded by Arthur Mitchell, a leading New York City Ballet principal, and Karel Shook, a widely experienced American dancer and teacher, the company of African American dancers developed from their Harlem ballet school in 1971. While Mitchell contributed the earliest ballets for the repertory, it was soon augmented by pieces from Balanchine and Robbins that were previously created for the New York City Ballet. Perhaps the Harlem company's most engaging ballet is a Creole version of *Giselle* (1984) staged by Frederic Franklin. While the choreography and score are traditional, the New Orleans–French Quarter locale for Act I and the typical New Orleans cemetery setting for Act II work well, reinforcing the ballet's timelessness. The bustling atmosphere of Louisiana urban life parallels the village wine festival in the 1841 production while the eccentrically picturesque funerary monuments in New Orleans' cemeteries provide a similarly poetic dimension to the Gothic graveyard of the original set. Dance Theatre continues to tour with its fifty-plus members.[26]

Shortly after Eliot Feld made his choreographic debut with *Harbinger* for American Ballet Theatre in 1967, he formed a short-lived touring company that made its debut in Spoleto, Italy. Following a brief period, Feld returned to American Ballet Theatre and worked as a guest choreographer in Europe and Canada. In 1974 he organized a new group named the Eliot Feld Ballet. The company has continued to be a showcase for his prolific creative output that represents a wide range of thematic matter. In the early 1980s Feld was instrumental in re-fashioning a New York theater into an excellent physical venue for ballet—the Joyce Theater.

The thriving Pennsylvania Ballet originally formed by Barbara Weisberger in 1963, and the Boston Ballet established by E. Virginia Williams in the same year have been built on strong organizational foundations. These companies had been awarded several Ford Foundation Grants, which gave them a certain amount of freedom from financial woes, and the liberty to further develop themselves and their regional public. Other American cities boasting major professional ballet companies are Houston, Cleveland, San Jose, Pittsburgh, Denver, Milwaukee, Miami, Seattle, Tulsa, and Atlanta. All these companies have substantial home seasons, largely supported by the proceeds of yearly *Nutcracker*

Dance Theatre of Harlem in Fokine's *Schéhérazade*. (Photo courtesy of Jack Vartoogian.)

performances. They also tour so that the dancers perform much of the year and are able to derive their livelihood from the profession.

Historical ballet companies like the New York Baroque Dance Company, the Court Dance Company of New York, and the Cambridge Court Dancers (Massachusetts) have made extremely important contributions to our understanding of Renaissance and baroque forms. Through the expert use of early notation, the choreography shown by these companies makes us more fully conscious of dance history, and with the current use of Laban notation, ballet continues to develop a written literature. Focusing on the richness of the past by accessing the early dance expertise that exists in the United States, both American Ballet Theatre and the Miami City Ballet have used specialists in historical choreography as consultants for new works.

As the second millennium draws to a close, there is a growing shadow casting itself across the face of American professional ballet. The tendency to take fewer risks in choreographic creation is a genuine concern for the future. The language of the marketplace is penetrating the art world, and profit-related imperatives are forcing ballet companies to become more populist in programming. The financial demands placed on all American troupes must be addressed first if they are to survive at all. Ballets like the Joffrey company's immensely successful *Billboards* (1993), much enhanced by the artistry of Elizabeth Parkinson, enjoyed healthy box office receipts that were vital to the enterprise's survival, but the work appealed more to large, nondance audiences who will never develop into balletomanes. The piece hardly advanced the quest for genuine artistic creation that goes hand in hand with great periods in art. While the National Endowment for the Arts continues its own struggle to survive, its presence has never produced American ballet masterpieces like *Serenade, Rodeo, Pillar of Fire,* or *Dances at a Gathering.*

## $\mathcal{R}$EGIONAL BALLET

Two major thrusts, in addition to the strong impact of the American professional ballet, contribute to the growth of the country's dance consciousness. They are the activities of the regional ballet movement present throughout the United States and the promising contributions put forth by the college and university setting.

The American regional ballet movement was born in 1929 when the Atlanta Civic Ballet hosted the first ballet festival in the country. Its guiding light was Dorothy Alexander (1904–1986), who taught and choreographed for her young company, the Dorothy Alexander Concert Group; she is credited with inspiring similar companies all over the country. Regional ballet companies are nonprofit, and were established throughout the country by dedicated teachers who wish to provide a professional environment in which choreographers and dancers can gain experience and develop performing skills. The presence of a regional ballet company enhances the art form by promoting community interest in ballet and in creating larger and more dance-educated audiences on the local level. At present, five general geographic areas in the United States represent the participation of numerous companies, both amateur and semi-professional. They are the Southeastern Regional Ballet Association, Northeastern Regional Ballet Associa-tion, Mid-States Regional Ballet Association, Southwestern Regional Ballet As-sociation, and the Pacific Regional Ballet Association; all are affiliated with the National Association of Regional Ballet.

334

Patricia Barker and Benjamin Houk in Balanchine's *Agon.* Pacific Northwest Ballet. (Photo courtesy of David Cooper.)

Following the example of Alexander's blueprints, regional ballet companies are composed of dancers from area schools who audition for apprentice or senior dancer status. The dancers then receive special training in addition to classes at their home studios from the company's staff, many of whom have had substantial experience with professional companies. Participants are rehearsed in ballets created for them and occasionally they also have the opportunity to learn the classics, depending on the company's level of development.

The principal activity of regional ballet is to present its companies in public performances, lectures, and demonstrations, which in turn increase civic awareness and appreciation of ballet. Every effort is made to prepare programs of the highest quality, and this is reinforced by yearly regional ballet festivals. Local choreographic works are adjudicated by invited professionals whose task it is to select the most representative ballets of a particular company to be shown at festival concerts. In addition to the participation in performances, series of classes taught by experts in ballet, modern, jazz, and ethnic dance are featured at the regional festivals. Participants benefit from workshops in choreography, lighting, and scenic design, as well as lectures geared to the rhythmic and musical needs of dancers and choreographers, and seminars on the care and prevention of dancer's injuries.

# BALLET GOES TO COLLEGE

A vibrant force in the growth of ballet consciousness in the United States is due to the dance activity generated on the American campus. Ballet in an extremely mild form first entered American college physical education departments when young women were increasingly admitted to higher education. Ballet teachers were called in to give "normal courses" in ballet to prepare physical education teachers for a segment of their teaching activities. Since the 1930s the recognition of the educational values of dance rapidly expanded in academic circles.[27] The presence of modern dance found support through its exponents who argued that dance contributed to the physical and mental well-being of the student, strengthening those aspects of personality development that contribute to the whole person. As a result, a number of colleges and universities instituted programs in dance education that were usually housed in physical education departments. From the beginning, college programs were enriched with the presence of professional dancers, such as Ted Shawn, Martha Graham, Doris Humphrey, and Hanya Holm. These artists greatly influenced the thinking and goals of academic dance educators during periods when they accepted invitations to teach and speak at professional meetings and workshops. By the 1960s dance on campus came into focus as an autonomous art form.

The professional dancer's accent on the technical discipline that underlies dance art, complemented the emphasis on individual creativity and freedom of expression in college dance. Therefore, classes in ballet were occasionally intro-

The University of South Florida Dance Department in performance. (Photo courtesy of Greg Fulton.)

duced with the intention of sharpening technical skills, as well as a way to augment the college student's level of endurance. While classes in ballet were meant to broaden the scope of dance programs and the range of the student's knowledge, their real value often lay in their unique service to the modern dance idiom. To a large extent this remains true today in that modern dancers, whether in the professional or collegiate world, actively seek the merits of studying ballet technique that produces greater strength and speed in the body.

The dance critic Walter Terry surveyed a number of college dance programs in 1947 to investigate the future trend of nationwide dance. Out of 105 colleges who reported they offered dance courses, only fifteen included genuine ballet classes. Terry's conclusion, however, was that dance in general was on an upward swing. By the late 1960s, the ballet boom that America had experienced in the 1950s infiltrated the campuses. While ballet courses designed to serve the general college student were popular, ballet major programs or those that emphasized ballet enjoyed healthy expansion. From hundreds of small colleges to the major universities, ballet established itself with an intensity not previously known to campus arts. Its locale varied, being housed in physical education, music, or theater programs, but in a number of institutions ballet classes flourish within a dance department.

Because of the inherent difficulty in the study of ballet, the level of achievement for the college student varies. It takes eight to ten years to become a fully developed ballet dancer, twice the time the majority of students spend on campus. Confounding the time problem, it is physiologically too late to begin to study for a professional ballet career in the freshman year. On the other hand, very good ballet dancers arrive at college with years of previous training, often having the privilege of dancing with regional ballet companies in their hometowns. Their abilities are absorbed into ballet programs, collegiate dance clubs, and campus performances, and serve to enhance the country's total dance picture.

A number of ballet departments place a strong emphasis on teacher training programs. Their systematic and comprehensive preparation of future teachers is perhaps higher education's greatest contribution to ballet. Many college ballet students, who are already excellent dancers, matriculate to prepare for other careers rather than pursue the life of a professional dancer. It is a unique aspect of higher education in the United States that students can attend college and still experience the joy of performing during their peak dancing years. Future dance historians will surely look upon campus ballet as a major American effort toward the expansion of the art. The long-range significance of ballet's presence in colleges and universities is undoubtedly the building of an enlightened new audience that will in turn generate a stronger nationwide appreciation of ballet.

# $\mathcal{R}$ETROSPECTIVE

Three hundred years after the first settlers established themselves on the North American Continent, classical ballet took a phenomenal hold on the nation's cultural psyche and became the country's most visible performing art. There had been social dancing and sporadic trickles of European theatrical dance from 1700 onwards, but the dancing masters and performing artists were foreign visitors. In the early 1930s an influx of Europeans, many of them veterans of Diaghilev's Ballets Russes, began teaching and educating American students in the traditions of schooled dance begun in France during the reign of Louis XIV.

Ballet was not a full-fledged art form in the United States until schools were effectively training a large reservoir of American classical dancers. The young Americans being turned out were the raw material of ballets, ballet companies, and future choreographers. Exhibiting the traits of high energy, optimism, and freedom of the New World, American dancers put the stamp of their own identity on the academic school. Continuous touring across the United States by the Ballet Russe de Monte Carlo developed an audience for the art. Guided by the Russian émigrés Mordkin, Bolm, and Balanchine, American Ballet Theatre and the New York City Ballet were the first national companies to appear and they, in turn, triggered the birth of successive ones like the Joffrey Ballet and Dance Theatre of Harlem.

Classical dance acquired a foothold everywhere in the country with regional ballet companies that were directed by dancers of the previous generation. Filled with eager youngsters, regional companies helped diffuse the art across the nation by encouraging the development of more dancers, and by opening up avenues where creativity for dance-making could prosper. By mid-century genuine classical ballet was entering schools of higher education on the back of its indigenous art, the modern dance. College and university programs have since generated thousands of dancers, choreographers, and informed audiences.

Even a brief survey of classical ballet from the post-Diaghilev era to the present serves to underscore the amplification of the art. The most advanced developments in this cultural explosion occurred largely in the United States between the 1970s and 1980s when dance became the country's number one artistic industry. Calling to its support tens of thousands of new adherents yearly, American ballet was internationally recognized, and New York City joined London as the Western dance capitals in just a few decades. The American ballet style, rich in the entire spectrum of classical dance's tradition, is a flowering unique in the history of the art. American ballet is rich in its heritage of numerous European stepparents, but it is also enervated and rendered enormously creative by American modern dance. Extended to millions through the medium of television, ballet continues to evolve in the public eye. The initial thrust that catapulted American dance into first place originated in the Old World, but over the years it merged and synthesized with the American experience into a uniquely fresh vision of movement expression.

The history of the classical ballet is one of an ever-expanding art form. The gradual emergence of its technique, firmly based on the classical Greek tenets of beauty, unity, and harmony, provides the ballet with infinite aesthetic possibilities, restrained only by the limitations of the choreographer's imagination and the dancer's body. The perfection of the theory underlying the ballet's pedagogical systems is timeless. Five centuries of human intelligence, accompanied by refined sensitivity and a profuse amount of collective energy, have molded an ingeniously contrived form of artistic expression that is rarefied and magical.

Classical ballet's inherently elegant character is ancient, connected to the very first expressions of dignity in the human spirit, but its energy is derived from living forces of the present world. That the heritage of classical ballet's theory and practice is useful as a successful means for expressing contemporary experience is witnessed by the fact that the ballet endures and yet continues to develop on the strength of its growing universal appeal.

338

# Chapter Notes

1. Charles Cyril Hendrickson and Kate Van Winkle Keller, *Social Dances from the American Revolution* (Sandy Hook, CT: The Hendrickson Group, 1992), pp. 5–6.
2. Lillian Moore, *New York's First Ballet Season 1738* (New York: The New York Public

Library, 1961), p. 5. (Horst Koegler gives the date as 1735 in *The Concise Oxford Dictionary of Ballet*, p. 427.)

3. Ibid., p. 5.
4. Winter, p. 145.
5. Hendrickson and Keller, p. 7.
6. Ibid., p. 6.
7. Ibid., p. 17.
8. Ibid., p. 16.
9. Migel, p. 279, note 97.
10. Guest, *Fanny Elssler*, p. 179.
11. Migel, p. 179.
12. Guest, *Fanny Elssler*, p. 136.
13. Mary Clarke and Clement Crisp, *The Ballet Goer's Guide* (London: Michael Joseph, 1981, p. 21). During the Nazi occupation of Paris, René Blum was arrested, deported to Auschwitz, and executed in 1942.
14. Information derived from personal communication with the dance chronicler Ann Barzel, and from Thomas Armour, who danced with the Ballet Russe de Monte Carlo during its many tours across the United States. Barzel noted that the Ballet Russe *Nutcracker* was slightly abridged, lacking the section with Mother Ginger, as well as the mice and soldier segments that required small children.
15. Anatole Chujoy, *The New York City Ballet* (New York: Alfred A. Knopf, 1953, p. 5).
16. Richard Buckle in Collaboration with John Taras, *George Balanchine: Ballet Master* (New York: Random House, 1988), pp. 84–88.
17. Ibid., pp. 96–99.
18. Ibid., p. 160.
19. Ibid., p. 322.
20. Clarke and Crisp, p. 21.
21. Judith Chazin-Bennahum, *The Ballets of Antony Tudor: Studies in Psyche and Satire* (New York: Oxford University Press, 1994.)
22. Ann Barzel, "Dance in Chicago," *Dance News Annual* 1953, eds. Winthrop Palmer and Anatole Chujoy (New York: Alfred A. Knopf, 1953), pp. 138–44.
23. Ann Barzel, conversations, 1997.
24. James Graham-Luján, "The San Francisco Ballet," *Dance News Annual* 1953, pp. 145–57.
25. Millicent Hodson, *Nijinsky's Crime Against Grace: Reconstruction Score of the Original Choreography for* le Sacre de Printemps (Stuyvesant, NY: Pendragon Press, 1996).
26. Lynne Fauley Emery, *Black Dance From 1619 to Today* (Princeton, NJ: Princeton Books, 1988), pp. 279–84.
27. Ann Barzel, conversations, 1997.

# CHRONOLOGY

| | |
|---|---|
| 15000 B.C. | Cro-Magnon people emerge as the first artists among primal societies. |
| 5000 | Ancient civilizations gradually expand the ritual importance of dance to formalized religion, education, sport, military training, and theatrical entertainment. |
| 499 | First stone theater erected in Athens. |
| 405 | Performances of highly refined Greek dance-drama of the classical age appear in Euripides' play *The Bacchae*. |
| 390 | Roman games are inaugurated in stone arenas to appease the gods and distract the volatile mob. |
| 322 | Alexander the Great's establishment of colonies spreads Greek culture throughout the Mediterranean area. |
| 240 | Roman actor Livius Andronicus invents the art of pantomime. |
| 55 | First permanent Roman theater is built at Pompey. |
| 22 | Pylades and Bathyllus are Rome's first professional mimes. |
| A.D. 33 | Crucifixion of Christ, and the beginning of the dissemination of the Christian message of faith, hope, and love. |
| 330 | Christian Emperor Constantine moves the capital of the Roman empire from Rome to Byzantium. |
| 426 | St. Augustine blames cruelty of the arena games and vulgar pantomimes on the debauched state of society. |
| 476 | Fall of the Roman Empire. |
| 530 | Christian Emperor Justinian I, from his seat of government in Byzantium, closes all public sites of entertainment. Mimes become official interpreters in a polyglot society. The Church uses mimes to act out religious doctrine in the effort to make converts and teach Christianity. |
| 544 | Childebert outlaws dancing in his territories. Theater people are cast out of Christian life and become wayfarers. |
| 600 | Population of Europe struggles to survive barbarian invasions, disease, and despair under the protective arms of the Christian Church. |
| 744 | The Papacy forbids all forms of dancing in Christendom. |
| 1000 | Sung and danced *caroles* appear as simple circle and line dances. Gothic cathedrals become sites for the era's greatest spectacle, the Mass. |
| 1095 | Returning crusaders introduce Eastern ideas to Europe. |
| 1120 | Provençal troubadours celebrate the beauty of human pleasures in their poetry, and oversee the song and dance at the courts of love. 1200A pagan carryover, the Feast of Fools parodies religious customs and the upper and lower classes mingle for merrymaking with singing |

and dancing. Wandering minstrels enter the houses of the nobility to educate, entertain, and refine the manners of the upper class. Peasant couple dances inspire elegant versions arranged by minstrels to add dignity and grace to castle life.

1347    The Black Death ravages Europe and fear is reflected in manic outbreaks of dancing; graphic and literary images of death dances become popular.

1393    The *Bals des Ardens* ends in a fiery tragedy.

1425    The persistence of dance in the lives of people is pictorially reflected in Fra Angelico's paintings of "dancing rounds of angels."

1430–1500    Activities of the dancing masters Domenico da Piacenza, Antonio Cornazano, and Guglielmo Ebreo make Italy foremost in dance.

1450    Dancing is tolerated in a modified and formalized state as part of religious services, such as in the *baile de los seises* in Seville's cathedral.

1452    Alberti constructs a theater in the Vatican for Pope Nicholas I.

1453    Fall of the Byzantine Empire scatters Eastern scholars and Greek learning westward to Italy.

1460    Humanistic values fortified with neoplatonic ideas gain importance and give rise to grandiose entertainments with dancing called *intermedii*.

1515    Battle of Marignano; French defeat the Italians, initiating the move of Renaissance culture northward.

1533    Catherine de Medici arrives in France and eventually becomes queen.

1555    Catherine invites the Milanese dancing masters Pompeo Diabono, Cesare Negri, and their colleagues to the French court.

1571    Jean de Baïf's Academy of Poetry and Music at Catherine's court attempts to reestablish the elements of harmony and unity fundamental to the laws of classical Greek art.

1572    Queen Catherine's dancing master, Balthasar de Beaujoyeulx, stages the *magnifique, Paradis d'Amour* to celebrate the wedding of her Catholic daughter to the Protestant Henry of Navarre; St. Bartholomew's Day Massacre ensues.

1573    Italian figure dancing in Beaujoyleux's *Ballet de Polonais* triumphs at Catherine's French court.

1580    Palladio's Teatro Olimpico in Vicenza is erected, inspired by Serlio's translation of an ancient Roman treatise on architecture.

1581    Beaujoyeulx's *Ballet Comique de la Reine* becomes the first genuine ballet with its cohesion of plot, poetry, music, dance, and decor.

1582    The scenario for the *Ballet Comique de la Reine* is documented and sent to the courts of Europe and wealthy families. The first example of festival literature, the handsome publication announces the superiority of French culture.

1588    Thoinot Arbeau publishes *Orchesography*, his comprehensive technical discussion of dancing that included a vocabulary of terminology.

1600    Highly amusing masquerade balls replace expensive *magnifiques* while equestrian ballets keep Henri IV's army in fighting form.

1609    At the English court of James VI, Ben Jonson and Inigo Jones introduce the antimasque in conjunction with the supremely elegant masque *Twelfth Night*.

1617    *Le Déliverance de Renaud* inaugurates a return to luxurious musical theatricals at the court of Louis XIII. As *ballets mélodramatiques*, they assist in establishing the concept of the divine right in monarchical rule.

1640　The concept of linear perspective and numerous mechanical inventions for the stage designed by Niccolo Sabbatini and Giacomo Torelli create a passion for theatrical illusion.

1645　Giuseppi Bianchi's company of Italian comedians, the *commedia dell'arte*, visits Paris.

1651　Louis XIV debuts as a dancer in *Cassandre*.

1653　Louis XIV triumphs as the Sun King in *Ballet de la Nuit*.

1661　Louis XIV founds the *L' Académie Royale de Danse* to regulate the teaching and licensing of dancing masters; this group was ineffective, but survived until 1780.

1662　Louis XIV sponsors an equestrian ballet, *Fête des Bagues* (Festival of Lies).

1664　Louis XIV magnificently entertains guests with an outdoors ballet, *Les Plaisirs des Iles Enchantées* (The Pleasures of Enchanted Islands), at the hunting lodge of Versailles.

1669　Louis XIV licenses Perrin to found the *L'Académie Royale de Musique*.

1670　Louis XIV retires from the ballet stage and begins construction to enlarge the hunting lodge of Versailles.

1672　Louis XIV authorizes Jean-Baptiste Lully to take over the music academy and to include dancing under its guardianship, becoming *L' Académie Royale de Musique et de Danse*.

1673　Lully designates Pierre Beauchamp as the Academy's chief ballet master who establishes the *danse d'école*, schooled dancing; over the next fourteen years they perfect the tragedy ballet form of court ballet.

1681　Mlle. Lafontaine becomes the first professional female dancer to appear on the French stage.

1687　The death of Lully and the retirement of Beauchamp leave the dancer and ballet master Louis Pécourt in charge of the Academy.

1697　The young Russian czar, Peter the Great, departs Moscow on an extended tour of Europe to observe its arts and sciences.

1700　*Opéra-ballet*, a new form of French ballet, evolves in conjunction with the *galant* music style.

1701　Raoul Feuillet's treatise on the art of choreography appears.

1713　Louis XIV authorizes a training school for novices.

1714　A danced duet by Françoise Prévost and Claude Balon that conveys a story without words is performed at an outdoor party at Sceaux.

1715　Ballet's first female choreographer, the Academy's ballerina Françoise Prévost, presents herself in a collection of twelve solos, *Les Caractères de la danse*.
　　　Death of Louis XIV.

1717　John Weaver stages the first example of wordless *ballet d'action* in London with *The Loves of Mars and Venus*.

1725　Pierre Rameau publishes *The Dancing Master*.

c. 1733　Ongoing rivalry between the expressive ballerina Marie Sallé and the virtuoso La Carmargo.

1734　Jean-Baptiste Landé arrives in St. Petersburg as ballroom dancing master to military cadets.

| 1735 | Opéra-ballet is perfected in the creation of *Les Indes Galantes*. |
|------|-------------------------------------------------------------------|
| 1738 | St. Petersburg Ballet School is founded by Landé. |
| 1743 | Debut of Jean Georges Noverre at the Opera Comique in Paris. |
| 1750 | Serf dancers of Russia learn the *danse d'école* technique. |
| 1755 | Noverre revives *The Chinese Metamorphosis* for English audiences. |
| 1757 | Franz Hilverding is invited to upgrade ballet in St. Petersburg. |
| 1760 | Publication of Noverre's definitive *Les Lettres sur la Danse et Ballets*; he begins his great reforms at the court of Württenberg. |
| 1761 | Gaspero Angiolini and Christopher Gluck collaborate on the wordless ballet, *Don Juan*, in Vienna. |
| 1766 | Angiolini succeeds Hilverding at the Imperial Ballet in St. Petersburg. |
| 1767 | Noverre becomes ballet master to Archduchess Marie Antoinette. |
| 1773 | Catherine the Great founds a ballet school in Moscow. |
| 1776 | Jean Georges Noverre's international reputation leads to his tumultuous years as director of the Royal Academy, the Paris Opera Ballet. |
| 1779 | Gennaro Magri publishes his detailed treatise on the techniques of theatrical dance and the grotesque style. |
| 1781 | Auguste Vestris inherits his father's title as "God of the Dance." |
| 1784 | Ivan Valberkh becomes the first Russian to head the St. Petersburg Ballet School. |
|      | A training school for children is formed within the Royal Academy. |
| 1789 | The premiere of Jean Dauberval's *La Fille mal gardée* celebrates the average person as a subject for ballet scenarios. |
|      | The French Revolution fosters a cataclysmic break with the past. |
| 1798 | Jacques-Louis David's post-Revolutionary clothing designs influence ballet costuming; masks, heels, *tonnelets*, and *paniers* disappear. |
| 1801 | Charles Louis Didelot arrives in St. Petersburg as a star performer, but remains to upgrade the schooling of Russian dancers. |
| 1803 | Publication of Noverre's *Lettres* in Russia. |
| 1810 | *Kinderballetten* flourishes in Austria and Germany. |
| 1813 | Influenced by Noverre's reformist ideas, Salvatore Viganò produces his complex *coreodrammas*. |
| 1815 | Napoleon is defeated at the Battle of Waterloo. |
| 1816 | After a brief time as the director at the Paris Opera, Didelot resumes his activities in St. Petersburg, concentrating on creating expressive dramatic ballets danced by Russian artists under his tutelage. |
| 1820 | Carlo Blasis publishes the first comprehensive book on ballet technique, *An Elementary Treatise upon the Theory and Practice of the Art of Dancing*. |
| 1825 | French and German poets and novelists influence the shaping of the format of Romantic ballet. |
| 1832 | Marie Taglioni revolutionizes female technique with her artistic mastery of *pointe* work and *ballon* in *La Sylphide*. |
| 1833 | Ascendancy of the ballerinas eclipses the male dancer. |
| 1836 | August Bournonville, ballet master and leading dancer of the Royal Danish Ballet, creates his version of *La Sylphide*. |
| 1837 | Taglioni and her father begin their five years in Russia, and initiate the flow of Romantic ballerinas and choreographers to the czar's ballet. |
| 1841 | Jules Perrot, Jean Coralli, Theophile Gautier, Adolph Adam, and |

343

Carlotta Grisi collaborate on the archetype of Romantic ballets, *Giselle*.

| | |
|---|---|
| 1846 | After the production of *Pas de quatre*, the Golden Age of ballet fades. |
| 1847 | Frenchman Marius Petipa arrives in St. Petersburg as principal dancer. |
| 1848 | Jules Perrot arrives in St. Petersburg as master choreographer. |
| | The post-Romantic epoch dilutes European ballet. |
| 1858 | Frenchman Arthur Saint-Léon assumes Perrot's post in St. Petersburg. |
| 1866 | Gautier admits that ballet in St. Petersburg is superior to Paris. |
| 1868 | Petipa takes over the helm of the Imperial Ballet. |
| 1870 | Saint-Léon creates his masterpiece, *Coppélia*, for the Paris Opera. |
| 1872 | Birth of Sergei Pavlovitch Diaghilev. |
| 1877 | Petipa puts the entire Russian *corps de ballet* on *pointe* in *La Bayadère*. |
| c. 1880 | First commercially blocked pointe shoes appear. |
| 1881 | Luigi Manzotti stages his extravaganza, *Excelsior*. |
| 1890 | *Sleeping Beauty* results in one of the world's greatest ballet collaborations when Tchaikovsky furnishes its score to Petipa's specifications. |
| 1895 | Lev Ivanov perfects the use of the *leitmotiv* in *Swan Lake*. |
| 1898 | Diaghilev founds and edits *World of Art*, which serves as a literary platform for advanced artistic ideas. |
| 1901 | Russians assume total responsibility for Russian ballet when Mathilda Kschessinska rallies on behalf of native artists. |
| 1903 | Petipa is forcibly retired. |
| 1905 | Isadora Duncan performs and lectures before Russian balletomanes. |
| 1906 | Mikhail Fokine's *Chopiniana* incorporates choreographic reforms. |
| 1909 | Diaghilev's Russian season in Paris returns the ballet to the West in a modernized form; the appearances of Vaslav Nijinsky causes a sensation and the male dancer resumes his importance in the foreground. |
| 1911 | Diaghilev's organizes the Ballets Russes, a permanent touring company with Fokine as its choreographer. |
| 1912 | Nijinsky's neoprimitive *Rite of Spring* establishes the Ballets Russes as avant-garde. |
| 1913 | Pavlova forms her international touring company. |
| 1915 | The Ballets Russes tours North and South America. |
| 1917 | French and Spanish composers and designers replace Russian artists in the Ballets Russes. Picasso introduces cubism into ballet with his decor for Massine's *Parade*. |
| | The Russian Revolution. |
| 1921 | Diaghilev produces *The Sleeping Princess* for London. |
| 1922 | The Soviet Government maintains ballet as a form of Russian propaganda. |
| | Bronislava Nijinska creates neoclassic works for the Ballets Russes. |
| 1925 | George Balanchine leaves Russia and joins Diaghilev's Ballets Russes. |
| 1926 | Marie Rambert forms an English ballet company with her students. |
| 1929 | Diaghilev dies and his company disperses. |
| | Serge Lifar becomes leading dancer and choreographer of the Paris Opera and dominates French ballet until 1958. |
| | Dorothy Alexander founds the regional ballet movement in Atlanta. |
| 1931 | Ninette de Valois moves her London ballet school to Sadler's Wells Theatre; the company becomes the Royal Ballet in 1956. |

| 1932 | A new Ballets Russes de Monte Carlo is established with the personnel and the remnants of Diaghilev's company. |
|---|---|
| 1933 | Nijinska and Balanchine choreograph brief ballet seasons in Paris. Léonide Massine creates his symphonic ballets for the new Ballets Russes. First visit of the new Ballets Russes de Monte Carlo to the U.S. San Francisco Opera Ballet is formed under Adolf Bolm. |
| 1934 | Lincoln Kirstein invites Balanchine to New York to establish a school and found a national company for America. Catherine Littlefield Ballet is formed in Philadelphia. |
| 1935 | Kirstein founds the American Ballet. |
| 1936 | The renamed *Ballet Russe de Monte Carlo* begins its years of touring in North America. |
| 1938 | Ruth Page and Bentley Stone establish their company in Chicago. |
| 1939 | American Ballet Theatre grows out of Mikhail Mordkin's school. |
| 1946 | Kirstein and Balanchine regroup their forces and establish Ballet Society from which the New York City Ballet emerges at City Center. |
| 1947 | Modern dance invades ballet when Valerie Bettis creates *Virginia Sampler* for the *Ballet Russe*; Bettis becomes a pioneer in television ballet. American higher education begins to offer courses in ballet technique. |
| 1956 | Robert Joffrey establishes his first touring company. |
| 1968 | Arthur Mitchell founds Dance Theatre of Harlem. |
| 1964 | Dance patron Rebekah Harkness forms the Harkness Ballet. |
| 1963 | Pennsylvania Ballet and Boston Ballet are shaped out of a grass roots movement begun by Alexander's efforts to establish regional ballet. |
| 1969 | Eliot Feld creates a touring company to showcase his choreography. |
| 1970 | John Cranko oversees the "Stuttgart ballet miracle." |
| 1976 | Modern choreographer Twyla Tharp creates *Push Comes to Shove* for American Ballet Theatre. |
| 1980 | Mikhail Baryshnikov assumes the leadership of American Ballet Theatre. |
| 1984 | Danish-trained Peter Martins becomes the director of New York City Ballet. |
| 1991 | Break up of the Soviet Union unleashes a worldwide flow of Russian ballet companies, dancers, and directors. |
| 1995 | Influence of American modern dance on ballet companies encourages formidable creativity in Europe. |

# GLOSSARY

**Académies**—Institutions officially created to protect the various arts in France.

**Allemande**—A moderate striding dance of sixteenth-century Germany and France that continued to go through various changes throughout the nineteenth century.

**Ambuettè**—A step listed by Gennaro Magri, related to the modern *embôité*.

**Anacreontic ballet**—A form of eighteenth-century ballet named for the ancient poet Anacreon that calls for pleasant situations shown in picturesque scenes, with sentiment, love, and grace dominating the stage.

**Antimasque**—Grotesque or comical aspect of the English masque, the opposite of the elegance and harmony of the masque proper.

**Aplomb**—A dancer's assurance and poise in presentation.

**Apollonian tendencies**—Characteristics of art objects or events that emphasize formal elements of beauty and harmony.

**Arabesque**—Classical ballet's hallmark pose with weight supported on one leg and other extended behind the body; term derives from Moorish ornamental design.

**Attitude**—A pose similar to arabesque, but with the extended leg slightly bent; Carlo Blasis said he derived it from Giovanni da Bologna's statue of Mercury. According to Magri's 1779 definition, attitude was a union of several poses of the arms, legs, head, and eyes that must express an emotional state.

**Avant-garde**—Pioneering innovations in art and literature.

**Baile de los seises**—Formal thirteenth-century Spanish dance traditionally performed in the Cathedral of Seville by ten young boys during Easter services.

**Baletomania**—Russian term for balletomania; originally, a condition describing a fanatical devotion to ballet on the part of gentlemen. The concept was born out of Didelot's intensive second period in St. Petersburg.

**Ballets à entrées**—Theatrical works consisting of three to five acts, independent of one another, but related by a theme stated in the prologue.

**Ballets burlesques**—Parodies of dramatic or lyrical works performed by nobles during the reigns of Henry IV and Louis XIII as subversive political statements.

**Ballet Comique de la Reine**—Called the first ballet (1581) due to its internal cohesion and balance; the word *Comique* is taken to mean "dramatic," not "comic."

**Ballet d'action**—Action ballet in which the narrative is advanced through gesture and pantomime.

**Ballet d'atmosphère**—A ballet in which the choreographic manipulation of classical steps and poses in their relation to plot, music, and decor creates a unique mood.

*Ballet de cour*—Entertainments of the sixteenth-century French court that were intended to influence domestic and world politics through a lavish display of artifice and power.

*Ballet d'epoque*—A ballet that evokes the ideas and feelings of other time periods.

*Ballet mascarade*—A private masquerade party that featured ballroom dancing, elements of improvisation, and often the *entrées* from *ballets burlesques*. They were temporarily substituted for financially ruinous court ballets.

**Ballet master**—Traditional European name for a choreographer, especially in Russia.

*Ballet mélodramatique*—A theatrical form that was dominated by diverse musical elements while containing a minimum of dramatic action and dance.

*Ballets sans paroles*—Eighteenth-century ballets without words; stylized gestures in between segments of dancing advanced their plots.

*Balli*—A sprightly fifteenth-century Italian ballroom dance form.

*Ballo lombardo*—Popular northern Italian social dance form that was comprised of pattens or figures that symbolized moral and aesthetic virtues, and required practice under the supervision of a dancing master.

**Ballon**—The bouncing quality that is prerequisite in the ballet dancer's jumping movements.

**Baroque**—Dynamic European style of art from 1600–1750 that was a reaction to the classicism of the Renaissance and the religious and social structure imposed by the Protestant Reformation.

*Bassa danza*—Italian term for a stately Renaissance form of social dance.

*Basse danse*—French term for a stately dance form of the late Middle Ages.

*Biedermeier*—Nineteenth-century decorative style favored by the middle class; named after a fictitious German poet.

**Bolero**—A Spanish folk dance introduced by Sebastian Zerezo around 1780 in which the dancer accompanies himself with castanets and song.

**Borders**—Strips of cloth above the stage space which hide lighting instruments and other forms of stage equipment from audience view.

**Boulevard theaters**—Privately run theaters in Paris where fresh ideas in artistic and technical production were not only tolerated, but expected of ballet masters.

**Bourbon**—Family name of the dynasty who ruled France between 1589 and 1830.

*Branle*—A collective term indicating a dance in which a hand-linked line of dancers sways from right to left; early French dances that were often accompanied by singing and indications of mime.

*Cachucha*—A Spanish folk dance of *tacquetée* steps, undulating torso, and special *port de bras*; performed with castanets and made famous by Fanny Elssler in the nineteenth century.

**Cancan**—A social dance introduced by Masarié around 1830 as a variation of the quadrille. Entering the dance halls mid-century, it had become increasingly rowdy when high kicking and frivolous displays of pantaloons and petticoats caused it to be outlawed.

*Canzos*—Provençal term for French *chansons*, Spanish *cansos* or love songs.

*Carole*—Earliest round or line dance; performed to unaccompanied singing and without a focal point.

*Carousels*—French equestrian ballets that became the foundation of the art of dressage.

**Character dancing**—A form of theatrical dancing derived from national and folk dances which played an essential role in Romantic ballets.

347

*Cheironomia*—Solemn symbolic gestures in the dance and mime of the ancient Greek theater.

*Choregus*—The leader of a chorus of dancers; in fifth-century Athens, a choregus was a wealthy citizen chosen to sponsor a play and its chorus.

*Chorus*—In fifth-century Athens, a group of up to fifty male actor-dancers who performed as a unit in comedies and tragedies; they did not take part in the dramatic action, but introduced or commented on it.

*Comédie-ballet*—A genre of ballet where dancing is perfectly integrated into the content of the prologue and three-act comic plays; danced *entrées* conclude each act. It was invented by Molière for *Les Facheaux* in 1661 and perfected by 1670 in *Le Bourgeois Gentilhomme*.

*Commedia dell'arte*—Improvised comedy with stock characters; originated in thirteenth-century Italy and perfected during the Renaissance.

*Constructivism*—Early twentieth-century Russian art movement in which mechanical objects were assembled into nonrepresentational and mobile structural forms.

*Convention*—Any element in the theater that is established over long usage by artists and accepted by audiences.

*Coreodramma*—A highly complex form of pantomime ballet named and perfected by Salvatore Viganò.

*Cosmic dance*—An antique element in Renaissance court dancing with philosophical overtones; its choreography reflected the harmonious movement of the heavens.

*Cothurns*—Grecian-style sandals in vogue after the French Revolution.

*Coup de théâtre*—A stunning and unexpected event in a theatrical production.

*Courante*—A dance form of the high Renaissance in France and in Elizabethan England that had originated in Italy.

*Czar, Czarina*—Titles of the emperor and empress of Russia.

*Dance notation*—The recording of movement through symbols on paper; systems currently in use are those of Rudolf von Laban and Joan and Rudolf Benesh.

*Dancing master*—One skilled at creating and teaching dances.

*Danse d'école*—Schooled dancing; requires instruction of a teacher to impart its classical rules formulated in the seventeenth century.

*Danse en l'air*—Aerial aspect of ballet style that resulted in the development of *ballon* in the Romantic ballerina's technique.

*Danse macabre*—A medieval literary and graphic rendering of dances representing death.

*Danseomania*—A spontaneous medieval dance craze born of massive superstition and widespread social malaise.

*Danse par haut*—Vogue for jumping steps encouraged by development of the *galant* style of musical composition.

*Danseur grotesque* or *comique*—Stylistic classification of a dancer outside the bounds of the *danse d'école* who exhibits acrobatic or exaggerated elements when representing a certain type of character.

*Danseur noble*—A classically proportioned male dancer who excels in the strict style of the *danse d'école*.

*Danseuse*—A female dancer.

*Démarche*—A backward moving step.

*Demi-caractère*—The middle ground classification of dancer who commands the dignified bearing of a *danseur noble* combined with the virtuoso technique of the *danseur comique.*

*Demi-coupé*—A principal eighteenth-century step that also entered into the formation of other steps.

*Deus ex machina*—God from a machine; a fifteenth-century mechanical device of ropes and decorated platform that lowered a theatrical deity to the stage.

**Dionysian tendencies**—Characteristics of art objects or events that emphasize the sensuous and irrational elements in their content.

*Divertissements*—A series of short dances within a classical ballet that are designed to display the unique talents of one or more soloists.

*Emmeleia*—Form of stately dances suitable for the tragic subject matter of ancient Greek drama.

*Enchaînement*—A combination of two or more steps designed to fit a phrase of music.

*En dedan*—Inward flowing movement; one leg, arm, or hand moves in a circular direction toward the front of the body.

*En dehor*—Outward flowing movement; one leg, arm, or hand moves in a circular direction toward the back of the body.

**Enlightenment**—Eighteenth-century empiricist philosophy that emphasized reason, idealism, and nobility of spirit over tradition and convention.

*En travesti*—Term used to describe masked and costumed dancers who appear in roles disguised as the opposite sex.

*Entrée*—A section of dance in a *magnifique, ballet à entrée,* or *opéra-ballet.*

*Entremet*—The first danced portion of grandiose French Renaissance entertainments.

*Épaulement*—A term indicating the elegant movement and placement of the upper torso.

**Equestrian ballet**—Form of elaborate Renaissance horse show descended from medieval tournaments.

*Estampie*—Early medieval dance performed by one couple at a time and directed toward a human presence.

*Farandole*—A hand-linked line of dancers following a leader in random winding figures or patterns; lifted arms allow the line to dance "under the arches."

**Festival literature**—A literary genre that resulted from official descriptions of Renaissance court ballets.

*Fête*—Variations of a highly formal Renaissance celebration to an informal lawn party in the eighteenth century.

*Fêtes revolutionnaires*—Massive pseudo-theatrical, political, and social celebrations that commemorated the values of the French Revolution.

**Figured dancing**—A genre of dancing characterized by Renaissance court dancers moving through numerous choreographed geometric floor patterns.

**Flamenco**—Spanish dances with Arabic and Moorish influences; originally from the Gypsy caves of Granada. A combination of fixed rhythms and individual improvisation provides drama and excitement.

*Fleuret*—An eighteenth-century step with three shifts of weight.

**Flies**—Holding space above the stage from which scenery is lowered within view of the audience.

*Gaillard*—Sprightly Italian and French court dance in triple time with complicated steps and surprising movements; the English equivalent was the Elizabethan volta.

349

*Galant* music—A light and free eighteenth-century musical form characterized by a strong beat and elaborate orchestration.

*Gavotte*—Eighteenth-century European court dance whose lively steps and rhythm originated in the Pays de Gap region of France.

*Gigue*—Popular French ballroom dance form of the eighteenth century that may have been inspired by the English, Scottish, or Irish jig. Earliest know gigues originated in Italy where they derived their names from *giga*, a small stringed instrument.

*Glories*—Noisy contraptions that lowered actors or dancers onto the stage to enter the dramatic action.

*Gothic*—A European style of art predominant from the twelfth to fifteenth century.

*Grotteschi*—Comic, acrobatic dancers of the Italian theater.

*Haute danse*—Sprightly French dance form influenced by the Italian Renaissance vogue for jumping steps.

*Hennin*—Old English word for a woman's cone-shaped head piece: literally, "steeple."

*Hopâk*—Energetic Ukrainian dance in double time; originally performed by men only.

*Hornpipe*—An English folk dance primarily associated with British sailors; danced to the accompaniment of a pipe fashioned from wood or animal horn.

*Humanism*—Renaissance philosophy of life primarily concerned with human rather than divine or supernatural matters.

*Intermedii*—The danced sections of elaborate Italian Renaissance entertainments.

*Islamic poets*—Flourished with the seventh-century rise of the Muslim empire; oriental nuance and exoticism of Islamic poetry strongly influenced the arts of the Romantic epoch.

*Joglars*—Provençal term for jugglers; the French term is *jongleurs*.

*Jota*—Colorful couple dance from northern Spain; dancers play castanets to the accompaniment of guitar and sing in triple time.

*Khorovod*—The most ancient Russian line dance performed by peasant women; translates as "lines and circles which move continuously."

*Kinderballett*—Popular eighteenth- and nineteenth-century children's ballet companies that were popular in Germany, Austria, and France.

*Kokoschniki*—Halo-like headdress that was part of the female national dress before the Russian Revolution; derived from the halos surrounding the likenesses of the Virgin Mary and Saints depicted on Russian icons.

*Kordax*—A dance form in Greek theater that was essentially vulgar or comical.

*Ländler*—Graceful Austrian couple dance that was the precursor of the waltz.

*Les Six*—Diverse group of early twentieth-century French composers initially led by Jean Cocteau.

*Livrets*—Lengthy program notes for eighteenth-century ballets usually penned by the choreographer.

*Ludi Romani*—Ancient Roman city games and various accompanying theatrical events.

*Magnifiques*—Magnificent entertainments with political overtones produced by Catherine de Medici; precursors of the *ballet de cour*.

*Masque*—Lavish English court entertainments laden with erudite poetry, dancing, scenic effects, and favored for beautiful costumes; contained some similarities to *ballet à entrée*.

**Maypole dance**—Ancient Druid tribal ritual; its external elements of circular dancing and merriment have been retained throughout the ages, while the symbolism of procreation in the spring of the year no longer figures into its performance.

**Melodrama**—A sensational dramatic work characterized by overwrought sentimentalism and histrionic appeals to the emotions; seeks to arouse audience identification, fear, and anxiety, but generally has a happy ending.

**Mime**—A nonverbal performer seeking to represent or imitate actual experience through gesture.

*Minnesingers*—Medieval German minstrels who were heirs to the troubadours.

**Minstrels**—Broad term for itinerant medieval entertainers who worked in the service of the aristocratic troubadours.

*Mise en scène*—Physical staging of any theatrical production; includes the use and concept of scenery, movement, composition, and visual effects.

*Moresques*—Also morescas, moriscos, and morris dances; widespread dance in 2/4 time; participants wore bells and disguises; the dance vaguely reflected the religious struggle between the Moors and Christians.

**Mythology**—Body of myths preseved in ancient Greek literature; it provided the chief source of inspiration for Renaissance and baroque artists, writers, and ballet masters who formulated the dramatic material for spectacles.

**Naumachia**—Costly mock sea battles staged in intentionally flooded courtyards of Renaissance palaces.

**Neoclassicism**—Revival of the classical treatment in art and literature; usually with a narrower critical interpretation of Greek or Roman models than they were subjected to in ancient times.

**Neoprimitivism**—Revival of the primitive in art.

*Nuvola*—Stage clouds made from white canvas stretched over wooden frames; they were lowered into the scene by ropes or rolled sideways in metal grooves onto the stage. Invented during the Renaissance, they were still used in the eighteenth century.

*Opéra-ballet*—An eighteenth-century form of theatrical dance characterized by three to five acts of unrelated plots held together by a theme announced in the prologue. Productions were greatly enhanced by the danceability of galant music and gorgeous decor. A number of early works were improperly named opéra-ballets; later, the term was used to distinguish lighter works from Noverre's tragic narratives.

**Pageants**—Late medieval religious and secular spectacles that moved through the streets mounted on elaborately decorated wagons.

*Panier*—Undergarment of wires and wooden stays that looked like an upside-down basket. It was worn around the waist to give broad form to the voluminous skirts of eighteenth-century high fashion.

**Pantomime**—Use of gestures and facial expression to convey dramatic meaning without speech; also a popular form of British Christmas theater based on fairy tales with music and comedy.

*Pas*—A simple step or a movement that involves a change of weight; also refers to a dance performed by one or more.

*Pas d'action*—A danced scene that conveys dramatic meaning through the use of gesture.

*Pas d'arms*—Skilled manipulation of men, horses, and weapons in equestrian ballets.

351

*Pas de deux*—A dance for two. A grand *pas de deux* is the climactic section of a full-length ballet when the dancers are presented in a dignified opening followed by virtuoso solos, followed by a rousing finale.

*Pas d'expression*—One or more steps danced in a certain way to convey emotion.

**Pastoral**—Eighteenth-century dance form featuring human happiness in peaceful and idyllic settings; evolved as a reaction to the formalized dignity of mythical deities in ballets of the same period.

*Pavane*—Stately court dance in double time; the Italian version is named for its origin in the northern city of Padua, while its Spanish name is descriptively termed *el pavo*, which suggests "strutting like a peacock."

*Pirola*—An early Italian term for *piroetta*, i.e., *pirouette*.

*Pirouette*—One or more complete turns of the body on the ball of the foot or full *pointe*; many variants.

*Poteshnaia palata*—Special rooms for entertainments in the imperial citadels of Russia.

*Plastique*—A French term indicating that the pliant and supple body is capable of being molded into any number of desired shapes.

*Pleiade*—Academic body assembled at Catherine de Medici's court to rediscover the ways and means of the perfect harmony of ancient art.

*Pliaski*—A genre of energetic Russian folk dance.

*Plié*—The bending of the knee to render the muscles pliable, the tendons flexible, and to create a sense of balance; one of the three most fundamental movements of the *danse d'école*, which are *plié*, *tendu*, and *sauté*. Bending, extending, and jumping are the common denominators of the classical technique from which all its steps and movements are derived.

*Pointe* **work**—A body of technique used by the female dancer that relies on reinforced slippers; *en pointe* is the ultimate stretch of the leg in a standing position.

**Polka**—A Czech folk dance in double time that became a popular round dance in ballrooms of the nineteenth-century bourgeois. Jean Coralli and his wife introduced it to the stage of the Paris Opera in 1844 with specially commissioned music by Friedrich Burgmüller.

*Port de bras*—Carriage of the arms; movement made by passing the arms through the classical positions stipulated in the *danse d'école* lexicon; involves the exacting and complex use of the head, shoulders, and upper back.

*Poulaines*—Excessively long and pointed men's shoes worn in the Middle Ages.

*Prisiadka*—A vigorous Russian folk step done in a squatting position in which a male dancer alternately extends one leg while the other is in the deepest possible bent position.

**Proscenium arch**—The architectural frame around the stage opening that separates the illusion of the stage from the audience in a theater; also serves to hide stage machinery and minimize backstage noise.

**Raked floors**—Stage floors that slope downward toward the audience in most European opera houses. They were intended to increase the illusion of depth and visibility of the central focal point; they require much getting used to for the American dancer.

*Regisseur*—The European term for one who schedules and oversees rehearsals in a ballet company; also stage manager, the person who directs the ballet production.

**Renaissance**—Fifteenth-century European revival of art, literature, and the human spirit according to classical models.

352

**Renaissance court theaters**—Built to house the growing demand for court entertainment within palace walls; served also as a mark of extreme wealth and power; construction was guided by translations of the plans of ancient architects for outdoor theaters and arenas.

*Révérence*—The elaborate bow of dancers meant to express appreciation for applause. The concept is derived from the opening and closing bows of early court dances when participants acknowledged and thanked each other.

**Rococo**—Ornamental style of decoration prevalent in late baroque art; involved asymmetrical designs of scrollwork, floral, and shell patterns.

**Romanov dynasty**—Ruling family of Russia from 1613 to 1917; munificent supporters of ballet from 1738 onward.

**Romantic era**—Nineteenth-century European art movement valuing emotion, intuition, and individualism; ballet was the period's most glamorous manifestation.

**Sacred representations**—Renaissance ceremonial processions with religious subject matter fostered by Lorenzo de Medici.

*Saltarello*—A lively Italian dance in which the 3/4 or 6/8 tempo accelerates; dates from the fourteenth century.

*Sarabande*—Stately seventeenth-century Spanish dance in triple time that became popular all over Europe.

*Sardana*—Traditional Catalan folk dance of the northeastern part of Spain; still performed on Sundays and holidays throughout the year.

*Scabella*—Ancient Roman percussion instrument used for its noisiness rather than as a rhythm-keeping device.

*Seguidilla*—A popular Spanish folk dance performed by couples in triple time; a number of versions of it are danced in most parts of Spain.

*Skomorokhi*—Thirteenth-century Russian entertainers who roamed the countryside and eventually found their way into the households of princes and wealthy boyars.

**Socialist Realism**—The official art style of the Communist party in the former U.S.S.R.

*Spiëlmann*—German minstrels who organized the dancing in the Jewish *tanzhäuser*; they were also entertainers at fairs and markets.

**Spotting**—A rapid movement of the head required in turning steps to prevent the dancer from becoming dizzy; Dervish dancers of Eastern Turkey are one of the very few groups who do not use the technique in turning.

**Stock characters**—Characters that exhibit stereotyped behaviors of people who are portrayed by actors, mimes, and dancers.

**Stuart**—Family name of the kings who ruled England from 1603 to 1714.

**Strike**—A term used in the theater to denote the taking down of scenery.

**Surrealism**—Early twentieth-century art and literary movement that attempted to explain the subconscious mind with the irrational juxtaposition of images, objects, and ideas.

**Sylph**—An elemental spirit of the air possibly extracted from previously living beings; one of many such beings who figured in the otherworldly domain of Romantic ballet.

*Tacquetée*—A term that indicates dancing *en pointe* with quick little steps that strike the floor in a staccato manner, such as *piqué*, *emboîté sur les pointes*, and *pas de bourrée*.

*Tanets*—Russian word for dance understood as a formal body of knowledge.

353

*Tanzhäuser*—Dance halls in the ghettos of German towns where the best fiddlers or "callers" arranged and oversaw dancing organized for the Jewish community.

*Tarantella*—A couple dance in accelerating 6/8 time that originated in southern Italy; according to fourteenth-century legend, if bitten by a spider from Taranto, one had to dance the tarantella until the poison was sweated out or else die of its effects.

*Teatralnaia khoromina*—Large wooden buildings set aside for theatrical performances that were open to the Russian public.

*Terre à Terre*—Ground to ground. A term used to indicate that in the exectuion of a step the feet stay in contact with the floor, as in *pas de bourrée*.

*Tonnelet*—Richly decorated costume of the male dancer with the lower half of the long fitted coat extended outward; first worn in the fifteenth century to suggest the heroic style of ancient Roman military dress. At the time of Noverre it had become a meaningless convention.

*Tordion*—French social dance from the late Middle Ages.

*Tragédie ballet*—The seventeenth-century supreme (noble) style of serious ballet intended to manifest the majesty of Louis XIV. Lully synthesized tragedy and ballet beginning with *Cadmus et Hermione* (1673) to create a new genre at the Royal Academy. Exalted antique themes were presented in five acts preceded by a prologue.

*Tragi-comédie ballet*—A genre of seventeenth-century ballet less serious than a tragedy, but more so than a comedy; it was distanced by time and space, often with a mythological setting as presented in Lavallière's *Psyché* (1671).

**Transcendentalism**—A nineteenth-century philosophy that holds that matter and objective things are products of the subjective mind; by transcending perceived reality, a follower becomes one with the divine.

*Trionfi*—Triumphal processions that the Renaissance modeled on ancient descriptions of returning victorious battalions of the Roman Empire.

*Tripudium*—A step characterized by three shifts of weight that originated in an ancient Roman military processional dance.

*Trompe l'oeil*—Designed to give an illusion of reality; literally, "to deceive the eye."

**Tudor**—Family name of the kings who ruled England from 1485 to 1603.

**Turnout**—Essential standing position of classical ballet in which the legs and feet are ideally rotated outward to a 90-degree position enabling the dancer to move with maximum freedom in every direction; its purpose is aesthetic as well as functional.

**Tutu**—The short, stiffened skirt of late nineteenth- and twentieth-century classical bal-let; its design was necessitated by the increased complexity of female technique.

**Valois**—Family name of the ruling dynasty in France from 1328 to 1589.

*Violin du poche*—A pocket-sized violin traditionally used by dancing masters to provide accompaniment for dance classes.

**Vomitorium**—Exit and entrance tunnels systematically built into ancient arenas to channel the flow of crowds.

**Wings**—Two-dimensional scenic pieces or curtains placed parallel to the proscenium line on a proscenium stage and located at the sides of the dancing space. They serve to hide lighting equipment and backstage activity, and create entrance ways to and from the stage. In the seventeenth and eighteenth centuries they were movable on tracks or hung in a receding manner to increase

# BIBLIOGRAPHY

Arbeau, Thoinot. *Orchesography,* trans. Cyril Beaumont. Brooklyn: Dance Horizons, 1965.

Baer, Nancy van Norman. *Bronislava Nijinska: A Dancer's Legacy.* San Francisco: The Fine Arts Museum of San Francisco, 1986.

———. *Paris Modern: The Swedish Ballet 1920–1925.* San Francisco: The Fine Arts Museum of San Francisco, 1996.

Bassompierre, Françoise de. *Mémoires contenant l'Histoire de sa vie.* Cologne: 1665.

Benois, Alexandre. *Memoirs: Vol. 2,* trans. M. Budberg. London: Chatto & Winders, 1964.

Binney, Edwin. *Longing for the Ideal: Images of Marie Taglioni in the Romantic Ballet.* Cambridge, MA: Harvard University Publishers, 1984.

Bland, Alexander. *The Royal Ballet: The First Fifty Years.* Garden City, NY: Doubleday & Co., 1981.

———, and Percival, John. *Men Dancing.* New York: Macmillan Publishing Co., 1984.

Blasis, Carlo. *An Elementive Treatise Upon the Theory and Practice of the Art of Dancing,* trans. M.S. Evan. New York: Dover Publication, 1968.

Bogin, Meg. *The Women Troubadours.* New York: W.W. Norton, 1976.

Bonilla, Luis. *La Danza en el Mito y en la Historia.* Madrid: Biblioteca Nueva, 1964.

Bournonville, August. *My Theatre Life,* trans. Patricia N. McAndrew. Middleton, CT: Wesleyan University Press, 1977.

———. *Études chorégraphiques.* Copenhagen, 1861.

Buckle, Richard. *Nijinsky.* New York: Avon Books, 1975.

———. *Diaghilev.* New York: Atheneum, 1979.

———, and Taras, John. *George Balanchine, Ballet Master.* New York: Random House, 1988.

Castiglione, Baldessare. *The Book of the Courtier,* trans. G. Bull. Middlesex: Penguin Books, 1984.

Chazin-Bennahum, Judith. *Ballets of Anthony Tudor: The Studies in Psyche and Satire.* New York: Oxford University Press, 1994.

———. *Dance in the Shadow of the Guillotine.* Carbondale: Southern Illinois Press, 1988.

Cheney, Sheldon. *The Theatre, Three Thousand Years of Drama, Acting and Stagecraft.* New York: Tudor Publishing Co., 1949.

Christout, Marie-Françoise. *Le Ballet de Cour de Louis XIV.* Paris: Editions A. et J. Picard & Cie, 1967.

Cocteau, Jean, and Alexandre, Arsène. *The Decorative Art of Léon Bakst,* trans. H. Melvill. New York: Dover Publication, 1972.

Danilova, Alexandra. *Choura.* New York: Fromm International Publishing, 1988.

355

Demidov, Alexander. *The Russian Ballet: Past & Present*, trans. Guy Daniels. Garden City, NY: Doubleday & Co., 1977.

de Rougemont, Denis. *Love in the Western World*. Greenwich, CT: Fawcet Publishers, 1966.

*Dictionnaire de la musique en France aux XVII et XVIII siècles*. Paris: Fayard, 1992.

Du Manoir, Guillaume. *Le marige de la music avec la danse*. Paris: Guillaume de Luyne, 1664.

Duchartre, Pierre Louis. *The Italian Comedy*. New York: Dover Publication, 1966.

Emery, Lynne Fauley. *Black Dance, from 1619 to Today*. Princeton: Princeton Book Co., 1988.

Fokine, Michel. *Memoirs of a Ballet Master*, trans. Vitale Fokine. Boston: Little, Brown & Co., 1961.

Franko, Mark. *Dance as Text: Ideologies of the Baroque Body*. Cambridge, England: Cambridge University Press, 1993.

Garafola, Lynn. *Diaghilev's Ballets Russes*. New York: Oxford University Press, 1989.

———. *Rethinking the Sylph*, ed. Hanover, NH: University Press of New England, 1997.

García-Márquez, Vicente. *The Ballets Russes: Colonel de Basil's Ballets Russes de Monte Carlo, 1932–1952*. New York: Alfred A. Knopf, 1990.

———. *Massine: A Biography*. New York: Alfred A. Knopf, 1995.

Gautier, Théophile. *The Complete Works,* trans. C. de Sumichrast. London: Atheneum Press, 1900.

Guest, Ivor. *The Ballet of the Enlightenment: The Establishment of the Ballet d'Action in France 1770–1793*. London: Dance Books, 1996.

———. *Ballet of the Second Empire: 1858–1870*. London: A. & C. Black, 1953.

———. *The Ballet of the Second Empire: 1847–1858*. London: A. & C. Black, 1958.

———. *The Romantic Ballet in Paris*. London: Sir Isaac Pitman and Sons, 1966.

———. *Fanny Elssler*. London: Adam & Charles Black, 1970.

———. *Fanny Cerrito*. London: Dance Books, 1974.

———. *Jules Perrot, Master of the Romantic Ballet*. London: Dance Books, 1984.

Hammond, Sandra N. *Letters on Dancing by E. A. Théleur*. Princeton, NJ: Princeton Periodicals, 1990.

Haskell, Arnold L. *Ballet Russe*. London: Weidenfeld and Nicolson, 1968.

Hendrickson, Charles Cyril & Keller, Kate Van Winkle. *Social Dances from the American Revolution*. Sandy Hook, CT: Hendrickson Group, 1992.

Hilleström, Gustaf. *Theatre and Ballet in Sweden*. Stockholm, Sweden: The Swedish Institute, 1953.

Hilton, Wendy. *Dance of Court & Theater: The French Noble Style, 1690–1725*. Princeton, NJ: Princeton Book Co., 1981.

Hindley, Geoffrey, ed. *Larousse Encyclopedia of Music*. Secaucus, NJ: Chartwell Books, 1977.

Jackson, George; Oberzaucher, Alfred; Raab, Riki; Schuller, Gunhild; and Spiel, Hilde. *Die Puppenfee*. Wien: Osterreichischer Bundestheaterverband, 1983.

Joel, Lydia. "Discovering Catherine de Medici." *Dance Magazine*, Parts I–IV, April–July, 1990.

Jordan, Stephanie; Grau, Andrée; editors. *Following Sir Fred's Steps: Ashton's Legacy*. London: Dance Books, 1996.

Jürgensen, Knud Arne. *The Bournonville Ballets: A Photographic Record, 1844–1933*. London: Dance Books, 1987.

Karsavina, Tamara. *Theatre Street*. London: Dance Books, 1981.

Kinkeldey, Otto. *A Jewish Dancing Master of the Renaissance: Guglielmo Ebreo*. Brooklyn, NY: Dance Horizons, 1972.

356

Kirstein, Lincoln. *Dance, a Short History of Classical Theatrical Dancing*. Brooklyn, NY: Dance Horizons, 1969.

———. *Movement & Metaphor: Four Centuries of Ballet*. London: Pitman Publishing, 1971.

Kochno, Boris. *Diaghilev and the Ballets Russes*, trans. Adrienne Foulke. New York: Harper & Row, 1970.

Krasovskaya, Vera. *Nijinsky*, trans. John E. Bowlt. New York: Schimer Books, 1979.

Lawler, Lillian B. *The Dance in Ancient Greece*. Seattle: University of Washington Press, 1967.

Lambranzi, Gregorio. *New and Curious School of Theatrical Dancing* (1716), reprint trans. by F. Derra de Moroda. Brooklyn, NY: Dance Horizons, 1972.

Lejeune, André and Wolff, Stéphane. *Les Quinze Salles de L'Opera de Paris: 1669–1955*. Paris: Bibliothèque de l'Opéra, 1955.

Levinson, André. *Marie Taglioni*. London: Dance Books, 1977.

Lynham, Deryck. *The Chevalier Noverre: Father of Modern Ballet*. London: Sylvan Press, 1972.

Macdonald, Nesta. *Diaghilev Observed: By Critics in England and the United States: 1911–1929*. London: Dance Books, 1975.

Magri, Gennaro. *Theoretical and Practical Treatise on Dancing* (1779), trans. Mary Skeaping. London: Dance Books, 1988.

McGowan, Margaret M. *L'Art du Ballet de Cour en France, 1581–1643*. Paris: Éditions du Centre National de la Recherche Scientifique, 1963.

Migel, Parmenia. *The Ballerinas: From the Court of Louis XIV to Pavlova*. New York: Macmillan Co., 1972.

Money, Keith. *Anna Pavlova: Her Life and Art*. New York: Alfred A. Knopf, 1982.

Moore, Lillian. *New York's First Ballet Season: 1792*. New York: New York Public Library, 1961.

Näslund, Erik. *The Art of Extravagance: Larinov, Bakst and Matisse*. Stockholm: Dansmuseet, 1996.

Nijinska, Bronislava. *Early Memories*, trans. and ed. Irina Nijinska and Jean Rawlinson. New York: Holt, Rinehart and Winston, 1981.

Noverre, Jean Georges. *Letters on Dancing and Ballets,* trans. C.W. Beaumont. New York: Dance Horizons, 1975.

Pellisson, Maurice. *Les Comédie-Ballets de Molière*. Paris: Hachette and Co., 1914.

Percival, John. *Modern Ballet*. London: Herbert Press, 1980.

———. *The World of Diaghilev*. London: Studio Vista, 1971.

Petipa, Marius. *Russian Ballet Master: The Memories of Marius Petipa*, eds. and trans. Lilian Moore and Helen Whittaker. London: Dance Books, 1958.

Pougnaud, Pierre. *Théâtres, 4 Siècles d'Architecture et d'Histoire, Tome I*. Paris: Moniteur, 1980.

Prudhommeau, Germaine. *Histoire de la Dance*. Paris: Éditions Amphora, 1989.

Prunières, Henri. *Le Ballet de Cour en France avant Benserade et Lully*. Paris: H. Laurens, 1914.

Rameau, Pierre. *The Dancing Master* (1725). New York: Dance Horizons, 1970.

Reynolds, Nancy. *Repertory in Review: Forty Years of the New York City Ballet*. New York: The Dial Press, 1977.

Rock, Judith. *Terpsichore at Louis Le Grand: Baroque Dance on a Jesuit Stage in Paris*. St. Louis: Institute of Jesuit Sources, 1996.

Roné, Elvira. *Olga Preobrazhenskaya*, trans. Fernau Hall. New York: Marcel Dekker, 1978.

Roslavleva, Natalia. *Era of the Russian Ballet*. New York: E.P. Sutton, 1966.

357

Rowling, Marjorie. *Life in Medieval Times*. New York: G.P. Putnam's Sons, 1968.

Sachs, Curt. *World History of the Dance*, trans. Bessie Schönberg. New York: W.W. Norton, 1963.

Saint-Hubert, Nicolas. *La Manière de composer et faire reussir les ballets*. Paris: Chez François Targa, 1641.

Saint-Léon, Arthur. *Letters from a Ballet Master*, ed. Ivor Guest. London: Dance Books, 1981.

Sasportes, Jose, and Pinto, Ribeiro. *History of Dance: Synthesis of Portuguese Culture*, trans. J.A. Ennes. Lisbon: Europalia, 1991.

Schneider, Ilya Ilyish. *Isadora Duncan: The Russian Years*, trans. David Magarshack. New York: Harcourt, Brace & World, 1968.

Sokolova, Lydia. *Dancing for Diaghilev*, ed. Richard Buckle. San Francisco: Mercury House, 1960.

Sorell, Walter. *Dance in Its Time: The Emergence of an Art Form*. Garden City, NY: Anchor Press/Doubleday, 1981.

Souritz, Elizabeth. *Soviet Choreographers in the 1920s*, trans. Lynn Visson. London: Dance Books, 1990.

Squarzina, Luigi. *Teatri E Scenografie*. Milan: Touring Club Italiano, 1976.

Spencer, Charles. *Leon Bakst*. London: Academy Editions, 1973.

Strong, Roy. *Art and Power, Renaissance Festivals: 1450–1650*. Suffolk, England: Boydell Press, 1984.

Swift, Mary Grace. *A Loftier Flight: The Life and Accomplishments of Charles-Louis Didelot, Balletmaster*. Middleton, CT: Wesleyan University Press, 1974.

Taubert, Gottfried. *Rechtschaffener Tantzmeister* (1717). Leipzig: Zentralantiquariat der DDR, 1976.

Tarasov, Nikolai Ivanovich. *Ballet Technique for the Male Dancer*, trans. Elizabeth Kraft. Garden City, NY: Doubleday & Co., 1985.

Terry, Walter. *The King's Ballet Master: A Biography of Denmark's August Bournonville*. New York: Dodd, Mead & Co., 1979.

Théatre National de l'Opéra, Editors. *Petite Encyclopédiede l'Opera de Paris*, Tome I. Paris: G.R. Joly, 1974.

Tomlinson, Kellom. *The Art of Dancing and Six Dances: London 1735 and 1720*. Brooklyn, NY: Dance Horizons, 1970.

Volkov, Solomon. *Balanchine's Tchaikovsky: Interviews with George Balanchine*, trans. Antonina W. Bouis. New York: Simon and Schuster, 1985.

Weaver, John. *Anatomical and Mechanical Lectures*. London, 1721.

Wiley, Roland John. *A Century of Russian Ballet: Documents and Accounts, 1810–1910*. New York: Oxford University Press, 1991.

———. *The Life and Ballets of Lev Ivanov: Choreographer of The Nutcracker and Swan Lake*. Oxford, England: Clarendon Press, 1997.

Winter, Marian Hannah. *The Pre-Romantic Ballet*. New York: Pitman Publication Corporation, 1974.

Wood, M. Melusine. *Historical Dances: 12th to 19th Century*. London: Imperial Society of Teachers of Dancing, 1972.

Wosien, Marie-Gabriel. *Sacred Dance*. New York: Thames and Hudson, 1974.

Yates, Frances A. *The French Academies of the Sixteenth Century*. Nendeln, Liechtenstein: Kraus Reprint, 1968.

# BALLETS

359

360

# INDEX

362

363

364

365

male dancing, 144, 151, 156, 168, 173, 235, 241, 306
Manzotti, Luigi, 175–176
Markova, Alicia, 268, 282
*Marriage of Figaro* (Mozart), 113
Martins, Peter, 326
Maryinsky Theater, 206, 211, 212, 215, 216, 220, 229, 231, 234, 242–245, 271
masks, 53–54, 60, 95
masquerades, 38, 41, 48
masques, 91–92
Massine, Léonide, 250, 255, 256, 258–269, 270, 280, 283, 319, 321
Matisse, Henri, 261
maypole dance, 10
Maywood, Augusta, 316–317
Mazilier, Joseph, 174
*mazurka*, 134
Medici family, 26–27, 28, 32, 37, 56
Medina, Maria, 115
melodrama, 140
Ménéstrier, Claude-Françoise, 79–80
*menuets*, 30, 70, 73, 74, 78, 82, 122, 313
Messerer, Asaf, 304
Metropolitan Opera, 256, 323
Middle Ages, 7–20, 53, 135, 136
Milhaud, Darius, 268
minstrels, 9, 13, 16
minuets, 313–314
Miró, Joan, 269
miracle plays, 19
*Mir Iskusstva* (Diaghilev), 229, 242
*misuro*, 31
*Mit Theaterliv* (Bournonville), 167
modern dance movement, 251, 297, 335
Molière, 74, 75, 76, 95, 98
Monaco, 288
Moorish culture, 19–20
morality plays, 19
Mordkin, Mikhail, 326–327
*moresques*, 19–20, 91
Moscow Art Theatre, 220
Moscow Ballet School, 192
*movemento corporeo*, 31
Mozart, Wolfgang Amadeus, 109, 113, 123, 144

Muravieva, Marfa, 204
musical comedy, 326, 329
musical notation, 28
music halls, 176–178, 220
Mussorgsky, Modest, 230
mystery plays, 19, 20
mythology themes, 29

Napoleon, 110, 133, 135, 137, 172, 192, 194
Narodny Dom, 215, 294, 300
*naumachia*, 56
Neary, Patricia, 297
Nederlands Dans Theater, 292, 294, 300
Negri, Cesare, 39, 54
Nemchinova, Vera, 255
Nency, Mlle., 106
neoclassicism, 262, 266–267, 270–273, 325
Netherlands, 291–294
Neumeier, John, 296
New York City Ballet, 273, 322–324, 325, 326, 331, 332
New Zealand, 284
Nicholas II, Czar of Russia, 215
Nijinska, Bronislava, 264, 265–269, 287
Nijinsky, Vaslav, 171, 233–234, 235–236, 239, 240, 241, 242, 244, 250, 254, 255, 260, 326; choreography of, 245–249, 256, 257, 266, 278
Noverre, Jean Georges, 94, 103–110, 115, 117, 120, 124, 127, 128, 137, 138, 146, 152, 164, 167, 181, 184–188, 195, 197, 203, 227, 241, 295, 302; writings of, 108, 110–112, 187
Novitskaya, Anatasia, 191
Nureyev, Rudolf, 282, 286, 287, 290, 330
*nuvola*, 57

*opéra-ballets*, 86–88, 94, 95, 102, 103, 104
*Opéra Comique*, 105
*Orchésographie* (Arbeau), 55, 80
oriental culture, 16, 105, 137
*Orpheus et Eurydice* (Gluck), 99

Page, Ruth, 330
pageants, 20
Palais Royal, 58–59, 76, 77
Palladio, Andrea, 57
*paniers*, 120, 183
pantomime, 168, 195; Roman, 4–6, 8, 16, 53
Paris Opera, 94, 99, 109, 121–124, 128, 129, 133, 138, 145, 150–154, 158, 168, 172–177, 181, 188, 202, 239, 284–288; Didelot at, 193–194
*pas d'action*, 152
*pas de basque*, 190
*pas de bourrée*, 78, 117, 190, 210
*pas de deux*, 89, 95, 96, 141, 142, 169, 190, 196, 244
*pas de trois*, 300
*pas d'expression*, 78
pastorals, 44–45, 48, 88, 89
Paul, Rose, 189, 190
*pavanes*, 55, 74, 78
Pavlova, Anna, 171, 221–223, 233–234, 235, 240, 241, 250, 268, 292, 318–319, 330
peasant dances, 19
Pécourt, Louis, 77, 80, 81, 86, 96
Pennsylvania Ballet, 332
Perrot, Jules, 8, 151–158, 165–167, 172, 176, 202–205, 213, 219, 227
Peter the Great, Czar of Russia, 182–183, 185, 201, 212, 229
Petipa, Jean, 205, 290, 317
Petipa, Lucien, 12, 54, 171
Petipa, Marius, 205–214, 220, 227, 230, 235, 237, 239, 243, 263, 264, 317
Petit, Roland, 286
Picasso, Pablo, 258, 259, 260, 261, 262, 268
*pirouettes*, 75, 78, 82, 88, 102, 117, 122, 124, 125, 147, 190, 191, 192, 211, 244
Pitrot, Antoine, 97, 98, 117, 148, 189
Placide, Alexander, 315
*plastique*, 236
*pliaski*, 182
poetic expression, 191–193

367

Titus, Antoine, 197
*tonnelets*, 98, 104, 105, 120
Torelli, Giacomo, 58, 59, 68
*tour en l'air*, 75, 78
tribal dances, 10–11
*trionfi*, 28, 34
troubadours, 15–17, 136
Tudor, Antony, 278, 279,
    327–328
Turnbull, Julia, 316
*Twelfth Night: A Masque of
    Blackness* (Jonson), 91

Ullate, Victor, 299
United States: development
    of ballet in, 312–338;
    French influence in, 254,
    255–257, 316, 317; profes-
    sional ballet across, 329–
    334; regional ballet in,
    329–335

Vaganova, Agrippina, 171,
    282, 305–309
Vaillande, Suzanne, 315
Vainonen, Vasily, 295,
    303–304

Valberkh, Ivan, 187, 190, 202
van Dantzig, Rudi, 293
van Hamme, Andries Voitus,
    292
van Manen, Hans, 293
Vasiliev, Vladimir, 305
Vazem, Ekaterina, 203, 204,
    207, 208
Verdi, Giuseppe, 298
Versailles, Palace of, 66–68,
    213, 230
Véron, Louis, 145, 156
Vestris, Armand, 126, 141,
    167
Vestris, Auguste, 110, 117,
    124–125, 147, 151, 155,
    167, 169, 172, 205
Vestris, Gaëtan, 94, 106, 107,
    124, 126, 127, 128
Vestris family, 104, 124–126,
    141, 188
Vienna Opera, 171
Vienna State Opera, 297
Viganò, Salvatore, 115–116
Vinogradov, Oleg, 305
Virgin Mary, cult of, 15, 18,
    155

Vitrivius Pollio, Marcus, 56–
    57
Volkova, Vera, 282, 283, 289
von Weber, Carl Maria, 244
Vsevolojsky, Ivan, 214

waltz, 121–123, 134
Weaver, John, 92–94, 102,
    103, 164
Western Europe, 277–301
Wigman, Mary, 251, 289
wilis, 136
William the Jew, 31. *See* also
    Guglielmo Ebreo
writings on ballet, 38–39, 51,
    54–55, 56, 70; eighteenth
    century, 79–83, 90, 93, 99;
    nineteenth century, 147,
    170–171; twentieth cen-
    tury, 229, 306, 308

Zambelli, Carlotta, 175, 176,
    210, 285
*zhar-ptitsa* theme, 239
Zucchi, Virginia, 210, 231

368

Banff City Library
WITHDRAWN
FROM STOCK